Islamic Roots of Capitalism
Egypt, 1760–1840

Modern Middle East Series, No. 4
Sponsored by the Center for Middle Eastern Studies
The University of Texas at Austin

Islamic Roots of Capitalism

Egypt, 1760–1840

BY PETER GRAN

Foreword by Afaf Lutfi Al-Sayyid Marsot

University of Texas Press, Austin & London

Library of Congress Cataloging in Publication Data

Gran, Peter, 1941–
Islamic roots of capitalism.
(Modern Middle East series; no. 4)
Bibliography: p.
Includes indexes.
1. Egypt—History—1517–1882. I. Title. II. Series:
Modern Middle East series (Austin, Tex.); no. 4.
DT97.G7 962'.03 78-16663
ISBN 0-292-70333-3

Printed in the United States of America

Contents

Foreword

In the past, eighteenth-century Egyptian history has been treated like an ill-favored stepchild. Scholars, with one or two exceptions, have treated it as an ancillary aspect of the Ottoman Empire or as a by-product of international relations. As a consequence, the basis for the history of the period has rested on two assumptions: first, that the period was one of chaos and anarchy in which little happened of historical interest other than internecine Mamlūk feuds; and, second, that it was an era of intellectual decline when nothing innovative was written, only endless commentaries and glosses of medieval religious texts. Zabīdī and Jabartī, the two intellectual giants of the later part of the period, were invariably described as unique and *sui generis.* Since hardly a scholar had read any of the glosses and commentaries, although many had read Jabartī and Zabīdī, the second assumption seemed safe enough to make. Moreover, the authors of the *Déscription de l'Egypte*, the standard reference work in the West for the period, had reinforced that opinion of the low state of Egyptian intellectual life.

Recent scholarship has begun to change that image. Scholars have gone back to the indigenous primary sources for their material: to archives, to *al-maḥkama, al-sharīʿa,* and *al-awqāf* documents, and to the commentaries and glosses of the time. The picture emerging from their efforts is a new and challenging one. André Raymond, in his masterly and brilliant work, *Artisans et commerçants au Caire au XVIIIième siècle,* gave us our first economic history of eighteenth-century Egypt. Peter Gran in this volume presents us with an equally exciting but certainly more controversial approach. His work asks questions not heretofore raised in a work on the Near East, even though such questions form the methodological apparatus of Western historical research. More important, he suggests answers to these questions on the basis of research in the commentaries and glosses. He shows that these works, previously ignored and despised, reveal an active intellectual life that mirrored the changing economic conditions of the day—that internal forces were pushing the country toward a capitalist transformation long before the advent of the Western entrepreneur. The intellectual developments of the period likewise show that, far from being *sui generis* in one case and mediocre repetition in the other, what was happening was well within an age of intellectual revitalization and was rich in secular ideas and rationalist interpretations of the economic changes Egyptian society was undergoing.

Peter Gran's hypothesis that the output of the *ʿulamāʾ* marked "developments in secular culture and were supportive of capitalism" is a challenge to past scholarship. It is one based on a rational premise that, since something does not arise out of nothing, there must be a historical pattern of continuity and an integrated framework for studying Egypt that would allow us to find reasons for events in historical terms rather than to label them in meaningless terms like "chaos" and "anarchy." Gran's attempt to find a pattern in over a century of Egyptian history is a remarkable work of scholarship. It will stir up controversy but will also open the eyes of scholars of the period to a totally new perspective—from within that society—an achievement in itself.

Professor Afaf Lutfi Al-Sayyid Marsot
Department of History
University of California at Los Angeles

Preface

This study is based on extensive use of books and manuscripts in the al-Azhar mosque center and the Egyptian National Library (Dār al-Kutub). Since the major figures of the eighteenth century who are studied here were all *shaykhs* of al-Azhar, and those of the Muḥammad ʿAlī period were nearly all *shaykhs*, the library of al-Azhar was very useful.

The criteria for identifying trends in various fields and for characterizing historical periods were developed primarily from the biographical dictionaries covering the principal figures of each period, and from manuscript catalogs. From these two sources, the books which were written during each period and their distribution according to subject matter were identified. The excellent manuscript catalogs of al-Azhar and Dār al-Kutub were a major source for delineating the character of the eighteenth-century revival. These catalogs date not only the original writings of different eras but also the copies of standard works. The demand for copies of various works is a reasonable indicator of the general direction which studies took at any given time. Of particular importance in the study of eighteenth-century culture is the section of any manuscript catalog entitled "Muṣṭalaḥ al-ḥadīth" (literally, the technical terms of *ḥadīth* studies); this section includes material on the subjects taught by each *shaykh* in the form of minor works called *sanad, thabat, ijāza, fahrasa,* and so on. For Turkey and Syria in the eighteenth and early nineteenth centuries, there are also outstanding biographical dictionaries and manuscript catalogs. For Damascus, there is the Ẓāhirīya library catalog with its supplements; and for Istanbul, I used a card file located in Dār al-Kutub which lists the contents of the private libraries in Istanbul, about thirty in number. Researchers needing individual call numbers for these manuscripts should contact me through the publisher.

I use a modified Library of Congress transliteration system retaining, for example, the spelling chosen by Arabic authors who write in Western languages, simplifying the system with respect to the different *alifs*, not underlining diphthongs like *sh, dh, th,* and so forth. In other cases, I emphasize the spelling over sound, such as *Sūhāj* for *Sohaj* and *Raḥman* for *Raḥmān*, and drop the *h* used for *taʾ marbūṭa*. I Turkicize only for Turkish writers in Anatolia.

The production of this book has also been a memorable experience. By its nature, it required a very stout heart and a large organizational approach. I owe a great deal to the mobilizing efforts of my colleagues Paul English and Robert Fernea, and from the technical and logistical end Barbara Burnham, Kristin Koptiuch, Scott Lubeck, and Barbara Spielman. Without the expertise of these latter, it is difficult to imagine how this would have come about.

This book was written over a long period of time and owes a great deal to people and institutions to whom I can scarcely do justice. Much of what I learned about Egyptian social history came from the seminars of the history department of ʿAyn Shams. Students and faculty there provided me with a critical and supportive atmosphere. The employees of the Ministry of Culture who work in the Manuscript Division of Dār al-Kutub and their counterparts in al-Azhar made great efforts to find and identify and explain points in manuscripts. Without the help of *shaykhs* and others who worked in these areas, it would have been difficult to proceed. My friend Aida Kershah helped me a great deal over several years while I was going through the corpus of Al-ʿAṭṭār's writings. André Raymond through his numerous writings and in my meetings with him gave me much of the framework. I owe a great deal to the institutions which permitted an extended stay in Egypt, foremost among them the American Research Center in Egypt; the Department of State, Bureau of Educational and Cultural Affairs; and the Arabic Studies Department of the American University in Cairo.

Among those who have read and commented on this manuscript in one stage or another are William Polk, Fazlur Rahman, Jaroslav Stetkevych, and Talal Asad. More recently I have received a number of very incisive suggestions from Rifaat Abou El-Hajj, who patiently helped me to tighten my argument and develop the framework of my ideas. I leave to last the mention of my wife, Judith Gran, and the two professors whose influence on this work the reader may see. Albert Hourani has encouraged my research since my student days. I thank him for this confidence in my work. Afaf Lutfi Al-Sayyid Marsot, unrivaled in her knowledge of Egyptian history, has given me enormous assistance over a long period of time. I want her to know how much I appreciate all her efforts. To Judith Gran I owe a great deal. She introduced me to social science and has had a great influence on my becoming a social historian. Her help in the elaboration of the argument over the last ten years, while it moved from dissertation to book, can scarcely be covered in a brief section of acknowledgments.

Introduction

This study seeks to redefine the relationship between the West and the Middle East in both cultural and material terms, using the industrial revolution as the period of concentration. It is an attempt at the reconstruction of knowledge. Traditional studies of Western civilization contain an implicit conception of Oriental civilization as an "Other." Thus Western definitions of its own civilization and of the civilization of the Orient have been developed through a series of positive and negative statements. On the one hand, Westerners see themselves as rational, democratic, and voluntaristic; while on the other, they perceive the Oriental as mystical, autocratic, and fatalistic.

This framework of perceiving Self and Other posits a nondialectical movement of culture; that is, history is perceived to be an undifferentiated totality in which there are no overlapping or interpenetrating areas of influence. European scholars have often argued that, in the Middle Ages, Europe merely received Hellenistic culture from the Arabs in toto, while in the modern period the Arabs received modern European culture in toto. Gustave Von Grunebaum, the well-known Orientalist, for instance, defined Islamic civilization as the brief period in which it embodied a form of Hellenism; this was the period between the ninth and eleventh centuries when the West was still barbarous, that is, still ignorant of Greek culture—a situation that was quickly reversed by the famous medieval European translation movement in which Greek classics were first translated into Arabic, then Arabic into Latin. Thereafter, Islam, its élan gone, was thought to be left in an existence alien and apart from civilization.

The most significant consequence of this kind of reasoning is the belief that the rise of the West implies a decline of an "Other." This model of cultural study crystallized in the early colonial period, 1750–1850. Logically, this dichotomous view takes precedence over the traditional mandate of the discipline of history, which is to explain actual change. The result has been the persistence of the simplistic notion that the course of Western history has been on the rise while that of Islamic and Arab history during the pre-nineteenth-century period has been on the decline. The theory of rise and decline has had negative consequences for the study of history. In order to sustain this view, a number of countries (Ireland, Greece, Portugal, and Spain, along with portions of the Baltic and Scandinavian countries) had to be dropped from the conventional curriculum of European studies, and various periods in the most representative societies had to be disposed of in a similar manner. The overriding theme of decline accounts for the cultural and material life of the Islamic world being considered unimportant or simply ignored and for outstanding figures from the region being cast into the role of "geniuses in a dark age."

This theory of rise and decline has never produced adequate paradigms for the study of the long centuries separating the Arab Golden Age of the tenth century and the modernization of the nineteenth century. Moreover, this model seems incompatible with our understanding of the nature of the social and economic relations between Europe and the Arab world. Trade was always important to both sides. As the West began to industrialize, it became increasingly dependent on cheap sources of food and raw goods as well as markets. The type of market which the industrial world required would not have come into existence without transformations in the countries of the Third World—the creation of new social classes and the mutation of old ones. Forces that opposed the industrial revolution from within Europe might well have gained the upper hand and blocked further development, particularly in France and other continental countries whose overseas options were much more limited in the late eighteenth century than those of Great Britain. Therefore, I contend that the non-Western regions collaborating in the larger social transformation of the late eighteenth century had indigenous roots for their own modern capitalist cultures, formed through processes of indigenous struggle and in some form of struggle with the European part of the system. I am convinced that, properly understood, the industrial revolution was a global event, and I question the strong tradition in the West to assume a proprietary relationship to it. This study seeks to examine these propositions through a detailed examination of the cultural and material life of Egypt, 1760–1840, in its international context.

Specifically, this is the study of the development of Egypt from the beginning of the impact of the industrial revolution to the defeat of the attempts of the indigenous ruling class to resist Western penetration and domination leading it to join in a loose set of dependent working relations. This study of Egypt between 1760 and 1840 is based on primary materials gathered in Egypt. It owes its inception to a reading of a series of articles written by Professor Afaf Marsot of UCLA in the 1960's. These articles made me aware of a contradiction between the generally held assumptions of centuries of unmitigated decline in al-Azhar, the famous mosque center in Cairo, and the reality of a too rapid creation, after the coming of the West, of a generation of students who could easily learn French, translate literature and medical textbooks, and participate creatively in a new economic infrastructure. This feeling of discomfort with the conventional framework grew when I found that the principal reform-minded figures were also prolific figures in what are usually called the traditional religious fields. In addition, I found upon surveying manuscript catalogs that the total number of books and the range of subjects covered appeared to be vastly greater in the later eighteenth century than in the well-known reform period of Muḥammad ʿAlī in the nineteenth century. The result of my reading a number of these manuscripts in traditional religious fields was the cardinal discovery that the title, often a gloss, was only in limited ways suggestive of the contents. It has been the common assumption of scholars to dismiss glosses as derivative by definition. No one has guessed that in the eighteenth century they disguised a new body of thought. Disguise is not a bad way of putting it, as invariably these works state that their major purpose is to clarify some earlier work or to expand on some well-accepted points. In fact these statements of self-justification were often followed by a most unexpected introduction of secular cultural matters in the midst of a religious subject. The repeated discovery of this among eighteenth-century books ultimately led to the hypothesis tested in this work that important developments in secular culture were taking place and these were supportive of capitalism.

What was the reason for this vast outpouring? Certainly it was not attributable merely to the development of new knowledge or even of polemical exchange, although these played a role. An explanation could only be found in the larger social historical context. The *ʿulamāʾ* of al-Azhar (a group of scholars) found themselves in the middle of the commercial revival of eighteenth-century Cairo which was threatening to tear the society apart. A number of the prominent *ʿulamāʾ* sponsored a revival of Ṣūfī *ṭuruq* (mystical confraternities) and pioneered methods of cross-class communication, trying to stabilize the lower classes, who were beginning to rebel as their situation deteriorated. I found that the *ʿulamāʾ* were central to the formation of culture. Their works taken as a whole have a logic firmly rooted in class structure. The Ṣūfī *ṭuruq* to which the *ʿulamāʾ* belonged were a main locus of cultural production and were the institutions which mirrored the processes of social change which Egypt experienced during this period. This was true exclusively for the eighteenth century; in the nineteenth century the *ṭuruq* gradually gave way to the reform institutions of the new bureaucracy.

How is the conventional picture of eighteenth-century Egypt in culture or economy to be reconciled with the views expressed here? First, supposedly, there was stagnation, then overrapid industrialization, and finally international debt. During the eighteenth century, most studies tell us, there was a decline in payments of tribute to Istanbul, and Upper Egypt broke away from Cairo. In 1798, Napoleon attempted some reforms and succeeded in registering private property, but with his departure chaos ensued. The rise to power of Muḥammad ʿAlī in 1805 inaugurated a period of reform and a rise in national income from the sale of cotton. However, Muḥammad ʿAlī squandered this income on unproductive wars and industrialization projects. Finally, Khedive Ismaʿīl's extravagance led to the financial problems of the mid-nineteenth century. Such studies, with their discontinuities in time and their apparent lack of any meaningful pattern as a result of their dynastic, racial, or ethnic foci, have dominated the historiography of modern Egypt.

The same events can be situated in a more integrated framework. Travel literature, consular reports, and general works on economic history suggest that toward the middle of the eighteenth century France became increasingly interested in Egypt as source of grain, especially to supply the region of Marseilles. Egypt also became attractive to France as a market for her finished goods. It is at this point that the modern world market began to have a direct impact. This impact fostered a commercial revival and encouraged growth of a new and increasingly non-Egyptian class directing an export-oriented economy.

The period of Muḥammad ʿAlī is thus basically a continuation of trends which began in the eighteenth century not a rupture with some millennial past. The capitalist sector grew but became increasingly dominated by Mediterranean commercial minorities which in liaison with the royal family were able to control the state. Egypt briefly retained economic and de facto political autonomy which it had enjoyed in the later Ottoman period. This opportunity was largely the result of international rivalries and of English politics of the 1820's and early 1830's, which discouraged Great Britain from exercising the economic and political influence on Egypt of which she was capable. When the rise of Muḥammad ʿAlī's power threatened the Ottoman Empire, which Great Britain considered to be a barrier to Russian expansion, Muḥammad ʿAlī was quickly broken. The Treaty of London of 1840–41 destroyed the monopoly system on which Egypt's development depended. The development of Egyptian monoculture, dominated by a large landowning class dependent on England, was thereafter a foregone conclusion.

The phases of the cultural revival termed neoclassical broadly followed socioeconomic change. In the first phase, a revival in *ḥadīth* (the studies of the sayings of the Prophet) accompanied and in important ways justified the activities of the commercial sector of the eighteenth century. In the second phase, there was a decline of *ḥadīth* studies and a rise in the study of *kalām* (speculative theology), which was used to justify the reform policies of Muḥammad ʿAlī. Finally, there was a return to *ḥadīth* after the breakup of Muḥammad ʿAlī's reformist bureaucracy. Each period also had a set of characteristic cultural institutions. In the phase of merchant capital, this institution was the *majlis* (salon) of the reform-minded Ṣūfī *ṭuruq*, the Wafāʾīya and the Bakrīya; in the phase of state commercial dominance, it was the printing press, the newspaper, and the translation bureaus. In the agrarian capitalist phase, it was the state school system.

The analysis of the eighteenth century concentrates on fields which were closest to *ḥadīth* studies: history, literature, and the philological sciences. These fields underwent great development characterized by the editing of texts and the study and emulation of classical models. Many of the models were drawn from the Mulūk al-Ṭawāʾif period of Andalusia and other medieval Islamic societies in which the commercial sector had played an important role. In the second phase, attention shifts to those fields which were important to the study of *kalām*: logic, argumentation, medicine, and the natural sciences. These fields enjoyed a local revival. They also continued to merge with various larger trends in science, as Europe, especially Mediterranean Europe, continued to evolve in the early industrial age.

The study of the development of culture in Egypt disclosed that the actual process of the development and reproduction and addition to that culture depended to a large extent on the interaction between the various centers of the Ottoman Empire, notably Damascus and Istanbul. Scholars traveled from place to place in the course of pilgrimages and trade and they studied in the various places they visited. This activity resulted from the different course of development of the raw-goods-producing periphery of the world market in contrast to the industrial center; in the culture of a city on the periphery a single modality of logic dominated a given center, influencing all the cultural production of a given period. For this reason, it is necessary to explore and develop at some length life in the centers other than Cairo as they form collectively a nexus. I have called this a de facto division of labor in the production of culture. This hypothesis facilitates the study of Ṣūfī orders, the crucial cultural institutions. I found that the Khalwatīya, an order spread through several countries of the Ottoman lands, while bound by the tenets of their most illustrious progenitors, were influenced by the more concrete activities in the societies in which they found themselves. While they were loyal to their confreres, across the Islamic world, the Istanbul Khalwatīya were concerned with the problems of the Ottoman elite and had a widely different position on theological and cultural questions from their counterparts in Damascus. The study of the life of a leading Egyptian intellectual, Ḥasan al-ʿAṭṭār al-Khalwatī, serves to clarify some of these processes.

Ḥasan al-ʿAṭṭār's formation in eighteenth-century Egypt, his travels to study in Damascus and Istanbul, and his return to high positions in Muḥammad ʿAlī's government serve to link eighteenth-century Egypt to nineteenth-century Egypt and Egypt to the larger Arabic-language Ottoman culture of his time.

Notes on Method

In this study, I found it useful to employ a series of terms which require a new type of index to help the reader. I find that such terms as *fiqh* or *ḥadīth* or *uṣūl al-fiqh*, which specialists know, must be redefined to convey the sense in which I found these subjects studied, thereby to escape from a misplaced staticness of definitions drawn from the seventh or the eighth century of our era and projected thereafter to cover the development of knowledge one thousand years later. Other terms which most specialists will feel less strongly about, such as the terms classicism and neoclassicism, but which have an assigned place in the study of the literature I find likewise to be both indispensable and in need of a redefining. For the general reader who has progressed this far, a short effort to explain some main concepts may be helpful.

The basic idea in Western Islamic studies that post-Caliphate orthodox Sunnī culture (post A.D. 1250) was a dry scholastic derivative enterprise on the whole simplistic is here challenged by the claim that this is both misguided in a very fundamental sense and self-serving. To begin afresh to enter into the writings of the period of the eighteenth century, one must accept the idea of the *ʿulamāʾ* as intimately involved in a period of momentous societal change which they interpreted and understood. The conclusions which they expressed in writing in one or more of the traditional fields studied here demonstrate this and show how different segments of the eighteenth-century *ʿulamāʾ* were aligned with and intellectually predisposed to defend either the commercial system in its unequal struggle with Western merchants, or the nascent landlord system especially after 1790, or the fate of the artisanate. This social context is a crucial component of the methodology for the study of culture and not merely a conclusion among many. The vast outpouring of books of the period came about because of this involvement. It is therefore crucial to read books, whether on grammar or in *kalām*, for what they tell us about the eighteenth century in which they were composed, to read them in the order in which they were written. I thus follow the development of the writer across the bounds of any given subject. Further, I take each work seriously. His decision to ignore or dismiss the classical rendition of a subject is approached as a problem of why. A brief survey of the works in the mosque available to him and of the high intellectual achievements demonstrated by the leading *ʿulamāʾ* of this supposedly dark age disabuses one of the ancient prejudice that ignorance accounts for abandoning classical models. A closer look suggests that what is taken from the past is self-consciously adopted in the eighteenth century, and this accounts for my claim, after giving many examples, that the eighteenth century saw the birth of neoclassicism in culture—not the mid-nineteenth century as is usually thought. In this respect the intellectual life of Cairo differs from that of Istanbul and Damascus which retained a late classicism in this period.

For Egypt in this period, *uṣūl al-dīn* (the roots of jurisprudence) represented the locus of ideological struggle for legitimizing different economic and social orientations. Again this is not included as a conclusion so much as to point out that the prevailing idea that the roots of jurisprudence exist as levels of reinforcement of a single doctrinal and social position is mistaken. *Ḥadīth* conflicts with *fiqh* not just in terms of what it rationalizes but in its epistemology. Thus, *ḥadīth* studies served the merchants and their need to justify profit in the eighteenth century within an orthodox framework. Philosophically, the collection of sound *ḥadīth* represented an orientation toward a truth which could be computed in such a way as to retain marginal qualitative distinctions. *Fiqh*, or systematic theology based on Aristotelian logic, not merely in practice justified the land system but approached the problem of justification in terms of universals and particulars, a structure of logic difficult to use in the particularistic relations of merchant and artisan, but suitable for the remote and abstract relations of administrator and peasant. These relations changed as the study progressed into the nineteenth century and therefore the particular conclusions cannot be generalized. What can be suggested is that the roots of jurisprudence contain at a given time in a given place an orthodox hegemony, which embodied within itself oppositional modes. The traditional idea of orthodox opposed by some remote Ṣūfī opposition must be sharply modified to appreciate this complex structure.

I claim that the study of culture is an integral part of the study of society and its dynamics. And this poses great difficulties for this book. There is no study of the mode of production in Ottoman Egypt. The efforts in recent years to study the Egyptian countryside have not been entirely successful. The study of Ottoman Cairo has however demonstrated that it provided half or more of the tax revenues coming to the central government. In this context, I decided to concentrate on the commercial sector and its internal class struggle. This choice is dictated by the belief, for which a lot of evidence exists, in the large role of early modern Mediterranean trade in promoting the transformations taking place in Egypt. Future studies will pick up the struggle of the rich peasant and will investigate the writings of al-Ṣiddīqi, a chronicler of the early seventeenth century who referred to the early seventeenth century as the period of the second Ottoman conquest of Egypt. At this point, it is possible to portray the struggles within the Egyptian commercial sector and to see at least the broad outline of the agrarian struggle.

Islamic Roots of Capitalism
Egypt, 1760–1840

Chapter 1
The Social and Economic History of Egypt, 1760–1815: A Study in Merchant Capital and Its Transformation

This chapter presents a socioeconomic interpretation of Egyptian history from 1760 to 1815. In the middle of the eighteenth century, the commercial revival which had received its impetus from the profits of the transshipment of coffee in the late seventeenth and early eighteenth centuries reached its peak and began to decline, only to be sustained and transformed by changes in the economic structure of Europe and in the development of the world market.[1] This chapter deals with the changes affecting Egypt on two levels: on the global level and within Egypt itself. In so doing, I contest the view that the origins of modern Egypt are to be found in the Napoleonic invasion. While I do not dispute the importance of European influence either in economics or in culture, I wish to argue the thesis that modern Egyptian culture has a coherent indigenous basis, and that this basis is rooted in social and economic changes which took place in the middle and late eighteenth century. In this chapter, I shall lay the groundwork for this thesis.

Trade (i.e., the international distribution of goods) took place throughout the history of medieval Egypt and included trade with Europe. Commercial revivals came and went. They permitted a few of the most successful merchants in different epochs to join the landholding aristocratic class. Trade was not transformative; it did not lead to a destruction of the guilds, to the uprooting of peasants, or, in short, to a capitalist transformation. This began to take place later and was due to a constellation of forces, some internal to the Ottoman Empire, such as the Porte's declining influence on Egypt, and others related to the progress of the industrial revolution in western Europe. The industrial revolution created a new type of goods and a market structure to sell them. There were also, of course, factors internal to Egypt which accounted for the breakdown of the Ottoman military corps which had been created in the sixteenth century.

The early 1760's mark two important events, one external, one internal, which serve to demarcate the beginning of our period. The external event is the conflict between England and France (1758–1763) during the Seven Years' War. The result of this war was a great setback for France: she lost much of her vast overseas empire and was shown to be weak on the seas. France turned to sources of raw goods closer at hand than those of the New World, including Egypt and North Africa. The internal event is the rise of the Mamlūk Beylicate, a semi-independent configuration of warriors with a strong commercial orientation, which marks the decline of the older Ottoman military caste system. The conjunction of these two factors accounts in large measure for the fate of the indigenous middle classes and the artisans whose religious and cultural life will be explored in the second and third chapters.

French involvement in Egypt, through its merchants' community, missionaries, and local minority groups, was an opening wedge for the expanded penetration of foreign capital into Egypt in the eighteenth century. I shall treat the social changes in Egypt which resulted from the impact of this penetration in conjunction with the evolution of internal forces.

The treatment of the upper classes focuses on the breakdown of the military castes, their entry into commerce, and their rivalries among themselves and with the European minorities. This chapter discusses merchant capital and its transformation to highlight the nature of commercial organization in this period and the growing impact which this capitalist sector had on the fabric of medieval society as a result of pressure of the world market.

We next study the middle classes and how by the end of the eighteenth century a small segment of the middle class was propelled upward into the landowning class, while the majority were depressed. From a study of the guilds and artisans, I have determined that, while their membership grew during the eighteenth century, their essential character changed for a number of reasons in the direction of wage labor. It is in this sense that we can speak of their decline, linked to market conditions.

Finally, we survey the Delta. In this region, the demand for rice and wheat was accelerating the trend toward monetarization and even, in isolated instances, toward a capitalist agriculture.

We begin with a brief discussion of the rise of Europe and the world market.

The Birth of the Modern World Market

By the end of the fifteenth century, European hegemony began to become apparent with the beginning of the successful expansion of European commerce to far-flung parts of the globe. Ocean voyages led to the conquest of the Americas and gradually to the overcoming of the obstacle or counterpressure of the Ottoman Empire, which had preserved a large share of world trade in Africa and Asia.[2] Europeans succeeded in Asian trade, not through superiority in commercial ability or organizational skill, but through use of superior weaponry. Their ships were strong enough to mount cannon effectively, and with them they could cripple other trading vessels. The effective use of naval artillery led to the setting up of coastal forts along the trade routes, thereby increasing the degree of control and the profitability of the trade.

The period from the end of the fifteenth century to the middle of the seventeenth was the one in which Asian trade was secondary. This was the period of the heyday of piracy of the mineral wealth of the New World. By the middle of the seventeenth century, the combination of new markets and the flood of gold and goods from the New World had greatly stimulated Western manufactures, contributing to the ascendancy of the bourgeoisie in Europe. With the rise of the middle class in western Europe, plunder ceased to be the most productive economic activity, as it interfered with planned growth. Even domination of trade routes was not profitable unless the trade itself was expanding; and in fact the profits from the East India spice trade declined by the middle of the seventeenth century, just as the flow of precious metals from the New World declined when the richest and most accessible mines became used up and the supply of Indian labor shrank.

The period from the mid-seventeenth century to the late eighteenth century, the period of commercial capitalism *par excellence*, was characterized by intensified rivalry among the leading powers of Europe, all of which sought new markets for their products, all of which needed raw goods. England gradually emerged during this period as the paramount sea power, breaking the Dutch monopoly.[3] By the end of the eighteenth century, the commercial expansion which had begun in the last part of the fifteenth century definitely appeared threatened. As Eric Hobsbawm has shown, in the second half of the eighteenth century even the prosperity of the triangular trade had begun to dry up.[4] The declining profitability of the colonies led to a renewed outbreak of warfare among the major powers in the mid-eighteenth century. In the Seven Years' War, France lost nearly the whole of her empire, while England doubled hers and gained concessions which opened up the road to India. The final confrontation between these two great powers took place during the Napoleonic Wars (1793–1815), which ushered in the Pax Britannica of the nineteenth century. The victory of England in the Napoleonic Wars led to a historical epoch of global dominance on an unprecedented scale. Dominion over the seas permitted Britain to colonize either directly or indirectly, or even to favor local independence movements, as in Latin America.

It was during the late eighteenth century that the commercial revolution gave way, first in England and then in other western European countries, to the industrial revolution. At home this meant a gradual decline of the royal companies and the growing power of the chambers of commerce, as in Marseilles or Manchester. Abroad, it meant new economic demands. Not only did the Europeans seek such products as sugar, spice, and slaves, as in the preceding epoch, but they also increasingly placed an emphasis on raw materials to be processed (cotton, oilseeds, dye stuffs, jute, metals, and food for the growing urban populations). The pressure within the European system and the availability of the technology led to attempts to capture control of capitalist sectors in African and Asian countries and to expand them.

During the eighteenth century, the Arabs of the Middle East felt the effects of the second wave created by the outward expansion of European commerce. The first impact had come at the end of the fifteenth century or shortly thereafter, when the Europeans rounded the Cape of Good Hope and gradually increased their dominance of the spice trade; probably this was a factor in the general economic standstill of the region in the sixteenth and seventeenth centuries. Direct English interest in the Arab countries and Egypt arose as a result of the expansion, in the eighteenth century, of the British East India Company. The growing British involvement in India, a region in which the French were already established, created a need for rapid communication as never before. Thus, affairs in Egypt, Syria, and Iraq became a matter of concern.[5] The British had previously depended on the Persian Gulf–Baghdad–Aleppo route, but this was increasingly uncertain because of the "instability" of the Pashalik of Baghdad and the raids of the neighboring Bedouins. An alternative route for the British was the Red Sea–Egypt route which ran through a shorter Bedouin-controlled stretch between Suez and Cairo. In 1768, ʿAlī Bey, the leading Mamlūk, seemed inclined toward trade and cooperation when the Scottish explorer James Bruce visited Cairo. Bruce's suggestions concerning the use of this route also interested the merchant community of Alexandria, and they lent their support, as did the British sea captains who found the Red Sea trade in a state of decay and thought that they might sell Bengal goods in the bazaars of Cairo. The East India Company and the Sultan, however, opposed it. The Porte was naturally concerned about the loss of revenue from the Ḥijāz region if trade should be diverted from Jidda to Suez; and the Company, on the defensive against free trade, was also reluctant "to have prohibited goods reach the Mediterranean."

Thus, when the British sought to send merchandise from Calcutta to Suez in 1774, the Sharīf of Mecca violently protested. The Turkish merchant community, which feared the loss of its Basra and Aleppo trade, strongly backed him. The Porte issued a firman banning this trade.[6]

It was not, however, merely concern for the Porte which deterred the British from establishing themselves more deeply in Egypt. Such involvement was also unprofitable. In Egypt, as in many other parts of the Levant, French cloth sold much better than English woolens. After 1750, English sales in Egypt dwindled to a mere twenty-five bales a year. In 1754 the Levant Company, England's representative in the Middle East, decided to withdraw to Cyprus, thus officially giving up, although for individuals who stayed, trade revived between 1757 and 1773.[7]

The Failure of French Agriculture: Search for an Overseas Solution, 1750–1815

France was the major power involved in Egypt and the other Arab countries during the second half of the eighteenth century; England's commitments were elsewhere. What was France seeking in Egypt? What impact did France have on Egypt during this period?

It will be recalled that France was decidedly weaker than England and that after the Seven Years' War she did not control overseas colonies; thus, she had fewer options for procuring raw materials and for marketing her manufactured products. In addition, France had a problem which England did not. Since she lacked control of the seas, a mounting urban population created for her a growing problem of inadequate food supply, especially in the south of France.[8]

In fact, it is not an exaggeration to say that France, in contrast to England, underwent a structural evolution in the eighteenth century which delayed the modernization of her agricultural sector and made her increasingly dependent on food imports in the late eighteenth century as the country became increasingly urbanized and mounted an army for war. This is clearly reflected in the nature of her trade with Egypt and would seem to have carried some weight in the risky decision to invade Egypt in 1798. A half-century of frustration in Egypt, combined with growing needs at home, created and sustained the hope that the destruction of the Mamlūk regime would break the monopoly which the Mamlūks held on the grain trade. If the French could gain access, it might even be enlarged by the introduction of some French production methods.

French agriculture at the beginning of the eighteenth century was dominated by royal absolutism. "The French landed upper classes adapted to the gradual intrusion of capitalism by putting greater pressure on the peasants, meanwhile putting them in a situation approaching *de facto* ownership."[9] This was because the impulse toward commercial agriculture had from the beginning of the century been weaker in France than in England, and not only among the French nobility. The problem of getting grain to the city was correspondingly greater in France than in England. The grain trade in France presented a picture of stagnation, broken by an impulse toward production for the market in the neighborhood of the big cities. There the wealthier peasants rather than the landed aristocracy appear to have been the main beneficiaries. The former were able to pass the costs of transportation on to the merchants. The early part of the century in particular was characterized by profiteering merchants who scoured the countryside to buy up food goods from the wealthy peasants. But later in the eighteenth century, aristocratic disdain for commercial agriculture did not hinder the nobility, especially in the Diocese of Toulouse, from making large profits in the grain trade. The incentive to grow grain was greater in southern France because of the rising population; local political pressures led to an improvement in transportation. However, unlike the English nobility, the French nobility who were involved in agriculture in the eighteenth century did not introduce any technological innovations.[10] Possibly the system of seigneurial obligation was an obstacle to technological change; possibly it was contrary to the interests of the rich peasants.

The end of the eighteenth century was marked by a long series of grain crises which, as can be seen from the preceding analysis, were clearly related to the failure of capital penetration into the French countryside—an aspect of the relative indifference of the French aristocracy to do more than live off their rents. Toulouse was the singular exception; here, however, the orientation toward increased marketing was related not to increased production but rather to a greater emphasis on medieval dues which the peasant had to pay. By the end of the eighteenth century, a vigorous reform movement had developed. The physiocrats were well aware of what was needed for agricultural reform, and as the grain crises continued, their number and influence grew at court. One particularly severe crisis occurred during the interval from 1787 to 1789, just prior to the outbreak of the Revolution. "A decree of 1787 removed restrictions on the grain trade, including those requiring the cultivators to bring their grain to the local markets. The harvest in the autumn of 1788 was disastrously short. The winter that followed was unusually harsh, while spring brought severe storms and floods. Natural disasters combined with political uncertainties and anxieties by the summer of 1789 to set off a series of panics and peasant uprisings in many parts of France."[11] Where the food problem was most acute, in the south, even the wealthy urban merchants supported the Gironde party and sought the Restoration.[12]

Agricultural reform began for the first time in 1794, when the disruptions created by the wartime situation helped the reformers to a certain extent in getting around the seigneurial system. However, in October 1795, inflationary pressure which was closely related to the price of bread led to revolts, the leadership of which was provided by the wealthy merchants.[13]

As the eighteenth century progressed, a relationship developed between French grain insufficiency and her trade policy of importing grain from wherever it could be found. It is clear that, by the end of the century, Marseilles was in a state of virtual dependence on foreign sources of grain. Egypt was a potential granary, although prior to the Seven Years' War this had not been the case. In fact, before the middle of the century, little can be deduced about the significance of French imports from the Middle East. Rather, the emphasis in a French consul's report of 1748 seems to be one of satisfaction with the great improvement in the sale of French cloth there. Whereas in the 1720's only the nobles could afford to buy it, now all the well-off families were able to purchase it, and the *beys* were dressing their slaves in it.[14]

Here the major concern was still that luxury goods might not find a broad enough market. This fear was put to rest by the phenomenon (which will be discussed below) of the sustained revival of the middle classes in Egypt. But by the 1760's, it is possible to detect a new and enlarged French involvement in Egypt. The direction this took is clear. Rather suddenly, France developed a local client community to carry on its trade. The support which France gave this group of traders, who were Christians and recent immigrants from Syria, permitted them to unseat the Egyptian Jewish community from its control of the lucrative *iltizām* (tax farm) of the customs *dīwān*.

The Egyptian Jewish community had received the nominal support of Venice. The principal support which France was able to give by virtue of her trade position was consular protection to merchants of her choice. This *beratli* status in turn gave the bearer an important advantage vis-à-vis the indigenous Muslim merchant community. The *beratli* merchant would pay one-half or less of the customs duties that an indigenous merchant would have to pay. The indigenous merchant community of Egypt was never again able to gain control of its own trade with Europe until the twentieth century.[15] The principal Syrians mentioned as working for the French during this period were Mikhāʾīl Fakhr and Yūsuf Bayṭār. In 1769 Fakhr took control of the Alexandria customs, and Yūsuf Bayṭār took over the Damietta customs. The Venetians immediately lost influence. Fakhr raised the import tariff on Venetian goods from the 3 percent, which was usual for European goods, to 5 percent.

The gross statistics provided by Paul Masson give a picture of rising trade between Egypt and France in mid-century, coinciding with the rise of the Syrians to influence. The Egyptians were purchasing some weaponry but mainly luxury goods; the French were buying mainly raw materials, including rice and wheat.[16] The reasons for the collapse of this trade have been presented in many works as due to Mamlūk misrule, which involved many discriminatory practices leveled against the foreign merchant community. A common example of the grievances which are frequently cited is the breakdown of the harbor facilities in Alexandria.[17] The collapse of the French merchant community did not of course signal the decline of Egyptian exports and French imports. The trade was now passing more and more through the hands of the minorities.

In 1797, a well-informed contemporary witness of Egyptian events, Jean-Baptiste Trécourt, wrote an interesting work on the economy of Egypt.[18] His aim was to discuss the procuring of Egyptian grain, which he foresaw would require political changes in Egypt, changes which France could bring about. Much of his book argues that these changes would greatly benefit the poor people of Egypt. Trécourt's book is highly polemical, but it is nevertheless very informative. He blames what he calls the general impoverishment of the people on the restrictions which the *beys* placed on the exporting of grain! He states that its export without tax was not permitted except to Jiddah and the Sharīf of Mecca, and that when it was permitted to other areas it was only with such "onerous restrictions" that no profits could be realized.[19] In years of privation, Trécourt argues, the ordinary Egyptian goes hungry despite the agricultural richness of his country. Because the cultivator knows that if he were to grow crops destined for local consumption he would receive a low price, there is no incentive for him to grow more than he requires for his own needs. In the event of crop failure, wheat is imported from abroad, and the differential in costs due to transportation and export duties makes it too dear for the poor people to buy it. This is the gist of his argument: widespread misery among the Egyptian people is the result of the Mamlūks' refusal to accept free trade in grain. It is clear from a close reading that the author was in fact projecting French problems onto Egypt. The problem of having to import grain at high prices was a real one for France but was purely hypothetical in Egypt. He refers to the "famine of 1784" in Egypt, but it is clear that in this year the "misery" came from the plague, not from the fact that the poor could not eat rice or wheat.[20] His real interest was in creating a free trade zone in Egypt which would ease the problem of French merchants and their subsidiaries in procuring grain. "The obstacles which I am speaking about are by no means the only ones which indicate the desirability of free grain sales. There is as well in Egypt a very ruinous monopoly, one of the principal consequences of which is to cause fluctuation in prices. I saw in the same year wheat selling for eight and for thirty-six piastres for the ardeb."[21] As Gaston Wiet remarks in his editorial notes, Trécourt was by no means the only Frenchman to complain about the grain production, which was sometimes even compared to the description given by Pliny of the grain trade.[22]

In the 1790's, economic restrictions imposed by the Revolutionary government in Paris made the local French trade situation even more difficult. In the summer of 1793, the Convention laid an embargo on the export of French goods and forbade the transmission of funds to foreign countries, thus making payment for imports impossible. In June 1793, the British declared grain and raw materials to be contraband of war. By September of 1793, France was almost cut off from world trade.[23] This almost certainly underlay the famous "vexations" of French merchants and is generally alleged to be one of the justifications of the Napoleonic invasion of Egypt in 1798. On the one hand, there was the fact that Egyptian wheat fed southern France; on the other hand, the French merchant community was unable to pay for the wheat.[24] This may explain, for example, the events of April 1794, when Ibrāhīm Bey "extorted" 14,000 patâques (!?) and subsequently pillaged French merchants' supplies, which led to their decision to leave Cairo.[25] Charles Magellon, the most experienced and most famous member of the French merchant community, returned to Paris and devoted himself to lobbying for an invasion of Egypt. Addressing the Commissioner of Foreign Relations in October 1795, he stressed the great value of Egyptian cereals and rice to France in those years in which the French harvest should be poor. After dwelling on the "tyranny" of the *beys* in yet another work, a *Mémoire sur l'Egypte* (February 1798), addressed to Talleyrand, he went on to describe the commercial and agricultural possibilities if France were to capture Egypt. The *Mémoire* included an estimate of the military expenditures required in such an operation.[26] This *Mémoire* appeared a year after the last diplomatic effort by France in Egypt, the Thainville Mission, which sought release of or recompense for a cargo of cloth which the head of the Egyptian customs had seized in March 1797. This mission ended in failure, and a year later the French sent an invading army. From all this it is quite clear not only that France had an objective need for grain, but also that a lobby existed in France composed of merchants and diplomats who, along with manufacturers from the south, pressured the French government to become involved. These groups desired to improve their situation in Egypt, but there were also in the background hopes of regaining France's position in India, which had been greatly weakened in the Seven Years' War. In the section below on the period from 1798 to 1815, emphasis will be placed on the almost single-minded concern with these issues, which continued to be paramount.

Egypt in 1760

What was the nature of the society which attracted France and which ultimately justified an overseas invasion at a time when France did not dominate the seas? The hypothesis developed here is that Egypt was a weak tributary formation. It was weak in the sense that the extraction of ground rent depended on the central government, and not on a seigneurial presence. It was weak in the sense that the reproduction of the system depended on the active cooperation of the rich peasants, who had to ensure the day-to-day maintenance of agriculture. Finally, it was vulnerable vis-à-vis Europe in the sense that its commercial sector, which was confined largely to the city of Cairo, was disproportionately large. This precapitalist commercial sector from Ayyūbid times to the early seventeenth century performed the functions of distribution and financing for the ruling class; thereafter, industry and trade came to account for half or more of the tax revenue and constituted a principal arena of struggle for domination by Mamlūks and Janissaries.[27]

The impact of the western European industrial revolution was to cause the value of agricultural land to rise and to intensify competition in the commercial sector, especially after the arrival of European merchants and Syrian Christians, who served as proxy for French capitalism. The year 1760 marks the date when struggle over distribution of the surplus began to result in a transformation of production. It marks the beginning of a long process in which the commercial sector was wrested from indigenous hands, a process in which other subordinate social formations, slave and tribal, likewise give way as capitalism developed. It is a convenient date to note the decline of pepper, spices, and coffee exports. Their displacement was critical for the city's economy.

The Ruling Class: Part One—The Mamlūk Elite, 1760–1798

The Mamlūk *beys* emerged as the political elite in alliance with a number of rich merchants who formed the economic elite after a series of internecine struggles between their rivals, the Janissaries and other feudal military groups. The Janissaries had been deeply involved in trade; and with the decline of coffee as an export commodity, their situation deteriorated in the early eighteenth century. The *beys*, whose wealth was in land and whose numbers were replenished from distant points, were isolated from the problems of Cairo. Their wealth rose steadily as the value of land rose. The strength of the Mamlūks lay in their alliances with indigenous and foreign merchants, an alliance constituted against the Ottoman presence in Egypt and against its rivals as well. The Mamlūks were able to control both their rivals, whose wealth they confiscated, and the Ottoman administrative apparatus, into whose ranks they introduced their personnel, whose procedures of land registration and taxation they circumvented, and whose chief officers existed only on their sufferance. As a result, the Mamlūks were far wealthier than their predecessors, the Janissaries. As a consequence of wealth and foreign connections, ʿAlī Bey, the leading Mamlūk, had access to new technology, especially weaponry.[28] This weaponry was extremely expensive in the short run and had a disruptive effect on the society in the long run.

ʿAlī Bey al-Kabīr became ruler in 1760, that is, Shaykh al-Balad, or the leading Mamlūk *amīr* (sometimes called simply *bey*). He was the first to attempt to work through the foreign merchant community and to attempt to reform key institutions, such as the army, by means of European advisors.[29] The Ottoman Pasha's significance was thereby reduced, but he was still a symbol of the legitimacy of the system, and as such a formidable figure. Not only did he possess a great deal of wealth, but it was still necessary that he be welcomed and courted and, if the *beys* found him to be dangerous, removed in a manner which was in no way critical of the Porte, whose personal appointee he was.

A Mr. Lusignan, a contemporary source, gives us a picture of the complexity of the competing economic and political orientations within the ruling class.[30] Upon being informed of the arrival of a new Pasha, the Shaykh al-Balad would send a party bearing gifts and spies to see what the Porte's intentions were. If they discovered anything discomforting, the Shaykh al-Balad would try to force the new Pasha to leave and at the same time write to the would-be Pasha. But, as Lusignan observed, if the Pasha was prudent, he could break the power of the Great Dīwān by gaining the affection of the Āghā of the Janissaries, the Kikhyā, and the Shawīsh and playing one *bey* against another, since each one wanted to be Shaykh al-Balad. According to Lusignan, the last Pasha who was able to accomplish this was Rāghib Muḥammad Pasha, the Pasha of Cairo from 1742 to 1749. After him it would seem that no Pasha gained power again, except for short periods when an Ottoman army was in Egypt. The revenue of the Pasha was great in absolute terms, but during the course of the eighteenth century it was continuously being limited by the Mamlūk *beys*.

"During most of the eighteenth century, the governors received an average of 15,000,000 para's from the sales of properties of deceased persons alone [*iltizāms* went as part of the governor's *khāṣṣ* revenues] but after 1779 the Mamlūk Amīrs seized this paying the governors an average of 1,500,000 para's."[31] While sources conflict on some points of detail, it is clear that the Pasha lost the bulk of the revenues of the customs house tax farm, which was worth some 12 million paras annually, after 1750.[32] Other income based on the collection of the *ḥulwān* (annual tribute to the Porte) was also greatly limited by the *beys*, especially after 1779/1193 when Egypt was ruled by Murād and Ibrāhīm.[33] Another loss of revenue to the Ottoman treasury in Egypt which affected the Pasha occurred when the Shaykh of the Hawwāra tribe of Upper Egypt, which had paid Cairo 150,000 ardebs of wheat during the first half of the eighteenth century, ceased to do so after 1769, when the Ṣaʿīd (upper Egypt) was in a state of "anarchy." This would seem to have left only the Pasha's minor revenues (e.g., investiture fees of officials, his annual salary from the treasury) free from the inroads of the Mamlūks in the later eighteenth century.[34]

The decline of the power of the Pasha was not an isolated phenomenon. The Mamlūks dominated all the ruling institutions of the society. Naturally, they sought to infiltrate the financial bureaucracy. In the early eighteenth century, the *efendis* of the financial bureaucracy passed their positions on to their sons; while the positions were tax farms, guild membership and attendance at the schools were nonetheless preconditions to access. Until 1775 the system remained intact; after this time the Mamlūks began to introduce their members into these posts. In 1798, when the French came, Ibrāhīm Efendī and most of his *efendis* and scribes fled to Syria with the *beys*, refusing the bribes offered by Napoleon and showing their loyalty to the Mamlūks.[35] Another example of Mamlūk interference in the treasury concerned the Maḥmal (sacred litter). The treasury had paid during the seventeenth and eighteenth centuries some 500,000 paras for the costs of the Pilgrimage to Mecca each year from Cairo through Egypt, and this was supplemented by *waqf* funds from the estates deeded by will. After 1775, the *beys* appropriated the funds to themselves. The *kiswa*, or cover, of the Maḥmal became increasingly threadbare, and for the first time Bedouin attacks on the pilgrimage route were a significant problem.

Another example of the breakdown of the system of extraction was a shift in taxation. The rate for those who paid in cash was far below the rate for those who paid in kind. This permitted large, untaxed profits on cash crops and encouraged speculation and the creation of an artificial scarcity.[36] Not only did Mamlūk capital penetrate the Ottoman financial administration, thereby altering the way in which it functioned, as in taxing, but on occasion it was also able to simply bypass it. One sign of this was the growth of *murattabāt*, which indicated that income was illegally being made into *awqāf* for individuals and institutions at the treasury's expense.[37] *Murattabāt* are an indication of an accumulation of capital.

A third important area of Mamlūk domination during the second half of the eighteenth century was within the military corps themselves. The seven Ottoman corps had never in practice been of equal strength of wealth, but their intact existence was a foundation stone of the medieval system and was symbolized by their equal representation in the Great Dīwān. As Stanford Shaw describes them:

> During the sixteenth and seventeenth centuries, the janissaries, ʿazab and mutafarriqa corps had the most men, revenue and power, and the others were subordinate to them. In the eighteenth century, as the mamlūk houses took over control of the entire Ottoman system, the corps as such, and the distinctions among them, became much less important, as they all became little more than vehicles for the maintenance and support of the freed mamlūks of the various houses in the mamlūk hierarchy. However, the janissary corps did retain somewhat more of an independent organization, and it usually was the chief weapon of the dominant mamlūk house, whichever house that might be.[38]

The Janissaries managed to gain part of the customs house revenue which had been taken from the Pasha during the second half of the eighteenth century. They then paid the Pasha a decreasing compensation, pocketing an estimated 25 million paras. Another source of revenue was derived from their work as the police of the city of Cairo. They could accept bribes from the artisans, merchants, and tavern owners and allow them to violate the various laws, and in this way collect an estimated 50 to 2,000 paras a month. The Janissaries also controlled the salt monopoly, which they had seized from the ʿAzabs in 1691. During the 1790's it was worth 1.6 million paras annually. Their monopoly of the slaughterhouse tax was worth about a million paras annually at the end of the century. Among the other tax farms which they controlled were the mint and the granary, which they had retained as a consequence of their basic function of policing the city of Cairo and the Citadel.

> After the middle of the century, the janissaries and the ʿazabs largely replaced the mutafarriqa corps as the principal sources of the new men sent to garrison the provincial fortresses. From the revolt of ʿAlī Bey al-Kabīr in 1183/1769–70 until the arrival of the French expedition, the Mamlūk amīrs who ruled Egypt based the power of their houses principally on the revenues and positions available to the janissaries and ʿazabs, in which they enrolled their men, while the other corps became little more than rewards for members of the janissary and ʿazab corps who were members of, or who supported the ruling mamlūk houses.[39]

From all this it is clear that the role of the Janissaries was subordinate to that of the Mamlūks, although sometimes they were in alliance with them. During the eighteenth century, the ʿAzab served mainly as subordinates to the Janissaries who guarded the police stations (*qulluq*) of Cairo. The ʿAzab also supplied most of the men for the forts in Upper Egypt; provided guards for the environs of Alexandria, Damietta, Rosetta, and Suez; and manned and guarded the boats sailing on the Nile and in the Delta.[40] The ʿAzab also retained several important tax farms, the one of greatest interest being the Amīn al-Khurda. This tax farm originally (in 1528) controlled public spectacles and entertainment, but by the late eighteenth century was only important as a way of entry into the guilds of Cairo.[41] This is the first direct evidence of the fate of some of the poorer and more subordinate corps. Their members, some of them undoubtedly Turks, others Egyptians, simply disappeared through intermarriage and economic associations into the indigenous population. A second tax farm retained by the ʿAzab, the Amīn al-Baḥrayn, carried with it the right to supervise, regulate, and tax the navigation on the Nile between the "two ports" of Old Cairo and Būlāq. A great deal of Cairo's grain trade passed this way, making it a very important office.[42]

In the second half of the eighteenth century, then, the Mamlūks were the backbone of the ruling class, a class which also included officials and even some wealthy Egyptians. The question we must answer—and it is a very difficult one—is: Who were the Mamlūks? The answer cannot be given, as it was above, simply in terms of the Mamlūks as a "corps" with their tax farms, because their economic function was now more complicated.[43] A standard response to the question of how to identify the Mamlūks has been to try to determine their social background, even though it obviously changed during the half-century on which we are concentrating.

The Mamlūks' social background in the mid-eighteenth century would seem to be well known. The Mamlūks came from territory ruled by Russia until the Empress Catherine prevented their leaving in the 1780's. A body of literature, some of which is discussed below, shows how they retained sympathies and perhaps even stronger links, with Russia. But, as a recent article shows, even during the pre-1780 period, the question of their identity was complicated. During the eighteenth century, the Mamlūk elite created for itself an elaborate mythology about its origins which had little to do with the reality of these origins, or with its professions of loyalty (or disloyalty) to the Ottoman Empire.[44] As P. M. Holt has shown, it was based on an obviously spurious genealogy which incorporated Egyptian Bedouin and classical Arabian tribal distinctions into Mamlūk history. The struggle between two Mamlūk houses in the eighteenth century, between the white flag (Faqqārī) and the red flag (Qāsimī), was related to a very early tribal conflict between the Tubbāʿī and the Kulaybī, then to the later struggle of the Yamanīs and Yazīdīs and to others from throughout Arab history. Another writer took this creation of spurious genealogy to be evidence of the "assimilation" of the Mamlūk elite into Egyptian society, a blurring of the difference between Mamlūk and non-Mamlūk; he also noted the rapid manumission of "slaves" attached to Mamlūk households which took place in this period.[45]

Undoubtedly, assimilation served a purpose of legitimizing rule as the socioeconomic structure changed. When English orientalist Edward Lane came to Egypt in the early nineteenth century, the distinction between a Turkish official and an Egyptian, even a prosperous one, was still clearly visible in the fact that the former rode a horse and the latter a mule. Lane arrived after the Mamlūk period. There is no doubt that legitimacy was a basic problem which confronted the Mamlūk *beys.* What was the basis of their claim to the loyalty of their members, or the loyalty of the society at large? In the later eighteenth century, when full-grown Mamlūks were being acquired from whatever region would send them, including Europe, traditional ties of a shared familial experience must in any case have been weakened, and ties based on ethnic solidarity were lacking. What then would hold the house together?[46] The houses were in fact not holding together; this is a corollary to the phenomena of assimilation, manumission, genealogy creation, and so on. Examples of treachery among the *beys*, of one killing another after having been his ally, abound in ʿAbd al-Raḥman al-Jabartī's account of the eighteenth century and in the European travel books of the period. Yet the system lasted into the first decade of the nineteenth century. There was no rising class within Egypt seeking to destroy it.

The question of what sustained the Mamlūk system before and after the 1780's can to a degree be studied separately. Between the 1760's and the 1780's, a number of sources link the Mamlūks to Russia. ʿAlī Bey was a prototype of the first period; Ibrāhīm al-Sannārī was a prototype of the second. During the "Russian period" (1760–1780), one finds a number of examples of Russian aid to the *beys.* One might question to what extent this aid was being given because of sympathy or to what extent Russia was simply interested in encouraging any anti-Ottoman rebellion.[47] After the 1780's, Mamlūks seemed to come primarily from the Sudan and even from Europe. French sources, reflecting the contemporary Frenchman's fear of the Russian fleet and of Russian diplomatic moves, tend to blur the distinction between Russian sympathy with anti-Ottoman motives and actual ethnic solidarity. Masson wrote that at the instigation of Baron de Thonus, the Russian consul, Murād Bey (who was of Russian origin) dunned the French merchants of 300,000 écus, a large sum, which they were unable to pay. Later, at Russia's behest, Murād demolished the French convent of the Fathers of the Holy Land (Couvent de Pères de la Terre Sainte).[48] Another French writer showed that in 1785 the Empress Catherine, anticipating war with the Porte, supported the *beys'* claim to independence. The Russian consul in Cairo was on this occasion given elaborate presents. Four years later, in 1789, however, the period of Russian influence was obviously over: Baron de Thonus was assassinated by followers of Ismaʿīl Pasha.[49]

But despite an exaggeration of Thonus' influence with the *beys*, one French writer does indicate quite concretely a way in which this influence may have been exercised: "One quarter of the 'New Houses' are truly Russian. The others are Georgian or Circassian, carry on as well through the Russian consul correspondance with their parents who are known to them and who have had them transmit quite large sums of money in recent times . . . Ibrāhīm Bey, son of a Georgian priest, can remember having served in the mass . . . he has written to the Baron de Thonus asking him to send five hundred Mamlūks and this consul has been charged with the task of convincing the Russian court to agree to this."[50]

The new Mamlūks of the end of the eighteenth century came from diverse sources, Africa being the most accessible. Of course, there were many holdovers. Muṣṭafā Āghā served Napoleon because he hated the Mamlūks of the family of Muḥammad Bey Abū Dhahab (Murād and Ibrāhīm), because Murād had killed his old patron, the Āghā ʿAbd al-Raḥman.[51] At the very end of the eighteenth century and in the early nineteenth century, a number of Mamlūks were clearly of Greek origin.[52]

If shared social origin does not explain how the Mamlūks' system survived, then it would be logical to postulate that the household of the *bey* represented during this period a rational unit of endeavor in economic terms or in military terms. A recent study argues that this was indeed the case, but points out that the household was always under strain because it was never quite sufficient. "ʿAlī Bey (1758–63), who was the first Mamlūk to recruit mercenaries on a large scale, began by seizing his opponent's lands and levying extraordinary taxes on the villages and the merchants and other groups in the towns. One of his successors, Murād Bey (1778–89), tried less short-term methods. He monopolized the customs and then began, forcibly, to purchase a large part of the wheat crop and to sell it for cash at a greatly increased price."[53]

The expense of hiring mercenaries was one of the chief causes of the economic strains which forced the Mamlūks to adopt short-run expedients to raise money. The mercenaries were of two types: first, the Maghāriba, who if not paid created havoc in the city (rulers, including Napoleon and Muḥammad ʿAlī, had to find special roles for them to keep them occupied); second, the European Mamlūks, who ran the navy and manned the cannon, whose service in war was a necessity but who were very expensive to maintain and in addition required expensive equipment. A few examples will make this clear. Among the great military and technical ventures of the late eighteenth century was the creation of a navy by Murād Bey. Using Turkish artisans whom he imported, he constructed several battleships at great cost. The largest of the ships was armed with twenty-four cannon and was moored at Giza in front of his palace. To run the navy, Murād relied on a Greek admiral, Niqūlā Raʾīs, and some three hundred Greek marines originally from the Archipelago. Niqūlā Raʾīs had previously served in the Ottoman navy and had deserted to the Mamlūks during the invasion of 1786. He was to desert again to Napoleon in 1798. Niqūlā had great power over the Mamlūks, who feared the consequences of being cannonaded.[54] They wanted him to stay because they needed his skills, for even the Europeans had respect for the quality of his artillery.[55]

Murād Bey also depended on the services of three Greek brothers, the Zantiots (Ibrāhīm, Aḥmad, and Ḥusayn). Ibrāhīm created an "artillery factory" for Murād Bey near his palace in Giza. Ḥusayn took charge of the artillery itself and took part in the defense of Upper Egypt against General Desaix de Veygoux. Later, however, he defected and served as a diplomat and intermediary between Murād and the French.[56]

As previously stated, the mercenaries had to be well paid for their services, and they also had to be equipped with the necessary technology. Fortunately or otherwise, Egypt possessed the saltpeter for making good gunpowder. This greatly interested the French, who, as stated above, had great trouble procuring an adequate supply during the eighteenth century and cast a longing eye on Egypt. "The fabrication of gunpowder was confided to the industry of a few foreigners who settled in Egypt . . . The gunpowder manufactured at Cairo appears to be good; the materials of which it is composed are excellent in quality . . . Gunpowder is not so dear at present in Cairo as it was in France anterior to the Revolution . . . The process employed here in the manufacture of saltpetre is exactly the same as that practiced in Europe."[57] But if Egypt possessed gunpowder, when it came to cannon another situation prevailed. Cannon began to be used in Egypt following ʿAlī Bey's unsuccessful siege of Jaffa. In 1776, an English artillery officer named Robinson was appointed to be a military advisor by Ismaʿīl, the Shaykh al-Balad.[58] In addition to the use of cannon, firearms became increasingly important to the Mamlūks in the late eighteenth century. As the Mamlūks insisted on retaining their basic identity as a cavalry force, they sought guns which were suitable for use on horseback, leaving to their servants the use of pistols which could be deadly at close range. A third category of fighter developed, servants mounted on horseback (*sarrājūn*), many of whom, as it turned out, were Christians pretending to be Muslims.[59]

Egyptian dependence on the French for their weapons was both expensive and, from a military point of view, unfortunate for Egypt. French iron and steel were of low quality; their artillery continued to be made out of copper as late as 1793. The fundamental weapon of land warfare for the French continued to be the smoothbore, muzzle-loading flintlock musket. The model of 1793 had not changed in principle for one hundred years.[60]

The Mamlūks, in addition to spending vast sums on the upkeep of their military establishments, and in engaging one another in small wars, were attracted to luxury goods on a scale which none of the other military corps had ever before indulged in. A study of the residential patterns of the Mamlūk aristocracy showed that the ruling elite left the austere Citadel, where they had lived in the seventeenth century, and in the eighteenth century built villas in the fashionable suburbs, where they lived a life replete with luxury.[61] One figure, Muḥammad Bey Abū Dhahab, more than any other came to symbolize the new way of life. He demanded of the French merchants on one occasion that they construct for him at their expense a four-wheeled gold carriage at an estimated cost of 7,200 French livres before shipping. Such was the profitability of the French position in Egypt that they proceeded to have the carriage made.[62] While Muḥammad Bey Abū Dhahab was a flagrant example, all French sources testify to the degree to which the *beys*, as well as the Egyptian middle classes, sought to acquire French cloth and luxury goods. These included silk scarves, muslin shirts, ivory-incrusted weapons, or weapons with coral inlay which the *beys* would pay for in pure gold. When the Napoleonic army captured some of these, there were several fights between the savants and various soldiers over whom this booty should belong to. French soldiers at the Battle of the

Pyramids pillaged the bodies of the dead Mamlūks, searching for sequins, the gold coins first struck in Venice. Berthier, a chemist, offered 10,000 francs for the blade of a sword made of black damascus and encrusted with pure gold. The sword of Murād Bey, which was much fought over, finally wound up in the Musée aux Invalides in Paris, as did other works of the famous craftsman Asʿadallah, the armorer.[63] The Mamlūks inherited aspects of the life style of the medieval knight. They had a similar idea of the well-rounded, versatile figure, skilled in war, in games of athletic skill, and in such pastimes as chess. They had an appreciation of luxury goods for which they paid dearly, as they did for their way of life as a whole,[64] but they sought to combine it with residence in a bourgeois suburb.

The breakdown of the Mamlūks' tributary system cannot be discussed properly apart from a discussion of ground rent, a theme no one has pursued yet. A few of the features to be discussed affecting the Mamlūks may be summarized as follows: The mounting costs of war placed severe strains on the Mamlūk households, which had to find new sources of revenue to meet them. While their involvement in commerce helped, it did not always suffice. At the same time, the new technology of war required a whole new set of personnel to employ this technology. The introduction of technology and personnel was not only a severe financial strain, but it also slowly undermined the primary rationale of the Mamlūk household, that is, as a basic fighting unit. The growing use of technicians and mercenaries, while rational from a military point of view, in the end called into question the basic legitimacy of the Mamlūk household as a pattern of organization.[65]

The Ruling Class: Part Two—The Rich Merchants, 1760–1798

A number of merchants can also be identified as members of the ruling class. They belong through ties of marriage and through wealth. According to André Raymond's analysis, the commercial elite of Cairo grew smaller in the late eighteenth century and was increasingly composed of members of the European-linked minority groups. Naturally there was an internal solidarity of the merchants which distinguished them from the Mamlūks and which occasioned interelite conflict. But before the end of the eighteenth century, ways of solving these problems were developed. The Shāh Bandar of the merchants, who was usually the wealthiest merchant, had links to the ruling *beys*, sometimes through marriage but always through trade and property.[66] The liquidity problems of the *beys* could for the most part be met by loans from the Jewish merchants, whose international contacts gave them liquid assets, and so it was not until after their decline, and after the gold shortage resulting from the decline of the Sudanese trade in the 1790's, that Mamlūk extortions from indigenous merchants, probably not elite merchants, became a regular event.[67]

Raymond finds a number of defects in the organization of the merchant community which he terms weakness of capital as opposed to liquid assets, reliance on word of mouth as opposed to written records, and reluctance to invest overseas.[68] These weaknesses were compounded by the tendency of the rich merchant to invest in land and not in workshops. If, however, one considers the rising value of land and the declining return on workshops due to the noncompetitive position of the Egyptian artisan, these trends bespeak a high degree of capitalist acumen.[69]

The structure of commerce, however parochial, must have contained an element of flexibility not always found in Europe or in other parts of the Arab world. Raymond mentions that, although Turks of the Ḥijāz region would not accept paper money from the French as late as 1730, this was not the case in Cairo and the Mediterranean countries. There was also the institution of the upper-class *dallāla*[70] as a seller of merchandise. The *dallāla* was a crucial part of the development of the world market which could only be played by women, for the *dallāla* had to pursuade the upper-class women to make fundamental alterations in their consumption patterns. They were successful in introducing French luxury products.

Still other evidence drawn from the lives of these persons indicates the changing role of the rich merchants in Egyptian history. They had, of course, a large number of personal attendants; but, especially in the first half of the eighteenth century, they exhibited a considerable trend toward buying and freeing slaves.[71] They aided in the construction of mosques and *zāwiyas* (monasteries). These were used for *ḥadīth* studies, which, as we will show in the second chapter, served as ideological supports for the merchants' activities.[72] Finally, the changing legal context of property in land was itself transformative.

The eighteenth century witnessed an increasing breakdown in the Ottoman land system which permitted all segments of the local ruling class to gain control of part of this important source of wealth. The breakdown of the *iltizām* system was officially recognized in 1728/1141 by the Ottoman financial bureaucracy in Egypt, the Ruznamjā. It had had a short and unsuccessful history, beginning in 1658/1069, when it was established as an alternative to a system based on government tax collectors. The *iltizām* system divided the land into tax farms to be awarded by the government or sold to the highest bidder. The government was to retain ownership, and all rights would revert to it upon the death of the *multazim* (tax farmer). The *iltizām* system depended for its successful implementation on the existence of a strong central government. With the weakening of the central government which took place during the eighteenth century, there was a rising trend toward the alienation of *iltizāms* which came to be known as *asqāṭ al-iltizāmāt* or *asqāṭ al-qura*. The land was alienated to individuals and did not revert to the government. The Ottoman financial administration, as has been mentioned above, began to try to deal with the problem of the loss of revenues in 1728. From this year onward the government maintained records called *Sijillāt asqāṭ al-qurā*. The weakness of the central government was a great advantage to the capitalist class, and there is substantial evidence that Mamlūk *beys*, perhaps in debt to merchants or in need of money, illegally alienated their *iltizāms* to merchants.[73] Thus a number of Egyptian merchants and even *ʿulamāʾ* acquired property in land which, given the weakness of the central government, they were able to transmit directly to their heirs by paying a fee called *badal al-muṣallaḥa*, creating an inherited tax farm; or, even more illegally, they could transmit it disguised as *waqf*. Trade revived, but as it did so, political and social conditions in Cairo deteriorated. Investment in urban real estate was risky, and investment in land was more secure.[74] To acquire land required some money. To make investment in land, for example, irrigation repairs, however, required very large capital investment. This was attempted by several *beys*, but it was an effort generally beyond the reach of the rest of the class.

The Egyptian Lower Middle Classes, 1760–1798

The indigenous Egyptian lower middle classes—local merchants, *ʿulamāʾ*, and artisanal elite—have not been heretofore discussed. They fall in Raymond's category of being worth above 5,000 but less than 50,000 paras. Through ownership, through possession of special skills, or through patronage they retained a solidarity with the ruling class which was absent among the wage-labor segment of the guilds of unskilled workers. This class emerged with and gained coherence from the coming of the French. After several decades of relative depression, it was again severely weakened by Muḥammad ʿAlī.

In the eighteenth century, this class was both a customer and a retailer of French merchandise, and procured goods needed by the French. Like the French, it was put at a disadvantage by the monopoly system of the *beys*, as well as by their policy of extortions and forced loans, and therein lay the rationale for the Napoleonic attempt at an alliance. Cairo merchants traded many products, some locally made, some procured with great effort from Africa, such as henna, or from Asia, such as spices.

The *ʿulamāʾ*, as did the merchants, benefited from this commercial revival. Some were merchants themselves or engaged in trades.[75] Others, many of whom were *shaykhs* in al-Azhar, were *nuẓẓār*, or superintendents of *awqāf*. These *nuẓẓār* became important officials due to their control of liquid assets and credit. It seems clear that the *ʿulamāʾ* were unsalaried and thus dependent on largesse. Apart from wealth they might have inherited, support from their relatives, and so on, the *ʿulamāʾ* made money from giving private lessons and copying manuscripts. Prior to the age of Muḥammad ʿAlī, it is claimed, a *shaykh* could live in luxury if he had only two students from the family of a moderately wealthy *fallāḥ*. These students would be expected to be his servants and provide him with free merchandise; one *shaykh* even had his home constructed through volunteer labor.[76]

Shaykh ʿAbdullah al-Sharqāwī, who died occupying the position of Shaykh al-Azhar in 1818, was a prominent member of this group. He was poor during his youth and depended on charity from the Syrian merchant community. After a psychological breakdown, he emerged as a powerful *Ṣūfī* leader of the Khalwatīya. Supporters gave him a house. When he became Shaykh al-Azhar, he automatically became the *nāẓir* of the very extensive *awqāf* of al-Azhar and grew increasingly rich. He had connections with the Mamlūks, who gave him some land in Sharqīya province, which he augmented during the French occupation when the land of the émigrés was being registered. Another *ʿālim*, or elite cleric, who rose to a position of great wealth and power through connections with the Mamlūks was Muḥammad al-Mahdī. Originally a Copt, he gained a position in the mint and slaughterhouse (and probably some degree of control over these tax farms). Later, because of his patronage from the *beys*, he won vacant *iltizāmāt* without paying the inheritance tax. He then turned to the raising of flax, cotton, and rice. When the French came, he further enriched himself, as did many of the well-off *ʿulamāʾ*, through tax-collecting activities and through participation in the Dīwān.

More important for our study are the *shaykhs* whose wealth came from affiliation with the major Ṣūfī orders of the upper classes. These *shaykhs* tended to play an important role in the cultural revival of the eighteenth century. We therefore turn to the information available on the most important of these, Shaykh Sijāda Wafāʾīya.[77] Shaykh Abū Anwār al-Sādāt, the great *shaykh* of the Wafāʾīya, received his *sijāda* from his maternal cousin, and wealth came to him with the title. His own father had been a tradesman. Upon becoming the *shaykh* of the order, he became *nāẓir* of several important *awqāf*, as well as *multazim* in the Ṣaʿīd and in Qalyūbīya. He acquired property in Cairo, as well as fruit gardens. During the Ottoman invasion of 1786, he protected the wives and property of a number of Mamlūks, for which he was rewarded with the charge of several major mosques in Cairo (that is, he became their *nāẓir*), including Sayyidnā al-Ḥusayn, Sayyida Nafīsa, and Sayyida Zaynab. He also took control of several shrines, including the Imām al-Shāfiʿī. He lived on into the Muḥammad ʿAlī period and ended his life as Naqīb al-Ashrāf. The Wafāʾīya included a number of merchants among their ranks; some of these merchants were *ʿulamāʾ* as well, such as ʿAbd al-Raḥman al-Ṣafāqsī, who was a leading Maghribī merchant in Cairo, Shaykh of the Riwāq of the Maghāriba in al-Azhar, and closely associated with Muḥammad Abī Anwār.[78]

Ṣūfī orders provided the chief network of horizontal communication among the various trading communities of Cairo. Otherwise, these communities were by and large self-enclosed and ethnically based, maintaining closer contact with the remote homeland whose goods these traded in than with the other Cairene groups. Such a community was the Maghribī merchant community. These North Africans had lived in Cairo a long time but were regarded ambivalently by the Cairenes as neither strangers nor one with them. Ultimately, the Maghribī community merged with the rest of Cairene society, but this was not until the nineteenth century. In the eighteenth century they were a distinct community and a force to be reckoned with because of their wealth and connections. A contemporary source offers some idea of their wealth, putting the value of their trade at 100,000 pounds annually.[79] If one takes the altercations between the Maghribī artisans, merchants, and students with the Cairenes as a rough index of the relative power of the former group, then the most violent period was around 1777. The students of the *riwāq*, defended by the Maghribī merchants, became "famous" for their unruliness.[80] Thereafter the Maghāriba are referred to as consisting of a troublesome lower-class element which was frequently used as mercenary soldiers and a small, wealthy commercial elite which lasted into the Muḥammad ʿAlī period.[81]

The upper strata of the artisans were craftsmen. They numbered some five thousand out of a total of fifteen thousand workers at the end of the eighteenth century.[82] Concentrated in certain crafts, such as sugar refining, brass, and woodworking, they constituted in the eighteenth century the poorest and most politically conscious segment of the middle class. As the eighteenth century progressed, these two traits were intensified.[83] There was little upward mobility in this segment of the class, especially in the later eighteenth century, although there is considerable evidence of downward mobility.[84] Many artisans not only produced but also hawked their own wares. In the latter part of the century, production was hampered by the uncertainties of the retail market, due to conditions in the city (see below). It was likewise concentrated in families and passed from father to son.

It is difficult to determine to what extent this segment suffered from the general collapse of the framework of guild life which affected the unskilled and less remunerative crafts and presaged the growth of free wage labor.

An important consequence of the fact that the Mamlūks and wealthy merchants were investing in land was that the city of Cairo became less important to them economically and was permitted to deteriorate.[85] This happened despite the fact that the majority of the middle-class merchants and *shaykhs* depended on the city as much as ever. The concerns of important merchants were frequently totally bound up with their quarter. For example, the cloth merchants of al-Ghūrīya promised Napoleon after the first Cairo revolt that they would seize the dissident elements *of their quarter.* The Shaykh al-Ḥāra was frequently the *shaykh* of the dominant trade guild located in the quarter (ḥāra). He had administrative powers, but they were purely local ones. With the decline in the power of the central administration during the later eighteenth century, and the shift of wealth to suburbs, garbage was dumped in the streets or in the Nile, and the city deteriorated physically, despite the presence of the middle and even some upper classes. In a number of instances the central authority came into collision with the still-powerful merchant community, as, for example, over the question of night lighting outside the shops. When the *muḥtasib* (market inspector) tried to enforce it, the merchants made him back down.[86]

The Urban Lower Classes, 1760–1798

At the lower level of the work force, the eighteenth century witnessed a marked growth in the service sector, which consisted of persons who worked for daily wages, and a general failure to incorporate this growing population meaningfully into guild or *ṭarīqa*. While the factors which conditioned the rise of the service sector have already been anticipated in the discussion of the enlarged middle class and their needs, it is necessary to stress the long-term internal breakdown of the corporate structure in Ottoman Cairo. Throughout the Ottoman period, there was a decline in the absolute number of guilds. There was also far less internal hierarchization within the Cairo guilds than that which existed in Damascus.[87] At the lowest level, there were guilds whose membership ranged into the thousands. They were frequently obliged to perform free labor for the government. Some, such as the "ambulatory or semi-licit trades" were only halfheartedly incorporated. At best, the *shaykh* of these service guilds could not protect his followers from market conditions.[88]

The history of the urban lower classes in Cairo reflects the relative stability of the urban economy in the middle of the eighteenth century during the rule of ʿAlī Bey, followed by the breakdown of urban life which characterized the period toward the end of the eighteenth century. A recent source described the period from 1735 to 1770 as one of relative economic stability and sufficiency of food. After 1770, the author found a re-emergence of economic problems and episodes of anarchy. During the period prior to the French invasion, there was extreme inflation,[89] which appears to have been caused by the vast sums of money spent by the middle classes on luxury goods.

The lower classes lived in certain very crowded quarters, such as Ḥusaynīya, in which the economy was closely linked to the production of primary food products. Ḥusaynīya was thus particularly susceptible to economic fluctuations such as occurred frequently in the latter part of the century when the *beys* would stockpile food outside Cairo and wait for its price to rise. The leadership of the Ḥusaynīya quarter seems to have been provided by the butchers' guild and the Bayyūmīya Ṣūfī order. Butchers were described as being physically strong, of strong personality, and highly organized.[90]

There were other areas of lower-class concentration around Ibn Ṭulūn mosque and Sulṭān Ḥasan mosque. The Ibn Ṭulūn area was known for its concentration of poor Maghāriba. The area was extremely volatile and probably well armed, as many of the Maghāriba served from time to time as mercenaries. The adjacent quarter of Khalīfa, which dealt in grain, was equally poverty stricken. Its leader at the end of the eighteenth century was Ḥajjāj al-Khuḍarī, the chief of the vegetable merchants' guild. He led his men in combat in 1805 and helped to put Muḥammad ʿAlī in power. Khalīfa, like Ḥusaynīya, was an intensely active Ṣūfī center. It contained the *maqām* of Sīdī Aḥmad al-Rifāʿī, which was noted for its tumultuous *mawlids*.

Raymond found that a certain political consciousness emerged among the lower classes during the last third of the century, through an awareness of the significance of the events of 1786. Where it was able, the middle class attempted to seize the leadership of this movement for its own ends.[91] In March 1796/1200, a revolt against the extortions of Murād and Ibrāhīm led to a confrontation between a Murādī *bey* and Aḥmad Sālim, which was resolved only through the intervention of Shaykh Aḥmad al-Dardīr. In July 1786, there was a protest in the Azbakīya quarter following the maltreatment of a gardener by a *bey*. In October 1787, the professional corporations protested against a new law of Ismaʿīl Bey. In 1788, the inhabitants of Bāb al-Shaʿrīya made a demonstration in protest against the summary execution of one of their own. In October 1790, a successful revolt in Ḥusaynīya led by Aḥmad Sālim al-Jazzār forced the *beys* to negotiate. In 1798, the arrival of the French transformed these struggles into patriotic struggles led by the middle class. Throughout the 1790's and the Napoleonic period, there had been a "decline of public order."[92] By 1798, Cairo was unsafe for the upper and middle classes at night. When Napoleon landed, bands from the lower-class citizenry forced into existence protection societies to carry lanterns and protect wayfarers.

The causes of lower-class agitation are not difficult to determine, and some have previously been mentioned. Inflation disrupted the economic existence of the lower classes, who were located mainly in fixed-income occupations, for example, the guilds and services. At the same time, inflation helped the merchants and *ʿulamāʾ*, who were receivers of merchandise and were paid wages in cash. At the end of the eighteenth century, there was an estimated total of fifteen thousand daily laborers, according to French sources, who had no source of income other than wages from daily labor.[93] Examining more specifically the situation of those groups who were alleged to have been involved in revolts, such as the Bayyūmī Ṣūfīs, we find that they were, even in comparison with their contemporaries, superexploited. Many of their members belonged to the guilds of water carriers. In times of shortage, these guilds were exploited by the authorities in the name of *ḥisba*. The guild was obliged to assist officials of *ḥisba* with the problems caused by incendiaries; the water carriers' drivers could be requisitioned by the Wālī during a time of crisis with no compensation. They were held responsible for bringing water of good quality which, considering the pollution of the Nile in the late eighteenth century, was an increasingly difficult task. The aquaduct which brought water from the Nile through Old Cairo to the Citadel was in disrepair from 1788 to 1808. This greatly increased the amount of work which the water carriers had to perform.

In general, the growth of a middle class involved in commerce greatly increased the needs for skilled and unskilled service industries. The weakness of the Ottoman central government in the late eighteenth century did not permit its effective intervention in a regulatory capacity, hence the development of private protection societies, the use of Maghribī mercenaries.

The Egyptian Delta in the Later Eighteenth Century

From the middle of the eighteenth century to the year 1811, Upper Egypt, the Ṣaʿīd, was not under the control of the central government. It was the Delta which was important, which interested the Europeans who were looking for grain. The high price of grain on the world market made the value of land rise; and with a weak central administration and many a cooperative *nāẓir*, *waqf* land became increasingly identical with private property. Moneylenders entered the Delta in the eighteenth century to lend money to the *fallāḥīn* at high rates of interest, which added to the problems which the *iltizām* system created for them.[94] Moneylenders regularly received 10 percent, and it is clear from one contemporary source that they sometimes took more. Moneylending continued into the nineteenth century, despite opposition from the Mamlūks and even from the Europeans.

Moneylenders had a special entrée in the cultivation of rice and other luxury export products which required a capital outlay. Damietta never exported less than 22,000 ardebs of rice in the 1790's and sometimes twice that. Her chief customers were the Greek Archipelago and Turkey. Indeed, there was no alternative source of credit for the *fallāḥ*. The Cairene could invest in land but not directly in agriculture. For example, the Bedouin made the trade routes insecure, political conditions were unstable, and so forth. When Napoleon came to Egypt, he could not eliminate the moneylenders, but he put the Damietta rice fields under a system of direct land administration. In Damietta, the French government made the investment, advanced the capital for seed, and secured the equipment. Napoleon administered the rest of Egypt through the "village chief system."[95]

To conclude this discussion of the social structure of the Delta during the late eighteenth century, it seems safe to state that, while the majority of the inhabitants were *fallāḥīn* rooted in the subsistence economy, the possibility of being uprooted from it existed as never before. One such case was that of al-Ḥājj Ṣāliḥ al-Fallāḥ, a poor merchant from al-Minūfīya who progressed from selling farm produce locally to selling slaves, and finally became a Mamlūk, in spite of the fact that he was an Egyptian.[96] How many others were able to take similar advantage of conditions in the Delta? Another case which suggests a similar evolution is that of Shaykh Ḥusayn b. Ḥasan al-Kinānī al-Ḥanafī (d. 1814/1203), who came to Cairo from Rosetta and changed from the Ḥanafī to the Shāfiʿī *madhhab* in order to study with the powerful Shaykh al-Sharqāwī. When Muḥammad Khūsraw Pasha, the Wālī, came to Egypt, Shaykh Ḥusayn went to him immediately and was rewarded with presents and made *nāẓir* of an important *waqf*.[97] Several members of the new bureaucracy of Muḥammad ʿAlī bore the name of al-Rashīdī (i.e., from Rosetta); undoubtedly a study of the social background of the members of this bureaucracy or the student missions to Europe (from among the Egyptians) would bring to light some relationship with this dynamic sector of eighteenth-century society.

If one looks at the social history of Damietta and Rosetta in the eighteenth century, one finds that what is most often commented on by Europeans is the hostility of the inhabitants to Europeans and their great reluctance to permit the export of rice to Europe.[98] The former point, that there was hostility to European involvement in marketing, seems the more valid; however, it is true that, as the Delta became more securely a part of the world market, Damietta still resisted the Europeans' establishing a consulate. Greeks and other minorities had established themselves there and the trade was, as the French viewed it, carried on by "indigenous hands."[99] The French gained decisive control of trade in 1776. Of eighty European boats which docked at Damietta in 1776, seventy-two were French. In 1778, the French established a vice-consul, M. de Kercy, in Damietta. How did the French get in? Prior to 1776, trade between Damietta and Marseilles was carried on indirectly and by subterfuge because the populace of Damietta would riot if they learned that rice was going to Marseilles.[100] What seems to have occurred to change the situation was that Muḥammad Bey Abū Dhahab had recently built a new chateau in Damietta. He also owned several villages in Damietta. This fact would be quite sufficient to explain the suppression of any local opposition to the French. But—who constituted the local opposition? Rosetta was a center of the Burhāmīya Ṣūfī order which was connected to the Zaghlūl mosque, but Damietta was not a major Ṣūfī center.[101] It is also clear that the riots in Damietta were not "food riots," because only the rural upper class, and not the poor, ate rice. The most probable explanation is that there was a struggle over who would be the middle men who controlled the marketing of rice. This struggle was also a communal struggle because it pitted the officials of the absentee landlords, the local rice merchants, and the rich peasants against the Greeks, the Syrian Christians, and finally the French. Damietta and Rosetta were both centers of communal conflict. In fact, Rosetta was rocked by communal conflict well into the nineteenth century. The convent of the Franciscans in Rosetta was ripped down a number of times until it was reconstructed once and for all in 1858.[102]

The impact of the beginning of private property and the commercialization of agriculture was, for the Egyptian Delta, as elsewhere, extraordinarily disruptive. The growth of a monetary economy created new possibilities of exploitation, as it created new dreams of social mobility. The commercial problems mentioned above reflect the reality that, in the eighteenth century, Europeans established a beachhead in the Egyptian Delta from which they were to steadily expand and finally control all of Egypt, economically at least, by the age of Isma'īl a century later.

The reader who has followed the argument will see that profound changes were underway in Egypt prior to the coming of Napoleon. How did the Napoleonic occupation affect these changes?

From the Napoleonic Era to the End of the Mamlūk Period: 1798–1815

The period in Egyptian history of 1798–1815 could easily be passed over lightly, if what is generally well known were not such a romantic distortion. To my knowledge, none of the standard works attempts to explain the motives of the French in terms of the economic and political realities governing Napoleon's strategy. Most works treat Napoleon's arrival in Egypt and his military encounters with the Egyptians as simply the total rout inflicted by a superior civilization on an inferior one. In reality, it was a complex effort by the French commander to pit one class against another when he was not in military control. His defeat is usually attributed to the English, to his subordinates, to anything but the Egyptians. Finally, these works regard the rise of Muḥammad ʿAlī, which is yet to be satisfactorily explained, as a new era. In fact, it was a continuation of the previous era. The importance of the Muḥammad ʿAlī period post 1815 was not his elimination of the Mamlūks, but rather that he himself ceased to be a Mamlūk, as he had been in significant ways during his early years in power.

A standard account of the reasons for the French Directory's approval of the invasion has been presented in many books. Basically, there were three: (*a*) to strike a blow at Great Britain by obtaining control of the best route to India, (*b*) to found a flourishing colony and exploit the best resources of Egypt, and (*c*) to provide for the scientific exploration of ancient and modern Egypt.[103] However, perhaps standard accounts should be taken with a grain of salt. As stated above, France was decisively defeated by England in the Seven Years' War. In various engagements of this war, it was obvious that France was weakest vis-à-vis England at sea. France had strong land armies, but England had the world's most powerful navy. Given these circumstances, the policy of the Directory and Napoleon generally called, in the 1790's, for expansion into regions like Spain, where the strength of the British fleet could be neutralized. Even so, there were dangers in this, as was shown by the support given to the Spanish by the British fleet. Why did the Directory agree, and why did Napoleon want, to risk a land army in unprotected boats in an overseas invasion? Did they really expect to obtain control of the route to India when they could not control the Mediterranean? One is strongly inclined to doubt it. They must have been prepared to take the risk of losing their fleet as soon as the English located it, and it must have been obvious to them that, with the loss of their fleet, they would be able to control only one portion of that route, which the British could bypass. Another reason which was offered also arouses suspicion. It is a truism that governments are rarely frank about their motives for going to war. The reasons which they give usually reflect their need for support from different sections of their societies. The most plausible of the reasons offered was that of establishing a colony.

We turn now to a brief account of those three years. In June 1798, Napoleon landed in Egypt, captured Alexandria, and began the march up the Nile toward Cairo. "When Murād learned of the capture of Alexandria, he went out from Cairo to meet Bonaparte. Tchesmelis seconded the advance of his commander by going down the Nile to the village of Shubrākīt, where he installed two batteries of nine-balls, and set up fortifications so that the village was on his left and the Delta was on his right."[104] When Napoleon's admiral, Perrée, who was leading the advance, arrived at Shubrākhīt, he was completely surprised by the withering artillery fire. Unable to fight back, the French sailors deserted a number of their ships. Luckily for Napoleon, there happened to be some infantry contingents in the vicinity near enough to bring up; when these arrived, they captured the gun batteries, permitting Perrée to recover his fleet. In this fierce but rarely discussed battle, each side lost about three hundred men. Even the capture of Alexandria was not as easy as the more romantic French sources have pictured it. A letter from a French soldier or officer dated July 6, 1798, spoke of the Mamlūks in Alexandria as having weak artillery but deadly musketry. One can judge from another comment in the same letter that the French did not get away unscathed. The Bedouins, this writer said, returned thirty French prisoners with an offer to collaborate against the Mamlūks.[105]

In the Battle of the Pyramids, Napoleon was much more careful and avoided the Mamlūk artillery. He concentrated his attack on the Mamlūk cavalry. In a letter to General Kléber on July 27, Napoleon estimated that a force of 3,000–4,000 Mamlūks had attacked 24,000 Frenchmen; that the French had lost 210 dead, 150 wounded; and that the Mamlūks had lost 700–800 men, many of these in swimming across the Nile. A further comment was made that many of his troops were suffering from severe diarrhea from drinking Nile water. In general, the military results of the first year did not convince the French that they were winning decisively.[106]

In fact, Napoleon soon changed his strategy from confrontation to one of trying to buy over his opponents, and in this he was reasonably successful. The Greeks served Napoleon after the defeat of the fleet as marines, as spies, and as merchants. Napoleon sought to revive the dying trade with the Archipelago because, with the exception of the goods specifically declared contraband, Greeks could get around the British blockade.[107] His support of the Greeks strengthened their position in Egypt, which in the long run was important. In the short run, they accomplished many things for him. A Greek priest in Damietta bribed a troublesome Bedouin chief. Murād's Greek general defected after the defense of Imbābā and thereafter served Napoleon by trying to win away other Greeks from the Mamlūks.[108] Napoleon was also able to enlist Maghāriba and Turks into his service in Egypt. However, most of the Mamlūks who were prepared to follow Napoleon to France were of Christian origin: Greek, Syrian, and Coptic.[109] But despite his successes in weakening the Mamlūks by winning contingents away from them, Napoleon could not defeat them outright. The old Mamlūk strategy of waiting in Upper Egypt, which had worked in 1786, as well as in the past, worked again.

Of more importance to this study is Napoleon's effect on the middle classes. From the time of his arrival in Cairo his proclaimed policy was directed toward winning their support, that is, the support of the merchants and ʿ*ulamā*ʾ. Once he was in Egypt, his own need for revenue came into conflict with the original idea of a broad-based trade alliance. Instead he became actively involved in the international trade of the elite. He sought to keep the Damietta trade from being impeded and tried to stop Ibrāhīm Bey's crossing the Egyptian border. He sent a messenger to Jazzār Pasha with some Syrian merchants, but this move turned out to be completely unsuccessful. When the mission failed, Jazzār Pasha killed the Syrian merchants.[110] Circumstances also frustrated other Napoleonic overtures. The Dārfūr caravan which appeared in 1799 was plundered by French troops at the village of Banī ʿAdī. Thus, although Napoleon wished to expand the scope of existing trade and corresponded with the Sultan of Dārfūr for this purpose, he was unsuccessful.[111]

Napoleon wanted to revive other trade routes, notably that through Suez. He began by lowering duties on the customs house at Suez and appointing a senior official, Possielgue, to be in charge of it.[112] But, as a recent study shows, Napoleon's policy here was perhaps too cautious. He overestimated the importance, in the Islamic world, of the Sharīf of Mecca, the Amīr Ghālib. Napoleon carried on correspondence with him for five months, from August to December 1798, before he ordered his Suez commander to try to gain as many merchants as he could from among the Ḥijāzīs, Yamanīs, and ʿUmānīs to trade directly with Suez.[113]

An active trade policy went hand in hand with support for the claims of the middle classes to the land. Registration of land gave Napoleon a weapon to expropriate Mamlūks who had fled, rewarding the upper classes whose support he needed, and at the same time laying the foundations for a more secure tax base. Through the land registration decree, Napoleon acquired some two-thirds of the land for the state, with the remaining one-third presumably already in the hands of members of this class, since the prominent *beys*, who were the major *multazims*, were all at war with him. Had this land registration of August 1798 been fully implemented, it could have destroyed the Mamlūk class. However, the registration required a degree of control which the French possessed only occasionally.[114] French military weakness, for example, led to increasing concessions to Murād Bey in the Ṣaʿīd, while in Cairo, ironically, the French ransomed his wife, Sayyida Nafīsa, for 120,000 talaris. But even in Cairo, the French could not always get their way. Ibrāhīm Efendī, a clerk in the financial administration upon whom the French depended to understand the *iltizām* system, refused to divulge the names of the remaining Mamlūks or to explain the Qirma notational system to them. When he was implicated in a treasonable act of supplying arms to and sheltering Mamlūks, the French nevertheless found it prudent not to execute him.[115]

Why, then, did the middle classes of Cairo turn against the French and provide support and leadership for the uprisings of Cairo which shattered the occupation? This question can be answered in many different ways. The behavior of the French soldiers, the many affronts to Islamic traditions such as occurred during Ramaḍān, the hardships suffered by the Cairenes from extortions, fighting, and so on can be adduced. A recent writer found that there was a close relationship between the uprisings of October 21–22, 1798, and the imposition of a graduated tax on urban property. This tax would have hit at the core of middle-class investments, especially those of the poorer merchants who were essentially shopowners, and would give them a strong motive to support the opposition to the French.[116]

In addition to the taxation of urban properties, the middle classes were adversely affected by the general stagnation of trade, both Middle Eastern and European. This was a consequence of the invasion and blockade. By 1805, direct trade with Marseilles was at a standstill,[117] meaning the long-distance trade was indirect and the Greeks were gaining a stranglehold.

The return of the Ottomans spelled further difficulties for the Egyptians. The Ottoman army was able to briefly impose a settlement on the *beys* but was unable to maintain it after a withdrawal of their forces. In July 1803, the Mamlūks accepted a treaty with ʿAlī Pasha Burghul, Wālī of Egypt, which permitted them to stay in Egypt on a fixed income but subjected them to paying an increased *mīrī*, or state land, tax. They also lost various subsidiary revenues which they had usurped from the Ottomans in the eighteenth century, such as the ports and customs revenues.[118] But when Yūsuf Pasha, *wazīr* (plenipotentiary) of the Turkish forces in Egypt, tried shortly before this to collect back taxes for the period from 1798 to 1801 from the *multazims*, they refused. The *wazīr* then sent Coptic tax collectors directly to the villages, but the *multazims* demonstrated and forced Yūsuf Pasha to back down.[119]

As was mentioned above, the elimination of the Mamlūk system by Muḥammad ʿAlī came during the Wahhābī war. Muḥammad ʿAlī's campaigns led to the formation of a new military structure. He had begun in the tradition of his predecessors: in order to pay his soldiers, he had extorted money from merchants and even whole towns; he had expropriated cattle and crops as needed. With the death of Alfī Bey in 1807 and the defeat of the British in the same year, Muḥammad ʿAlī finally gained control of the Delta. Realizing that his army of ten thousand men could not be supported by the existing system of taxation, he began, first on a small scale, a series of financial reforms which were all more or less in the tradition of ʿAlī Bey. During 1806–1808, he removed the tax collectors; during 1807–1809 he gained control of monies from *waqf* land and Uṣīya land. In 1810 he launched an attack on the Coptic clique in the financial administration. These moves, combined with his first high profits from trade (1810), permitted him to abolish the *iltizām* system, replacing it with a system of government officials. Trade financed the recapture of Upper Egypt, which had been outside the effective control of the central government since the time of ʿAlī Bey. The traditional refuge of the *beys*, Upper Egypt was also important for the control of the African trade.

Muḥammad ʿAlī's attempt to increase revenues through the control of trade increasingly brought him into alliance with the foreign and indigenous commercial groups and one step nearer to the new system. In 1810 a French consul estimated that Muḥammad ʿAlī had made more than three million francs selling wheat to the English, and this more than quadrupled in the period from 1810 to 1813 (during the peninsular campaign), until the resumption of Russian wheat exports brought an end to the boom. Throughout this period (1810–1813), Muḥammad ʿAlī was deeply involved in the mechanics of trade—hiring or purchasing ships, appointing commercial agents in Malta, Portugal, and Spain. He acquired the grain monopoly for himself and drove off a number of speculators. As a consequence of these efforts, the Egyptian national income, which had been estimated at four million francs in 1798, rose in 1812 to thirty or forty million francs.[120]

When war was thrust on Muḥammad ʿAlī by the Porte, he entrusted the organization of the Wahhābī campaign in 1811 to the leading merchant of Cairo, who had large investments in the Meccan trade, Sayyid Muḥammad al-Maḥrūkī.[121] A contemporary observer writing in 1814 noted that, when Muḥammad ʿAlī deposed the Sharīf of Mecca for his "Wahhābī views," it was obvious that he was trying to get at the Sharīf's alleged wealth, which was thought to have been hidden. He also thought that Muḥammad ʿAlī was disposed to undertake the capture of the Waḥhābī capital, an achievement which was difficult from a military point of view, because of the rumors of the wealth of Al-Darʿīya.[122] One must conclude that the merchants felt they had a large stake in the outcome of the war and hence lent their support to Muḥammad ʿAlī. The Waḥhābīs certainly were known for creating havoc on the trade routes; but perhaps it went beyond this. Lane wrote that, in the theology which the Waḥhābīs actively propagated, coffee (a Yamanī product) was permitted, while tobacco (a Syrian and Turkish product) was forbidden. This brand of theology boded ill for the Cairo merchant community.[123]

By 1815, Muḥammad ʿAlī once again expanded his agriculture monopolies, which he financed through state revenues; previously, production had been financed by local merchants. The expansion of the monopolies to cover the vast majority of the crops grown in the Delta occurred hand in hand with the introduction of costly and important reforms in the army which would put it on a European basis. As this occurred, and the new structures grew in strength, the remaining Mamlūks, including the European ones, faded from the scene.[124] A new era was dawning.

The Middle Classes: 1798–1815

There have been frequent references to the role of the middle classes in the Napoleonic invasion, vis-à-vis the Ottomans, and in their original support of Muḥammad ʿAlī and the Waḥhābī campaign. The elite commercial elements, the landowners, and many of the *ʿulamāʾ* opposed Muḥammad ʿAlī and hoped for an Ottoman return. The principal trend during the period between 1798 and 1815 was that the commercial minorities and the foreign trading community grew stronger, while the majority of the indigenous middle class grew weaker. Splits appeared that had been covered up by the *ṭuruq* in the eighteenth century, which permitted one element of this class to be played against another, a tactic used by Napoleon as well as Muḥammad ʿAlī.[125] By 1815, the question had clearly been resolved. A strong figure, Yūsuf Būghus, an Armenian merchant from Smyrna, had been appointed, first, chief dragoman, or interpreter, then minister of trade. Shortly thereafter, many of the remaining merchants of Cairo moved to Alexandria. On abolishing the *iltizām* system, Muḥammad ʿAlī felt obliged to offer land to only a few of the former landholders. Some received pensions; a majority received only promises which amounted to nothing. He threatened the *shaykhs* with the loss of still further revenues for their "malversations" as *waqf* superintendents. In 1814, the land was examined, and if the land was declared in excess of the written amount, it was removed and given to the village, while the rest was taxed unless the owner had a special deed from the Ottoman *wazīr* Yusuf or from Sharīf Efendī. The *shaykhs* made a few halfhearted protests and retired into subdued silence.

The women of the middle classes at this point made one violent strike against Muḥammad ʿAlī, and they were put down with force. For women like the wife of ʿAbdullah al-Sharqāwī, who ran her husband's financial affairs and made a fortune in the process, and others who were entrepreneurs in the eighteenth century, the coming of the Muḥammad ʿAlī bureaucracy was a crushing setback.[126] Finally, in 1815, some *shaykhs* warned the Kikhyā *bey* that this last tax would induce the ruin of the mosques and the collapse of Islam. The Kikhyā told them that the responsibility lay with the Pasha and his tax agents, Maḥmūd Bey and al-Muʿallim Ghālī. These latter criticized the *shaykhs* for obstructing the financing of a holy war. Another, and last, protest in June 1815 was met by the army, and the demonstrators were beaten.[127]

Thus, between 1798 and 1815 the indigenous middle class was seriously weakened in power and wealth while the Levantine foreign middle class was strengthened; this was a continuation of trends which had been noticed in the 1780's and thereafter. One can conclude that the Mamlūk system broke down between 1798 and 1815, not for want of recruits, nor even of skilled ones, but because in terms of mounting an effective army, this type of system, by its nature divided at the top, could not solve its attendant financial problems. Basically, the Mamlūk system broke down because the pressure of Western trade and technology was relentless and in the end too strong to be resisted. It had to be effectively incorporated. Muḥammad ʿAlī, in shifting to the use of Western advisers, was acknowledging the new realities of power and was conducting a self-conscious policy which balanced the factors favoring greater independence against those militating in favor of dependence. In the Delta, the lower classes were suffering from the breakdown of the subsistence economy. Increased demands were placed on them for production, and a cash economy placed most of them in a situation in which they were probably worse off than they had been before the middle of the eighteenth century. The same was true of the urban poor, who lived in an increasingly deteriorating physical environment during the late eighteenth and early nineteenth centuries in Cairo and who entered in increasing numbers the ranks of the conscript army, a sign that no better occupation was open to them.

These, then, were the main trends of the social and economic history of Egypt from 1760 to 1815. These trends had their beginnings around the middle of the eighteenth century and progressed relentlessly through the last few decades of the eighteenth century into the nineteenth century. In retrospect, the Napoleonic interlude was far less significant for Egypt than the lopsided capitalist development of France in the eighteenth century.

The period of sixty-five years between 1760 and 1815 represents a unit as well as a part of a larger whole in Egyptian history. These sixty-five years saw the gradual breakdown of the Ottoman system. With the internationalization of the commercial sector and the rising importance of the agricultural exports, the composition of the ruling class changed. A rebirth of politics took place, as Mamlūks and others struggled to secure the new sources of wealth; old solidarities based on corporate structures began to break down and were replaced by new ones more characteristic of an urban class structure. This process of transformation lasted until around 1860, for one hundred crucial years in which the basic framework of modern Egypt was created.

Chapter 2
The Religious Framework of The Eighteenth-Century Revival

A great religious revival accompanied the commercial revival which affected not only the Mamlūks and the middle classes but the artisan community as well. This revival took the form of a renewed involvement in Ṭarīqa Ṣūfism. Old, established orders experienced a sudden burst of energy, grew in membership, and played important roles in cultural and social life. New ones emerged, especially among the lower classes. The approach of this chapter is to study the Ṣūfī revival as both a socioeconomic and a religio-cultural phenomenon. As a socioeconomic phenomenon, the *ṭarīqa* constituted during the period of the revival the modal social institution for the middle and upper classes during the transition from a society based on medieval corporate institutions to one based on a modern class structure. By "modal" it is meant that a study of the range of the existing *ṭuruq* will find that their structures closely approximated existing social and economic realities, and that their milieu was the most active focus of social and cultural life in the society. For the lower classes, the popular *ṭuruq* were an additional shield at a time when the guild structure was being eroded. For both the upper and lower classes, the high point of *ṭarīqa* activity as measured in terms of outstanding leaders and important writing was the period between approximately 1760 and 1790. After this date, the growing gap between wealthy and poor broke down the solidarity within the *ṭuruq*. The celebrated case of ʿAbdullah al-Sharqāwī is presented in some detail as an example of this process.

Until the beginning of the eighteenth century, Egypt was a medieval society dominated by a set of institutions each of which was self-contained and characterized by a vertical structure. The head of a guild or the *muftī* of a rite presided over a hierarchy through which he mediated between the members of his corporation, on the one hand, and the rest of society, on the other. The latter phase of the commercial revival broke down the authority of these corporate structures without, of course, destroying them or replacing them in any sense.[1] Al-Azhar and the guilds continued to exist, but there was a general felt need to participate in social groups which more nearly reflected the changed social situation, a situation in which artisans of a given trade, merchants in a particular community or of a particular ethnicity, or Mamlūk warriors of a given house could no longer always identify with "their own" group. The emergence of urban class structure, which gave wealth or the promise of wealth to some while withholding it from others on a new basis, needed legitimation. This fact played a large role in the revival of Ṭarīqa Ṣūfism. The new economic differentiation expressed itself during this period for the first time in the creation of suburbs where wealth, not occupation or origin, was the sole criterion for admission. The internal structure of the Ṣūfī *ṭuruq* mirrors this transition. I make this claim on the basis of the information which the historical sources contain about the lives of particular Ṣūfīs in this period, taking this as the primary data, rather than the somewhat idealized schematizations which are to be found in the manuals for their followers, the *murīdīn*, in the nineteenth century. These later works, which are often quoted by scholars, impose a picture of the organic unfolding of the *ṭuruq*, of an internal logic of organization which was apparently based on simple symmetrical patterns. The latter writings actually reflect the more static institutional conditions of the nineteenth century.

Concentrating on the contemporary historical evidence, one finds that in the "elite orders" a group of wealthy figures surrounded a *shaykh*, who was also usually quite wealthy. A few "pure intellectuals" with compatible views may have received patronage. These "prominent" members of the *ṭarīqa* included a mixture of Mamlūks, rich merchants, *ʿulamāʾ*, Ottoman bureaucrats, and others. Sometimes these members appeared to offer a sort of collective leadership of the organization, to judge from specific events and literary evidence. Sometimes they submerged their personalities into an organization under the guidance of the *shaykh* in the sense in which the *murshid-murīd* relationship between members and initiates have traditionally been understood. This tension between the vertical and the horizontal increased as a class structure imposed greater and greater strains on the functioning of the *ṭarīqa*. By the end of the eighteenth century, strains in certain elite *ṭuruq* were easily discernible. While a *shaykh* would not leave al-Azhar, nor would he leave a *ṭarīqa*, his behavior vis-à-vis these institutions would change as he forged a set of social bonds along class lines. The popular orders from the middle of the eighteenth century appear to follow the opposite path. The role of the *shaykh* was initially much more important. He was sometimes credited with supernatural powers and sometimes permitted a role as a political leader. By 1798, the role of these *shaykhs* was more limited.

In what sense can we speak of the *ṭarīqa* as a socioeconomic unit? One must readily admit that hard evidence is difficult to find: there are no membership lists, and it is difficult to ascertain the relative sizes of different *ṭuruq*. Moreover, since there is little hope of finding such records, the best that can be hoped for is more information from wills and property records on the nature and size of a *ṭarīqa*'s wealth.

This problem can nevertheless be surmounted. If one takes the prominent figures about whom information is already accessible as a definable collectivity, one may discuss the *ṭarīqa* as a group whose identity, behavior, and degree of solidarity is that of a given historical epoch about which we also have some knowledge. The prevailing assumption is that the popular orders were "large," with multiple memberships common. The size of the elite Ṣūfī orders, the Bakrīya-Khalwatīya and the Sādāt al-Wafāʾīya, which are identified in this study as the most important orders patronized by the upper class and the wealthy middle classes, was obviously much smaller. They were in fact continuations of indigenous salons now caught and partly transformed by the new religious fervor, that is, the older Bayt al-Ṣiddīq and Bayt al-Sādāt.

The specific problem of this chapter, then, is to define the relationship of the *ṭarīqa* to the social history of the period. We turn first to the *ṭuruq* of the elite. It seems that, as the corporative nature of all social institutions began to "break down" at the end of the Egyptian "middle ages," the Islamic intellectual elite reconstructed itself, using the Ṣūfī *ṭarīqa* as a dam against the new seductive ideology of bourgeois individualism and utilitarianism. The consequence of this for members of these two orders has already been indicated. For those in higher positions, the pull of the new economic nexus led to the acceptance of this new "ideology," which in turn undermined the earlier solidarity of the order. Where this occurred, the breakdown of religious solidarity and its replacement by more secular loyalties was nothing short of spectacular. This can be seen in al-Jabartī's account of the case of al-Sharqāwī and his followers. It can be shown that the *ṭarīqa* in general, though not fully a "class" institution, was developing consistently in that direction.

How did changes in the *ṭarīqa* affect its religious and cultural mission? The principal data on such matters can be found in the pietistic writings by Ṣūfīs, notably in the field of *ḥadīth.* Over and above the requirements of ritual, there was an enormous revival of interest in *ḥadīth* studies by the Bakrīya and the Wafāʾīya and other orders. One finds in these *hadīth* studies and in the Ṣūfī manuals comments—sometimes direct, sometimes indirect—which illuminate the normative process by which Ṣūfīs adjusted to the existing economic and social realities. Problems relating to commerce and profit were raised in numerous *ḥadīth* manuals. For example, these manuals promised that *tawakkul,* trust in God often manifested in withdrawal from earthly affairs, was not an obstacle to gainful activity. This was a revolutionary promise. Book after book contained particular points of emphasis which were not stressed in earlier or later works in *ḥadīth*. One theme which was emphasized during this period was the concern that the chain of *ḥadīth* transmitters, the *rāwīs,* be unbroken back to the beginning. There is of course nothing new in this. But the particular emphasis which it received in this period is indicative of the hold the Ṣūfīs tried to maintain over their *ṭuruq* and vis-à-vis the growing popular orders which also found in *ḥadīth* a justification for their own beliefs. It is for this reason that *ḥadīth* studies are included here and not in a chapter devoted to cultural works. *Ḥadīth* studies were more than just by-products or reflections of the age. They were an integral part of the collective religious consciousness and performed a role analogous to *al-dhikr* (meditation) and *al-inshād* (recitation). The writers were motivated by religious fervor; sometimes they achieved fine results in scholarship, but like the Qur'ān reciters, and the *murshidūn* (spiritual mentors) at a *dhikr*, their work should be understood as part of a larger whole. To apply "modern" methods to the study of *ḥadīth*—especially those which treat any book as "literature"—blurs the crucial distinction between law and culture. Not all works stand in the same relation to their society as others. As we shall explain, *ḥadīth* studies was an integrative force which contributed to the internal juridical development of Islamic history.

The spiritual designation of the *ṭuruq* as "orthodox" or "popular" can to some extent serve as a guide to an analysis of the *ṭuruq* as part of social history.[2] Although these terms do not carry any normative or social consequences a priori, they do suggest a sort of social map. Another approach which is useful to the social historian of religion is to study the mode of expression of piety, for example, activist or quietist, and whether or not this is orthodox expression. What follows is an attempt to use both these approaches.

Within the same social class, there were different spiritual orientations, and these were embodied in different *ṭuruq*. We shall study here two fundamentally opposite orientations, represented by the Bakrīya and the Wafā'īya. The first was a movement led directly by the merchants. The second was based on upper-class merchant patronage relationships. While both orders participated in the cultural renaissance and both enriched themselves immeasurably from the commercial revival, their mystical theological orientations differed. Both movements produced great works in *ḥadīth*, and *ḥadīth* served them well as a medium of debate. A pioneering study of Egyptian mystical theology has characterized the differences between them in the following ways: Among these conservative, Sharī'a-minded *'ulamā'*, the soul might seek illumination through either (*a*) the quietist way (illuminationist, or *ishrāq*) or (*b*) the activist way (*jalā'*). The first was the way of the Wafā'īya, the second that of the Bakrīya.[3]

Sādāt al-Wafā'īya

We turn first to the Sādāt al-Wafā'īya, the order which made the most important contributions to the cultural revival of the eighteenth century. This order was a patron-client order, whose harmonious social relations with the upper classes brought at various times material rewards. It was made up of a small group of prominent intellectuals who lived from patronage which they received both in Egypt and from abroad. The peculiar characteristic of their structure, derived from the absolute spiritual reverence paid to their *shaykh*, Muḥammad Abī Anwār, was no doubt related in complex ways to this fact of patronage.[4]

The relationship between the *murīdīn* and the charismatic *shaykh* was defined unilaterally in the *taknīya* ceremony in which honorific names were bestowed. Other aspects of internal organization were not rigidly maintained. The principal theme in mystical thought which the Wafāʾīya stressed was the special role of Ahl al-Bayt as the figures whose lives embody the highest moral examples. This theme was linked to the assertion of the religious obligation of visiting the tombs of the *ṣaḥāba* buried in Egypt, which naturally led to an emphasis on the spiritual efficacy of the visitation of tombs. These themes, to be discussed in detail later, served not only to reinforce the image of Muḥammad Abī Anwār as the continuator of the Ḥaqīqa Muḥammadīya but also to distinguish the Wafāʾīya from its rival, the Bakrīya. In contrast to the focus on Ahl al-Bayt, the Bakrīya, as their name implies, claimed that their spiritual genealogy extended back to the caliph of the Rāshidūn era.[5] The visiting of the tombs of the *ṣaḥāba* is broadened in Bakrīya writings to include later figures. In one sense the factor of rivalry or coexistence over a long period of time accounts for the choice of opposite motifs. But there was also a more organic basis, a basis which sustained the "quietist" orientation, a religious environment appropriate to its material and spiritual situation.

The Wafāʾīya had come to Egypt from North Africa in the eighth century and had taken up residence first in Alexandria, then in Cairo.[6] In the seventeenth century, their salon was praised by both al-Khafājī and al-Nābulusī for its poetry, when they maintained a fashionable residence in Birkat al-Fīl.[7] In the eighteenth century, the transformation of the order began with the rise of the Shaykh al-Ṭarīqa, Muḥammad Abī Anwār al-Sādāt, whose charismatic personality drew major intellectuals from the Islamic world to him, and whose name was referred to with the greatest respect by most of the poets and writers of Egypt late into the nineteenth century, long after his death and the decline of the order. His father was a merchant, but not well-off. Abū Anwār's success was apparently a consequence of his education and his family connections, in other words, the patronage which he received. He studied with his maternal uncle Shams al-dīn M. Abī al-Ashrāf b. Wafāʾ and others in the *ṭarīqa*, as well as with his paternal uncle ʿAbd al-Khāliq. By birth he was connected to the order on both his father's and his mother's sides.[8] Not much exists in the literary sources of the period to indicate how he rose to become Shaykh al-Sijāda, the position which he "inherited" in 1772/1182 from Muḥammad Abī al-Ashrāf. In 1775/1190, his relations with the Ottomans were such that he approached the Ottoman *raʾīs al-kuttāb*, ʿAbd al-Rāziq Efendī, for funds for the repair of the *zāwiya* of his ancestors, and they were granted. Muḥammad Murtaḍā al-Zabīdī was appointed to head the *zāwiya*. ʿAbd al-Rāziq was at the time a student of al-Zabīdī. The grant of funds permitted the enlargement and decoration of the Riwāq al-Kubrā; later, houses and palaces were constructed around the *zāwiya*.[9] Abū Anwār also expanded his influence among the Mamlūks in Egypt by protecting their wives during the Ottoman invasion of 1785. This saved a number of prominent *beys* large sums in ransom, and for this he was remunerated by being appointed *nāẓir* of a number of important mosques in Cairo.[10]

As mentioned previously, what was distinctive about the Wafāʾīya in the late eighteenth century was their concern with the theme of Ahl al-Bayt. The tradition of the Āl al-bayt (ahl al-bayt) served as a point of reference for the Wafāʾīya in their mysticism and poetry, just as the Rāshidūn did for all the Bakrīya.[11] It was said to have been derived from the principal literary source of the Wafāʾīya, a book entitled *Al-Kashkūl*, by Bahāʾ al-dīn al-ʿĀmilī, who lived in the sixteenth century. It was claimed that a particular *qaṣīda* (classical form of Arabic poetry) in this book was the beginning of the use of the theme of Ahl al-Bayt.[12]

The Ahl al-Bayt theme was closely related to the custom of visiting the tombs of the *ṣaḥāba* who were buried in Egypt. The *ṣaḥāba* were an earthly embodiment of the Prophet's divine nature, the Ḥaqīqa Muḥammadīya. Meditation at the tomb in time of crisis gave the most immediate spiritual contact with the Prophet, the Messenger of God. ʿAbdullah al-Shubrāwī, a Wafāʾī *shaykh* who died in 1758/1172, wrote about two of the *sahāba*, Āl Ṭaha and Āl Aḥmad; al-Idkāwī, another Wafāʾī *shaykh* (died 1768/1182), wrote in praise of Fāṭima al-Zuhrā, citing *ḥadīth* which were apparently from Shīʿite writings.[13]

The concept of Muḥammad Abī Anwār as the *imām*, as continuator of the Ḥaqīqa Muḥammadīya, a concept which is drawn from *Al-Kashkūl*, was repeated in various ways. He was referred to as Ṣāḥib al-zamān (Lord of His Time), al-ʿUrwa al-wuthqa (The Most Firm Bond), and so on. Many of the poems written in praise of Muḥammad Abī Anwār contain similar expressions.[14] Ismaʿīl al-Khashshāb, a poet and a mystic, developed the imagery further than any other writer, claiming that God had praised Sādāt in the Qurʾān; this is identical to the Shīʿī claim concerning the *imāma* following Ibn Hānī al-Andalūsī's praising of al-Muʿizz li-dīn allah al-Fāṭimī. By this he meant that the Qurʾān praised the Ahl al-Bayt in its descriptions of their *ṭuhr* and *barāʾa* (purity and innocence). Al-Khashshāb believed in the Shīʿī theory of Waṣīyallah, which he applied to Muḥammad Abī Anwār, saying that, if he had been present at the time of the Prophet, he would have gone to Heaven with al-Ḥasan and al-Ḥusayn, the sons of Imām ʿAlī.[15] Al-Khashshāb further claimed that al-Sādāt knew the *ghayb*. Other poets pursued similar themes of praise. The Shaykh Riwāq al-Maghāriba, ʿAbd al-Raḥman al-Ṣafāqsī, wrote in a poem that he was al-Mahdī al-Muntaẓar (the awaited *imām*). Muḥammad ibn Shabānat (Shubāna) claimed that Sādāt's lineage stretched back to the Imām ʿAlī, and cited *ḥadīth* for this. Yet another writer claimed that a visit to Sādāt was more obligatory than the Pilgrimage itself. Still another described him as the faithful guardian of the secret of the Messenger of God.[16]

The theme of the *imāma*, as the continuation of the Ḥaqīqa Muḥammadīya, combined with the emphasis on the Ahl al-Bayt, led naturally to another important doctrinal point—the obligation to perform *ziyārāt*, or visitations to the tombs of the saints, especially those of the *ṣaḥāba* buried in Egypt. An extensive medieval literature existed on the subject of *ziyārāt*. Conservative Muslims, among whom were doubtless many Sunnīs who were free of any "superstitious" beliefs, approved of such practices because of the inner religious strengthening (*tabarruk*)[17] which they encouraged. In Egypt, *ziyārāt* served as a principal focus of spiritual and intellectual activity during the eighteenth century. Writings on *ziyārāt* gathered together information concerning the special virtues or the miracles attributed to the visiting of certain tombs. Such studies were carried on in Egypt within the context of renewed interest in the study of *ḥadīth*.[18] The most influential Egyptian who wrote on *ziyārāt* was Shaykh Muḥammad al-Ṣabbān. Muḥammad al-Ṣabbān was honored by the Wafāʾīya in the *taknīya* ceremony, by which he became known as Abūʾl-ʿIrfān, possessor of the mystical knowledge. On al-Ṣabbān's death in 1790/1205, the al-Sādāt family honored him and recalled his praise of them in one of his books, where he spoke of the honor of being initiated into the way of the Wafāʾīya. "I learned," he said, "to take as an example the way of our master, the Wafāʾ, for whom God has willed that they drink peace in their cups. The continuator of their line, a beacon light to the great and small, is Muḥammad al-Sādāt, may God protect him and us all by virtue of his ancestor the Prophet."[19]

Al-Ṣabbān's formal education was extensive within the conventions of the times. He concentrated on *ḥadīth* studies and read the basic texts from a number of different teachers. He also excelled in language sciences, which for him was closely related to his *ḥadīth* studies. A third area in which he studied was science (*al-hayʾa* and *al-mīqāt*, astronomy with geometry and science of time measurement), with Ḥasan al-Jabartī. The texts he read were the well-known works of the later Middle Ages, which included material from *al-ḥikma* (gnosis).[20] One of al-Ṣabbān's major books linked the theme of *ziyārāt* with that of the special virtues of Ahl al-Bayt.[21]

> I wrote the book on Sīra al-Muṣṭafā and the Faḍāʾil Ahl al-Bayt. . . . the third chapter deals with the group of notables of the Ahl al-Bayt who are buried in Egypt, about whom I have been inquiring. . . . [a list] But there are different points of view on the locations of their burial sites. Some rely for their evidence on eye-witnesses [*arbāb al-baṣāʾir*]. Sīdī ʿAbd al-Wahhāb al-Shaʿrānī, in a section in his text (may God permit it) devoted to visiting the tombs of the Ahl al-Bayt buried in Egypt, stated, I visited them three times a year for the sake of obtaining the mercy of the Messenger of God. But I do not see any one of my associates there. As for the claim that there is no proof for their burial in Egypt, this is indifference on their part, for indeed there is sufficient reason to hold this. So I have presented an account of these tombs, one part commenting on the Amīr al-Muʾminīn, another on his wife, Sayyida Fāṭima al-Zuhrā, and another on her son Abī Muḥammad al-Ḥasan. I enlarged on this in Chapter Two in discussing the Imām (al-Mahdī al-muntaẓar). And I proceed in Chapter Three to

> discuss al-Sayyid Muḥammad al-Bāqir and his son Jaʿfar al-Ṣādiq and his son Mūsā al-Kāẓim, may God be satisfied with all of them and with our Umma![22]

A student of al-Ṣabbān named ʿAbd al-Raḥman al-Jabartī had a somewhat similar formation. In his youth he was attracted to the Shādhilīya Ṣūfī order and received from them a *shahāda*, attesting to his spiritual progress. In 1775 he decided to make a tour of Egypt to familiarize himself with the tombs and shrines of his country. In the Delta, in Rashīd, he stopped to study the "Arbaʿīn" in *ḥadīth* with Shaykh Aḥmad ʿAlī al-Khuḍrī, as well as other books. He also attended the Mawlid al-Badawī in Ṭanṭā. His later teachers included Ṣūfī travelers, mainly al-Zabīdī, but also ʿUmar al-Qināwī al-Ḥusaynī.[23]

By the late 1780's, the Wafāʾīya appeared to lose some of its internal cohesion as an organization, from which its power had come. Muḥammad Abī Anwār attempted to form political alliances with certain Mamlūks and to conduct "international diplomacy" with Jazzār Pasha. The strains imposed on the members of the *ṭarīqa* are represented by Ismaʿīl al-Khashshāb, the main Wafāʾī poet of the post-1790 period. Al-Khashshāb, by ever magnifying the powers attributed to Muḥammad Abī Anwār, implicitly enhanced his claims to authority, at a time when his actual power was receding. This would especially seem to be the case with respect to the claim that Muḥammad Abī Anwār was "al-Mahdī al-Muntaẓar" (the awaited *imām*). The concept of the Mahdī almost necessarily implied a political role. Al-Kilānī claimed that Muḥammad Abī Anwār quietly encouraged this, and gave his support to al-Zabīdī rather than encouraging an internal strengthening of the organization through liturgical devices or otherwise. Al-Zabīdī's major function within the organization was his ability to use his great intellectual prestige to propagate the idea of the Ahl al-Bayt. The Wafāʾīya, as continuators of the Ahl al-Bayt (the *ḥukamāʾ al-ʿAluwīya*), were making in Al-Kilānī's opinion a certain claim to the right to rule. They had not done so at the beginning of the reform movement, if one were to judge from the selections in "al-Lawāʾiḥ al-Anwārīya." Possibly Muḥammad Abī Anwār, like the other great Ṣūfī leaders who were his contemporaries, thought that he had an assured social basis of support within the society through his order, and that he could freely pursue the accumulation of wealth through the new economic structure. Perhaps he did not realize that this wealth could undercut his popular support.[24]

The Khalwatīya-Bakrīya

In the middle of the eighteenth century, a missionary of the Syrian branch of the Khalwatīya arrived in Egypt and "created" an orthodox Ṣūfī *ṭarīqa* which we could term a merchant-scholar order, an order distinct from the older Egyptian Bakrīya which continued as an aristocratic salon.[25] The reform doctrine of the new Bakrīya was in fact a conservative restatement of Sharī'a-minded Sunnī orthodoxy of the older Bakrīya and of the Egyptian Khalwatīya. What was notable was the practice. Muṣṭafā al-Bakrī and his Egyptian *khulafā'* (lieutenants) concentrated on the development of *tahdhīb* (spiritual training). *Tahdhīb* was the program of discipline along which the soul progressed on the spiritual path. The elaboration of the steps of *tahdhīb* and the setting up of the appropriate organizational form for the order were among the principal activities of the early Bakrīya reformers. After Muṣṭafā al-Bakrī's death, his tomb and the "fact" of his descent from Abū Bakr took on a certain significance.

Clearly, in the middle of the eighteenth century, many Khalwatī merchants felt a heightened sense of piety and an intense yearning for moral regeneration. They participated in the *dhikr* and, unlike the Wafā'ī, submitted to individual spiritual examination as well. The best-known aspect of the *tahdhīb* was the practice of seclusion, or *khalwa* (literally, a cell). These periods of spiritual meditation constituted something of a novelty for modern Egyptian Ṣūfism. There were few well-known recluses in late-eighteenth-century Egypt. Unlike the recluses of early Islam in Egypt, the Khalwatīya of the eighteenth century sought *khalwa* according to a ritual calendar, and they did so as a group, although each member presumably went to a private cell. In certain instances, the withdrawal probably represented a moment of heightened religious consciousness and clarification, but the routinized fraternal character of the practice lends itself to other interpretations. Although the *ṭarīqa* was a collectivity and its ritual a group expression, one should note that the *khalwa* had its individualistic side. In fact, in Khalwatī devotional writings, the collectivity of the Rāshidūn, like that of the *ṣaḥāba*, was more veneer than substance. Khalwatī books were, in fact, mainly devoted to individual biographical episodes. The normative value of these episodes for the collective ideal was strongly felt and obviously implied but never spelled out. This tension in religious thought mirrored the tension in the material situation of the members. They felt themselves to be mere individuals, and as such they were powerless. They could protest the new order in an individualist manner, for example, by forbidding a Muslim to visit a Christian shrine. The Bakrīya *jihād* (holy war) was thus directed inward. It could not be organized and directed outward.

The main Khalwatī figure of the eighteenth-century revival was Shams al-dīn Muṣṭafā al-Bakrī (died 1748/1162). He had been a student of 'Abd al-Ghanī al-Nābulusī and was a disciple of 'Abd al-Laṭīf b. Ḥusām al-dīn al-Ḥalabī. Al-Bakrī had a range of influence along the trade routes through his three principal disciples. One, a Turk, founded the Kemalīya branch (Mehmet Kemaleddin Bakrī, died 1784/1199); the second, an Arab, founded the al-Sammānīya at Mecca (Muḥammad b. 'Abd al-Karīm al-Sammānī, died 1775/1189); the third, an Egyptian, founded the Egyptian branch sometimes called the Ḥifnāwīya (Shams al-dīn Muḥammad al-Ḥifnāwī, died 1767/

1181).[26] Al-Ḥifnāwī's father was a tax collector for the *beys* and not wealthy. The *beys* or some wealthy individuals gave the son money with which he built a house.[27]

According to Hans Kissling's account, al-Ḥifnāwī had two principal disciples, al-Kurdī and al-Dardīr. Al-Kurdī had one principal disciple, Aḥmad b. Muḥammad al-Tijānī, the founder of the Tijānīya.[28] Besides these men, one must include the figure of Muḥammad b. ʿAbd al-Raḥman al-Azharī, an Algerian born in 1720 who spent twenty-five years in Cairo, many of them as a *murīd* of al-Ḥifnāwī. Later, he founded the Raḥmanīya order as a sub-branch. It spread rapidly along the North African trade routes: a *zāwiya* was opened in Tunisia in 1784/1199, and a century later it was one of the principal orders in Tunisia. But despite the tendency of new orders to break away from the parent body, the Tijānīya and the Raḥmanīya remained somewhat intertwined. However, it is the internal problems of the Khalwatīya reform movement which are of greater significance for this study, especially the conflicts within the organization which marked the final years of the eighteenth century. The organization as centered in Cairo was theoretically a pyramid. Each *khalīfa* had a *shaykh* above him and deputies beneath him, organized by region; and around each *khalīfa* in a given locale were the disciples. The Shaykh al-Ṭarīqa thus relied on his *khulafāʾ* and they in turn on those below them. This was how orders were transmitted, supervision maintained, and deviation prevented.[29] In this period, however, the structure was better characterized as rather egalitarian and, as the life of al-Sharqāwī would indicate, fissiparous.

Al-Sharqāwī was born in a village in 1737/1150. As a youth, he memorized the Qurʾān and came to al-Azhar, where he was a very successful student. He soon became a teacher in the *madrasa*, or training school, system of al-Azhar. He then became a Khalwatī and followed the path with al-Ḥifnāwī. Shortly thereafter, he had a mental breakdown (*ikhtilāl fī ʿaqlihi*) and went to a *māristān* (hospital; actually, a Ṣūfī *tekke*, or monastery), where he recovered. He then went back to teaching and to Ṣūfism. He went to the *khalīfa* of al-Ḥifnāwī, al-Kurdī, and under him took the "names," symbolizing that he undertook the discipline prescribed by the Khalwatīs, as opposed to the merely credal elements indicated by his earlier *ijāza*. Al-Sharqāwī had been poor in his youth, and when he began to teach in the *madrasa*, he received presents of food and invitations from wealthy patrons to carry on his spiritual revival work. When his *murshid*, al-Kurdī, died, al-Sharqāwī succeeded him as *khalīfa* and met every night with the *murīdīn* for Qurʾān reading and for *dhikr*. By this means he gradually enriched himself and finally bought a house; his nightly visits to other people's homes (where he had received free meals) occurred only rarely. As a consequence of his having become a *khalīfa*, wealth was showered on him and he "ceased to be virtuous"; he began to concern himself with his appearance and his clothing. In 1794/1207, on the death of Shaykh al-ʿArūsī, al-Sharqāwī became Shaykh al-Azhar in a victory over his rival, Muṣṭafā al-Ṣāwī. Muṣṭafā al-Ṣāwī was also a leading Khalwatī, the *khalīfa* of Aḥmad al-Dardīr. In the resolution of this conflict, al-Ṣāwī was given another position, one which was usually part of the responsibility of the Shaykh al-Azhar, namely, the teaching in the Madrasa al-Ṣalāḥīya, which was located near the mosque of Imām al-Shāfiʿī. The struggle between al-Sharqāwī and al-Ṣāwī over teaching in al-Ṣalāḥīya was instigated by the retainers of al-Sharqāwī, who claimed that the position of the rectorship lacked integrity without the duties of this post. From this argument, one might fairly guess that its endowments made the post a lucrative one. The struggle was resolved through the outside intervention of Shaykh Muḥammad al-Jawharī and Ayyūb Bey al-Daftardār, who found the two principals basically in agreement and inclined toward a settlement. But al-Ṣāwī was angry with al-Sharqāwī, and when al-Ṣāwī's supporters assembled for a lesson in al-Ṣalāḥīya, they advised him to take his revenge. This led Shaykh al-Ṣāwī's supporters to contact Riḍwān Katkhūdā and Ibrāhīm Bey al-Kabīr, with whom he was on friendly terms. Besides, they owed him money and were further indebted to him for cures which he had worked for them. Riḍwān and al-Ṣāwī met and the outcome of their discussion was that the debt was reduced and Riḍwān Bey became actively involved in the affair. He went to see al-Sharqāwī, and after several discussions, al-Sharqāwī gave up his rights over the *madrasa* and al-Ṣāwī stayed there until his death. With the death of al-Ṣāwī, al-Sharqāwī then took back the teaching position. This happened to take place during a time in which he was somewhat unpopular. Various of the *ʿulamāʾ* seized on this act and raised the matter with the Pasha, insinuating various falsehoods against al-Sharqāwī. This resulted in the Pasha's removing him from the rectorship. The Wālī, however, saved al-Sharqāwī by interceding on his behalf through the chief Ottoman judicial official in Egypt, the *qāḍī*. When he returned, he ejected his interim successor, Muḥammad al-Shubrāwī. This occurred in 1794/1209, during the time of Ṣāliḥ Pasha. In 1800/1215, al-Sharqāwī became rector again. In the meantime he had established a firm relationship with Napoleon.

An incident which occurred after Muḥammad ʿAlī came to power is very instructive as to the nature of the Khalwatī organization and the nature of the power relationships which existed within it. This incident involved the building of the *riwāq* of the Sharāqwa, in which ʿAbdullah al-Sharqāwī was actively engaged. The decision to build this *riwāq* resulted from a fight which had broken out between some of the followers of Shaykh al-Sharqāwī and some members of the *riwāq* of the Muʿammar. A number of Sharqāwī's followers lived in this *riwāq* and worked in its warehouses. After this fight, the *naqīb* of the *riwāq* of the Muʿammar, Shaykh Ibrāhīm al-Sijīnī, ordered that the followers of al-Sharqāwī be expelled from the *riwāq* and from the Madrasa Ṭaybrisīya. Thus, a new *riwāq* was constructed for the followers of al-Sharqāwī. What is interesting is the way in which the costs were defrayed. Al-Sharqāwī received financial assistance from a *bey* whose wife attended his lessons. This *bey* gave him lands and a *muqaṭāʿa* (tax area).

He was Ibrāhīm Bey (known as the Wālī); his wife was ʿAdīla Hānim bint Ibrāhīm Bey. Ibrāhīm Bey, the patron, also procured building materials for the *riwāq* and took rocks and pillars of marble from the mosque of al-Mālik al-Ẓāhir Baybars outside al-Ḥusaynīya. The *nāẓir* of this mosque was none other than Shaykh Ibrāhīm al-Sijīnī. Al-Sharqāwī also bought provisions for it, and these were distributed to persons whom he chose from among his countrymen.[30] Al-Sharqāwī was ably assisted by loyal attendants in his every endeavor. He relied heavily on al-Sayyid Muṣṭafā al-Damanhūrī, an assistant, to carry on his correspondence with the notables and even to write *fatāwī* (legal opinions on points of *fiqh*) in his name, for he was as well an able systematic theologian (*faqīh*).[31] But al-Sharqāwī broke down the order which had fostered him. When he grew wealthy, his peers were Mamlūks and other rich merchants. They mediated each others' disputes. His money turned his *murīdīn* into a personal retinue, which in turn developed certain expectations not dissimilar to those of the Mamlūks in a household. The Ṣūfī *ṭarīqa* could not control the divisive influence of these trends. Al-Sharqāwī did not, of course, leave the *ṭarīqa*. He remained an influential teacher and writer, with all the ambiguities which this entailed.[32]

In considering the consequences for the Khalwatī's *tahdhīb* of pressures from without and dissensions from within, it is worth noting a change in the technique of the *dhikr.* (There may also have been a revival of spiritual medicine in the *tekke.*) As was mentioned above, Muṣṭafā al-Bakrī had been a student of ʿAbd al-Ghanī al-Nābulusī, who was a famous continuator of Ibn al-ʿArabī. A number of al-Bakrī's works deal with problems in this tradition, while others were conditioned by his quarrels with the Naqshbandīs, influential elements in the major reform-minded Ṣūfī order of later Islamic history. In his most controversial work, "Al-Fatḥ al-qudsī," he argued against the Naqshbandīs that the spoken *dhikr* was superior to the silent one. This met with severe opposition both from within his order and from without, especially from the Ahl al-Ḥadīth, whose importance was rising in Damascus in the eighteenth century. The transfer of the Bakrīya to Egypt facilitated the development of the spoken *dhikr* and also encouraged the introduction of music into the *dhikr.* When, however, a disciple of al-Ḥifnāwī visited the Yaman and attempted to introduce music and voice technique into the *dhikr*, he met with sharp opposition from other Ṣūfīs.[33]

We conclude this section by returning to a discussion of the social significance of the *khalwa*, which was the most notable feature of Khalwatī *tahdhīb*. It has been said that the Khalwatīya, unlike the mystics of early Islamic history, did not seek to idealize the figure of the recluse, although they did hold up as an example the saint Sīdī Muḥammad al-Khalwatī, who lived in a *khalwa* for forty years.[34] The practice of *khalwa*, while rooted in Islamic tradition, owed something to the peculiar circumstances of the eighteenth century. It represented, in this view, a symbolic withdrawal. Where capitalist formations were retarded, as in eastern Europe, mystical thought has long flourished. Where capitalism marched triumphantly forward, religion has emphasized the appropriate worldly orientation. Calvin's congregation in Geneva consecrated Sunday to God, while maintaining a continuous routine of work congruent with the ever-expanding scope of opportunities which lay open to the diligent and thrifty family capitalist of the period. The *khalwa*, on the other hand, represented a withdrawal from economic life in another sense. The indigenous Egyptian Muslim middle class was blocked from the most profitable trade (i.e., trade with Europe). The *khalwa* would seem to symbolize the powerlessness of the affluent Khalwatīs, as, on the one hand, a worldly presence was not really needed and, on the other, one could not reach God except through God's grace. Moments of ecstasy, such as were experienced in the popular orders, were, for the Khalwatīs, merely moments of delusion, drug-induced flights from reality.

Reaction to and differentiation from the popular orders and their piety were as central to theology as the corresponding social differentiations created by the emergence of class. Popular orders moved quickly to enter the swelling ranks of day labor which developed in Cairo in the later eighteenth century. The growth of these "popular" orders naturally threatened to undercut the influence and authority of the *ʿulamāʾ* of al-Azhar among the masses. The existence of these large "popular" orders which engaged in social protest and propagated heterodox religious views was an ever-present threat to middle-class merchants and *ʿulamāʾ* as well as, of course, to the Mamlūk elite. The revival of the "popular" orders was one of the consequences of the breakdown of traditional corporate structures.

In the first chapter, the Bayyūmīya was briefly mentioned as a prototype of the "popular" order. I will now discuss its distinctive doctrines. Two of the most important elements of doctrine were, first, that of the *imāma* (or the *shaykh*), that is, of the *imām* as a figure who could perform miracles by virtue of his *baraka* (power); and, second, the vows of mutual assistance to fellow members in times of need. The profound contrasts in religious outlook between the Bayyūmīya, on the one hand, and the Bakrīya or Wafāʾīya, on the other, should explain the religious anxiety and atmosphere of strain, as well as the need for revival, felt by the conservative *ʿulamāʾ* in their *ṭuruq*.

The Bayyūmīya appears to have been one of the breakaway orders from the Khalwatīya reformers. Its founder and chief expounder of doctrine, Shaykh ʿAlī al-Bayyūmī (1696–1769/1108–1183), received a scholastic education in his youth, when he shared the characteristic preoccupations of the scholastics of that period in their studies of *ḥadīth*. In fact, he taught the famous work in *ḥadīth*, "Al-Arbaʿīn," by al-Nawawī. But he subsequently broke with this milieu and turned his attention to the lower classes. He formed his own *ṭarīqa* of highwaymen and water carriers. The break with Sharīʿa-mindedness in his writings parallels this break. In his work "Sharḥ asmāʾ al-Suhrawardī," the *murīd* is provided with a vivid description of the stages of the mystic path to their apex.[35] The "Sharḥ" began with a biographical note on the origins of his ideas (p. 229), which he claimed he received as the latest in a chain of Ṣūfī *shaykhs* stretching back in an unbroken line to ʿAlī b. Abī Ṭālib through Ḥasan al-Baṣrī and then a series of Maghribī *shaykhs.* He then turned to a discussion of problems in mystical theology: There were three levels of association with the names of God. The first level (*martaba*) deals with the meaning of names as they can be comprehended by reason. The second level (which he calls *al-takhalluq*) deals with the meanings of names, their essences, and what God has created through them. The third level (*martabat al-taḥaqquq*) concerns the seeking of annihilation through the name. Al-Bayyūmī stressed that there is no short cut to the established, gradual method based on discipleship of *murīd* to *shaykh.* But he held out that those who were accomplished in the names (p. 230) could read them twice and conquer an enemy; three times and settle an important matter; four times to meet a king; five times to seek wealth or to get someone out of prison (!); six times to bring those who were not present or to defend himself against being robbed, and so on. Al-Bayyūmī then mentioned a special form of supplication for help, beginning "O! Opener of the doors, O! Causer of that which is caused, O! Stirrer of the hearts and bringer of the proofs . . ." and concluding with the reading of *iḥbāb al-asmāʾ*, a document of numbers and letters.

In another text, he claimed that the "selling of water is agreed by all schools to be forbidden."[36] The water carriers believed that those who could pay should pay, but that those who could not should receive water anyway. This attack on the sale of water would suggest that the practice existed. This would seem natural, given the polluted state of most of the available water in Cairo and the breakdown of the aquaduct. Some indirect evidence suggests that commerce in water existed, although whether it took place in Cairo itself is unclear. In the biography of Shaykh Muṣṭafā b. Aḥmad, known as al-Ṣāwī, al-Shāfiʿī al-Azharī (died 1802/1216), it was stated that his father was one of the leading merchants of Egypt and that when he went to Suez he was buying water.[37] If we imagine a situation in which a leading merchant was able to bring in and sell pure water to the classes who were capable of paying, one could also imagine the added financial strain imposed on the local guilds of water carriers, who might otherwise have expected to receive some money for the sale of the local water to these classes.

In another essay, al-Bayyūmī defended the legitimacy of the developing religious counterculture. In this work, "Risālat al-faḍl waʾl-minaḥ," he began with a defense of the *awliyāʾ* (saints) "who are on earth," based on *ḥadīth*.[38] In chapter 3 of the same work, he emphasized protecting the rights of one's brethren, an emphasis which is not apparent in the writings of the Khalwatīya or Wafāʾīya.[39] The most important part of this essay is al-Bayyūmī's discussion of the importance of poverty. On this subject he cited the Imām Jaʿfar al-Ṣādiq (the seventh *imām* in Shīʿī theology), who stated

> that he had served six hundred *shaykhs* and asked them on four matters, but none had given his heart a cure, until the Prophet of God came to him in a dream. He said, "O! Prophet of God, what is *tawḥīd*

> [theology of unity]?" And the Prophet replied, "O! Jaʿfar, all that is said concerning this is imagination, God is different . . ." [Finally, Jaʿfar asked], "What is poverty?" and the Prophet of God said, "O! Jaʿfar, poverty is a secret among the secrets of God which he promises to those who, by serving him, make him the seal of prophecy and who are his people and remain with him; because God almighty has ordered the prophets to mix with the poor and to be with them as [a source of] patience to them in their loneliness and misery."[40]

Although later Bayyūmīs of the period of the Napoleonic invasion were apparently more revolutionary than ʿAlī al-Bayyūmī, their writings could not be located. The writings of ʿAlī al-Bayyūmī, however, are sufficient to show the vast gulf separating the religious world of the popular orders from that of the conservative middle classes. Something of the intensity of middle-class feeling against the popular orders can be found in the writings of the Shādhilī ʿAbd al-Raḥman al-Jabartī. He attacked them repeatedly and called them the *ashāwīr*, referring to the banners which they carried in their processions. He also referred to them as the rabble and as the masters of the vulgar crafts (*arbāb al-mardhūla*), who claim association with the lords of the famous shrines (*awliyāʾ*).[41] The harshness of al-Jabartī's views reflected perhaps the growth and relative importance of these classes in the late eighteenth century.

The Revival of Ḥadīth *as the Primary Legal Juridical Expression in Late-Eighteenth-Century Egypt*

Heretofore I have introduced *ḥadīth* studies to illustrate conflict mirrored in Ṣūfī traditions. In this section I take up the legal and philosophical consequences of the *ḥadīth* studies of this period and make some observations on the use of *ḥadīth* in this period which affirm the value of trade and the making of a just profit from trade.

By the phrase "revival of *ḥadīth*" it is not meant that al-Azhar and other centers of Islamic learning had been neglecting fundamental works in *ḥadīth*, such as the *Ṣaḥīḥ* of al-Bukhārī, but rather that in this period there occurred a burgeoning of scholarship based on *ḥadīth* sources as data. A comparison of the writings in *ḥadīth* studies in the seventeenth and early eighteenth centuries shows that previously *ḥadīth* studies had played a far more limited role. In the later eighteenth century, writings in the field of *ḥadīth* not only were directed to devotional or liturgical purposes, but also branched out seeking to clarify points of historical, philosophical, or literary importance. *Ḥadīth* had become the point of reference, the primary approach to truth.

Ḥadīth studies has a logic, as well as a method, which is distinct from *fiqh* (systematic theology), even where *fiqh* does not depend on *kalām*. In the eighteenth century, as *ḥadīth* studies turned to the battles of the Prophet and the lives of the *Ṣaḥāba*, there was a subtle shift in this logic. Whereas, previously, *ḥadīth* studies exhibited a contextual logic among Ṣūfī authors, it turned now more and more to the accumulating of discrete truths. Thus the Bakrīya, in contrast to al-Nābulusī and others in the Ibn al-ʿArabī tradition, would deem as true a proposition which was supported by a majority of the relevant *ḥadīth*. Quantity mattered. In addition, the use of *taʾwīl*, or derived meaning, was restricted in favor of literal meaning. Similarly, the role of analogy was sharply curtailed. In contrast to the universalistic logic of Aristotle to which we now turn, the logic of the specialists in *ḥadīth* studies, the *muḥaddithīn*, evolved under the impact of the Western industrial revolution toward positivism, the basic epistemological outlook of capitalism.

Fiqh as it was studied in the eighteenth century in Egypt was based on *kalām*, that is, ultimately on Aristotelian logic. Aristotelian logic, unlike the logic of context and unlike positivism, is grounded in the absolute, the eternal. This was pre-eminently the logic of administration, the logic of a state. When the state was strong, *fiqh* had a systematic character and flourished; but as the central state weakened in the later eighteenth century, *fiqh* and Aristotelian logic were reduced to a more and more elementary position in the *fahrasa*, the courses taught by the *shaykh*. Aristotelian logic did not find a significant development in all places in which theology was highly developed. This leads to the surmise that the relationships created by this logic, the absolute polarities, had a varying relevance to concrete social situations. On the whole, precapitalist commercial centers with their large artisanal populations were not characterized by social relationships which could not be subsumed in this framework. Perhaps it is thus not accidental that the later Andalusian, Fāṭimid, and Safavi periods appropriated Aristotle in ways quite different from the writers of Baghdad in the age of translation, the era of an agrarian tributary predominance. One could contrast *falsafa*, or peripatetic philosophy, with the use of reason by Ibn Ḥazm. Aristotelian logic was at a low ebb in Egypt during the period of commercial predominance. It recovered in the early nineteenth century as the state took over the capitalist sector and subsumed it under its administration. Its recovery occurred as the actual social relationships shifted to the polarity of bureaucrat and peasant.

There is evidence among a number of *muḥaddithīn* of the eighteenth century, and progressively so as the century developed, both of a rising literary production and of a deepening critical consciousness in scholarship as well. For example, this is reflected in the analysis of *ḥadīth*. The new focus on analysis with all it implied concerning the efficacy of human involvement contrasted with Ashʿarite theology, which stressed the more nearly total determination of God's will in human affairs. It reflected the Māturīdite reformism which had arisen in Naqshbandī circles several centuries earlier among merchants threatened by the development of the world market.

Ḥadīth *and Trade*

Both Qur'ān and *ḥadīth* look favorably on the quest for profit, on commerce, and on production for the market. Witness such sayings as "The sincere, the faithful merchant will on the Day of Judgment be among the prophets, the righteous, and the martyrs," as well as "The trustworthy merchant will be seated in the shadow of the throne of God on the Judgment Day," and "Merchants are the couriers of this world, and the faithful curators of God on earth." According to a sacred tradition (*ḥadīth qudsī*), commerce is a privileged way of earning a living: "If you make a profit in a permissable way, your action is a *jihād*, and if you use it for your family and those near to you, it will be a charitable work, and in truth a *dirham* which comes legally in commerce is worth more than ten earned in other ways."[42]

Certain commercial practices were forbidden by the Qur'ān and *ḥadīth*, but in every case there was an element of ambiguity which permitted a certain liberality in practice. Even in the celebrated case of *ribḥ* (interest), the meaning was by no means clear. The variety of points of view which were expressed, especially by the Muḥaddithīn, was quite extensive. In fact, the enlargement and explication of the concept of *ribḥ* were from the point of view of commerce undoubtedly carried out more satisfactorily in *ḥadīth* than in *fiqh*. Likewise, in matters concerning the regulation of property, the *sunna* part of *ḥadīth* was more precise than the Qur'ān; where legal devices existed in *fiqh* which were useful to merchants, such as *ḥiyal* (a device for getting around the prohibition of interest),[43] they were vigorously rejected by the Ahl al-Ḥadīth. Al-Bukhārī and his commentators attacked Abū Ḥanīfa on the question of *ḥiyal.*

In eighteenth-century writers in *ḥadīth*, one finds strong support for trade and opposition to *ḥiyal.* Al-Zabīdī described *ḥiyal* as a way of getting what one wants secretly; and God is severe with those who resort to secrecy.[44] But in the same work, when he turns to the concept of *kasb* (gain), al-Zabīdī quotes Ibn Jānī, who stated that, while *kasb* was good, *iktisāb* (excessive profiteering) was immoral; the judgment hinges on the dialectical conception that past a certain point gain would imply the use of immoral means. In this context, al-Zabīdī himself quoted a number of *ḥadīth* which supported *kasb.*[45] Elsewhere, in his commentary on the *Iḥyā' 'ulūm al-dīn li'l Ghazzālī*, al-Zabīdī indicated his attraction to the honest merchant. In one passage he speaks of the *jihād* against evil which the merchant wages confronted by the devil in the form of his weights and measures.[46] From this one can see that al-Zabīdī exceeded al-Ghazzālī in his degree of approbation of commerce. Al-Ghazzālī had said that one's earthly livelihood is a means of attaining bliss in the hereafter. Commerce is in this respect like any other occupation. If it grants a sufficient livelihood, it is better than begging. In categorizing types of trade, al-Ghazzālī suggested, however, a certain negative attitude. The two basic types of trade, in his view, were trade which is injurious to the individual and trade which is injurious to the society. The market place was, as al-Zabīdī's anecdote indicated, a place of *jihād* within men's souls. Certain types of men, al-Ghazzālī urged, would do well to refrain from trade; for example, the pious, the mystics, the learned, and the officials.[47] Al-Zabīdī's approval of commercial activities was, however, that of a learned, pious Ṣūfī in close contact with, and benefiting from, the involvement in trade of the local officialdom of his day.

Al-Zabīdī was not alone among the leading Ṣūfī reformers in supporting trade. The Shaykh al-Azhar, ʿAbdullah al-Sharqāwī, quoted a *ḥadīth* from Ibn ʿAbbās to the effect that, if Adam was an artisan, Noah a merchant, Idrīs a tailor, and Moses a herder, this shows that profit cannot be a denial of religiosity.[48] Al-Sharqāwī's position on the "most beneficial of occupations" is an interesting equivocation. The choice he poses is between trade and farming. In turning to *ḥadīth* literature, al-Sharqāwī took it up in order to discuss which was best: work by hand or work by craft. He concluded that, while some say that agriculture is best from the point of view of general utility, this differs according to circumstances; for example, while there are large numbers of people involved in some cases, in other circumstances this is not the case.[49] That the Bakrīya should in their writings justify their commercial activities would seem obvious from the previous discussion of the period. On occasion it was referred to in passing as a matter of course.

Muṣṭafā al-Bakrī, the reformer who renewed the order in Egypt, wrote in one essay: "And then we passed by the tomb of the Shaykh, the reformer, the beloved, the possessor of good fortune, ʿAlī the owner of a cow, may God protect his soul. And this cow was buried next to him. We read in this place the fatiḥa imploring God Almighty that our trade should be profitable."[50] Al-Bakrī also claimed that visiting tombs was important because anything we pray for from a saint at the tomb is from God, because saints do not cut their relations with this world after death.[51] An even more radical statement of this type comes from the son of an eighteenth-century Ṣūfī. He claimed that a mosque was like a place of trade (*maḥall tijāra*) in which is present the voice of God and Islam and in which both the rich and poor benefit.[52]

More examples could be adduced from the *ḥadīth* literature of the period, defending or praising commerce. One can also find a number of examples of *multazimīn* who studied *fiqh* rather than *ḥadīth*. Here the distinction between Ṣūfī and non-Ṣūfī does not seem to have been so important.[53] Among those *multazimīn* who were prominent *fuqahā*ʾ (systematic theologians) was Muḥammad al-Amīr al-Kabīr, a Ṣūfī who also wrote works in *ḥadīth*. Muḥammad al-Amīr was of Maghribī origin, but for two generations his family had been *multazimīn* in Upper Egypt, in the village of Ṣanabū near Asyūṭ. Muḥammad al-Amīr studied Ḥanafī *fiqh* and other rational sciences with Ḥasan al-Jabartī and with al-Jabartī's student Muḥammad b. Ismaʿīl al-Nafrāwī. He became *muftī* of the Mālikīs and wrote a number of works in Mālikī *fiqh*, such as "Al-Majmūʿa," and even a commentary on Ḥanafī law.[54] Ḥasan al-Jabartī was a Ḥanafī *faqīh*. He was a *multazim* in the village of Abidūs in Upper Egypt and independently wealthy, or so one infers from his numerous "withdrawals" from teaching at al-Azhar. His decision to teach at home was based on his possession of a large family library.

There were others who appear to have been landlords and students of *fiqh* rather than *ḥadīth*. One was Mūsā al-Sirsī al-Shāfiʿī al-Azharī (died 1804/1219). He studied the rational sciences and grammar. Thereafter he bought land in al-Minūfīya, including mills and farmlands, and became al-ʿArūsī's expert on writing *fatāwī*.[55]

An Effort to Measure the Revival

The Bakrīya Khalwatīya and the Wafāʾīya were more actively involved in the study of *ḥadīth* than in any other subject. From a statistical point of view, there is no doubt that *ḥadīth* studies was by far the most popular field in eighteenth-century writing.[56] Within *ḥadīth* studies, collections of *ḥadīth* were by far the most numerous, but a number of specialized studies also appeared. The principal works of *ḥadīth* used in the eighteenth century were those by al-Bukhārī; Muslim was much less used. Following the listings of the "Ṣaḥīḥ" of al-Bukhārī in the annotated catalog of al-Azhar, one finds listed some 384 copies. The great bulk of these date from after the advent of printing (i.e., from the late nineteenth century) and can thus be ignored for our purposes. With regard to the manuscript copies, which date back to the sixth Islamic century, it is noteworthy that the vast majority date from the twelfth Islamic century. Between 1737/1150 and 1814/1230, there are twenty-five copies. Between 1494/900 and 1688/1100, there are two. There are ten from the ninth Islamic century (this number would be increased by four if the end of the eighth century and the beginning of the tenth century were included).[57]

A similar trend is noticeable in the commentaries on al-Bukhārī. Al-Qastallānī's "Irshād al-Sārī" has fourteen copies from the twelfth Islamic century, none from the period between 1511/917 and 1680/1091. The mosque's holdings of other commentaries are much smaller. In the case of Ibn Ḥajar, "Fatḥ al-Bārī," only four out of forty-three manuscripts are dated. Of these, two are from the ninth century, one from the eleventh century, and one from the early twelfth century. Al-ʿAynī's "ʿUmdat al-qāriʾ" has a total of thirty-five copies, mainly printed, and no dated manuscript copy.[58] From these findings it is clear that, insofar as number of copies from a given period indicates use, and use indicates importance, the fifteenth, the eighteenth, and the late nineteenth centuries were the periods of most active interest in the principal works on *ḥadīth*.

A search through the catalog for the works in *ḥadīth* studied in Egypt during the seventeenth century led to the conclusion that, apart from such major collections as al-Bukhārī, there was only one work of major importance in the entire century, the *Bayqūnīya.*[59] This book is three pages long in a printed edition, written in rhymed prose. It briefly mentions the different types of *ḥadīth*, for example, strong and weak *ḥadīth*, broken and unbroken chains of transmission, and so on. The book was obviously a primer, meant to be memorized, and perhaps was modeled on a famous work of the late seventeenth century in *ʿaqīda* (dogmatics), the *Jawhara* of Ibrāhīm al-Laqānī. The *Bayqūnīya* remained a standard work until at least the early nineteenth century in al-Azhar and the mosque centers of the Maghrib.[60] Many commentaries were of course written on this elementary work, for it was necessary to expand upon and explain the material. The most important seventeenth-century commentary on the *Bayqūnīya* was written by Sīdī Muḥammad al-Zurqānī. Al-Zurqānī, who wrote in 1667/1080, stated that the purpose of the field of *ḥadīth* was to deal with literally everything from the whale in the sea to the bird in the sky. In undertaking the commentary, he stated that, despite his training, he had no other works available.[61] More advanced students had to go beyond the capsulization for the sake of memorization, and in the course of the eighteenth century this led to a number of long explications or glosses (*ḥawāshī*). The absence of these in the seventeenth century is an indication that *ḥadīth* studies had, with a few exceptions, declined to an elementary level.

The Rise in Critical Consciousness in Scholarship

There were several manifestations in the later eighteenth century of a rise in critical consciousness. We shall explore them here through a discussion of the single best-known figure, Muḥammad al-Zabīdī, a Māturīdite *muḥaddith.* In al-Zabīdī one finds the origins of the nineteenth-century scientific outlook of figures like Ḥasan al-ʿAṭṭār and Rifāʿa al Ṭahṭāwī. To attempt to give an account of the single most important writer of this period, even in *ḥadīth* alone, would be a very large undertaking, so great was the number of his writings, so numerous his students, so extensive his travels and contacts. It is clear from his own statements that he studied *ḥadīth* in India with Shāh Walīʾullah, from whom he received an *ijāza*, and that he had also studied in the Ḥijaz.[62] His arrival in Cairo in 1754/1167 was portrayed by al-Jabartī as one of the great moments in the intellectual life of the eighteenth century. Al-Jabartī, his student, may have exaggerated,[63] but exaggeration or not, the range of his activities and the number of his students were certainly very considerable. This is apparent even from the few sources which have been located.[64] Unlike most other *ʿulamāʾ*, he had Turkish and Mamlūk students: for example, ʿAllāma Muṣṭafā Efendī al-Qayṣūrlī,[65] Amīr Ḥasan Bey Sirbawwābīn,[66] and Shaykh Yūsuf al-Diyārbakarlī (died 1193), who came in his very old age.[67] Another student was Muṣṭafā Efendī, known as Bek Zadeh, who studied *al-Ḥadīth al-musalsal biʾl-awwalīya* with him, with all its conditions (*shurūṭ*).[68] Among his Egyptian and Arab students in *ḥadīth* were Shaykh Ibn al-Ikhlāṣ b. Salīm b. Salāma b. Yūsuf al-Wardānī al-Shāfiʿī al-Muḥammadī;[69] Muḥammad Ṣādiq

b. Aḥmad al-Nakhlī al-Ḥanafī, who came to Egypt to study with al-Zabīdī;[70] and Muḥammad b. Yūsuf al-Firqī al-Zakī, who studied *al-Ḥadīth al-musalsal bi'l-awwalīya.*[71] Another was ʿAllāma Yūsuf b. Aḥmad al-ʿAqqād al-Dimashqī.[72] Three Egyptian students are mentioned: Aḥmad al-Sijāʿī, Sulaymān al-Akrāshī, and Muṣṭafā al-Ṭā'ī.[73] Al-Zabīdī traveled extensively in both the Ṣaʿīd (with which he maintained close relations and visited at least three times) and the Delta. On these trips he wrote and taught a volume which has been lost containing an Ijāza Rashīdīya (an academic diploma to the people of Rosetta or Rashīd) which was supposedly reproduced in his "Alfīyat al-samt."[74] Apart from his teaching, al-Zabīdī was also famous for his research in *ḥadīth*. His research led him to write reference books which focused on questions relating to *nasab* (genealogy) and the meanings of words and terms.

Al-Zabīdī's great erudition and distinctive manner of teaching are often referred to as the reasons for his eminent stature in late-eighteenth-century Egypt. He used to teach *ḥadīth* presenting the complete chain of *rāwīs*, which he knew by heart, and following it by reciting lines of poetry.[75] As al-Zabīdī's reputation grew in Egypt, he shifted from the recitation of *ḥadīth* to the analysis of *ḥadīth*. This made for brilliant lectures which he would often give of an evening in the home of a notable. Another noteworthy feature was the presence of women and children in these sessions. The scribe would record whether they participated or merely listened.[76]

A number of Wafā'ī Ṣūfīs who were influenced by al-Zabīdī participated in the revival of *ḥadīth* studies through their travels, which aided them in the study of *ḥadīth*, and through the study of ancillary disciplines, such as history, literature, and the language sciences. Among them, Muḥammad al-Ṣabbān was outstanding. So thorough are his works in grammar and the language sciences that they are still used, or at least well known, in Egypt today.[77] Al-Ṣabbān indicated that his intention in writing his main essay in *ḥadīth*, the "Manẓūma . . . fī ḍabṭ asmā' rijāl ṣaḥīḥayn," was to correct the mistakes which he found in copies of Muslim's *Ṣaḥīḥ* and Mālik's *Al-Muwāṭṭā'* in the names of *rāwīs.* He said "I chose to focus on the problems concerning the *rāwīs* which I found in the books of the 'Thalāthiyāt,' and to correct them, that is, apart from mistakes in the copying. There are names which involve the use of non-Arabic letters, names which resemble other names . . . and we wish to give what is generally known about the name, its *laqab* [honorific name] and *kunya* [surname] and its lineage."[78] Al-Ṣabbān's criteria prefigure modern critical scholarship.

The Bakrīya *shaykhs* were also extensively engaged in *ḥadīth* studies. Muḥammad al-Ḥifnāwī (also called al-Ḥifnī) taught Muḥammad b. Muḥammad al-Bidīrī al-Dimyāṭī (known as Ibn Mayt) such works as the *Iḥyā'* of al-Ghazzālī; the *Ṣaḥīḥ* of al-Bukhārī; the *Saḥīḥ* of Muslim; the *Sunnat Abī Dā'ūd* and *Al-Nisā'ī* of Ibn Māja; the *Al-Muwāṭṭā'* of Mālik; the *Musnad* of Ibn Ḥanbal; *al-Maʿājim al-kabīr*, *Al-Awsāṭ*, and *Al-Ṣaghīr* of al-Ṭabrānī; the *Ṣaḥīḥ* of Ibn Ḥaban; the *Mustadrik* of al-Nisabūrī; and the *Ḥilyat* of Ḥāfiẓ b. Naʿīm.[79] A disciple of al-Ḥifnāwī stated in the introduction to another book that he (Aḥmad al-Dardīr) had been asked to specify the *asānīd* (chains) of the sound works in *ḥadīth* for an Ottoman *reis ül-kuttāb.*[80] This book dealt with *ḥadīth* by topics, for example, ritual purification, fasting in Ramaḍān, and so on. Another Khalwatī who has been referred to above, ʿAbdullah al-Sharqāwī, wrote a three-volume study based on *ḥadīth*, stating that "the best of sciences, after the Qurʾān itself, is the study of the *sunna* of the Prophet, because it is on this that the principles of judgment in the Sharīʿa are built." He then listed a number of *ḥadīth* which give the science of *ḥadīth* study, *ʿilm al-ḥadīth*, priority over or equality with *fiqh*, for example, from Sufyān al-Thawrī.[81] His scholarship combined rigor with pragmatism.

Conclusion

This chapter surveyed the religious framework of the cultural revival of the eighteenth century. The principal religious phenomenon of the period was the revival of Ṭarīqa Ṣūfism which took place during the second half of the eighteenth century. An analysis of this revival showed that it was juridically a reflection of the commercial revival of the same period. The characteristic form of literary expression among Ṣūfīs was in *ḥadīth*. This was linked to the new commercial ethos in content and method.

The revival of the study of *ḥadīth* and the general rise in standards of religious scholarship were built on a broad scholarly foundation. *Ḥadīth* studies depended on a range of ancillary disciplines, including literature, language sciences, and history. As a consequence of the need for more specialized knowledge in these fields, religious scholars organized a new cultural institution within the *ṭarīqa*, the *majlis*. The function of the *majlis* was to serve as a meeting place for scholars and litterateurs. The role of the *majlis* and the developments which it encouraged in various fields is pursued in Chapter 3.

Chapter 3
The Cultural Revival of the Late Eighteenth Century: Literature, Language Sciences, and History

Ḥadīth studies has always been one of the most difficult of the fields within medieval religious studies. The process of evaluating the "soundness" of a given *ḥadīth*, which is sometimes criticized for its narrow formalism, nonetheless required a wide knowledge of a range of scholastic disciplines. Among the most important were those relating to language. These included in a formal sense the "language sciences," but more broadly literature and history. With the revival of the study of *ḥadīth* in the eighteenth century, there came a corresponding revival in these fields. The revival of their study marks an important turning point in the cultural history of Egypt. In this study, it is referred to as the indigenous origins of modern secular culture. The revival of these studies among the Wafāʾīya and Bakrīya reformers turned their *majlis* into a religiocultural institution, a literary salon. These *majālis* permitted the coming together of Azhar *shaykhs*, literary figures from outside the Azhar, and traveling scholars for frank interchanges free from the artificialities of formal situations.

While the main contours of the cultural revival were determined by the needs of the *ḥadīth* revival, as the movement progressed and patronage was increasingly extended (at least prior to 1790), developments in different fields can be seen which clearly go beyond fulfilling the needs posed by the revival of *ḥadīth*.

In literature, we find that the original purpose of the *majlis* (to revive literature in order to aid *ḥadīth*) was accomplished by a revival of the *Maqāmāt* of al-Ḥarīrī, which was studied and commented upon by several writers during this period. This led to several other developments: first, the study of the pre-Islamic sources of al-Ḥarīrī, which was necessary in order to understand him. Second, it led to individuals' emulating the *maqāma* as a model for a prose form. While the first such efforts were naturally clumsy, by the end of the eighteenth century a prose work of some merit had been produced. Likewise, the poetry of this period showed development. Alongside the dominant forms of insincere praise or mourning written in a heavy *sajʿ* (rhymed prose), there developed a poetry in which the poet wrote about his own feelings with obvious sincerity. In linguistic fields, a particularly large number of works were composed as "transmitted" sciences; for example, in lexicography writers produced works which emphasized the importance of the original sources for the meanings of words, and the knowledge of the chain of authorities through which the original sources had been received. The study of grammar, in the hands of its leading student, likewise underwent a critical development. In some writings, there began a utilitarian critique of later medieval accretions and imprecisions in the grammar books which could be detected with a precise knowledge of *ḥadīth*. The sciences of language style, especially rhetoric, made a dramatic revival during the eighteenth century. These were particularly needed for the *talqīn* (instruction) in the *inshād* (recitation). Historical studies also made a notable revival during the eighteenth century. The first major theme which was developed, through the study of the Battle of Badr, was the unique importance of the *ṣaḥāba* al-Badrīyīn. (The battle is discussed more fully later in this chapter under "History.")

As the middle class prospered and the salon flourished, the medieval court culture began to give way. The *maqāma*, as will be shown in Chapter 4, began to develop toward something like a novel. History became the history of the middle classes and even of the guilds. It was no longer merely dynastic history. Language sciences began to be related more to language as it is and has been and not language as it should be. The most important general development was the nascent sense of critical consciousness which was to grow and guide the neoclassical revival. These were some of the main attributes of the first phase of the indigenous development of a modern culture in Egypt.

Literature

The first phase of the revival of Arabic literature reflected very closely the milieu in which it was being studied. The dominant note of *ḥadīth* studies created the direction and mood. Judging from some of its poetry, the *majlis* of Riḍwān was still like the Bakrīya of the late seventeenth and early eighteenth centuries. Its poetic expression contained much of the artificiality and dull repetition of the poetry of formal occasions. With the rise of the *majlis* al-Wafāʾīya, a very considerable broadening of literary activity took place. The needs of the *ḥadīth* movement had a certain precedence, but the developments resulting from the studies of Ḥarīrī which were pursued in the service of *ḥadīth* studies were significant. The *maqāma* began to emerge as a prose form. The tradition of poetry of praise was continued but with the difference that in the context of the Ṣūfī *ṭarīqa* it did not have the same artificiality as it did in a court.

The first literary salon to be organized, the *majlis* of Riḍwān, lasted some fifteen years (from 1738/1152 to 1753/1167). It was founded by Al-Amīr Riḍwān al-Jalfī, who offered annual prizes to poets. Many of the participants were early students of the Bakrīya-Khalwatīya *shaykh* Muḥammad al-Ḥifnāwī: for example, Muḥammad b. Riḍwān al-Suyūṭī (died 1766/1180), who wrote wine poetry in imitation of Abū Nuwwās. Al-Suyūṭī reserved his best panegyric efforts for the Khalwatī *shaykh*.[1] Another prominent member of Amīr Riḍwān's circle who studied with al-Ḥifnāwī was Aḥmad

ʿAbdullah b. al-Salāma al-Idkāwī (died 1770/1184). He wrote *maqāmāt*, including two for his patrons, ʿAbdullah al-Shubrāwī and Muḥammad al-Ḥifnāwī. He was described as the "poet laureate" of the salon; among his literary activities was the collecting of the poems written in honor of the Amīr Riḍwān, which he gathered together in a work called "Al-fawāʾiḥ al-jinānīya fīʾl-madāʾiḥ al-Riḍwānīya." This book contained only some of these poems, for it is described as being a collection of those poems which were written by the Amīr's North African guests. Al-Idkāwī also attempted to imitate the *Maqāmāt* of al-Ḥarīrī, although poorly, and he composed a work called "Bidāʿt al-arīb fī shīʿr baḍāʾi al-gharīb."[2]

Shaykh Muṣṭafā Asʿad al-Laqīmī al-Dimyāṭī, who wrote wine poetry, also frequented the salon. There were many other figures, but by mid-century these had nearly all died, and the circle presumably collapsed sometime after 1753/1167 with the death of the Amīr.

The formation of the Wafāʾīya salon, the first modern cultural institution of Egypt, occurred very soon thereafter. Although the salon of the Wafāʾīya was smaller, there can be no question that it played a more significant role in the history of Egypt than did its predecessor, notwithstanding that some of the same figures participated in both.[3] The *majlis* al-Wafāʾīya was characterized by two emphases, its interest in later Andalusian culture and its interest in mystical poetry, especially that of Fāṭimid Egypt. This latter interest gave to some of the poems of the Wafāʾīya an extraordinary emotionality and a sense of drama generally lacking in the dominant rhymed prose (*sajʿ*) for which poets in the later courts received patronage. This is not to say that a master of *sajʿ* could not use it with a biting realism but that, in general, poetry and prose became richer and more complex in cultures which had a strong middle class, and conversely. This dual-cultural orientation mirrored the division within the salon between Egyptians and Maghāriba. As Maghribī power declined generally in Cairo, the salon became "Egyptian."

One of the main figures of the Wafāʾīya salon was al-Ḥasan b. ʿAlī al-Badrī al-ʿAwḍī (died 1809/1224). Al-Ḥasan was an Egyptian Qurʾān reciter who followed his father in this profession. He spent his life in al-Azhar in the Riwāq al-Arwām. He also taught in the neighboring mosque of Sayyidnā al-Ḥusayn, which came under the influence of the Wafāʾīya after the Ottoman invasion of 1786. Among his students was ʿAlī Bey al-Daftardār. The extent of al-ʿAwḍī's understanding of Wafāʾīya mysticism is not known, apart from a brief reference to his knowing the "names" and his capacity for *kashf* (illumination). Al-ʿAwḍī was a scholar of literature. He compiled one of the most important works of the period, "Al-Lawāʾiḥ al-anwārīya" (Dār al-Kutub manuscript 1419 Adab). This work collected the major poems written in praise of Muḥammad Abī Anwār al-Sādāt. Al-ʿAwḍī's other writings included a number of essays and a Dīwān, which remain unlocated. He was also remembered for a quarrel with Muḥammad al-Amīr, the *muftī* of the Malikīs. Al-ʿAwḍī is said to have remarked that al-Amīr's surprise at his own view on the matter of *al-najāsa* (ritual impurity) was related to the fact that al-Amīr was a foreigner![4] Al-ʿAwḍī was a close friend of several other literary figures who collectively formed the *majlis*, for example, Qāsim b. ʿAṭāʾullah, who was known for literary activity. Qāsim was widely read in literature and history, apparently a result in part of his studies in *ḥadīth*, a field in which he was also distinguished. In his youth he memorized *Al-Mulḥa*, *Al-Alfīya*, and other works in literature and the language sciences, as well as popular Arabic poetry forms of *zaghal* and *muwashshaḥa*. In the latter he became known as the most famous of his generation. In the book of al-ʿAwḍī mentioned above, Qāsim's poetry in praise of Muḥammad Abī Anwār reflects his mastery of these genres and of the mystical themes of the Wafāʾ. He referred to al-Sādāt as the center of the Aqṭāb of his age, as possessing a *wilāya* (guardianship) on the authority of the *ṣaḥāba*, that is, Āl Ṭaha. This poetry, which was written in the *majlis*, contrasts sharply with the conventional literary products of the day, such as his early poem praising Riḍwān Katkhūdā al-Jalfī.[5]

A third literary friend of al-ʿAwḍī and the others who frequented the *majlis* al-Wafāʾīya was Muḥammad b. Riḍwān al-Suyūṭī, known as Ibn al-Ṣalāḥī (died 1766/1180). He came from the Delta; his mother's family had wealth in Damietta, where he was born in 1727/1140. Among his teachers was Muḥammad al-Ḥifnāwī, with whom he studied literature, handwriting, and lexicography. He was a friend of one of al-Zabīdī's students named Aḥmad al-Sijāʿī, and on al-Sijāʿī's death he wrote a *qaṣīda* of mourning. Earlier he had had a literary encounter with al-Sijāʿī on the subject of "*al-lughz al-Damāmīnī fīʾl-fāʿil*," in which he addressed the *ʿulamāʾ* of India and al-Sijāʿī replied in an essay which has never been located. There is a *qaṣīda* praising Muḥammad al-Ḥifnāwī, another praising Muḥammad Abī Anwār. Two poems cited by al-Jabartī refer to coffee drinking. They are complemented by some wine poetry and even love poetry built on the imagery of *ḥashīsh*: "*alqāki wa fī ḥashīshatī al-ashwāq*." Couplets in *rajaz* metre which were recited in the *majlis* al-Wafāʾīya are quoted.[6]

The last person to be dealt with here was a member of the salon in later years. He was one of its most significant poets and one of the most committed followers of Muḥammad Abī Anwār. He was Ismaʿīl al-Khashshāb, or Ismaʿīl Wahbī (died 1815/1230). We shall deal here with his *Dīwān*, which shows his imaginative abilities and may be used to show the impact of the *majlis* al-Wafāʾīya on the development of the younger writers of the late eighteenth century, among whom were also Ḥasan al-ʿAṭṭār and ʿAbd al-Raḥman al-Jabartī.[7]

The most important part of the *Dīwān* was the poetry in which he praised Muḥammad Abī Anwār al-Sādāt. It is poetry written by a young man to an older man whom he loved and admired, and despite the *sajʿ* form, al-Khashshāb achieved a warmth and sincerity rarely found in eighteenth-century poetry. He praised al-Sādāt's house as a center of civilization, a place of relaxation for the traveler. He called al-Sādāt the leading spiritual figure of his age and referred to him as the chosen legatee of the divine (*al-wārith al-mukhtār*), the one who has been appointed by God to lift the gloom of the Eastern night. He also alluded to his divine spiritual powers (*awwalī al-taqwa, dhū ʾl-ʿulyā*). Referring to al-Sādāt's connection through the house of Wafāʾ to the Prophet, al-Khashshāb spoke on the occasion of the birth of a son to al-Sādāt of the child's inheriting the light from his father.[8] These and many other images were used by al-Khashshāb as he sought to describe al-Sādāt and the Ṣūfī literary milieu of the Wafāʾ. Al-Khashshāb possessed a degree of aesthetic sensibility which responded to the imagistic possibilities in mystical life; he conveyed these as vividly as his craft permitted. Al-Khashshāb, however, like others of his age, was struggling not only with the enormous problem of the fitness of language, but also with the fact that no public existed outside the small salon to read what he had written. He worked all his life in government employment and wrote numerous poems in traditional genres for those who paid him to do so.

The tragedy of the late eighteenth and early nineteenth centuries which affected the creative lives of both al-Khashshāb and al-ʿAṭṭār was the weakening of the indigenous segment of the middle class, which had supported the salon tradition, and with this decline the reversion to a "court culture." This occurred in the time of their early manhood. Al-ʿAṭṭār left Egypt for Turkey and Syria, where he stayed thirteen years, during which he haphazardly studied literature and wrote less and less, as we shall see in Chapter 5. Al-Khashshāb stayed in Egypt and died in 1815/1230. After the death of al-Khashshāb, new genres entered the literature, such as the poetry of the bureaucratic age, the *waṭanīyāt*; but it would be difficult to find an Egyptian poet again before the middle of the nineteenth century who struggled so hard and so sincerely to express personal feelings.

The salon had served as the principal vehicle through which literature was revived, discussed, and in many cases emulated. An outstanding example is the *maqāma* of al-Ḥarīrī. Its study was revived in Egypt by a Maghribī litterateur in the late seventeenth century. For certain linguistic purposes, al-Ḥarīrī served throughout the eighteenth century. Interest in the *maqāma* form steadily developed. Religion was scarcely the reason for the choice of a Jewish Andalusian model by one Egyptian *shaykh* for editing and by another for emulation. Even al-Zabīdī, who did much to train students in linguistics by having them memorize parts of al-Ḥarīrī, revealed at the time of the death of his wife that it was the pre-Islamic tribal background in al-Ḥarīrī which drew him.

The classical *maqāma* was a prose form in which jugglery of words and verbal gymnastics dominated concern for content. According to modern scholarship, its greatest practitioner was al-Hamadhānī.[9] Significantly, however, al-Ḥarīrī enjoyed the greatest popularity, especially in the post-caliphate period. After a general decline in the writing of Arabic commentaries on *maqāmāt* literature in the thirteenth century, there was a revival of studies on al-Ḥarīrī in Egypt in the late seventeenth century. The initiator of this revival was Shihāb al-dīn al-Khafājī (died 1653/1069), who wrote on al-Ḥarīrī and also composed *maqāmāt* of his own.[10]

In the eighteenth century a large number of writers turned their attention to al-Ḥarīrī's *Maqāmāt*, such a large number that the phenomenon deserves special attention.[11] Leaving aside for a moment the contribution of the main figure in this revival, Muḥammad Murtaḍā al-Zabīdī, we shall begin with other writers of the same period. Muḥammad b. Muḥammad al-Kuthnāwī al-Dānirānkawī (1742/1155) memorized the *Maqāmāt* for linguistic reasons with Shaykh Muḥammad Fūḍū, who taught him literature and grammar for four years. This student became a teacher and later a timekeeper.[12] Ḥasan al-Jabartī wrote a long commentary on the *Maqāmāt* which he taught to the *beys.*[13] The son of ʿAbdullah al-Shubrāwī possessed numerous copies of the commentaries on the *Maqāmāt al-Ḥarīrī*, such as the one by al-Zamakhsharī and others.[14] Another person mentioned above in connection with the salons, a poet named Aḥmad b. ʿAbdullah al-Salāma al-Idkāwī, also memorized parts of the *Maqāmāt al-Ḥarīrī.*[15] Yet another person was Alī b. Abdullah al-Rumi, originally the Mulla Darwish Agha, known as Muharram Efendi Bash. In his youth he studied handwriting as a craft with the famous teacher Ḥasan al-Ḍiyāʾī, taking an *ijāza* for his skill. When he came to Egypt he had serious discussions with a student of Shihāb al-Khafājī named Muḥammad b. ʿUmar al-Khuwānkī, called the *adīb*, or litterateur, of his age. Al-Rumi memorized parts of this man's writings, including a historical work called "Asmāʾ ahl al-Badr," along with parts of the *Maqāmāt al-Ḥarīrī.* He also edited al-Zabīdī's work on the Battle of Badr (see below) and studied *ḥadīth* with him.[16] Another student of al-Zabīdī was ʿAlī b. ʿAbdullah b. Aḥmad al-ʿAlawī al-Ḥanafī (died 1784/1199). He studied language and literature with al-Zabīdī; among the works he studied was the *Maqāmāt al-Ḥarīrī.*[17]

Finally, there was al-Zabīdī himself. Al-Zabīdī drew vast numbers of students to his lectures. One account which is much celebrated in the biographical literature is that of the decision of a high Ottoman official to come to Egypt in order to study with al-Zabīdī. It is said that this person, ʿAbd al-Rāziq Efendī, would go to al-Zabīdī with the difficult passages after he had finished his lessons with other *shaykhs.* He read the *Maqāmāt al-Ḥarīrī* with al-Zabīdī, who would simplify it for him.[18]

Al-Zabīdī's study of al-Ḥarīrī led him to study the pre-Islamic and early Ommayad sources of the Arabic language which al-Ḥarīrī himself had drawn on.[19] When his wife died, al-Zabīdī mourned her in poetry written in the fashion of Majnūn Layla, which was unheard of in Ottoman Egypt to that point.[20] Al-Zabīdī's study of Majnūn Layla in the Jāhilīya (pre-Islamic) period brings out the more radical equality of sexes found in tribal contexts than in some urban situations. While it was shocking to al-Zabīdī's contemporaries, it was symptomatic of trends in sexual relations in the later eighteenth century. In this unusual period, women did appear in the chronicles. In the reversals of the nineteenth century, this ceased to be the case. Al-Zabīdī in fact wrote numerous works on tribal history and genealogy, drawing information from his travels among the tribes. The tribes who spoke a purer Arabic than that of Egypt in his day also supplied him with information on language, which was vital to his *ḥadīth* studies.[21]

The revival of interest in al-Ḥarīrī had another consequence for the development of eighteenth-century literature, namely, the revival of the *maqāma* as a literary genre. Not surprisingly, the early attempts at emulation were generally disappointing, although not more than two or three have been studied by modern scholars. From those which have been surveyed, it is a great leap to the brilliant prose work of al-ʿAṭṭār, *Maqāmat al-ʿAṭṭār* (which will be discussed in Chapter 4).[22]

In the eighteenth century, literature in Egypt was studied and composed by *shaykhs* of al-Azhar. Despite the participation of the Ṣūfī salons in the literary culture, it bore the marks of its scholastic environment. While this environment was not the most conducive to creativity, it was a supportive environment for the writing of commentaries on classical and literary works and for the editing and reintroduction of old texts. One example of this was the work of Shaykh Aḥmad al-Sijāʿī, who wrote "Bulūgh al-ārāb bi sharḥ qaṣīda min kalām al-ʿarab (Qaṣīdat al-Samuwʾal b. ʿĀdīyāʾ al-Ghassānī al-Yahūdī)" (1763/1177).[23]

The Language Sciences: Lexicography, Grammar, and Style

In the study of lexicography, al-Zabīdī retained close and continuous relationships with travelers to and from North Africa. In grammar, Muḥammad al-Ṣabbān wrote on the Andalusian Ibn Mālik. The object of his very popular work was the commentator al-Ashmūnī, much more so than the text, which had in any case been criticized in North Africa by figures like Ibn Khaldūn. Muḥammad al-Amīr, who did retain close links with his North African origins, wrote on Ibn Hishām. But his interest seemed to be more the critique of the commentator Khālid al-Azharī. Al-Ṣabbān's discussion focused on the use of *ḥadīth* by al-Ashmūnī. Finally, with regard to style, the principal writings reflected the use of these works within Ṣūfī circles. The new epistemology of the *ḥadīth* movement emerged clearly in all these fields. These works mark a break with the past.

Philological control over the meaning of individual words was always much less than that over the rules of discourse. Thus in lexicography, al-Zabīdī taught the classic lexicographers, such as al-Thaʿālibī and al-Bāqillānī, who argued that the knowledge of conventional meanings is not enough for making proper word combinations; one must also know the actual usage.[24] In the early nineteenth century, Ḥasan al-ʿAṭṭār, whose studies were primarily in the rational sciences, avoided lexicography.[25]

The heightened interest in lexicography in eighteenth-century Egypt can be witnessed from the fact that six out of the ten copies of a standard dictionary in al-Azhar's library were made in the eighteenth century. This is a large number in view of the small total number of dictionaries.[26] The study of lexicography in eighteenth-century Egypt was integral to the work of the *muḥaddithīn*. It was characterized by the same concern for precise linkage of meanings to their origins. It sought to achieve this through the study of literary sources and the observation of actual usage.

Chronologically, the first student of lexicography was Muḥammad b. al-Ṭīb al-Fāsī (1698/1110–1756/1170). He lived most of his life in Madīna, where he studied *ḥadīth*. He wrote a major work on lexicography, and his principal student was al-Zabīdī.[27] Al-Ṭīb began his study by stating that when defining words his intent was to give the most important meaning and to avoid strange and remote meanings, such as one would find in some of the glosses. This was because he wished to facilitate the study of *ḥadīth* and *tafsīr* (commentary on the Qurʾān). He further stated that he wished to correct the mistakes which he found in these two fields in particular, which he called the noble sciences, the "*ʿulūm al-sharīfa*."[28] He then began the commentary on the basic text, on which he had grave reservations. Al-Ṭīb differed markedly with al-Firūzabādī, the author of the great medieval dictionary, the *Qāmūs*, over the value of the *Ṣiḥāḥ* of al-Jawharī. The disagreement centered on the use of *ḥadīth* sources.[29]

The commentary on the *Qāmūs*, called *Tāj al-ʿarūs* by al-Zabīdī, is one of the most important works of the eighteenth century. Moreover, it has been in continuous use up to the present day among students and scholars.[30] Al-Firūzabādī had modeled his work on the *Ṣiḥāḥ* of al-Jawharī but included numerous root combinations which al-Jawharī had omitted. These were written in by al-Firūzabādī in red. Al-Zabīdī carried this process further and included root combinations which al-Firūzabādī did not include. The issue at stake concerned the problem of the genuine existence of a word. For al-Zabīdī, as for other philologists, especially in the context of the religious revival, the language of the Qur'ān was nearly as sacred as the revelation of the Qurʾān. Lexicographers had been led by this belief to calculate the possibilities in each known root. Al-Zabīdī sought to trace the source of every single word. In addition, he sought to overcome the traditional conflict between the conventional and actual meanings of words. Al-Zabīdī's preoccupation with the reconciliation of this conflict led him to undertake empirical research on a scale unparalleled in later Islamic history. When travelers came to Cairo, he would inquire of them their names, their tribes, and information on their origins. In this way he established such close relations with the North Africans that it became proverbial among them that to visit Cairo was to visit al-Zabīdī. The breadth of these contacts was illustrated on the occasion of the completion of one of his major works, when he sent copies literally across the Islamic world.[31] Prior to his sojourn in Egypt, al-Zabīdī had traveled widely in the Arab world, especially among the tribes, where in his day the language was less corrupted than that which was spoken in the cities.

What degree of success al-Zabīdī had in his investigations of language among the tribes is not known. As has been pointed out in a recent article, the Ḥijāzī tribes, like the Quraysh, who were frequently used by philologists as a reference, had extensive "foreign" contacts; hence, their language might not be the purest. On the other hand, the study of the tribes and of tribal culture might show that their sense of history and their own historical mission served to keep them highly self-conscious in matters of language. The Wahhābīs, for example, were widely respected for their knowledge of language and *ḥadīth*. The Quraysh might have preserved their language more successfully than tribes in the Arabian interior which had never played a similar historical role. In any case, it would be wrong to maintain that the "remote" tribes were not also used by philologists: among those that were studied were the Qais, Tamīm, and Asad.[32]

Al-Zabīdī was the last lexicographer to cite his authority for every piece of information which he records. Many of these references were to previous lexicographical works, some fifty in all.[33] Al-Zabīdī's concern with the criteria of an acceptable entry led him even to list the chain of transmitters from himself back to Ibn Ḥajar, who took it orally from al-Firūzabādī.

Al-Zabīdī's criticism of the *Qāmūs* was that it sacrificed clarity for the sake of brevity. This made it difficult to use, at least in the fashion that al-Zabīdī wished to use a dictionary. His *Tāj*, with the text of the *Qāmūs* inserted in brackets, is about five times the size of the earlier work. Al-Zabīdī reinserted the *shawāhid* (sources), along with quotations from geographical and medical authorities, thereby increasing the amount of information on place names and persons beyond that given in the *Qamūs*,[34] making the *Tāj* comparable to the O.E.D. in function.

Al-Zabīdī's profound influence on the development of lexicography in Egypt continued long after his death. This was especially true among later students of *ḥadīth*. However, he was not alone.[35] Al-Ṣabbān, who studied with al-Zabīdī, also combined *ḥadīth* studies with philology. Another writer contemporary with al-Zabīdī who worked in lexicography and *ḥadīth* was Fakhr al-dīn b. Muḥammad Ṭuwayh, who wrote "Majmaʿ al-baḥrayn wa maṭlaʿ al-nīrayn" (1757/1171), which was composed to cover the obscurities in the Qurʾān and *ḥadīth*.

While the early Ottoman period produced few really distinguished Egyptian grammarians, there was, however, a continuous production of treatises on grammar at al-Azhar. The main grammarians discussed by Carl Brockelmann—al-Zabīdī, al-Ṣabbān, and the seventeenth-century scholar al-Khafājī—are all from the later Ottoman period. The following chart gives the distribution of manuscripts which Brockelmann lists, by the century in which they were written.[36]

	Century		
	16th	*17th*	*18th*
Supplement edition, vol. 2	5	10	12
First edition, vol. 2	5	6	7

From this listing, the importance of the later period can be deduced. Even for the field which was traditionally most aligned to the rational sciences, it would seem that al-Ṣabbān was the most prominent grammarian of eighteenth-century Egypt. His works were used in the nineteenth and even the twentieth centuries.

The works of Ibn Mālik were studied intensively throughout the entire Ottoman period, if one may make a rough estimate from the number of dated manuscripts in the catalog of al-Azhar. The *Sharḥ al-Ashmūnī*, on which al-Ṣabbān wrote a gloss, was only one of many, although it was the most popular. The other principal work which was used in the eighteenth century in the field of grammar was written by Ibn Hishām and commented upon by Khālid al-Azharī. In addition, there was a second work by Ibn Hishām which was also commented upon by Khālid, and a third work by Khālid which was a commentary on a composition of his own.

The school of Ibn Hishām was continued by al-Amīr in the 1790's. In the early nineteenth century, it was represented by Ḥasan al-ʿAṭṭār. At the same time, al-Ṣabbān had found Nūr al-dīn al-Ashmūnī "lean in understanding" and subject to "delusions of the mind" in his approach to grammar. He was particularly critical of al-Ashmūnī's treatment of *ḥadīth*.[37] In the following generation this critique was continued, although the points of concern were reversed. Al-Ṣabbān's student Ḥasan al-ʿAṭṭār was a *mutakallim*, a student of speculative theology. With al-ʿAṭṭār, as I show in Chapter 4, the progress of utilitarianism becomes marked.

In the field of rhetoric, in particular, it would appear that the need to revive the study of this discipline in Egypt grew out of the requirements of *al-inshād* and *al-dhikr*. Prior to the eighteenth century, during the Ottoman period, there were very few writings in this field. In the eighteenth century, however, both the copies of classical works and the number of "independent" writings increased considerably. Prior to the eighteenth century, nearly all the glosses on the basic text of the postclassical period which was used in Egypt, the *Talkhīṣ al-miftāḥ* of al-Qazwīnī on the *Miftāḥ al-ʿulūm* of al-Sakkākī, were by non-Egyptians. In the eighteenth century, *ḥawāshī* were composed by Muḥammad al-Ḥifnāwī and his brother Yūsuf (who were leading Khalwatīs), by Muḥammad al-Ṣabbān (a Wafāʾī), and by Muḥammad ibn ʿArafa al-Disūqī (whose teacher in theology had been Aḥmad al-Dardīr).[38]

Three Ṣūfī writers in eighteenth-century Egypt wrote on more limited themes and built on the medieval texts. Their works enjoyed a large popularity until the end of the nineteenth century. The first of these writers was Aḥmad al-Sijāʿī, who composed two works on the use of metaphors. Both were commentaries on his own compositions. A gloss was later written on one of them in the nineteenth century. The two principal figures were, however, Muḥammad al-Amīr and Muḥammad al-Ṣabbān. Al-Amīr's commentary on the text called *Al-Samarqandīya* (1778/1185) was frequently used. The writing of subcommentaries was common into the nineteenth century. The most influential work in this field was al-Ṣabbān's "Risāla fīʾl-bayān."

One last work which was both the longest and one of the most detailed studies of the period was based on the *Talkhīṣ al-miftāḥ*. It was written in some fourteen hundred pages and was finished three years before Napoleon invaded Egypt.[39] Other Egyptians who wrote during the eighteenth century and contributed to the revival of this field included Aḥmad al-Damanhūrī, Muḥammad al-Kafrāwī, ʿAbdullah al-Shubrāwī, and Ḥasan al-ʿAṭṭār.

In conclusion, the revival of the study of style in the eighteenth century was part of the larger body of "new" writings by Ṣūfī *shaykhs*. In some cases their practical application is particularly clear. The art of rhetoric was of great importance in the context of the Ṣūfī *dhikr*. In fact, Muḥammad al-Ḥifnāwī, the famous *khalīfa* of the Bakrīya, was himself responsible for a number of innovations in communication in Egypt. It is said that he turned to the use of *mawwāl*, colloquial poetry often sung to the accompaniment of a reed pipe. Al-Ḥifnāwī's solution to the problem of effective communication across class lines was a considerable achievement. Before the eighteenth century, the Azharīs had never had to confront the lower classes in large numbers. One may infer what was meant by the description of a basic text in *ʿilm al-waḍʿ*, the rules of composition, as written for the sake of "matters related to the hearts" in this context.[40] A parallel conclusion is that, because other fields, such as the formal rules of poetry, did not share the needs for cross-class communication, they did not participate in the eighteenth-century revival.[41]

History

In the eighteenth century, Egypt began its transition from a tributary mode to modern periphery capitalist society. Two types of historical writing coexisted during this era and reflected this transition. One school represented the old ruling groups which were suffering upheaval; the other reflected the rise of the new, commercially oriented middle classes.

In their pure form, these two principal genres reflect, both in method and in content, different social realities. The chronicle of the deeds of the upper classes, written in imitation of Turkish dynastic history, recorded the sequence of events (*akhbār*) during the reign of each Ottoman Pasha. The middle classes, on the other hand, were interested in explaining their own changing situation rather than in writing chronology. As has previously been mentioned, their mode of analysis was derived from *ḥadīth* studies. Their concern was with morality, both individual and social, although there was no artificial separation in their thinking. The social aspect (insofar as practices were concerned) has been discussed above. Here our concern will be with awareness of the historical decline of Islam and its contemporary weakness. The middle-class study of history, unprecedented in its choice of subject matter and the intensity of its commitment, was an attempt at self-understanding through focusing on the Battle of Badr, which for the first time in Islamic history was studied, in Egypt, as an independent subject. The concern of these historians was to learn how the Prophet was able to emerge victorious from adverse conditions. The deepening of an analytical approach to history led to a revival of interest in the historical writing of Ibn Khaldūn. The naturalism of Ibn Khaldūn within a religious framework was acceptable to the Māturīdite outlook of the eighteenth century.

The reader may rightly ask at this point, why are studies in *ʿilm al-ḥadīth* being grouped with chronicle history during the eighteenth century, especially in view of the fact that the one grew out of the other in early Islamic times? The treatment of both types of writing as antecedents to modern historiography is deliberate. It reflects a conviction that the chronicle is the antecedent of only one kind of modern history. If one understands modern history as essentially a sequence of events and dates, then the chronicle form can rightly or wrongly be understood as a primitive antecedent of it. However, if one understands by modern history a science striving to achieve a holistic understanding of the human condition, then the choice of medieval antecedents would naturally be quite different. The latter concept of historical writing is not so tightly bound to a linear notion of time as is the "positivist" tradition of historiography.

In post-tenth-century Islam, a great concern with an integrated vision of reality was shown in the writings of Ṣūfīs. In the Ṣūfī revival of the eighteenth century, a number of central themes from the life of the Prophet were revived. Through these themes, an attempt was made to understand the historical predicament of the eighteenth century. It is for this reason that these works are studied along with the chronicles.

The revival of interest in Ibn Khaldūn, al-Ṣabbān's concern with the careful use of *ḥadīth* in grammar, and al-Khashshāb's sincerity in poetry were manifestations of what has been called in Chapter 2 the rebirth of a critical consciousness among writers of the middle classes.

The chronicle literature of the Ottomans in eighteenth-century Egypt reflected the decline of the old order. Two works by members of the ʿAzab corps, written during the eighteenth century at a time when the corps was extremely weak, create a romanticized image of society according to the norms of Ottoman rule a century earlier. One of these chronicles was written about 1751/1165 and begins with the author's explanation of why he was moved to write it: "I was asked by some comrades about the events of Egypt which concerned the Sanājiq, the Āghawāt, the Ikhtiyārīya . . . from the time of Sultan Sulaymān Khān down to Sultan ʿUthmān in 1754/1168, may he continue victorious; and I was asked about those who were sent as Pasha during this time to Egypt."[42] The principle of organization was cyclical. The new Pasha would arrive in Alexandria on a given date with his entourage. He would then make his procession up the valley of the Nile through Rosetta to Cairo; this was a biennial reconquest of Egypt on a symbolic level. Along the way the officials and notables would make their gestures of obeisance. The only concession to Egypt, again purely symbolic, was the custom which apparently began in the eighteenth century, of his visit to the tomb of the Imām al-Shāfiʿī. The chronicle then relates the major events of the Pasha's "reign."[43]

One does not find in the Ottoman-style chronicle, as one does with al-Jabartī and the middle-class milieu, a particular concern with written sources. The Pasha's contact with "Egyptians" was very limited. One of the few references to an Egyptian was to an unnamed Naqīb al-Ashrāf, who was also the Shaykh al-Rifāʿīya (a Ṣūfī order). Commerce was not discussed, but there were references to the land tax.[44] A second work which dealt with the Pashas who served during the reign of each Sultan presented less the Ottoman theory of government and more the reality in its treatment of subjects, such as the rivalries of Dhū'l-Faqqār and the Qāsimīya and the attacks of the Bedouins.[45] The historical chronicle as a genre survived into the nineteenth century. One writer wrote a chronicle history of the Ottomans for the French and a similar chronicle for an Ottoman patron.[46]

Middle-class historians wrote on historical themes which interested them directly. One such theme was the Battle of Badr. The historical details of the Battle of Badr were well enough known, and they do not fully clarify the reason for the singularly widespread interest it evoked in this period. In March 624/Ramaḍān of the year 2, a battle took place between Muḥammad's troops and the Meccans. Although outnumbered by perhaps one thousand to three hundred, Muḥammad was able to rally his army and put the Meccans to rout. Some seventy Meccans and fifteen Muslims were killed. Seventy Meccans were taken prisoner. The battle confirmed the Muslims' faith in Islam and perhaps should be seen first of all in this light. One theme which ran through the eighteenth-century writings on the Battle of Badr was the concern to ascertain the exact number of those who were fighting on the side of Muḥammad. In general, the eighteenth-century authors lowered the totals compiled by previous writers. These previous writers were not discussed: who they were and what their motives might have been for attempting to show that there were larger numbers of participants were not really dealt with. Is it possible that the eighteenth-century writers on the Battle of Badr felt a renewed sense of identification with the forces of Muḥammad? Did they feel that they, too, were struggling in a rather hostile environment against powerful odds?[47]

Before considering whether this is a logical interpretation, we will present some examples of these writings. Muḥammad al-Ṣabbān wrote a short essay on this subject in 1757/1171 called "Manẓūmat asmā' ahl Badr."[48] Al-Ṣabbān also wrote a commentary on this work (the commentary was not located), and his student Muṣṭafā al-Banānī wrote a subcommentary on that.[49] Al-Banānī began his work by listing the sources which he intended to use. These included the "Sīra" of Ibn Sayyid al-Nās called Nūr al-Nirās. He also stated that he would draw on his other teachers—ʿAbdullah al-Shubrāwī, Muḥammad al-Ḥifnāwī, and Shihāb al-dīn Aḥmad al-Ḥadramī. On folio 78B he begins a biography of al-Ṣabbān based on al-Jabartī and states that al-Ṣabbān studied the *Tafsīr al-Bayḍāwī* with al-Shubrāwī and the *Ṣaḥīḥ al-Bukhārī* with al-Ḥifnāwī, as well as the *Miʿrāj* of al-Ghayṭī. On folio 79, he includes some of al-Ṣabbān's poetry in praise of Muḥammad Abī Anwār. The tone of this work is very different from that of the original:

the sense of urgency expressed by al-Ṣabbān in the earlier period is missing. From folio 82A on, al-Banānī follows al-Ṣabbān's organization, explaining the *aḥādīth* which al-Ṣabbān chose.

In another work on the same subject which was written in 1748/1162, the time of Muḥammad and the author's own era are linked through a general history of Islam from the time of the Battle of Badr until the age of Sultan Maḥmūd in 1748/1162.[50] The author stated that he intended to give the number of the companions of the Prophet, their names, what had been said concerning their divine blessings (*karāmāt*), and their fates. According to the author, the work was composed at the request of the Ottoman Pasha ʿAbdullah in the year 1750/1164. He said on page 2, "It is said that a man reads what has happened in the past to know that which makes it unique and distinguishes it from what has existed from the beginning of time; so I put forward this collection, as examples." Chapter 2 dealt with the names of the Prophet's companions. Al-Shubrāwī stated that certain Ṣūfīs had achieved spiritual cures through the recitation of these names, and that such recitation had helped merchants to succeed in commerce.

Muḥammad al-Ḥifnāwī, who wrote on the same theme sometime around 1759/1173, invoked the "path of guidance" for those who are engaged in a *jihād* for God's sake. Then he stated that he "had read some writings connected with the names of the Ahl al-Badr and that from among these writings were some which condensed or abridged the account without maintaining the necessary precision; while others were too long and went off the subject."[51] He describes the Badrīyīn as the noblest group (*ʿaṣaba*) which has ever existed. "I chose to take as an example some of the most illustrious so as to dispel illusions." His method of concluding an argument was quite didactic: "Know that it has been agreed concerning the Badrīyīn that their number is 313, and whoever contests that is in opposition. Awṣil b. Sayyid in his book *ʿUyūn al-athīr* found 363, including those who were martyred during the Battle and those who died after it. But of the latter there were only 14; six from the *muhājirīn* and 8 from the *anṣār*."[52] His line of attack was to challenge earlier works to explain how their total was arrived at, a total which should have been no more than 327. Al-Ḥifnāwī cited another source (Shaykh Aḥmad al-Munīnī al-Dimashqī) which listed 352. According to al-Ḥifnāwī, al-Munīnī was silent about the nature of his evidence.

After the initial discussion of sources, al-Ḥifnāwī discusses the Badrīyīn as individuals, using *ḥadīth* material. For example, there was ʿAbdullah b. Suḥayl, who was said to have died at the age of sixteen after proclaiming his desire to fight for God (p. 27); also Abū Ayyūb Khālid b. Zayd al-Najjār, who went to the Prophet of God in Madīna, built a mosque and houses for him, and made his *jihād* for the Prophet until he died in the attack on Constantinople, where his tomb became a famous shrine which people visit seeking blessings—it is famous for its responses to petitions.

Methodologically, individualism is apparent in the approach to history taken by the eighteenth-century *ḥadīth* writers. The life of each of the

Badrīyīn is individually discussed. Only one author, in a very early Khalwatī work, referred to, much less treated, the Badrīyīn as an ʿ*aṣaba*. Through the reading of all the *ṣaḥāba*'s lives and virtues, a composite picture of human greatness emerges. No claim is made to its universality; no common theme is pursued in a linear fashion; no deductions or comparisons are permitted. This is the logic of context, which strives to create a coherent meaning out of particulars.

The impact of the *ḥadīth* revival went beyond those historical works which had an obviously pietistic inspiration. As in the case of literature, the religious revival provided a context in which a discipline began to emerge which was based increasingly on the study of classical models. In the case of history, this development was also stimulated by the demands of tribal chiefs for studies of their own family genealogies. The principal sources from which these works could be compiled were part of *ḥadīth* literature. However, the spirit of these genealogical works was distinctly secular.[53]

One of al-Zabīdī's principal students was Muḥammad Abī Raʾs al-Muʿaskarī (died 1822/1239). He was known for many works in *fiqh*, *adab*, *tārīkh*, and *nasab*. He traveled widely in North Africa, the Arab East, and Turkey. His works included a *riḥla* (spiritual travel literature), two tribal histories, a work on the *ṣaḥāba* in the Maghrib, and one on *nasab*.[54]

Apart from tribal genealogies, al-Zabīdī composed other more general works which transcended in breadth and vision the needs which religious scholarship per se would have imposed on them. Al-Zabīdī's dictionary has been mentioned as an example of scholarship in philology; in history, his works include an enumeration of all the Ṣūfī orders of his day and a biographical work on travelers of the twelfth Islamic century.[55]

The most important historian of the late eighteenth century besides al-Zabīdī was another Māturīdite reformer named ʿAbd al-Raḥman al-Jabartī. In style and outlook, al-Jabartī's main writings represent a synthesis of the two major trends in eighteenth-century historiography. At the same time, he marks a distinct step in the development of the neoclassical revival of Arabic culture.[56]

His principal work was a chronicle which dealt in great detail with the history of the *beys* in the eighteenth century. But it also contained *tarājim*, which were organized according to death dates and presented at the end of each year. These sections were written in the style of the *tarājim* literature. Writing shortly after the French invasion, al-Jabartī was particularly explicit in the introductory passages of the first volume in his explanation of his concept of history.

> It should be known that history is the science which determines and transmits knowledge of the conditions of different peoples, of their countries, their customs, their industries, their origins and their ends. . . . the first who established the chronological science in Islam was ʿUmar b. al-Khaṭṭāb, upon receiving a letter in which Abū Mūsā al-

> Ash'arī drew his attention to the difficulty of determining dates.[57]

As for his own "utilitarian" intentions in writing history:

> The majority of these events [of twelfth and thirteenth century A.H.] are the cause of the unhappiness which we have suffered. . . . I wanted to make a collection of these few notes and to classify them chronologically in order to facilitate research, and so that the reader, by being instructed of past misfortunes, could find a salve for his suffering, finding as well the necessary experience to struggle against bad fortune![58]

Al-Jabartī was committed to working within the tradition of the chronicle despite the technical problems involved in writing in this genre in an age in which few such works had been composed, and those by Turkish soldiers and of little value. But al-Jabartī balanced his commitment to include a totally different historical tradition: one which was preoccupied with the moral and intellectual utility of the study of history. Its spokesmen were the *muḥaddithīn*. "[History] has as its object of study past generations: prophets, elected persons, *'ulamā'*, sages, poets, kings, sultans, and others. Its intent is to do research on the facts and circumstances in which [these] figures arose. Its utility lies in learning from the examples and from the counsel of history as well as the experience acquired from the study of diverse events."[59]

In his stress on the utility of the study of history for its lessons and on the efficacy of struggling against bad fortune (a pagan concept), al-Jabartī naturally had to make some conscious reconciliation with the dominant Ash'arīte tradition. Such a reconciliation was also needed to free him from the suggestion of Mu'tazilite learnings, a trend once known for speculative thinking untempered by dogmatic theology. This was the general problem of the Māturīdī reformer, and this explains his defense of the study of history in terms of its service to the religious sciences; his reaffirmation, albeit vague, of God's intervention in human affairs; and his concluding comments on God's kingdom on earth.

> History is, besides, the source of several other sciences which could not exist without it. These include the study of *ḥadīth* sciences. It is the source for the reciters of the Divine Word, and for the commentators on it; for the study of the Companions, [*ṣaḥāba*], for jurisprudence, grammar, wisdom, literature, medicine, the study of the lives of the prophets . . . the lives of good men, of the sayings of kings, anecdotes, accounts, advice, instructive examples and proverbs, voyages, discussions of caliphs.[60]
> [And so]
> The science of history is therefore a noble and edifying one which offers the wise man instructive examples drawn from the lives of people who have existed before him on this earth: God himself has mentioned in his Holy Book the history of the ancient nations, stating

> that it was filled with instructive examples for the man endowed with sense. The prophet, too, has recounted several matters which belong to the history of past generations, such as some matters concerning the Israelites and the changes which they made in the Bible and the Gospels; and several other strange matters concerning the Arabs and other peoples. The Imām al-Shāfiʿī, may God be satisfied with him, also stated that the study of history develops the intellectual faculties.[61]

Finally, al-Jabartī discusses his concept of the social order. Society was a divinely ordained scheme which included five categories of man, hierarchically arranged. The first category are the prophets, God's apostles who bring messages. The second category are the *ʿulamāʾ*, who are continuators of the tradition of the prophets and carry out their mission in their own lives by propagating the faith, "but occasionally corrupted by love of riches as in our own day!" The third category are the kings and other rulers; they create order and maintain justice and equity. This concept rests on the idea that man is by nature unjust. If he does not commit injustices, this is because he has been prevented from doing so: "Thus the principle of all government is justice, whether it be a Muslim government or not; and it is equally the source of all happiness." The fourth category contains those whom al-Jabartī classifies as being in the middle: that is, they observe justice in their relations with others; they render good for good and evil for evil. The fifth category includes those whom God has placed on earth who are still seeking for self-mastery, or attempting to establish control over their own passions.[62]

It should now be clear that al-Jabartī's writing is characteristic of the eighteenth-century revival, and that his major work was in fact a "fusion" of previously existing trends. Thus, he is not, as is often claimed, a "unique" figure. In most important respects as a thinker and writer, he was a continuation of Māturīdite reformism. A study of his ideas on history and the relationship of history to other disciplines clearly locates him within the late-eighteenth-century revival. In this period, a revival of classical fields was taking place in a profoundly religious atmosphere which nevertheless permitted elements of naturalism to enter.

Al-Jabartī's history clarifies certain points about the culture of the commercial revival which could not be settled from a study of the Badrīyīn. It did so by situating biography within an ordering of events based on the calendar year. Al-Jabartī further suggests that the true order of history (the history of God on earth) requires a radical reassertion of the power of the *ʿulamāʾ*, the continuators of the divine prophecy. Al Mawardī and most of "feudal" Sunnī political thought saw the kingship as the fusion of the secular and the spiritual, of *mulk* and *imāma.* Al-Jabartī, writing in an atmosphere of religious fervor, conditioned by the onslaught of the commercial age, separates the two, choosing perhaps influenced by Wafāʾī ideology and/or by a realization of the actual weakness of the central authority.

Al-Jabartī's greatness as a writer lay first in his presenting the fullest and most coherent expression of the social ideas of the Egyptian commercial revival. Judged in this way, his work is the crowning masterpiece of the eighteenth-century reform movement of the *ṭuruq*. In depth of analysis and sustained presentation, it surpasses even the writings of his teacher al-Zabīdī.

As a work of history, it has been approached by modern scholars, unaware of the unique methodological problems of his age, and as a result compared to classical or modern models. Where al-Jabartī was scrupulously honest in portraying (and portraying in minute detail) events which did not fit his main historical concerns—for example, in his account of the coming of the Europeans—he has been severely judged.[63]

The question of style is somewhat beside the point—an observation I made in commenting on the eighteenth-century *maqāma*. The initial effort, artistic and otherwise, of locating, reading, and trying to evaluate classical models of culture was itself a stupendous achievement. It would seem that both al-Jabartī and al-Zabīdī were able to produce monuments far greater than their more polished and better known successors in later generations of the neoclassical revival.

Thus, while it lasted, especially during the years 1760–1790, a remarkable, and largely unstudied, cultural revival took place in Egypt. The range of subjects, the number of participants, and the rise in critical consciousness in scholarship which have here been sampled in a limited way make necessary a reinterpretation of the development of modern culture in Egypt. Clearly, the commercial revival of the eighteenth century triggered a renewal of vitality in the religious life of Egypt, which in turn gave birth to a nascent secular culture. Much remains to be said about the nature of secular culture and the trajectory of its development in a developing country. Such a discussion cannot be launched until the role of the indigenous reform movement and the role of the European cultural movement in Egypt have both been assessed, for secular culture is a resultant of both these two.

The logical continuation of this chapter is a chapter bridging the gap between the cultural revival of 1760–1790 and the succeeding phase in which the development of secular culture continued. This second phase took place during the Muḥammad ʿAlī period, and more specifically during the period of reform-minded bureaucracy from 1815 to 1837. The analysis also requires greater depth, for the argument from socioeconomic factors to cultural developments leaves out biography and simplifies the struggles within the period, as well as the tensions within individuals lives, for the sake of concentration on the main trends.

The fourth chapter will begin a detailed biographical study of one of the major figures of nineteenth-century cultural reform in Egypt. He is virtually unknown to most of his own countrymen, except for some minor poetry which he wrote and for one or two isolated statements about reform. For almost a generation, vast attention has for various reasons been lavished on his student (one might almost say his disciple), Rifāʿa al-Ṭahṭāwī. Little or none of this attention has worn off on the teacher of al-Ṭahṭāwī, Ḥasan al-

ʿAṭṭār. Al-ʿAṭṭār is equally little known abroad, despite the fact that he had contact with numerous Europeans, wrote more than fifty books, and occupied an important position in his society. In al-Azhar itself, he is still known, for several of the textbooks which he wrote for his students are still used or have been used until recently. But the use of his texts, now 150 years old or more, has not awakened in the *shaykhs* of al-Azhar or the scholarly community at large a sense of the intellectual revolution which al-ʿAṭṭār represented during the first quarter of the nineteenth century.

Chapter 4
The Decline of the Eighteenth-Century Cultural Revival: The Formation of Shaykh Ḥasan al-ʿAṭṭār

The major period of the eighteenth-century cultural revival was between 1760 and 1790. From 1790 to 1815, conditions in Cairo made scholarly life difficult. The warfare of the *beys* increased, and this in turn increased the social and economic problems faced by the rest of society. An inflationary situation was brought on by the artificial concentration of wealth in the form of unearned income in the city of Cairo at a time when there were no commensurate possibilities for investment. The inflow of foreign luxury goods and the growth of the service sector both served to undermine the artisanate; it was further beset by the inflationary situation. Finally, manipulation of food prices and hoarding of food outside Cairo created almost chronic social unrest. These conditions helped usher in a period of partial anarchy after the French invasion and then a further decade of instability during which a new social formation emerged. The indigenous middle classes in particular were deeply affected by the deterioration of commerce. While they had struggled in uneven competition with the foreign commercial nexus before 1790, after that date the breakdown of market conditions within Egypt precipitated a very sharp decline in their position. It was also in the 1790's that the foreign commercial nexus began to emerge and to impinge directly on the affairs of state. Greek merchants and others dictated to their Mamlūk lords. They gained lasting commercial advantages from the performance of their services. As early as 1790, the strains of warfare began to show themselves in diverse ways. In cultural fields, patronage sharply declined, a fact which one can deduce from the decline in the number of books which were written in the 1790's as compared to the 1780's. Cultural life, it would seem, became increasingly confined to the minimum required to support religious life. Even the *majlis* al-Wafāʾīya seems to have been affected by the decline in the power of the middle class and the waning of the religious revival which it had fostered. What became of the younger generation who had entered the *ṭuruq* in their youth and now, in early manhood, faced the conditions in Egypt during the 1790's? This chapter seeks to provide some answers. It studies in detail the life of Ḥasan al-ʿAṭṭār, along with his friends ʿAbd al-Raḥman al-Jabartī and Ismaʿīl al-Khashshāb. The three together represented the most important continuators of cultural life in Egypt, and while only al-ʿAṭṭār remained active as a teacher with students, all three had a pronounced influence on the culture of the early nineteenth century.

Al-ʿAṭṭār's youth fell in a period in which the uneven rhythm of the expansion of the world market had the effect of dismantling the indigenous commercial community, which was also the bearer of the classical cultural heritage. In the space of a scant one hundred years, a middle class arose and was disestablished in Egypt; a bureaucracy was installed and then dismantled in favor of a large landholding class; and, finally, this too was modified and a bureaucracy again was introduced. Throughout this state of flux, so unlike the almost organic unfolding of western European history, the Egyptian intellectuals "maintained" and "adapted" their intellectual traditions. Many similar cases could be drawn from Africa, Latin America, and Asia. How was continuity maintained under these conditions? What is the meaning of the term "cultural continuity" in this context? I shall try to explore this question as far as possible through a discussion of the life of Ḥasan al-ʿAṭṭār.

Al-ʿAṭṭār emerged during a period in which the institutions of patronage which had served the eighteenth-century revival were breaking down with no new ones to take their place. Much of his youth was taken up with an unsuccessful quest for patronage, which was needed for al-ʿAṭṭār to continue his education. During this period, he was obviously striving to achieve and to be accepted. Given the historical situation, failure was bound to be the outcome. The alternatives for his generation, in fact, were either struggle or passive surrender to an unfavorable situation. The life of ʿAbd al-Raḥman al-Jabartī contained moments of both alternatives. Al-Khashshāb's represented more the motif of surrender. For al-ʿAṭṭār, the failure to succeed led to dissatisfaction with the existing intellectual life, then increasingly to rebellion against it. A certain bitterness was inevitable for all three men. The principal focus in this chapter will be on the attitude represented by al-ʿAṭṭār. I shall explore the nature and the degree of rebellion which he expressed and attempt to explain its main outlines in terms of the history of this period.

Biographical Summary

It is necessary to give a chronological account of the main events in the life of Ḥasan al-ʿAṭṭār, then a more detailed account of the events of his youth, before proceeding with an analysis. Al-Khashshāb and al-Jabartī will necessarily occupy our attention as well, but their lives and writings have already been discussed in Chapters 2 and 3.

Chronology of the Life of Ḥasan al-ʿAṭṭār

1766 approximate date of birth (in Cairo)
1786 first composition in grammar
1798 flight to Asyūṭ
1799 return to Cairo; writing of the *Maqāma*
1802 departure from Egypt by way of Damietta for Turkey

1804 first composition on medicine (in Istanbul)
1807 visit to Alexandretta
1810 trip to Damascus; mystical studies
1811 trip to Palestine
1814 completion of main works on medicine, essays on *kalām*, glosses on *ādāb al-baḥth* (argumentation) in Damascus
1815 return to Cairo as teacher and writer
1820–25 composition of works in logic; royal tutor
1828 Arabic editor of the Egyptian Official Gazette (*Al-Waqāʾiʿ al-miṣrīya*); beginning of major work in *uṣūl al-dīn*
1831 appointed Shaykh al-Azhar; completion of the work in *uṣūl al-dīn*
1835 death

The information available on al-ʿAṭṭār's family is unfortunately very limited. According to ʿAlī Mubārak, who relied for his information on al-ʿAṭṭār's son Asad, Asad's grandfather was named Muḥammad and was called Muḥammad Kutn, taking the name of al-ʿAṭṭār as a *nisba*, or attribution, of occupation.[1] Ḥasan al-ʿAṭṭār signed his works Ḥasan b. Muḥammad al-Shahīr biʾl-ʿAṭṭār, suggesting that this addition was of recent vintage. Perhaps it dated from the time when his father became a druggist. It is also indicated that al-ʿAṭṭār's father came to Egypt from the Maghrib. Little other reliable information can be found on his origins. Concerning his early education, ʿAlī Mubārak presented al-ʿAṭṭār as having had friends who attended al-Azhar while he himself had to work at his father's trade. He memorized the Qurʾān to "qualify" to enter the mosque university and thereby persuaded his father to permit him to carry on with his studies. This picture of his father as an uneducated man who discouraged his son's efforts to obtain an education is belied to some extent by the indication that, when al-ʿAṭṭār did memorize the Qurʾān, it was regarded as a triumph and celebrated as a milestone by both father and son. It opened doors to him, but at the same time it created expectations which were increasingly unrealizable in the particular period in which he lived.

From the earliest records available, al-ʿAṭṭār is pictured as intellectually gifted. He memorized the Qurʾān without assistance while he was working for his father; when he was young, he sought opportunities to go to al-Azhar informally with some of his friends; when he entered al-Azhar, he completed the elementary syllabus very rapidly but then sought to pursue other subjects rather than seek immediate employment as a lower religious functionary. In this we see him breaking with the milieu of the artisan community. It would not have been at all difficult for him to have secured a lower post. It was the fact that he sought a higher education and thus higher social status which makes clear the problems created by the social context of his day.

The problem of patronage was clearly on his mind even during his teens. It was roughly on his twentieth birthday, in 1786, that he wrote a short grammatical work in rhymed prose for an unnamed Turkish patron, perhaps a member of the Ottoman forces invading Egypt.[2] In any case nothing came of it.

The first person known to have been a friend of al-ʿAṭṭār was a singer who was also noted as a prominent writer and grammarian. In the year 1787–88/1202, al-Jabartī mentions that Khalīl Efendī al-Baghdādī was unmarried and visited his friend Ḥasan al-ʿAṭṭār to get his clothes washed. Al-Baghdādī had come originally from a prominent Iraqī family and knew many of the *beys* of Egypt (e.g., ʿAbd al-Raḥman Bey). He was especially close to Murād Bey, who studied handwriting with him. Al-Baghdādī's reputation in Egypt stretched over some forty years, from the year 1730/1145, when his poem on the death of the Wazīr al-Makrum ʿAbdullah Pasha al-Kiwārlī brought him fame. His life, however, was destined to end in misery with the exile of Murād. Despite his friendship with the *beys*, al-Baghdādī must have been regarded as something of a curiosity in Egyptian society. He must have been one of the few independent figures in Egyptian cultural life, and perhaps for this reason al-ʿAṭṭār was attracted to him.[3]

Al-ʿAṭṭār's friendship with Ismaʿīl al-Khashshāb and al-Jabartī began around 1790. Al-Jabartī was impressed with al-ʿAṭṭār and commented that he was "a good-looking youth, broadchested, clear-eyed, of North African origin but wearing Egyptian clothes and speaking with an Egyptian accent."[4] From this comment one gains some insight into al-ʿAṭṭār's efforts to achieve mobility through assimilation into Egyptian society. Formal education in the Arabic language, that is, philological studies, was one vehicle; but in the final analysis it was not enough.

It is not known how al-ʿAṭṭār and al-Khashshāb met, although the most probable place was the *majlis* al-Wafāʾīya. It is known that in the *taknīya* ceremony, al-ʿAṭṭār was given the name of Abū Saʿādāt, and al-Khashshāb the name Abūʾl-Ḥasan. This probably took place in the late 1780's.[5] Al-Khashshāb's background was similar to al-ʿAṭṭār's. His father was a carpenter and petty shopkeeper in the lumber trade near Bāb al-Zuwayla. He, too, had studied with the prestigious *shaykhs* of the reform movement, perhaps to a greater degree than al-ʿAṭṭār. In the course of his studies with al-Zabīdī, he undertook a small commentary on part of al-Ghazzālī's *Iḥyāʾ ʿulūm al-dīn*, on which al-Zabīdī was himself writing a commentary. Al-Khashshāb was likewise a close friend of Muḥammad Abī Anwār and was with him constantly. After the death of al-Zabīdī, al-Khashshāb no longer advanced in scholarly and Ṣūfī circles. He began instead to seek employment and worked as a clerk for the Ruznamjā. Al-Khashshāb's situation, especially after 1790, was therefore quite similar to that of al-ʿAṭṭār. Both were frustrated.[6]

Al-Jabartī, the mutual friend of al-ʿAṭṭār and al-Khashshāb, was no less affected by the turn of events around 1790 than they were. With the death of his teacher al-Zabīdī and of al-Murādī shortly thereafter in Damascus, al-Jabartī realized that he was the chief repository of the knowledge of the history of the previous generation. This time also brought to an end the days of his youth when he had toured the Delta and studied *ḥadīth* with Ṣūfī *shaykhs* in Rosetta and Ṭanṭā.[7] Al-Jabartī had grown up among the *beys*, who came to his father for instruction. When he went to al-Azhar as a student, he studied Ḥanafī *fiqh* with ʿAbd al-Raḥman al-ʿArīshī, Shaykh al-Riwāq of the Syrians, an *ʿalīm* like his father with close connections to the Ottoman Porte.[8] With the crumbling of the Ottoman presence in Egypt, the al-Jabartī family found their relations with the *shaykhs* of al-Azhar increasingly strained. Ḥasan al-Jabartī quarreled with the other *shaykhs* and finally withdrew himself from al-Azhar altogether.[9]

Thus, with the decline of the cultural movement, ʿAbd al-Raḥman al-Jabartī went into the state of semiretirement in which he was to pass much of the last thirty years of his life. Always the weight of the past obsessed him; and although, as did al-Khashshāb and al-ʿAṭṭār, he sought patronage and new opportunities, his life was different from theirs, being a part of the declining gentry.

In the 1790's, both al-Khashshāb and al-ʿAṭṭār apparently sought the patronage of Muḥammad Bey al-Alfī. Al-ʿAṭṭār wrote poetry praising the beauty of his new house. Al-Khashshāb was a friend of his. Al-Jabartī, too, preferred him over Muḥammad ʿAlī. Little is known about this man. In 1803, when he visited London, British sources describe him as a collector of astronomical instruments and as interested in mysticism.[10]

With the coming of the French in 1798, al-ʿAṭṭār, al-Khashshāb, and al-Jabartī boldly turned to them in search of the patronage which they had not found elsewhere. Al-Jabartī worked for them and served in the Dīwān. In his main chronicle, he revealed a considerable familiarity with their activities. Al-Khashshāb wrote for them a short history of Egypt.[11] Al-ʿAṭṭār exchanged lessons with them, as will be discussed below. For all three, these efforts were unproductive; in the case of al-ʿAṭṭār, they were quite detrimental. Al-Jabartī and al-Khashshāb survived the ensuing embarrassment from their friendly interchange with enemies of the state. Al-ʿAṭṭār apparently could not and left Egypt. Of the three, al-Jabartī was in the most secure position. He had performed an important role in society during the 1790's, he was well-off, and he was able to bask in the continuing prestige of his father.[12] When the French left and the Ottoman army arrived, his family connections in Istanbul stood him in good stead. The commanding officer of the Ottoman army, Yūsuf Āghā, turned to him to write a history of the recent troubled times. Al-Jabartī wrote the book which Yūsuf Āghā requested and included in it material by al-ʿAṭṭār, perhaps as a way of rehabilitating his friend.[13]

Intellectual and moral conflicts have been mentioned in the preceding discussion of merchants and Ṣūfīs, but I have not concentrated on the psychological problems. Before proceeding with a discussion of al-ʿAṭṭār's writings, it might be well to note that, at the end of the European middle ages, a period in Western history which is perhaps analogous in certain ways to eighteenth-century Egypt, the transformation which led to the emergence of an economy based on commerce and the cultural changes which resulted from this transformation caused exceedingly severe feelings of dislocation.[14] Both societies saw a great flourishing of mystical centers, institutions partly for the care of those who were mentally or morally deranged. ʿAbdullah al-Sharqāwī, one of al-ʿAṭṭār's teachers, had had a mental breakdown during his youth and had been treated and cured in a *tekke.* The period of al-ʿAṭṭār's youth followed the peak period of mystical culture, but preceded that of the switch to rationalist theology.

If one were to pursue a "psychological" analysis of al-ʿAṭṭār's youth, the theory must be modified to fit the historical era. The ego psychology of the modern West is written in terms of the relationships within the modern nuclear family. In a situation in which father-mother-child relationships are mediated by the extended family, the possibility of total rebellion and individuation is much less likely to be realized. Even if these processes were to occur, they would not necessarily occur at the same pace as in modern times, for the whole concept of the child, the adolescent, and the process of "growing up" was alien to the medieval world. The child went to work at an early age and was soon regarded as a young adult. If al-ʿAṭṭār "rebelled" against his father, it was surely not against his father as an individual but against certain values associated with his father's occupation and social class. It was a forceful rebellion, but at the same time it was an ambivalent one. In rejecting his status and seeking upward mobility, al-ʿAṭṭār ultimately abandoned the Maghribī community, and finally left Egypt altogether. At the same time, he was greatly drawn to the popular Andalusian culture of his own social group. He missed its warmth and spontaneity when, in later years, he had risen to the status of a high official.

One could argue that the phases of psychological development were themselves conditioned by the nature of the times. The need to rebel and to seek upward mobility in order to enjoy an intellectual life was characteristic of a society which was developing rigid class barriers. A generation earlier, the pursuit of intellectual life, even physical medicine, the field which drew al-ʿAṭṭār, would not necessarily have depended on the prior acquisition of a high socioeconomic status. The need to rebel was also conditioned by homosexuality, which made al-ʿAṭṭār's chances in the less liberal environment of the 1790's distinctly poor.

The breakdown of the indigenous economy in the 1790's limited social mobility by sharply limiting the accessibility of patronage. A number of the leading figures of the reform movement died during the period between 1789 and 1791, and those who replaced them were no longer motivated to pursue scholarship to the same degree, if one can judge from the decline in the writing of books. At the same time, increasing numbers of Europeans were coming to Egypt, many in technical capacities which were clearly transforming society. Yet in the face of this challenge, the older generation of *shaykhs* remained rather passive and continued to live from their trade, their landed wealth, and whatever gifts they received. In retrospect, it is difficult to see what alternatives existed for the indigenous merchants' community, but from the perspective of Ḥasan al-ʿAṭṭār in the 1790's, it is not unlikely that he blamed his teachers for his difficulties. At least, it is not difficult to find examples of his rejection of their views. They in turn did little to help him and thereby created in al-ʿAṭṭār a personal basis for criticism and rejection of the dominant *ḥadīth* movement. This was fed by the general ethos of the expanding commercial sector which promoted a growing orientation one might call "scientific" in every sphere of life, including culture. Thus, it would seem reasonable to interpret al-ʿAṭṭār's own desire for (as well as his own conception of) intellectual development in terms of the study of the rational sciences as a desire promoted by forces within his own life—in his background and scholarly associations—as well as by the emerging social reality of a dominant capitalist sector.

Al-ʿAṭṭār's education in al-Azhar centered on the philological sciences, and his first writings were mainly in these fields. His principal teachers in philology were Muḥammad al-Ṣabbān and Muḥammad al-Amīr. Both had been among the leading figures of the reform movement: one was a symbol of the *ḥadīth* movement in Egypt, the other was the representative of "higher" Maghribī culture in Cairo in his day. Al-ʿAṭṭār's decision to study the rational sciences and to abandon the Maghribī community and try to assimilate into Cairene society should be seen through the eyes of these two men. How noticeable it must have been to al-Amīr, who outlived al-Ṣabbān by many years, that al-ʿAṭṭār had modified his dress and his accent in order to assimilate into Cairene society.[15] In al-Ṣabbān's last years, al-ʿAṭṭār was beginning to read texts in logic. After al-Ṣabbān's death, al-ʿAṭṭār turned to Muḥammad al-Disūqī, a scholar of logic. This relationship was, however, short-lived, as al-Disūqī died soon thereafter.

In 1786 al-ʿAṭṭār, barely twenty years old, wrote his "Manẓūma fī ʿilm al-naḥw" in two days, as he rather boastfully claimed. It was written for a patron and in the accepted manner (rhymed prose, religious justifications, etc.). It is from this time that one is alerted to the problems which al-ʿAṭṭār confronted. Eight years later, in 1794, al-ʿAṭṭār had finished the draft of his first scholarly book, a work indebted to al-Amīr.[16]

Al-ʿAṭṭār's independence from his teachers (in this case, from al-Ṣabbān) was first clearly asserted in a work in rhetoric which was written in 1797–98/1212.[17] In this work, he broke with some of the literary conventions of his day. Instead of beginning with the traditional ritual praise of the religious virtues of studying the field, al-ʿAṭṭār inserted a history of the development of the discipline. Al-ʿAṭṭār began with a didactic couplet of his own composition, listing the components of the *ʿilm al-bayān* part of rhetoric. He then proceeded to describe the field as it finally culminated in the writings of ʿAbd al-Qāhir al-Jurjānī.[18] Al-ʿAṭṭār then gave an account of one of al-Jurjānī's most important predecessors, Abū ʿUbayda, and cited as his source "the historians." He suggested that the term *al-balāgha*, which indicated the general field of rhetoric, dated from a later period (when the discipline was differently organized), citing such works as the gloss of al-Suyūṭī on al-Bayḍāwī. These later writers (after al-Suyūṭī) based their writings on the ideas of the great writers, copying in imitation of their lively minds. And that is the way it is to our day—this sort of imitation. Knowledge is a shelter to which the dull cannot find their way—it mocks them with a smile.[19]

In the late 1790's, al-ʿAṭṭār returned to the study of grammar, renewing and intensifying his critique of the later continuators, notably Khālid al-Azharī.[20] Al-Azharī was perhaps the most influential later figure, apart from the Imām al-Suyūṭī. Al-ʿAṭṭār saw al-Azharī as an uncritical compiler who "mixed" his sources, unaware that some were *uṣūliyīn* (traditional jurisprudents), some *muḥaddithīn*, some *ḥukamāʾ*, and some *mutakallimīn*; and that, being insufficiently aware of these intellectual currents, he made errors in analysis by drawing material on various questions without understanding the consequences of working within one tradition or another.[21] Al-ʿAṭṭār himself attempted to separate and distinguish these different trends, paying particular attention to the logical implications of questions in grammar which al-Azharī ignored.

Al-ʿAṭṭār made similar criticisms in another work on grammar which was written shortly thereafter.[22] This manual was intended for more advanced students. Advanced manuals tended to go deeply into the quarrels of the medieval grammarians, making many erudite points during the process, but al-ʿAṭṭār resisted this temptation. In one place he actually praised al-Azharī for limiting the number of punctuation marks, comparing him favorably to the Imām al-Suyūṭī, who in a certain book listed more than thirty.[23]

Al-ʿAṭṭār's commentary on *Al-Azharīya* was not only a critique of Khālid al-Azharī; it was also a critique of al-ʿAṭṭār's teacher Muḥammad al-Amīr. Al-Amīr had earlier inspired him to write a commentary in 1794 on a text of Khālid al-Azharī. But in the work on *Al-Azharīya* and in the "Risāla . . . ʿalā al-ājurrūmiya," al-ʿAṭṭār criticized books which al-Amīr had praised.[24] In addition, al-ʿAṭṭār, according to his own claims, was teaching the *Azharīya* in al-Azhar while al-Amīr was there, even before 1798.[25]

Finally, the neoclassical revival involved not merely a critique of later figures, but also an effort to uncover a wide range of the classical writers, such as the grammarian al-Azdī, who was the inspiration of "the teacher Abūʾl-Ḥasan b. Asfūr, the teacher Abīʾl-ʿAbbās b. al-Ḥājj, the teacher Abū Zakariyā b. Dhūʾl-Nūn, the teacher Abū Jaʿfar b. Raqīqa, and other *shaykhs* of grammar. According to what we have learned, none of these *shaykhs* of grammar has let down his reputation. I have collected some thirty students of his in grammar, and every one of them became famous."[26] From al-ʿAṭṭār's account of the life of al-Azdī and his students, whom he called here "our teachers," it is clear that the neoclassical revival was still gaining momentum, even during a period of relative cultural decline. Figures who were then known only at second and third hand were now freely praised and held up as a model. This is in clear contrast to the early part of the eighteenth-century revival, when only a few texts of great fame were revived. Progress can also be seen in the extent to which al-ʿAṭṭār presented a secular image, both in the above account and in his discussion of *balāgha* which was quoted previously.

In general, al-ʿAṭṭār's critique of philology (be it in the form of praise or blame) was on the level of particulars. Formal logic and utilitarianism entered in, but they did not transform his process of thought. He was not yet *mutakallim*, although he was beginning to read the basic texts in logic.[27]

Al-ʿAṭṭār's study of the rational sciences long preceded his capacity to effectively internalize them. This took place only during the Muḥammad ʿAlī period. However, in his early writings, when his own efforts at criticism were closer in structure and content to those of the *ḥadīth* revival than to nineteenth-century *kalām*, he clearly began to reject the preceding generation in the most fundamental sense: its insistence on verification exclusively in terms of the past. The reasons for this derive from particular factors in his life, together with the social changes of the 1790's.

Al-ʿAṭṭār's Study of Literature

A study of al-ʿAṭṭār's literary formation is perhaps the clearest way to understand the struggles and conflicts in his own life, conflicts which involved ethnicity, class, and status. It is legitimate to say that in his youth he was a product of two literary cultures, both of them Andalusian-Maghribī, each of which denied the aesthetic and linguistic premises of the other. Al-ʿAṭṭār grew up in the "low" culture of the coffeehouses and remained a part of it until he left Egypt. At the same time, he had been exposed to the "high" culture of the Maghāriba, probably through the *majlis* al-Wafāʾīya but in any case through such teachers as Muḥammad al-Amīr.

During the particular period of al-ʿAṭṭār's youth, popular culture was perceived as more and more of a threat by the conservative *ʿulamāʾ*, given the general social context of upheaval. For al-ʿAṭṭār to openly identify with it, therefore, would have been very dangerous to his career as an *ʿālim*. Given the attraction which it held for him, this was an acute problem.

Al-ʿAṭṭār's formation in the "high" culture and literature coincided of course with his attendance at al-Azhar, with his study of philology, and, as was noted in the preceding sections, with his efforts to assimilate into middle-class Cairene society. The fact that literature was not officially taught at al-Azhar was not a major problem. More important was the changing situation of the Maghāriba and of their culture in the Cairo of the 1790's. Here a brief review may be useful. In Chapter 1, it was argued that, on the basis of the outbreak of student disorders, the peak of Maghribī power was in the 1770's or even earlier. This was more or less confirmed, as noted in Chapter 3, by the changing composition of the *majālis*, which became more Cairene-Egyptian and less Maghribī during the latter part of the century. By the 1790's, the situation of cultural studies in general and Andalusian culture in particular was on the defensive. Where al-ʿAṭṭār's teacher Muḥammad al-Amīr had made fairly extensive use of Andalusian literary works in his philological studies,[28] al-ʿAṭṭār was criticized even by his friends when he sought to do the same. Al-Khashshāb criticized al-

ʿAṭṭār, even though both al-Khashshāb and al-ʿAṭṭār studied with Muḥammad al-Amīr. In the 1790's, the Cairene al-Khashshāb rejected the characteristically North African form of the *muwashshaḥāt*, making plain in so doing that he was criticizing al-ʿAṭṭār for adopting it.[29] Another figure who took the same position was an important Egyptian Ṣūfī musician, which leads one to assume that this conflict extended beyond the bounds of literature per se.[30]

The degree of rejection, however, is very difficult to determine. Al-ʿAṭṭār and al-Jabartī might write about the people of Egypt, "Ahl Miṣr," but what cultural boundaries this implies are vague. For example, *ghazal*, or love, poetry, which the Maghāriba also favored, apparently did not pose any similar problems for al-ʿAṭṭār despite his predilection for Andalusian models. In the absence of al-ʿAṭṭār's "Dīwān," I shall turn to a work which he edited and for which he wrote a most informative introduction and conclusion. This work was completed in 1814/1229, which makes it necessary for me to take certain liberties with the strict periodization which I have been following. The spirit of the work conforms so perfectly, however, to what one would expect of the literary situation of the 1790's that it seems justified to do so by including it in my discussion of al-ʿAṭṭār's youth. The year 1814 still fits quite well into the larger periodization of the life of al-ʿAṭṭār, for the main dividing line separating the writings of his youth from the labors of his mature years comes in 1815, at which time or shortly thereafter he entered into the ethos of the new reforming bureaucracy of Muḥammad ʿAlī.

The *Dīwān* of Ibn Sahl represented something of a mockery of fate, a fate to which al-ʿAṭṭār was nonetheless prepared to bow.[31] It shared this characteristic with the earlier *Maqāma*, which will be discussed shortly. The author of al-ʿAṭṭār's text was a Jewish convert to Islam, an Andalusian poet, and a figure whose reputation was always linked to the ambiguity of his religious commitments. It was not wrong to have chosen a figure of Jewish origin, whether a convert or not. Such works had passed unnoticed in the preceding generation.[32] But the decision to reintroduce a writer who had made a joke of his conversion at a time of heightened communal tensions was decidedly an ostentatious act.

> This is what came to me of the poetry of Ibrāhīm b. Sahl al-Mālikī al-Ashbīlī al-Andalūsī after an intense search. After asking people from many lands, a copy, i.e., of his "Dīwān" finally reached me from some part of Africa upon my asking some of their *ʿulamāʾ* for it. . . . This copy is in Maghribī script, which makes reading difficult, and there are inaccuracies [*taḥrīf*] in some of the verses. I made this copy and removed what was included in it of the biographical sketch of Ibn Sahl . . . and concentrated on the poetry, writing an explanation in the margin where I felt it necessary to deal with the defects.[33]
>
> [Al-ʿAṭṭār saved the difficult matter of the author's biography to the end.]

The author was educated under Abū ʿAlī al-Shalūbīn and Ibn Dajjāj and others. Islam by its nature includes into itself and does not abominate or discriminate against non-Muslims. Thus the matter was closed. But then some of the Maghāriba asked how he could write such delicate poetry, and he answered that "it was because he wrote poetry like the gentleness of love and the softness of the Jew."[34]

[The argument proceeds in the dialectical style of the eighteenth-century *ḥadīth* movement.]

And when he drowned, some of his famous contemporaries said, "a pearl has returned to its homeland." And al-Ḥāfiẓ ʿAbdullah Muḥammad b. ʿUmar b. Rashīd al-Fakhrī mentioned in his travel book . . . that there was a disagreement among the Muslims over the nature of Ibn Sahl's true convictions in his innermost soul [*bāṭinan*]. There was written the following on the margin of this copy by the Khaṭīb Sīdī Abū ʿAbdullah b. Marzūq in which he stipulated that what he understood from our teachers was correct, that he died a Muslim. But in some of the literary books of the Maghāriba [it was related] that there was once gathered a group with Ibn Sahl in a friendly meeting. They asked him, when they had taken their wine, whether he was outwardly and inwardly a Muslim or not. He replied that it was for man what is outwardly apparent and for God what is veiled. . . . Some of them found proof of his Islamicity in his words "I console myself in Moses out of my love for Muḥammad," and others by "I am guided as if God were not there as a model of right guidance to me, and what occurred to me, in my insignificance, was that the law of Moses was suspended by Muḥammad."

And al-Rāʿī said, may God have mercy on him, I heard from our teacher Abīʾl-Ḥasan ʿAlī b. Simāʿa al-Andalūsī, may God have mercy on him, that there are two things which are not known to be certain: the Islamicity of Ibrāhīm b. Sahl and the repentance of al-Zamakhsharī from writing *ghazal*. It is a matter of two stories. Regarding the first, I believe Ibn Sahl, but regarding the second, I doubt it. . . . and al-Rāʿī also certified that the incomparable Ibn Sahl was joking with Shaykh Abūʾl-Qāsim when he irritated him by saying "Is not Moses at once all and part of the truth? And is not a metaphor the whole and the part?"[35]

[Al-ʿAṭṭār attempted to bring the reader to his own conclusion:]

With this proof one can see that the Andalusian Jews were accustomed to writing in Arabic. If Ibrāhīm uttered the above two verses before converting to Islam (and God Almighty knows), Ibn al-Maqqarī has said, "His family related to us that he died a Muslim, drowned in the sea. . . ." Abu Ḥayyān reported on the authority of Qāḍī al-Quḍāʾ [Chief Judge] Abū Bakr Muḥammad b. ʿAbd al-Nāṣir al-Fatḥ b. ʿAlī al-Anṣārī al-Ashbīlī [in Grenada] that Ibrāhīm b. Sahl was a Sevillian

> poet, originally Jewish, who converted and praised the Prophet of God, may God bless him and peace—and he showed that in his inimitable *qaṣīda.* Abū Ḥayyān said, "I paused over it, for it is one of the most amazing of those created in its type. . . . Before his death, he used to recite his prayers with the Muslims and mix with them."

Al-ʿAṭṭār then closed the book with one of the author's most famous *muwashshaḥāt.*[36]

Al-ʿAṭṭār used the traditional device of saving his best for last—namely, the opinion of a major historian, a contemporary of Ibn Sahl, and a major literary figure of the following generation. This approach partly nullified the effect of the many amusing and ambiguous comments for which Ibn Sahl was known.

More characteristic than the work on Ibn Sahl was a book such as al-ʿAṭṭār's gloss on *Al-Samarqandīya,* a work which was previously mentioned in the section on language sciences. From *Al-Samarqandīya,* one infers two other aspects of the literary climate in Egypt in the 1790's. First, the study of classical literature was still severely handicapped by the non-availability of many of the basic texts during this phase of the neoclassical revival. Many works were known only at second hand, through biographical and historical literature. Second, one can see the extent to which literature had reverted to its role as an adjunct to the study and mastery of a sacred language. That such an approach was uncongenial to al-ʿAṭṭār scarcely needs repeating. Also, the problem of acquiring the original *dīwāns* of poetry, which was mentioned in the case of Ibn Sahl, was a very considerable one. It was obviously one of the limiting factors in the study of classical literature. For example, in presenting illustrative material to explain a major figure, al-ʿAṭṭār introduced eight lines of a poet who he said was magnificent in his ability to describe gardens and ponds and who was renowned as well for his prose, but whom, it would seem, al-ʿAṭṭār did not know at first hand. For, as he mentioned, he took his material on this poet, Abū Ishāq b. Khafājī al-Andalūsī, from the history of al-Maqqarī called *Nafḥ al-ṭīb.*[37] So it was with many other Andalusian figures of whom he had heard. An exception was undoubtedly Abū Ḥayyān, who had also been one of the main sources for his essay on Ibn Sahl. Al-ʿAṭṭār stated clearly that he had studied Abū Ḥayyan "from the mouths of my Andalusian *shaykhs.*"[38] Elsewhere he claimed that he drew much of his material from that author's book "Al-Tashīl" when he was studying the literary figures of Seville.[39]

Up to now the emphasis has been placed on the retreat from secular culture in the 1790's and on the conflict which this caused for those determined to pursue the work of cultural revival. In concluding this section, I would like to draw attention to the literature during this period. The chief examples are also drawn from the poetry of al-ʿAṭṭār, but many similar examples might have been chosen from al-Khashshāb or al-Jabartī. They reflect a reversion to what may be termed "court culture," as evinced by a renewed emphasis on the decadent *saj*ʿ. If one were a litterateur, it was necessary to write in *saj*ʿ whenever a patron demanded it; the *majālis* were no longer a counterforce.

Al-Jabartī has recorded several such poems by al-ʿAṭṭār, and it is perhaps for this reason that al-ʿAṭṭār is unfortunately best known as a poet of this type. In his "official" poems, al-ʿAṭṭār, as did other writers of his period, severely limited himself, not only in terms of the use of language, but also to certain themes and images which could be embellished. In 1799/1214 a Maghribī merchant who was a friend of al-ʿAṭṭār and al-Jabartī was appointed Shaykh Riwāq al-Maghāriba. Al-ʿAṭṭār was on poor terms with his predecessor, who happened to be a blind man. Al-ʿAṭṭār's poem celebrating his friend's appointment began "wake up, for the armies of darkness have gone away, and the morning has come up unveiled," and continued in this vein, relying on the images of flowers, pearls, and so on.[40] A second example of this can be found in the conclusion of the same poem, where al-ʿAṭṭār refers to his subject as "*mawlāna*," our lord or master. As the man was not one of al-ʿAṭṭār's teachers, did not write books, was not a Ṣūfī master, and indeed led a most ordinary and unimportant life, merely having accumulated enough money to qualify for this minor tax farm, the term was clearly mere flattery.[41] Al-Jabartī, writing for a court audience at the beginning of the nineteenth century, included many such poems in his history of Egypt and favored them over any other kind.

Earlier in the same year (1798/1214), when the French came to Cairo, they used their artillery in the area of Birkat al-Azbakīya, destroying some of the beautiful homes there, such as the home of Ismaʿīl Kāshif. Al-Jabartī was saddened by this and included at the end of his account a poem on al-Azbakīya by al-ʿAṭṭār in rhymed prose. The mood of the poem alone is a clue to the fact that it was not written against the background of these events. Rather, it was written to praise the beauty of the view from the house of one of the Mamlūks, who had solicited the poem. ʿAlī Mubārak republished this poem, and it has become the single best-known poem of al-ʿAṭṭār. In it he conveyed the effect of the beautiful grass, trees, and pools. Such poems as the one on al-Azbakīya were numerous, and the element of competition which sometimes led the poet to write a poem answering one by another author or trying to outdo another author by elevation reflected the negative side of the patronage system of the period.[42]

I now turn to the other side of al-ʿAṭṭār's literary formation, the result of his immersion in the popular culture of the Maghāriba.

Popular Andalusian Literature and the Youth of al-ʿAṭṭār

Maghribī "low culture" was historically the product of an artisanal class. Here one may imagine that restraints on wine imbibing and narcotics were relaxed, while cultural and spiritual activities provided a release from the hard restraints of life. Here music and secular literature, as well as folk stories, had (and still have) an important role. The culture of the masses was by its nature most free from literary artifice—the most given to warmth, spontaneity, and an unself-conscious appreciation of beauty traits which we find only occasionally in the writings of later *ʿulamāʾ*, heterosexual or homosexual: "Êtes-vous enclin à l'amour? Vous avez là un être svelte, de nationalité Turque, au visage éclatant comme la lune; il semble d'être tout entièr composé de perles; il a l'oeuil noir, la joue vermeille et une bouche dont la salive possède la saveur de nectar et la suavité de parfum."[43]

During his youth, response to beauty, the desire to capture it in words, the writing of poetry, and the study of Andalusian literature were fused in al-ʿAṭṭār's personality. It is easy to see from the suggestive images concerning wine and illicit relationships which abound in his writings that al-ʿAṭṭār, when not writing the official *sajʿ* poetry, wrote for the coffee shop, a place where poetry and song, wine and ḥashīsh united people from different walks of life. An encouragement to such indulgence came from the *ṭuruq* themselves. That he frequented this milieu there is no doubt. In the *Inshāʾ al-ʿAṭṭār*, he included a letter to a Ṣūfī *shaykh* in which he wrote of a "perfumed night of wine drinking . . . reminding me of moonlit nights in which the wine glass was merciful until I saw with the eye of a lover. . ."[44] The same imagery of wine, taken from Andalusian poetry, is included in an example of an *ijāza* which al-ʿAṭṭār wrote.[45]

The main literary work of the period in which elements of popular culture find a sustained presentation in a classical literary form was, as I have mentioned, the *Maqāmat al-ʿAṭṭār*, which was written in 1798 or 1799. The background of this work in terms of al-ʿAṭṭār's literary background has been discussed. I turn now to the activities of al-ʿAṭṭār during the composition of the *Maqāma* in an attempt to determine his state of mind when he wrote it. It is clear at the outset that the coming of the French to Cairo had a highly destabilizing effect on the life of the city. This was particularly true of the *ʿulamāʾ*, who found themselves in a very difficult situation. Quite a number, in fact, eventually compromised themselves.

In 1798/1215, with the coming of Napoleon, al-ʿAṭṭār and a group of *ʿulamāʾ* fled to Upper Egypt. Al-ʿAṭṭār remained in the Ṣaʿīd for approximately eighteen months, fearing the French army and seeking refuge in an area controlled by Murād Bey.[46] Al-ʿAṭṭār's fright was much greater and his self-imposed isolation much longer than that of the other *ʿulamāʾ*. Al-Jabartī also fled to his village to prevent any breakdown of landlord authority, but his absence from Cairo was much shorter and less unpleasant than that of al-ʿAṭṭār.[47]

Napoleon's rapid stabilization of commerce and the land won the cooperation of most of the Egyptian middle classes. After a short period, al-Jabartī received a letter from Shaykh Sulaymān al-Fayyūmī and Muḥammad al-Ṣāwī inviting him to return to Cairo to serve in the Dīwān. There then took place a correspondence between al-ʿAṭṭār in Asyūṭ and al-Jabartī in Cairo, selections from which al-Jabartī drew in his writings on this period. From these letters we can deduce that for al-ʿAṭṭār this was a period of considerable suffering, that he lived in isolation from the events in Cairo except for the occasional letters of his friend, that he sought to come back as quickly as possible but the imposition of the quarantine because of the plague delayed this, and that, finally, when he and some other *shaykhs* did come straggling back they had to overcome en route dangers from the Bedouin.

Returning to Cairo in the middle of 1801/1215, al-ʿAṭṭār found a situation in which the normal sanctions of social behavior were relaxed. In some cases, reversals of the norm had had immediate political repercussions, such as the much-discussed persecution of the Muslims during Ramaḍān by some Copts. Al-ʿAṭṭār's impression of the Europeans underwent a significant transformation in the context of these new conditions. In 1798 he had written a poem, "The French in Egypt have lost their money between bars and donkeys; soon they will face a disaster in Syria where they will find their end," which reflected the contemptuous attitudes of al-Azhar.[48] But when al-ʿAṭṭār returned, "circumstances were different," permitting respectable people to make contacts with them.

Al-ʿAṭṭār swung wildly from extreme to extreme. The painfully maintained identity resolution which had been sustained over the years simply gave way. What appeared when this façade was lifted was more or less genuine. Al-ʿAṭṭār turned to composing poetry freely. He sought to understand the new technology and practical arts of Europe, and he sought the social mobility which had been denied him in the 1790's. When, in the wake of his decision not to press too far in his social relations with the French, he wrote down in his autobiographical fragment an explanation of his motivations, he did so in the same free-spirited fashion (see Appendix I). This account incorporates some remarkable statements. The first is al-ʿAṭṭār's claim that the French were "peaceful" rather than "cruel," that is, al-ʿAṭṭār's ability to see them in human terms; second and more important, historically speaking, was the statement stressing the fact of their love of philosophy and their willingness to discuss it.[49]

Al-ʿAṭṭār then presented his account of his first meeting with the French. In this account, the broad outline of al-ʿAṭṭār's defense of himself becomes clear. Al-ʿAṭṭār was emotionally overwhelmed and did things out of love which he later regretted; intellectually captivated, he overdid his contacts with the French scholars. Having spent a traumatic year and a half in the Ṣaʿīd, al-ʿAṭṭār had suddenly returned to Cairo, finding for the first time the chance for free expression of his emotions in poetry and the unrestrained pursuit of new forms of intellectual life. The forcefulness with which al-ʿAṭṭār described these moments of liberation, his degree of self-awareness, and his candidness give this short piece psychological as well as historical significance.

As a form of self defense, or mea culpa, the *Maqāma* would seem to have been a total failure. Al-ʿAṭṭār's honesty in defending foreign knowledge, even philosophy, and his frank acknowledgment of having been attracted to Europeans which ended in a criticism of himself rather than the Europeans were in striking contrast to the analogous works of al-Sharqāwī and al-

Jabartī. The *Maqāma* could also be seen as a defense of the study of literature and the natural sciences, subjects which had been declining in Cairo in the 1790's, subjects which required an openness to foreigners. One can only surmise how negative an effect this work must have had at the end of the French occupation—a period marked by extreme antipathy to Europeans—written by a *shaykh* in al-Azhar.

Al-ʿAṭṭār, writing of this period years later (1815) in Damascus to explain to his Syrian students his work on *Al-Azharīya*, was in a very different situation; thirteen years of exile had made him very homesick. "I had been gathering glosses on the commentary of *Al-Azharīya* in the field of grammar when I was teaching it in al-Azhar to some students; then I made my analysis and was about to make the final draft when the disasters which befell Egypt from the French *kāfirs* happened. I left, fleeing Egypt for Turkey, seeking my companionship in this rough draft and some of my other books."[50] Elsewhere in the same work he states: "I finished the rough draft of this gloss in the end of Dhūʾl-Qaʿda in the year 1217, and I was at that time in the fort at Damietta on my way out of Egypt to Turkey."[51]

In conclusion, we might find many incentives, both negative and positive, to explain why al-ʿAṭṭār fled from Egypt at the end of the French occupation. His desire to pursue the rational sciences was a long-term source of frustration to him. The flow of historical events, especially the French occupation, transformed circumstances by relaxing previous taboos and creating certain expectations and caught al-ʿAṭṭār by surprise; when the occupation was over, he found himself compromised by it and was forced to flee. His general state of alienation was a factor. Another important reason for leaving Egypt was that there would be few or no stable sources of patronage in the near future. Al-ʿAṭṭār left for Turkey, the most developed part of the Ottoman Empire, taking his skills in Arabic philology and seeking knowledge in the natural sciences. The departure of al-ʿAṭṭār presaged the end of further cultural development until a new constellation of historical forces reshaped Egyptian society.

Chapter 5
Turkey and Syria in the Early Nineteenth Century: The Travels of al-ʿAṭṭār and the Preparation for Egyptian Reform

This chapter continues the analysis through the reform period from 1815 to 1837 and the culture which it produced. During this period, the modern Egyptian state was formed. Several studies of the period have stressed the important role of western Europeans in the process of state formation in Egypt. In this study the role of Egyptians is central, that of the Ottoman reform movement is secondary, and that of Europeans is only tertiary.

This chapter begins with an analysis of the socioeconomic structure of Turkey shortly after the reform period of Selim III, followed by a similar analysis of Egypt in 1815. This analysis explains why the development of Egypt, a breakaway province of the Ottoman Empire, was actually aided by experienced Turkish personnel, both through their actual defection from the Ottoman Empire and through their contribution to the education of Egyptians who played an important role in the new state structure. The ruling elite in both Istanbul and Cairo during this period of the early nineteenth century shared a common theological-juridical orientation, and there was some similarity in intellectual trends in both cities.

The principal development in theology during this period was the revival of *kalām* by members of the ruling elite. This was especially noticeable in Egypt. There was at the same time a sharp decline in the use of *ḥadīth*, and in fact the *mutakallimūn* explicitly criticized the use of *ḥadīth*, after a generation in which *ḥadīth* studies had been the overwhelming preoccupation of the dominant class. This trend is of great interest to this study, for it is a phenomenon which may be interpreted on several levels. First, it was a reflection of social conflict. Middle-class Egyptian merchants and artisans now struggled to survive in a regime dominated by Turks, Europeans, and a few Egyptian *mutakallimīn*. This suppressed middle class continued to engage in *ḥadīth* studies, as is evident from the writings of the majority of the Azharī *shaykhs* of the period. Second, it was a reflection from within the structure of elite religious thought of the growth of utilitarian rationalism. This tendency opposed the Ashʿarite tendencies of the seventeenth-century *muḥaddithīn*. Finally, the criticism of the arguments of the *muḥaddithīn* sustained and reinforced an interest in history, philology, and literature, as well as logic, science, medicine, and related fields which attracted the *ʿulamāʾ* who participated in the reform movement. The main line of development in these fields is a search of the Islamic past for a range of models appropriate to the conditions of the early nineteenth century. The rationalist foundations for *kalām* came primarily from India.

The legal-juridical framework thus juxtaposed and combined two incongruous elements which have escaped scholarly attention in the past. On the one hand, the revival of Islamic rationalism meant a revival of the Aristotelian framework. Yet this revival was partial and selective. The principal feature of Aristotelian logic which concerned Ḥasan al-ʿAṭṭār, the chief *mutakallim* in Egypt, was argument by analogy. Argument by analogy and discussions explicating the nature of analogy and how it should be applied demonstrated that it, too, could serve as a vehicle for utilitarianism for reform-minded intellectuals. This is important, for theories of modernity frequently stress the apparent wholesale rejection of the indigenous past. Neoclassicism, which was at the base of the cultural revival of the eighteenth century, continued in the nineteenth century, expanding into areas of Egyptian thought in which it had not previously been significant. Finally, different fields proceeded at different rates of development under the general influence of neoclassicism.

This raises the question of why neoclassicism played such an important role in the development of Egyptian culture during this period. The simplest answer is that neoclassicism as a conscious elite endeavor was, both in the eighteenth and in the nineteenth centuries, an efficient vehicle of cultural domination. Indigenous traditions supporting reform were often more persuasive and inspired less conflict and confrontation than did European traditions. Neoclassicism was not the only option, as we can see through a comparison between Egyptian and Ottoman culture. The Ottomans maintained a high level of awareness of developments in European technology and medicine, and until the eighteenth century they found no great difficulty integrating these developments into the rationalist framework of late medieval thought. (This may sound odd, but as Hossein Nasr has observed, Ibn Sīnā, the symbol of medieval medical thought, was also taught in German medical schools into the beginning of the nineteenth century.) A historian of Turkish literature in the nineteenth century has even observed that the transition from Ottoman literature in the early nineteenth century to European-dominated styles did not mark a radical break in the expression of the concrete, an interesting statement which attests to the vitality of a supposedly "decadent" period.[1] Again, the simplest answer to the question of why classicism was not continued in Egypt may be that the opponents of the reform movement had taken it over, and they had become a formidable force.

The cultural elite of the reform period was composed almost entirely of Egyptians. But Egyptians were at that time denied access to the dominant military and political elite which was initially monopolized by Turks. Neoclassicism asserted the value of Arabic high culture over against Turkish. It also served to retain Islamic culture in a court increasingly dominated by European influence. The development of the Arabic language to meet the new challenges of the age, as well as the assertion of Islamic tradition, strengthened the Egyptian position within the ruling class. Neoclassicism was a means of self-assertion and, ultimately, one of the foundations of nationalism.

During the reform period, neoclassicism advanced in different fields at different rates. In some areas there were vast outpourings, in others repression. In the age of the printing press, significant works remained in manuscript form, although they were written by such a prominent figure as Ḥasan al-ʿAṭṭār. Why was this so? Perhaps because there was no place in Cairo for such a work as al-ʿAṭṭār's in the field of physical medicine (a book he wrote in Damascus). It could not be introduced in al-Azhar, and there was no alternative in Egypt to Western medicine, which had been in use since the eighteenth century. As a result, a work of potentially great interest to modern scholarship remained a manuscript. In his work, al-ʿAṭṭār shows that the tradition of Ibn al-Nafīs, a medieval writer who is said to have anticipated Harvey in the theory of the circulation of the blood, did not die out in the later Islamic world. He also shows that there were Muslims who apparently supported a rebuttal of the central ideas of Ibn Sīnā against the majority. This important general discovery for the structure of the history of medicine is important in clarifying the role of neoclassicism in Egypt.

This chapter further examines the intellectual formation of Ḥasan al-ʿAṭṭār, who played a central role in cultural reform in Muḥammad ʿAlī's Egypt. In the process, it examines intellectual life in Turkey and Syria, to explain not only al-ʿAṭṭār's development but also the development of those Arabs and Turks who flocked to Egypt to participate in what was in effect a breakaway reform movement. Finally, it seeks to clarify the relationships among Turkey, Syria, and Egypt in this period. I shall explore the relationship between the Ottoman heartland and its provinces in the light of the development of the world market and its progressive impact on Turkey.

Turkey had the earliest and most sustained relationship with the capitalist West of any of the Middle Eastern countries. But Turkey was protected from the full impact of capitalism because it was the seat of an empire based on tributary relationships. This allowed capitalism to develop in Turkey over a long period of time without the radical institutional transformations which occurred in Egypt. Modern historiography of the Ottoman Empire has emphasized this continuity to such an extent that the decisive change from one precapitalist phase to another is still unclear. For the purposes of this study, Istanbul in the late eighteenth century represented the Ottoman Empire's state commercial sector. Landowning bureaucrats used precapitalist means of coercion, including state power, to produce crops for sale on the world market. This landlord bureaucratic class openly allied itself with the commercial minorities. The latter conducted marketing operations for them and performed other services. It is often assumed that the commercial state sector was less evolved in the Ottoman Empire of the early nineteenth century than the analogous formation in Egypt during the period 1815–1837. In the time before the Tanzimat reform period, the Ottoman *aʿyān* (provincial notables) were able, through alliance with disaffected elements in the city of Istanbul, to overthrow sultans and to block technicalization, institutional reform, and other measures which would have contributed to the development of a capitalist mode of production. In Egypt, there was greater centralization, and political opposition was less organized, as we shall show in Chapter 6.

Turkey's integration into the world market encouraged the cultivation of a reformist Māturīdite theology among the leading *ʿulamāʾ* of Istanbul. The existence of regional centers of power in Turkey, along the caravan routes, created the political context for a theological (and in effect a juridical) opposition. This opposition differed from that of the popular orders in Istanbul. Its orientation was not toward heterodoxy but toward orthopraxy. The movement called the Ṭarīqa Muḥammadīya, which exaggerated the performance of ritual, made its last stand in these years. With the Tanzimat reform period, these regional centers no longer could challenge Istanbul. Ḥasan al-ʿAṭṭār was among those *fuqahāʾ* who began their careers in speculative theology with a polemic against the revival of this movement.

In the early nineteenth century, Damascus was a precapitalist commercial center which differed from Istanbul and Cairo in being wholly based on trade, with a very limited agricultural hinterland. Damascus was more organically commercial. Its ideological orientation and culture were less eclectic than those of Istanbul and Cairo. Damascus symbolized Muslim commercial power and sheltered a highly developed form of mystical life. It was both a center of mystical learning and a source of recruitment for many leading Ottoman personnel. It had been important for the Egyptians in the eighteenth century at the time of their merchant commercial revival, when Muṣṭafā al-Bakrī came from Damascus to Cairo to develop the Khalwatīya-Bakrīya reform movement which was discussed in the first chapter.

The early years of the nineteenth century marked the end of an era for Damascus, too. Three factors began to undermine Damascus' commercial position: the disruption of trade routes caused by the prolonged Wahhābī wars, British commercial penetration of India which undermined the Indian end of the Indian-Syrian luxury trade, and, finally, the development of the French commercial position in the Levant, which was discussed in Chapter 1. By the 1820's a defensive orthopraxist movement found a home in Damascus with the rise of Shaykh Khālid.

Al-ʿAṭṭār's studies in Damascus from 1810 to 1815 highlight the crises in mystical theology confronting reformist theology in Istanbul and Cairo. In Istanbul, Māturīdism was becoming an intellectually fragmented body of thought, susceptible to the influence of positivism. In traveling from Khalwatī reformist circles in Istanbul to the more-inward-turning mystical circles of the Khalwatīya in Damascus, al-ʿAṭṭār discovered the conflicts which divided the people of his age as they were reflected in different tendencies in the confraternity in which he had grown up.

Holistic and integrative thought flourished in the precapitalist commercial sectors. This had made such towns as Damascus into important intellectual centers. With the development of modern capitalism through the world market, not only were the traditional commercial centers displaced, but also the new Muslim capitalist elite, like the landowning bureaucracy of Turkey and Egypt after 1837, abandoned this mode of thought. For these latter, the urge toward a synthetic understanding was replaced by a drive toward unitary accumulation of parts of a whole which they could not comprehend, over against which they felt powerless. Some of the most important intellectual struggles which took place in Turkey in the late eighteenth and early nineteenth centuries, struggles which the Syrians entered in a highly partisan fashion, centered around the acceptability of the Wujūdī position. The Wujūdī position was a holistic synthesis, more or less pantheistic, of man and nature. The forces which opposed the development of agricultural capitalism in Turkey championed it. The reform movement destroyed certain Ṣūfī movements in Istanbul which had championed the Wujūdī position. In so doing, it displayed the class dynamics which underlay apparently abstruse points about the nature of man and God. A movement which espoused a rather less pantheistic version of the same doctrine existed in Damascus, where it continued well into the nineteenth century.

The bourgeois class which triumphed in Turkey and Egypt during the nineteenth century did so during periods of rapid reform which seemed to rise and fall with an individual ruler. These periods of reform were moments of effective alliance between Western technocrats and the indigenous political elite, which succeeded in weakening the indigenous opposition. Reform in the nineteenth century did involve extensive institutional change. This affected the development of culture very directly, for patronage was virtually controlled by a few bureaucrats. Of equal consequence for the development of culture, the rise of the central state power coincided with a decline in *ḥadīth* as the official juridical expression of the state *ʿulamāʾ*. *Ḥadīth* was replaced by *fiqh*. This did not, of course, mean a cessation of either the obligatory religious or intellectual activities that characterized the first phase but rather that these activities were placed in a new context.

Some of the reasons for these changes are self-evident. In the case of Egypt, the commercial sector gained political control of the state, and in so doing took over responsibility for law giving and, hence, required the participation of *fuqahāʾ*. It is interesting to note that the dominant class abandoned *ḥadīth* studies, the arena of intellectual conflict of the previous era, and left it to the suppressed middle class. The ruling class relied on *kalām*, at least during the period of "reform." This phase, when class cleavage was sharpest and polemics most bitter, was the heyday of the state commercial sector. *Ḥadīth* studies had been most congruent with merchant capitalism; *kalām* was most congruent with state domination. One might also note that the merchant class abandoned the Māturīdite theology to the new dominant class, although in the period of its own ascendance it had initiated the introduction of Māturīdite theology against Ashʿarite theology.

Māturīdite *kalām*, fully developed, provided the appropriate religious climate for the reform movement of this period. Māturīdite *kalām* was an effective weapon in the hands of the regime's spokesmen. In this regard, the state commercial sector differed from the agrarian capitalism which arose after 1837, which for totally different reasons reverted again to *ḥadīth* studies. A well-known example of these changes from Egypt may be found in the life of Rifāʿa al-Ṭahṭāwī. He was the son of a merchant from the Delta who was displaced by the rise of Muḥammad ʿAlī. In his youth he studied *ḥadīth*, but when he became a member of the new reform bureaucracy, he became a *mutakallim*, as is evinced by his essay on *ijtihād*, reliance on self-judgment in theological matters. Later, following the development of agrarian capitalism in the third phase (after 1837), he produced his major religious work, and it was a study of *ḥadīth*.

A reliance on Māturīdite *kalām* imposed the need for the study of certain ancillary disciplines, such as logic and rhetoric, and these fields were revived; in addition, a new relevance was found for the study of the traditional Aristotelian corpus during that period. Certain topics in logic or geometry recur many times; among these were discussions of argument by analogy. The explanation for this was a social one, a reflection of the contradiction between the mode of production and the mode of distribution. We are accustomed to conceiving of all modern cultural history in terms of the center of the world market. Not only does such a conception exclude indigenous non-Western traditions, but it also gives an unbalanced perspective by which to judge the development of Western culture outside the West. If, however, we shift our focus to the problems of adaptation, adjustment, and implementation in precapitalist regions which fell under Western influence, having struggled unsuccessfully to control the industrial revolution, we can see why the framework of empiricism which was central to Western thought at the beginning of the industrial era was confronted by a framework which now grew to place great stress on deductive reasoning and argument by analogy.

Al-ʿAṭṭār's period of study in Turkey and Syria represented a time of preparation for the tasks he undertook on his return to Egypt in 1815. While Turkey was in a period of regressing away from "reform," a number of individuals and institutions, including libraries, existed which made the study of the rational sciences possible. While we do not know how, it is clear from his writings that he finally secured the patronage he had long sought and never found in Egypt. References to his associates in Turkey include a number of highly placed figures. In both Turkey and, later, Syria, he is identified with Khalwatī circles, and they certainly represented in terms of outlook and range of interests something fairly close to what al-ʿAṭṭār himself did. The numerous interconnections between Syria and Istanbul and the paucity of biographical sources make it difficult to determine his motives for going to Damascus in 1810. What is fairly clear is the nature of the work he undertook there and, to a certain extent, its relationship to his earlier studies in Turkey. I would like to speculate: One motivation may have arisen from his studies in Turkey in the natural sciences. In reading the later commentaries and the achievements of different ages, he did not find himself drawn to the classical period, although he obviously had read widely, noting, for example, the importance of the translation movement in Dār al-Ḥikma. What held his attention was the work in the astronomical observatories of Samarqand and Marāgha. This work, which was carried out by such figures as Nāṣir al-dīn al-Ṭūsī, was largely accomplished under the aegis of a Shīʿī ethos. The intensified communal feeling made it difficult in all probability to use such sources for teaching purposes without some theological justifications. Al-ʿAṭṭār, in fact, made recourse to a rather strange justification for his reliance on al-Ṭūsī. In any case, it was in Damascus that al-ʿAṭṭār turned to reading Ibn al-ʿArabī with a specialist, and it is at this point that his own views on Ṣūfism crystallized, insofar as we can use this expression; for he retained all his life an ambivalence toward mystical experience, which he found essentially alien to his soul. A second reason may have come from his studies of logic and *kalām*, which began in Turkey. Again, his interests were focused on the postclassical commentators, whose merits he freely discussed. The majority of these commentators were Indian. Al-ʿAṭṭār praised the virtues of the Indian rational tradition several times and compared it to the feeble condition of rational studies in al-Azhar. Nearly all these commentators were Ṣūfīs, most of them Naqshbandīs. In coming to Damascus, al-ʿAṭṭār would find the center of the Indian Naqshbandī-based Māturīdism in the Arab world. A third reason might simply be that he returned with a Syrian who was his friend and colleague in Istanbul and found Damascus a very congenial place. For the last time he was free to study Andalusian poetry. He even composed some poetry of his own; but unfortunately, while he was there, he lost the only copy of his "Dīwān."

Istanbul

Istanbul represented the most advanced center of capitalist development in the Middle East prior to the Muḥammad ʿAlī period. The conflict between urban and rural interests in the Ottoman Empire had been developing for more than a century. Local notables struggled against higher bureaucrats in Istanbul, each seeking to control the wealth which accrued from trade. Throughout this period, the balance of power seesawed back and forth as different regimes rose and fell. Muḥammad ʿAlī's regime (1805–1848) was a case of more absolute dominion in the Middle East, for he was actually able to uproot the peasantry. In Turkey, periods of domination were relative. When the higher bureaucrats and the Sultan held the upper hand, there were periods of "reform"; foreigners were given commercial privileges vis-à-vis indigenous merchants and foreign experts were brought in to create a new army which would support the government in its policy of attempting to gain monopolistic control of the wealth from commerce. During periods of dominance by the local notables, the Janissaries and the popular Ṣūfī orders, such as the Bektashis, thrived and the urban structure reverted away from class relations.

The commercial sector of Istanbul in the late eighteenth and early nineteenth centuries was more dependent on Europe than that of Cairo during the same period. The expansion of European trade after the Renaissance had made a deep impact on Turkey far earlier than it had on Egypt. Strains on the indigenous artisanal community were noticeable from the seventeenth century, when the rising demand for raw silk in France and other more advanced countries caused them to turn to Turkey. The government export of raw silk proved to be a very great hardship for the Turkish silk industry. Artisans in this basic industry of medieval Turkey found themselves both with a shortage of raw silk and forced to compete with silk products which undersold their own. The Ottoman government was unable or disinclined to control its own standards of production; nonguild merchandise, illegally produced and generally of inferior quality, proliferated in the seventeenth century. In the early eighteenth century, the Turks imported artisans to improve the quality of production from the Morea, but nothing stemmed the export of raw silk. In the later eighteenth century, Turkey was forced to make a series of economic concessions which undermined her economic independence. Until 1777 it had been forbidden for foreigners who became naturalized citizens to pass their merchandise directly to French citizens representing the Marseilles firms in Turkey. In 1777 this ban was lifted.[2] This greatly strengthened the foreign commercial sector and its indigenous tributaries at the expense of local trade interests. In 1806, the Turkish government attempted to impose a quota for the export of raw silk from Bursa, but by then it was too late to salvage the position of the artisans. In 1818 came the Anglo-Ottoman Treaty of Commerce which further limited the tax on imports while keeping the tax on exports at a high level.[3] The ruin of the indigenous urban economy was impassively described in the celebrated travel account of M. A. Ubicini. He chronicled the decline in the number of looms in Anatolia, Syria, and Iraq between the late eighteenth century and the 1840's. Similar declines were noted across the board in other artisanal wares.[4]

Simultaneous with the undermining of the artisanal economy (which proceeded throughout the eighteenth and early nineteenth centuries), corresponding changes took place on the higher levels of the bureaucracy. These changes reflected the new wealth and power which accrued to these officials. Class relations emerged; corporativism was replaced by economic individualism. If the *ʿulamāʾ* had represented a unity until the middle of the eighteenth century, this rapidly gave way during the next half century to patron-client relations, as a great gulf emerged between a few wealthy religious bureaucratic officials (*mollas*) and the rest of the Turkish *ʿulamāʾ*. The Sultan intervened with a number of firmans ordering the Qāḍī to uphold the Sharīʿa and to desist from the sale of legal decisions to the highest bidder.[5]

The last years of the eighteenth century, during the reign of Selim III, witnessed another abortive reform period in Turkey. Characteristically, the gap between the rich and poor widened, and it was in this period that such popular institutions as the Janissaries and the Bektashis were "discredited." Selim was overthrown in 1807 by a coalition of popular forces, including Janissaries but also a sizable number of *ʿulamāʾ*. Reasons given for the revolt of 1807 explicitly include the distress of the people under the weight of rising prices as well as revolts in other parts of the Empire.[6] An examination of the policies of Selim can be found in a book inspired by one of his leading religious spokesmen, the Muftī Durri Zadeh. In this work, a much-praised collection of *fatāwī*, the preoccupation of the regime with the interests of the landlord and foreign merchants is massively evident. Commerce remained virtually unregulated; it was the age of laissez faire.[7]

When the "reform" movement of the landowning class was resumed in the 1820's, the trends of the late eighteenth century resurfaced. The Janissary corps was destroyed in 1826, opening the way for the orthodox *ṭuruq*, whose members were prominent in the ruling class, to expropriate the wealth of the Bektashis and put a number of the latter to death. One writer estimated that the destruction of the Janissaries was followed by the killing of some seventy thousand Bektashis, the destruction of a large number of *tekkes*, and the turning over of a great deal of Bektashi wealth to representatives of the elite Ṣūfī orders, the Naqshbandīs and the Khalwatīs. Only in the 1850's did a more conservative Bektashi organization begin to revive.[8]

The shift in balance of power was already reflected in the Anglo-Ottoman Treaty of 1818–1820. The indigenous merchants and artisans had been seriously weakened by the unequal competition with European industry; the Janissaries, too, had been weakened in wars against Russia. Seventy thousand craftsmen were expendable, and the regime was so strong that whatever protests ensued could be ignored. The year 1826, which witnessed the destruction of the Janissaries and the massacre of the Bektashis, rightly marks a turning point; never again, except briefly after World War I, was the balance of forces in Turkey ever in doubt.

Before turning to a study of cultural institutions and leading intellectuals at the time of al-ʿAṭṭār's studies in Turkey, I shall proceed with a socio-economic analysis of a formation characterized by a proportionately larger commercial sector than Istanbul or Cairo, a more limited agrarian hinterland, and an enduring sense of corporate identity, far stronger than that of either Cairo or Istanbul. This was the city of Damascus.

Damascus

The factors which have previously been mentioned conspired to undermine the commercial position of Damascus, but they did so in a fashion which prolonged the existence of a medieval sense of corporate identity. The reason for this is that the threats (the Wahhābī wars, British commercial activity in India, and growth of French commerce in the Levant) were external, and the resistance which was made was against common foes. The livelihood of the artisans, as well as that of the merchants, was jeopardized by these developments.

In the eighteenth century, the French presence in Syria was noticeable only in Aleppo, where a community of European merchants lived in relative isolation.[9] Much of their work was performed for them by the *beratli* community of Syrian Christians, mentioned in Chapter 1. For their labors the Syrian Christians were rewarded by guarantees of protection which they received through the capitulations agreements. From the middle of the eighteenth century, the Syrian Christians rose in importance; in fact, they dominated the important littoral trade between Syria and Egypt.[10] As they did so, the Syrian Muslims relinquished their hold. Muslims in the late eighteenth century dominated the *wikālāt*, or wholesale trade houses, of Ṭuffāḥ, Junīya, and Ḥamzāwī, but the most famous merchant names of the period, such as Faraʿūn and Ḥanna Fākhir, were Christian.[11]

I now turn to a second area of confrontation, the Wahhābī campaign. Among the chief events of the late eighteenth century was the rise of the Wahhābīs as a threat to Syrian commerce. The Arabian Wahhābīs actually raided in Syria in 1793. In that year they succeeded in overrunning the bordertowns of Ṣūb, Dūmat, and al-Jundal. In 1797/1212, Ḥajīlān b. Ḥāmid, the Amīr al-Qaṣīm, raided the Wādī al-Shārārāt, taking much of its wealth. This had the effect of convincing a number of the Bedouins of Syria to come to his side. Despite the absolute silence of Damascene sources, there was, in the death notice of a writer who died in 1803/1218, a passing reference to the departure of a caravan of tribute to the Wahhābī capital from Aleppo, indicating that at least some parts of Syria were under effective Wahhābī control during the 1790's.[12] By 1800, the Syrian-Istanbul pilgrimage was being intercepted—an event which had wide repercussions in trading circles, albeit a more precise knowledge of Syrian rural economy would help in understanding its significance. Further Wahhābī raids on the Ḥawrān and Jabal al-Shaykh regions were, moreover, practically unopposed. In fact, the Syrians, divided among themselves, were not able to make any effective response. The Wahhābīs were reformers, and in their political and military strategy they sought to drive a wedge between the wealthy merchants of the cities (and the regimes which supported them) and the poor. The Wahhābīs made inroads into Syria and, as will be shown, into Egypt, charging that the commercial elite represented corruption and decadence. But the Wahhābīs were suppressed militarily, and they failed at least in Damascus to shake the regime from within.

Paradoxically, the underlying cause of the Wahhābī campaign was itself conditioned by the same economic factors which had had such a profound effect on Damascus. As has been shown in Chapter 1, the Indian spice trade, which included indigo and textiles, contracted sharply during the second half of the eighteenth century as the British began to dominate the Indian economy.[13] The decline of the Gujerat–Red Sea trade impoverished the Sharīf of Mecca. When he lacked the money traditionally used to bribe and buy the services of the tribes, the Wahhābīs arose in this hinterland as its economy in turn declined. The decline of the Indian trade to the Arab world, which Das Gupta has discussed, also had staggering effects on the Syrian merchant elite.

A traveler's account of the Indian trade from the vantage point of the 1830's suggested that it was in such a state of decline that the making of silk and gold fabric was finally being undertaken locally in Aleppo, as India was no longer a dependable source of supply. However, in recent years, even the number of Syrian artisans engaged in this craft had shrunk to no more than one thousand artisans, 20 percent of what their number had been before.[14]

Given the difference in the socioeconomic framework, it is not surprising to find that the reform-minded Ṣūfīs who lived in the respective centers had quite different orientations. Naqshbandīs and Khalwatīs in Istanbul were oriented toward the sciences, history, and government service. In their writings of the eighteenth century, one finds a number of attempts to integrate the findings of Western positivist science into a holistic framework. Ṣūfīs of these two orders in Damascus were not touched by these problems even in the early nineteenth century. In Damascus, systematic thought like the writings of Ibn al-ʿArabī was prized, while Ibn al-ʿArabī had long since lost his appeal among the upper class Ṣūfīs in Istanbul. In Istanbul the Ṣūfīs studied the scholastic sciences (*ʿulūm*), whereas in Damascus mystical experiences were reported, as were numerous lives given over to various forms of rigorous self-denial. With all this, Damascus was the freer literary environment.

An important point to note is the interconnectedness of Damascus and Istanbul in the period which we study. Numerous Damascenes went to Istanbul, became doctors, stayed, or returned to the Arab provinces. A number of Turks are reported who went to Damascus for study and who, as did one official, chose to be buried in a shrine of Ibn al-ʿArabī.[15]

Al-ʿAṭṭār in Turkey, 1802–1810

The effort which I have undertaken here to demonstrate the relationship between Damascus and the study of mysticism, between Istanbul and the rational sciences, the role of travel, and the importance of the major *ṭuruq* in the support of intellectual reform helps to explain the travels of *shaykhs* like Ḥasan al-ʿAṭṭār. It is no exaggeration to claim that the development of the indigenous culture was intimately related to the *ṭuruq*, as one can tell from a glance at the number of writers and poets who belonged to them, or from a consideration of those who supported the reform of Selim III, Mahmud II, or Muḥammad ʿAlī. The intellectual orbit created by the Ṣūfī *ṭuruq* continued to show great vitality at the end of the eighteenth century and during the early years of the nineteenth century, before the industrial age had fully undermined the traditional crafts and the regional commerce which supported the *ṭuruq*.

Al-ʿAṭṭār spent eight years at the beginning of the nineteenth century (1802–1810) in Turkey studying the rational sciences and then five years in Damascus, which were at least partly taken up with the study of Ibn al-ʿArabī. In this section an effort to reconstruct those years is undertaken. Al-ʿAṭṭār becomes both focus and example. The sources for this period in his life, that is, prior to his return to Egypt in 1815, are very few, and, worse, they contradict one another. The following itinerary, however, seems the most probable one. When al-ʿAṭṭār left Damietta in 1802, he went directly to Istanbul, where he occupied himself with the continuation of his still-uncompleted work on *ʿilm al-handasa* (geometry, including topics in astronomy and engineering). Al-ʿAṭṭār is known to have been in Istanbul in 1804.[16] He himself stated that when he left Istanbul he went to Alexandretta, a town on the Turkish coast.[17] His writings from Alexandretta permit this visit to be dated fairly precisely as having occurred during 1806–1807, the period in which he finished writing a grammar text.[18] Elsewhere in the same text, al-ʿAṭṭār indicated that in 1807 he traveled from Alexandretta north to the Black Sea coast. He also visited Izmīr and made a serious commitment to study medicine.[19]

The desire to study medicine would logically induce him to return to Istanbul (or its suburb Scutari). Approximately in 1808, al-ʿAṭṭār's first writing on medicine, a work on anatomy, appeared. While this cannot be proven from the text itself, there are several indirect pieces of evidence. First, his student Muḥammad al-ʿAṭṭār studied medicine in Istanbul. Second, Ḥasan al-ʿAṭṭār, in his major work on medicine, mentioned his interest in the work of European doctors and hospitals, which he stated were located in Istanbul or its suburbs. This leads us to conclude that between 1808 and 1810 he was in the Istanbul area studying medicine, on which he later wrote when he was teaching medicine in Damascus. Of the other works which he wrote (which were not located), notably, the "Tuḥfa," the most logical time of composition would be between 1803 and 1806. The success of this work, of which he was to boast many years later, might well have facilitated his obtaining a post in Alexandretta and perhaps also eased the situation when he wanted to study medicine. In 1810 (there is no doubt about this date), he left Turkey for Damascus (see Appendix II).

Al-ʿAṭṭār's Associates in Turkey

In Istanbul, al-ʿAṭṭār knew several of the leading intellectuals of the period. At the time of his arrival or shortly thereafter, the group which he knew manifested strong opposition to Selim, even helping to bring about his overthrow. Al-ʿAṭṭār also entered another circle, which included some Europeans, while he was living in the house of the Hakimbashi and studying medicine. How he met these people, and how easily he adjusted to his new situation, is not known. We do know that he studied Turkish while he was there, but how far he progressed is again not known. In one work, we find praise of a certain Turkish grammar book.[20]

A prominent Ottoman who knew the writings of the Wafāʾīya in Egypt very probably knew al-ʿAṭṭār; at least, among his works is a translation in which some of al-ʿAṭṭār's writings appear. This was the Mulla Ahmad Asim Efendī (1755–1819/1169–1235), a writer and translator. He translated al-Zabīdī's dictionary, "Tarjamat al-qāmūs li-Firūzabādī," and it was published in Turkey. He composed his own works in the Arabic language and wrote on Ottoman history. In 1810/1225 he finished the translation of al-Jabartī's *Maẓhar al-taqdīs bi khurūj ṭāʾifat al-Faransīs*, which contained selections by al-ʿAṭṭār, as has been previously noted. Ahmad Asim was a chronicler of the period of Ottoman history through which he was living; and from his work, one can identify his sympathies with Mehmet Ataʾullah (died 1811/1226), a person with whom al-ʿAṭṭār definitely had some relationship.[21] Al-ʿAṭṭār's attraction to this group is understandable on several grounds. Neither he nor they were opponents of reform—quite the contrary—but they did oppose the giving over of real power to foreigners and the needless breaking with indigenous reform traditions which Selim permitted.[22] From everything we know of al-ʿAṭṭār's later life in Egypt, he stood for very much the same principles while he was in the service of Muḥammad ʿAlī. No doubt his contact with these religious officials had occurred in his first stay in Istanbul, during the period when he was studying and writing on *ilahīyāt* (theology).[23] Al-ʿAṭṭār makes clear that when he was in Istanbul studying medicine, he was living with a Hakimbashi. This would clearly seem to be the "second stay."[24]

As al-ʿAṭṭār indicated, he had sought to study medicine in his youth, but this was not possible for him in Egypt. Among his earliest writings in Istanbul, which he wrote after leaving Egypt, was a work based on Ibn Sīnā. This work, a study of anatomy, was completed in 1803/1223. Later, his friend and student Muḥammad al-ʿAṭṭār undertook to write a commentary on it.[25] After writing this work, al-ʿAṭṭār began to learn of advances in European medicine and other medical traditions in Islam. He became encouraged to criticize Ibn Sīnā. He told of this change in his major work on medicine, written in 1814, which included some of his experiences in studying medicine in Istanbul:

> Concerning the study of the structure of the human body, to see how it is composed of tissues, nerves, and other things: this is done through dissection, that is, through cutting it up into pieces, just as one examines meat. This dissection is done up until the present time in . . . the European countries. At the time I was in Istanbul, I asked some European doctors about it, and they informed me that in their country there is a place called the dissection room [Tashrīḥkhāna]. The doctors go there for their meetings with their students and bring the dead which had died during the day—ignoring whether or not the dead

person was famous or the reason for his death. Then they dissect him piece by piece, using special instruments. The students take the pieces in order to learn—some the head, others the hand, others the intestine, and in this way they proceed in their training. Many of the European and Turkish doctors continue this tradition, and they have persons who are skilled [*ashkhāṣ*, perhaps assistants] who study what they have observed of the body's structure.

Some of the Muslim doctors also have skilled personnel in the medical school in Istanbul—and there remains in this school [after dissection takes place] only some veins, bones, and leftover pieces from corpses, which are then placed in a spot in the school for the qualified people to examine. When I used to read books in that school at various times, I tried not to look at these displays, as to look at such things made me depressed.

Al-Qurashī said in his commentary on the *Qānūn* that dissection of bones and joints and what lies next to them is simple in dead persons regardless of the cause of death. . . .

Al-Anṭākī said that, according to Ibn Sīnā, the most conclusive approach to anatomy is through reading the well-established findings of a skilled man with precise knowledge in it. By this he meant that the usefulness of anatomy is the deductions [*istidlāl*] from the findings of a man who knows everything well. . . . It is known, however, that dissection begins with the observation of the strange things of kings and kingdoms and with the making known of the secrets of the divinity; and it is a science which cannot seriously be pursued except with one's two eyes. What one learns by way of logical proofs [*barāhīn*] is not useful. We have been dissuaded from the pursuit [of the empirical approach] because it has been considered an obstacle to God's law and to faith, and an impediment to His Mercy and Charity which dwells in our hearts.

But for this reason it might be said that there exist two sciences, the careful study of which leads to a growing certitude concerning the wonders of Creation and the masterful skill of God—and these two fields are *ʿilm al-hayʾa* and *ʿilm al-tashrīḥ* [astronomy and empirical anatomy]. And I say that these two fields transform the mind, but that precision in the knowledge of them is concealed from the masses. For that reason you will see that the majority of distinguished people in our time have not been influenced at all by these two fields. In fact, these fields are almost nonexistent now, except among a very small number of people, who save us from ignorance.[26]

Additional comments on his contacts with Europeans and European medicine appear in the same work, giving us a small clue to the way in which he met the Europeans during his stay in Istanbul. He stated that he lived with a Hakimbashi while he was in Istanbul, and that he had a very enjoyable time with him. He studied with him and made considerable progress.

Among the works which he read with the Hakimbashi was the "Mūjaz al-qānūn," a shortened form of the main work of Ibn Sīnā, by Ibn al-Nafīs. He also read the commentary literature on Ibn Sīnā.[27] In another passage, in a discussion of the difficulty of deducing clear medical conclusions from the pulse, he returned to the subject of foreign doctors. "And when I was in Istanbul all the doctors of different nationalities used to frequently meet in a place where I was staying in the house of the chief of the doctors [Dar Reis ul-Atibba, i.e., the Hakimbashi's house]. I used to ask them about the pulse, but I did not find a single one of them who was certain about it. I asked some who were well versed, and they said that it was not known about except by a very few individuals who were to be found in Europe."[28] One Hakimbashi, Mehmet Ataullah, at this time gained some fame through his son Shaykh Shani Zadeh, whom he sent to Italy to study medicine, and who returned to write the first modern textbook of anatomy written by a Turk. Whether this Hakimbashi was the same one whom al-ʿAṭṭār knew cannot be determined, but it seems probable.[29]

Al-ʿAṭṭār in Syria, 1810–1815

In 1810/1225, al-ʿAṭṭār arrived in Damascus and took up residence in a Ḥanafī *madrasa*, the Madrasat al-Badrʾīya, which, he stated, was well organized and at the same time offered seclusion.[30] He had barely been there a month, during which time he was writing a work on *ādāb al-baḥth* (argumentation), when an opportunity arose for him to visit Jerusalem. "After my return to Damascus from Turkey, I had begun writing [a certain book] until Rabīʿ al-Thānī 1225 [May 1810], arriving at the chapter titled 'Taqsīm'; and then the opportunity arose to visit Jerusalem. So I left what I wrote in Damascus and visited the Bayt al-Maqdis on the 16th on Shaʿbān 1225 (September 16, 1810); and then I traveled about in this area, returning to Damascus in Rabīʿ al-Thānī 1226 (May 1811), and completed the work with waning energy and growing laziness on the 24th of Shaʿbān (September 13, 1811)."[31] Al-ʿAṭṭār went with some Syrians who were traveling on horseback. They proceeded first to Maʿn, then to Hebron where al-ʿAṭṭār stayed for ten days, and then proceeded to Jerusalem where al-ʿAṭṭār stayed with the Naqīb al-Ashrāf, al-Sayyid ʿUmar Efendī.[32]

Probably at the time of his return to the Madrasat al-Badrʾīya, there occurred the incident involving Shaykh Muḥammad al-Miṣīrī. He was a friend of al-ʿAṭṭār, and his stay in the same *madrasa* for a period specified as having been two months was a source of great happiness for al-ʿAttār. As it is estimated that al-ʿAṭṭār stayed for no more than one month in the *madrasa* in 1810, this event must have occurred somewhere between 1811 and 1815. Muḥammad al-Miṣīrī was one of the few Egyptian *ʿulamāʾ* who had intellectual relations with the French during the Napoleon invasion of Egypt. He wrote a letter to Napoleon describing the treasures of Egypt (which he said were "greater than musk and amber"), notably the archeological remains of

Pharaonic times. He urged Napoleon to make a law to stop the pillaging of these ruins, which Napoleon did. Napoleon reported meeting Shaykh al-Miṣīrī and discussing religious matters related to the celebration of the birthday of the Prophet. He was one of the principal *shaykhs* of Alexandria, and these contacts did nothing to tarnish his reputation. In fact, he played an active role at the time of the British invasion of Alexandria.[33]

After al-Miṣīrī left the *madrasa*, he sent a *qaṣīda* from Bayrūt praising Damascus, its *ʿulamāʾ* and merchants with whom he had been staying. A part of this poem was not acceptable to the *ʿulamāʾ* of Madrasat al-Badrʾīya because of its wording and its rhyme schemes, and it caused a great stir.[34] If it could be located, this poem might be found to be a part of the intellectual development of Egyptians who, as did al-Disūqī or Barbīr, went to Damascus as rebels against Egyptian culture as they found it.

Other biographical information included in the last of the books which al-ʿAṭṭār wrote in Damascus (the commentary on al-Anṭākī) shows that he stayed in the *madrasa* until he departed for the Ḥijāz in 1813/1228, or slightly later, making the Ḥijj on the way home to Egypt.

Al-ʿAṭṭār had two main students in Syria, although many others doubtless attended his courses. The more devoted of these two was Muḥammad al-ʿAṭṭār (Muḥammad b. Ḥusayn al-Ḥanafī, died 1827/1243). He had known Ḥasan al-ʿAṭṭār from Istanbul as well as from Damascus. In his commentary on al-ʿAṭṭār's essay on anatomy, he included a biographical fragment on his teacher which has previously been mentioned. In this biography, he stated that Ḥasan al-ʿAṭṭār had asked him to write this commentary; later, in Damascus, Ḥasan al-ʿAṭṭār was also to write a commentary on his own text. Muḥammad al-ʿAṭṭār, as did Ḥasan al-ʿAṭṭār, studied the natural sciences and medicine in Istanbul. Ḥasan al-ʿAṭṭār assisted him in writing a commentary on a text in medicine. Muḥammad al-ʿAṭṭār assisted Ḥasan al-ʿAṭṭār in his writing and teaching of *ādāb al-baḥth*, and loaned him several books to help him understand the Walādīya text. Muḥammad al-ʿAṭṭār, whose main reputation was in the natural sciences, as will be discussed in Chapter 8, had one student in the natural sciences who was quite well known. His name was ʿAbdullah Efendī al-Asṭuwānī (died 1845/1262), called al-Fālakī.[35]

While Muḥammad al-ʿAṭṭār studied medicine and science, Ḥasan al-Bayṭār al-Naqshbandī (died 1865/1282), Ḥasan al-ʿAṭṭār's other principal student, studied *fiqh* and the legal sciences. Ḥasan al-ʿAṭṭār was described as being a father and spiritual guide to him. He gave him much of his time. He even taught him *ḥadīth*. It was at this point that al-ʿAṭṭār, far from Egypt, wrote his only work (which has not been located) on *ḥadīth*, "Ḥāshiyat al-nukhba fī ʿulūm al-ḥadīth," drawn from the Imām Ibn al-Ṣalāḥ (perhaps from his *Muqaddima*). Al-ʿAṭṭār also taught him *fiqh*, a field in which he made such rapid progress that he was sought after to perform public functions before he had reached the age of thirty. Al-Bayṭār, like al-ʿAṭṭār, had important connections in Istanbul. In later years he was a friend of Şeyh ul-Islām Arif Hikmet Bey, with whom he shared an interest in *ḥadīth* and *tafsīr*. It was perhaps not a coincidence that his Shaykh al-Islām had been Ḥasan al-ʿAṭṭār's student in Egypt during the 1820's, when he was then the Ottoman Qāḍī in Egypt. Al-Bayṭār, too, had students in *fiqh*, among them a Shādhilī Ṣūfī named Saʿīd al-Khālidī (died 1877/1294), who traveled in Azerbaijan.[36]

While in Turkey, al-ʿAṭṭār had decided to go to Damascus in order to meet the Khalwatī Ṣūfī Shaykh al-ʿĀrif biʾllah al-Shaykh ʿUmar al-Yāfī, who was deeply versed in the study of Ibn al-ʿArabī. When al-ʿAṭṭār arrived in Damascus, it was al-Yāfī who wrote in praise of al-ʿAṭṭār's essay against the *Ṭarīqa muḥammadīya*.[37] Al-Yāfī, as it turned out, was a specialist in literature. His interests in Ibn al-ʿArabī were at least partly literary. He himself wrote wine poetry and *muwashshaḥāt*. Al-Yāfī was a disciple of a person who was well known in Egypt, Muṣṭafā al-Bakrī, founder of the Bakrīya. This social link, combined with an interest in literature, made him naturally a person to whom al-ʿAṭṭār might gravitate. Al-Yāfī had a number of students and close associates who formed a circle in Damascus at the beginning of the nineteenth century. A limited amount of information makes it possible to reconstruct this circle. His most devoted follower, and his inseparable companion, was Shaykh Muṣṭafā Zayn al-dīn al-Ḥimṣī, a musician as well as a student of poetry and history. Al-Ḥimṣī traveled with his *shaykh*, al-Yāfī, to Istanbul. Shaykh al-Ḥimṣī was a friend of an Ottoman *wazīr* named Abdullah Pasha. Through his good offices, it was possible for the two of them to meet Sultan Abd ul-Aziz, who honored them. A second student of al-Yāfī was ʿUmar al-Mujtāhid b. Shaykh Aḥmad al-Midānī. He became a Khalwatī from al-Yāfī and then a Naqshbandī from Khālid. He also studied with al-ʿAṭṭār's student Ḥasan al-Bayṭār, and was known for his piety.[38] A Khalwatī *shaykh* bearing the name Ṣāliḥ al-Yāfī lived in the same *madrasa* in Damascus as Ḥasan al-ʿAṭṭār. He wrote numerous works and had students. What his relationship to ʿUmar al-Yāfī or al-ʿAṭṭār may have been is not known.[39]

The main influence of al-Yāfī was obviously literary, if one is to judge from al-ʿAṭṭār's achievements while in Damascus. First, while in Damascus, al-ʿAṭṭār edited the *Dīwān* of Ibn Sahl. He also composed some original poetry which is lost; some of this was wine poetry, some *muwashshaḥāt*, like the poetry of his teacher and like that of Ibn Sahl. When he referred to Ibn al-ʿArabī, he referred to the latter's poetry in *Sharḥ turjumān al-ashwāq*, not to theology.[40]

Damascus was not reputed to have been a center of the rational sciences or medicine in the eighteenth century.[41] In general, it can be stated that, since Damascus was a center for mystical studies (while those Syrians who were interested in the study of physical medicine generally gravitated toward Istanbul), it would have been a very inhospitable atmosphere for the findings of Western medicine which interested al-ʿAṭṭār. Yet, al-ʿAṭṭār had many students there in his courses on anatomy, among them one *shaykh* who became a leading doctor in Syria. Al-ʿAṭṭār was not the only teacher of medicine. There was also Shaykh Ibrāhīm al-Khulāṣī (died 1840/1255), who was described as a specialist on the pulse and eyeballs and had written a book on these subjects. This may account for al-ʿAṭṭār's reticence on the subject of the pulse.[42] Shaykh Ibrāhīm, his brother Ṭālib (died 1877/1294), and ʿAbd al-Qādir al-Khulāṣī (died 1868/1282) were all from a family in Aleppo which produced a number of famous doctors.[43] Ḥasan al-ʿAṭṭār's student ʿAbd al-Qādir was also the student of his father, Ibrāhīm. A medical diploma from Ḥasan al-ʿAṭṭār to ʿAbd al-Qādir still exists.[44] Al-ʿAṭṭār also helped his friend and student Muḥammad al-ʿAṭṭār write a commentary on the *Qānūnjā* of al-Jaghmīnī. According to his son, he wrote other works as well, but these have not been located. It is clear from al-ʿAṭṭār's main work that, as long as he taught in the holistic framework of Ibn Sīnā, he did not have to agree with him, even in Damascus, just so he was tactful.

A study of the social history of Istanbul and Damascus clarifies a point of considerable importance to Egyptian intellectual history, the fate of the Ṣūfī intellectuals. In Egypt, they declined with the suppression of merchant capital. It is difficult, especially in the Muḥammad ʿAlī period, to find their views expressed. In Turkey, the conservative orders were secure members of the state bureaucracy. A comparison is thus possible between the Naqshbandī and Khalwatī Ṣūfīs of the early nineteenth century, bureaucrat versus merchant. In Istanbul, Ṣūfīs worked in the state bureaucracy and appeared to lose contact with experiential mysticism. They suffered a fragmentation in thought. This did not happen to Ṣūfīs of these same orders who lived and worked in Damascus. The "experiential" Ṣūfism was possible only as an opposition force in modern Turkey and Egypt; and as such it has played an important role, especially in the twentieth century.

A number of Ottomans came to Egypt and helped Muḥammad ʿAlī carry out his reforms. From a survey of the social history of Turkey, it is striking to find that reformists in Turkey encountered many frustrations. In fact Egypt could appear to certain Turks, as it later did to Saint-Simonians, as a place for a fresh start. The dominant state commercial sectors of Turkey and Egypt, post-1815, contained a number of similarities which permitted Ottomans to move easily from Turkey to Egypt. The life and writings of Ḥasan al-ʿAṭṭār during his formative years in Istanbul offer striking evidence of these trends.

By this, I am suggesting that the study of the individual has a larger significance which justifies the attention to biographical detail. How do the countries of the periphery restructure themselves as the world market continues to evolve? Clearly they do not have a structure which would simultaneously permit divergent cultural trends. This leaves travel and foreign education as a very important avenue of change. Al-ʿAṭṭār's early life shows alienation with the conditions prevailing in Egypt during his youth. His travel to Istanbul and his association with the intellectual elite during the period of his study of rational sciences were obviously part of a very common pattern for intellectuals from the Ottoman provinces. His subsequent efforts to integrate the new knowledge into a holistic framework in Damascus was also quite common, as I will show in Chapter 9. Damascus represents for al-ʿAṭṭār a parting of the ways with his own past. He takes his last steps in late Andalusian literature and gradually abandons it for fields more congruent with the new, more hierarchically organized, pragmatically oriented age of reformism. The travels of al-ʿAṭṭār draw attention to a point which heretofore has not been stressed in scholarly writings, notably that a de facto division of labor in culture existed among the principal centers of the Ottoman Empire in the eighteenth and early nineteenth centuries. Travel in this context was the norm for the scholar; the study of cultural development in any one center must take cognizance of this larger totality. The importance of travel for intellectuals in the periphery is suggested already in a main argument of the second chapter of this work, where I argue that later Sunnī societies are rooted in a single modality of logic embodied in a single prominent root of Islamic jurisprudence at any one given time. Where one finds in the industrial heartlands the seeds of an opposition culture emerging and presaging social change within the framework of national culture, transitions in the periphery from one social formation to another, from one cultural pattern to another, do not have this attribute. The inorganic character of this change no doubt presents opportunities to groups possessed of certain traits of flexibility, traits shared particularly by the minorities of the Mediterranean. The biographical details of al-ʿAṭṭār's adjustment to the new age are not full enough for me to show that he redeveloped a very profound aesthetic. In the ninth chapter there is a discussion of science and music. Al-ʿAṭṭār, writing as a bureaucrat in the reform movement, states that music is dangerous, as it appeals to the passions. Perhaps music is not wholly bad, for its use is sometimes necessary in order to inspire soldiers in battle.

Chapter 6
The Muḥammad ʿAlī Period, 1815–1837: State Commercial Sector and the Second Phase of the Cultural Awakening in Egypt

This chapter continues the analysis begun in Chapter 1 of the socioeconomic formation which characterized the Muḥammad ʿAlī period, a formation dominated by a state commercial sector. This represented a precapitalist formation which was a transitional stage in Egypt's integration into the world market as a peripheral capitalist formation. During this phase, precapitalist and peripheral capitalist elements interpenetrated. The state was chief employer and paid cash wages: high wages to factory workers and students in the missions, and low wages to workers in the agricultural sector. Wage labor predominated throughout the economy, which was buffered by state policy from the direct impact of the world market. On the other hand, the major state projects relied on precapitalist relations of production, for example, the corvée, which was a throwback to the *wajba* of Ottoman times. Likewise, in industry the social relations of work corresponded more to the craft world than to the world of industry at the center of the world market. As the upper classes assimilated the technical progress of Europe, they became increasingly dependent on Europe. Revolutionary technology did not accompany the rise of a new class but prodded the evolution of an old one.

The regime's official ideology reflected these realities. The ruler appealed to his subjects, who were neither citizens of a nation-state nor members of a medieval millet, through the *ʿulamāʾ* chosen to speak for the regime. Medieval religious and cultural forms were followed when exhorting the draftees in the army, or to warn society at large of the dangers of the powerful Sānūsīya confraternity (which opposed the capitalist transformation), because these forms still adequately corresponded to social reality for the majority of the population. Ḥasan al-ʿAṭṭār was the most prominent example in the early bureaucratic period of an *ʿālim* who served the new regime and helped to forge its institutions and cultural direction. It is therefore appropriate to conclude the chapter with a section on his activities and those of his associates during this period.

The most important innovations in cultural life of the reform period were the new schools, the missions, the translation movement, and the corps of European technical advisers. These developments have not been sufficiently studied in terms of their contribution to the existing cultural life of Egypt. In order to understand this period in indigenous Egyptian terms, it is necessary to begin with an analysis of its religious framework, for this continued to be the primary framework of thought and culture for all classes. To these two points of reference, Europe and Islam, should be added the rise of the Arabic language as a rival to Turkish as the language of the ruling class.

I shall begin with a brief discussion of religion and culture as an introduction to the work of reformers, such as Ḥasan al-ʿAṭṭār, during the period from 1815 to 1837. In succeeding chapters I shall deal with jurisprudence, language sciences, literature, and the natural sciences in much greater depth.

The breakdown of the *ḥadīth* movement of the eighteenth century and its replacement by *fiqh* and *kalām*, which were revived during this particular historical period, encouraged the development of the rational sciences and a logical-deductive approach to all fields of learning in general. The reasons for this revival derive from economic development, as Egyptian merchant capitalism yielded to a state mercantile sector. The emergence of a dominant state capitalist sector necessitated a commitment to the explicit articulation of the law and, hence, a commitment to the study of theology. The theology which emerged was Māturīdite. It was built on rationalist tendencies which existed during the later eighteenth century and have already been discussed in the second chapter, but it took these tendencies much further than did earlier writers, such as al-Zabīdī, in response to changing social realities. In the eighteenth century, mechanisms of control were reinforced by religious culture and presupposed a degree of shared values which corresponded to the norms of the corporate age. During the reform period, law no longer functioned as the authoritative evocation of a moral image; it had to command an earthly loyalty, an obedience which it could not depend on without recourse to coercion; hence, the emphasis on *kalām*. Muḥammad ʿAlī himself, of course, tried, as I have shown in chapter one, to wear the mantle of religion, that is, to blur the fundamental social changes; but with the emergence of class relations, the traditional social bonds dissolved and, with that, the whole nature of authority and legitimacy changed.

While there had been *qāḍīs* in eighteenth-century Egypt, they had represented a system whose legitimacy was on the wane. In practice, order was maintained by the dominant class. In the reform period, there was an explicit institutionalization of authority, and the regime required official spokesmen, such as Ḥasan al-ʿAṭṭār, for its legitimacy. *Fiqh* became the basis of the culture of the ruling class, a culture which was permeated by the logical-deductive outlook which originated in its theology. In opposition to the culture of the ruling class was the culture of the depressed middle classes and artisans, based on *ḥadīth* and the popular Ṣūfī culture.

In the eighteenth century, the elite Ṣūfī orders represented the dominant Muslim elite culture. The ruling Mamlūks had become partially fused with certain segments of the middle classes, so that all the groups involved in the commercial revival were represented in the *ṭuruq*. In the reform period, as I have already shown, the division between the ruling class and the indigenous middle class was the fundamental cleavage in the society. The importance of the popular culture lay only in its relation to the middle class, and it scarcely touched the elite at all. Thus, for the reform period, I shall concentrate on the culture of the ruling class. After 1830, the economic basis of the ruling class was weakened, and the Egyptian middle classes made a limited revival. This fact probably explains the resurgence of *ḥadīth* after the death of Ḥasan al-ʿAṭṭār.

The first impression one might receive after surveying the cultural and religious writings from 1815 to 1837 is that the shift to an emphasis on *kalām* and the methods of the rational sciences greatly broadened and deepened the possibilities inherent in the neoclassical revival. This was true in the case of a small number of intellectuals, such as al-ʿAṭṭār, who consistently enjoyed the patronage of the authorities. But one cannot escape the fact that the number of books written during this period was very modest by comparison to that of the eighteenth century, and the literary production that did exist was more intensively channeled into fewer directions. It seems that the patronage that was available was administered far more rigidly than in the eighteenth century, and that this rigidity was in fact a benign manifestation of how the ruling class needed to function to adjust its production to the demands of the world market. The general pace of cultural life slowed, and there is no doubt that it deteriorated. Not only did no one produce a history on the scale of al-Jabartī's or a dictionary based on the scholarly learning of such a figure as al-Zabīdī, but also the general quality of textbooks declined. The fields of literature and philology in particular suffered severe dislocation, despite the efforts of al-ʿAṭṭār and others to keep on teaching these subjects in the spirit of the eighteenth-century *majlis* and to prevent the emergence of a debased court culture.

The Arabic language suddenly became necessary for running the state. The use of Ottoman Turkish as the language of administration and government, which had been the practice for three hundred years, was largely abandoned in the space of a few years. The ethnic cleavage on which the use of Ottoman was based, and which was beginning to give way in the eighteenth century, gave way to a class cleavage. Arabic developed with incredible rapidity, but it did not develop freely or organically. Its development, like that of theology, was conditioned by the needs of the ruling class. The chief centers for literary production under the regime of Muḥammad ʿAlī were journalism and the press. This had the effect of flooding the language with neologisms and transliterated terms, while no corresponding development either in the rules of language or in style (philology and literature) took place. Certain problems had to be solved quickly, while others were ignored. When the students returned from their mission in Europe, they could not translate their new knowledge into a suitable form of Arabic. It required Arabic literary editors to make their efforts comprehensible and precise. Analogous problems existed in journalism. In the two areas of professional and literary editing, there existed the necessary institutional basis, however limited, for a continued pursuit of Arabic studies, and talented figures in Arabic philology and literature were drawn to it. This work was extremely demanding, for it required a vast knowledge of terms in medieval technical fields, a capacity for linguistic innovation, and a sense of style and presentation, if need be, of unfamiliar subjects. Ḥasan al-ʿAṭṭār was the leading figure in this group until 1830. In studying this period of his life, one gains a deep insight into the second phase of the indigenous cultural revival.

The New State Commercial Sector, 1815–1837

After the destruction of the Mamlūks, the new upper class was comprised of those groups whose services and loyalties Muḥammad ʿAlī's Turco-Albanian bureaucratic elite could depend on. These were groups which opposed the Egyptian middle classes. In fact, the principal dialectic in Egyptian history from the rise of Muḥammad ʿAlī in 1805 to 1815 and even afterward was Muḥammad ʿAlī's relationship with the indigenous middle classes which had brought him to power. When Muḥammad ʿAlī reconquered the Delta and the Ṣaʿīd, and eliminated both the Mamlūks and the Albanian soldiery from the scene, he was able to turn directly against the middle classes and expropriate their wealth. But prior to this there were many signs of an impending collision. The crisis which precipitated this collision was the prolonged and indecisive Wahhābī war, which drained Egypt and weakened Muḥammad ʿAlī. Muḥammad ʿAlī was of course unable to refuse the Ottoman demand that he prosecute this war, but at the same time he was unsure of the loyalty of the home front. Thus, for both economic and political reasons Muḥammad ʿAlī took direct control of the country's agricultural production in 1815. Government financing of agriculture had important social consequences, for it eliminated the role of the local merchant as financier.[1] This was particularly important in the Delta, which produced many raw materials and was the most important agricultural area in the country. Muḥammad ʿAlī virtually tried to replace the Egyptian Delta merchants with government officials and foreign merchants[2] whom he selected. This lower officialdom was drawn from a class traditionally antagonistic to the merchants: the village *shaykhs.*

The composition of the ruling class between 1815 and 1837 has been described in most historical studies in terms of ethnic cliques. The groups considered to have been the most powerful changed every few years. It would seem that, despite the array of different ethnicities which had some power in the government, the general policy of the government was altered more as a consequence of material constraints than by considerations of ethnic solidarity of any given clique. Hence, it would seem that whether Muḥammad ʿAlī favored his "old lions," the Albanians, who had been with him from his days in the Boyük (soldier band), or the "Moreates," who came later, policy changes did not emanate from this fact alone.[3]

A key characteristic of this period was that the ruling class retained power by avoiding a direct confrontation with the Europeans, a mistake which cost the Mamlūks dearly. It did so by making concessions and by playing one power against another. The institutional structure imposed by the ruling class was dictated by the general contours of the society, a society composed of a depressed middle class and a large peasantry. The large new bureaucracy reflected the efforts of the small ruling class to mobilize the society, structured as it was to extract the greatest possible wealth from the peasantry. Changes were introduced selectively so as to preserve the general structure of the society; it was only as a result of lack of alternatives that in the 1830's the government was obliged to promote many more Egyptians within the structure to promote necessary efficiency.

Some studies of this period have devoted considerable attention to the monarchical form of the ruling class, insisting that the important decisions were made by the ruling family. Indeed, Muḥammad ʿAlī and his son Ibrāhīm, and certain trusted military men, held the highest ranks and gradually amassed large landholdings. But this group did not possess technical skills. They were largely bypassed in military affairs by junior technical officers, and in civilian affairs (at least, during the period from 1819 to 1837) for the same reason. They do not stand out as having had a monopoly of effective power. One is led to suppose, thus, that the wealth which they received was not absolutely indicative of their capacity to influence the course of events in the society.

A more accurate picture of the ruling class which had emerged by 1830 would thus include the family of Muḥammad ʿAlī, the Turkish and Albanian commanders, foreign technocrats, and representatives of the new Chamber of Commerce.[4] The continuing necessity to increase state revenues forced the government to attempt to increase agricultural productivity. This involved the regime in agrarian problems, the solution of which necessitated an expansion of the bureaucracy and an inclusion of a larger number of Egyptians in it. The formation of the Council (Majlis al-Mashūra) in 1829, which was made up largely of Egyptians, is frequently pointed to as a counterweight to Turks and foreigners. One might note, however, that no evidence has been given to support the view that its behavior in any way justified such a claim. It was composed of 146 members who served the government as consultants: 23 high functionaries and *ʿulamāʾ*, 99 notables and *shaykhs* from the provinces, and 24 *maʾmūrs* (administrators) of the provinces. The vast majority thus came from the village *shaykhs* or notables, a group which was among the earliest supporters of the regime of Muḥammad ʿAlī. Perhaps one should argue that for the most part this assembly was "anti-Egyptian," because it brought together the forces in the society which exploited the peasantry and blocked the growth of the Egyptian middle class.[5]

The final phase which the ruling class underwent in the reform period was its own transformation from a bureaucratic class into the beginnings of a large landholding class. The land was still theoretically owned by the state. After 1837, however, it could be willed to one's heirs, not as private property but as the right to the wealth from the land which was still nominally the possession of the state. What had happened to permit this is well known: Muḥammad ʿAlī suffered defeats as the Europeans rapidly expanded in Syria and other areas. The central government had grown weaker. As a consequence, the bureaucracy could no longer attempt industrialization, and it even ceased to provide an efficient managerial arrangement for an agricultural economy. For the period had seen a rapid development of a financial system which could provide for agricultural credit and further improvements in agricultural technology, at the same time permitting a considerable degree of decentralization.[6] The breakdown of the bureaucracy meant the breakdown of the cultural movements which the bureaucracy represented in the assimilation of foreign knowledge and the neoclassical revival. A third phase reached its culmination a generation later under the bureaucratic regime of Ismaʿīl.

The Old Middle Classes

The socioeconomic situation of the old middle classes in the reform period remains unstudied, and what has generally been stated about the situation of either the Egyptian merchants or the *ʿulamāʾ* as a whole is based on very few examples. The contemporary European writers had few contacts and were much less interested in these groups than in the government itself. A small amount of information is to be found on the merchant elite which had grown out of this class because it was actually a part of the government.[7] For example, one can learn that the president of the Chamber of Commerce in Cairo in 1833 was Aḥmad al-Gharbī and that his brother Muḥammad was also a Cairo merchant; also, that this family maintained close ties with the Maghrib and its politics and that Aḥmad had loaned money to various persons there.[8] The Maghribī merchants invested by proxy in the Indian trade route to Jidda through the main merchants in Jidda, who in 1830 were two Maghāriba named al-Jaylānī and al-Saqqāṭ. These merchants apparently accepted investment from the Cairo Maghāriba but not from the Syrian merchants in Cairo. They were also heavily involved in the coffee trade, although they did not sell to Egypt because Muḥammad ʿAlī's blockade was still strong enough for him to resist West Indian coffee and to buy Yamanī coffee instead.[9] But apart from a few references to this elite, no clear picture of the merchants can be drawn from the published sources, foreign or indigenous, for the reform period except for those in the Sudan trade.[10]

The other main component of the urban middle classes, notably the *ʿulamāʾ*, has been frequently discussed. The Egyptian *ʿulamāʾ* have recently been contrasted with their contemporaries, the Turkish *ʿulamāʾ*, on the issue of reform. The Turks supported reform whereas the Egyptians did not. The reasons which are given for this difference vary. One is that Muḥammad ʿAlī ignored al-Azhar and ruled around it rather than reforming it from within. He honored the *ʿulamāʾ* but never gave them any effective power.[11]

This view is correct, but the reasons why the *ʿulamāʾ* chose not to support Muḥammad ʿAlī from the beginning and why he opposed them need a deeper analysis.

From what is known about the *ʿulamāʾ* in the eighteenth century and the early nineteenth century, it seems that they had deep-rooted relationships with the world of commerce and the guilds. A few of the most wealthy held *iltizāms.* When the government took control of trade, removing it from the hands of the merchants, and when it placed a new administrative structure in control of the guilds, it was striking at the heart of the economic world of the majority of the *ʿulamāʾ*. Some *ʿulamāʾ* were themselves merchants, involved with the guilds. Many derived their income from serving as *nuẓẓār* of the *awqāf* of religious buildings and institutions. When the ruling alliance took over the administration of these buildings, it deprived them of this source of wealth. Thus, there were objective grounds for the outright opposition of the *ʿulamāʾ* to the ruling alliance, their opposition to its policies being but the most visible expression of the opposition of the entire middle class.[12]

But if the ruling alliance could control the wealth of the *ʿulamāʾ*, why was it not able to break them entirely and force them to either emigrate or accept reform? One must conclude that, despite the inroads which it made in their wealth and power, it was not strong enough vis-à-vis these legitimizers of its authority to break their power completely. There was no strong external or internal threat, as in Istanbul, which forced the *ʿulamāʾ* to side with the rulers. The conscription policy of the new ruling class removed any internal threats from the lower classes, who could be transferred easily to foreign battlefields. Still, the ruling alliance had to listen to the "complaints" of these *ʿulamāʾ* and go through the motions of extending certain honors to them. This would seem to reflect a power relationship in which, although it had the upper hand, it could not do without the *ʿulamāʾ*.

Muḥammad ʿAlī appointed a number of *shaykhs* to the key position of Rector, or Shaykh, of al-Azhar. It has been observed that for the most part they were either too old or too weak to organize effective opposition to Muḥammad ʿAlī, even if they were so disposed. No inquiry has been made, however, as to what was their probable attitude toward Muḥammad ʿAlī and the new regime. While I have no direct evidence, there is considerable indirect evidence from literary sources. All those who were chosen, with the exception of Ḥasan al-ʿAṭṭār, grew up in the circles of *ḥadīth* study of the late eighteenth and early nineteenth centuries. They had thus spent their lives among persons who later opposed Muḥammad ʿAlī. Muḥammad ʿAlī was aware of the futility of attempting to co-opt them and merely sought to neutralize their opposition. He permitted the *shaykhs* to choose elderly men, whose death in any case made for a large turnover.

Only Ḥasan al-ʿAṭṭār tried to function as one of Muḥammad ʿAlī's "men," and this was at the height of the regime's power. Even then Muḥammad ʿAlī did not make the appointment until 1831.[13] As will be shown below, the *shaykhs* ganged up on al-ʿAṭṭār, and his period as rector, until his death in 1835, was singularly unproductive as well as personally uncomfortable.

In 1838, Shaykh Ibrāhīm al-Bājūrī came to power as rector as the result of an explicit compromise. He had made a written promise to al-Bakrī that he would keep out of Ṣūfī affairs and that he would not act in matters concerning al-Azhar without first conferring with the other *ʿulamāʾ*. This shows clearly enough that the power of the *ʿulamāʾ* vis-à-vis the government had slightly increased.[14]

Returning to the "complaints" of the *ʿulamāʾ* to which Muḥammad ʿAlī listened, one can find a number which have a fairly clear relationship to social and economic cleavages. In 1822, some *ʿulamāʾ* opposed the building of a hospital in Alexandria by the French at the Couvent de Pères de la Terre Sainte, citing a law which forbade the enlargement of monasteries. Muḥammad ʿAlī intervened, financing the building of the hospital, insisting for the sake of the *ʿulamāʾ* that a wall be built between the hospital and the convent.

Opposition to foreign penetration in the Delta caused a series of incidents which were simultaneously communal and economic. The Zaghlūl mosque in Rosetta figured as a rallying point, and Rosetta was the scene of recurrent opposition to the Franciscan missionaries from the Vatican. The Delta was at the same time experiencing an intensive penetration of foreign capital. One suspects that the importance of the region to the new regime led Muḥammad ʿAlī to take steps to ensure his control. Muḥammad ʿAlī concentrated most of the new institutions in the Cairo area, but he chose to locate the School of Arts and Crafts, founded in 1831, in Rosetta. Earlier, the Veterinary School founded by P. N. Hamont was also located there.[15] At the same time that Muḥammad ʿAlī made concessions, he also strongly attacked those who opposed him. In his observations on Egypt, written about 1830, Edward Lane discussed the prominence and strength of the Disūqīya (Ṣūfī order), who were based in Rosetta. The *ʿulamāʾ* of Cairo "condemned" the practices of the Disūqīya as being contrary to Islam. At the same time, Muḥammad ʿAlī went out of his way to mention his support for the Naqshbandīya, a conservative and Sharīʿa-minded order which numbered among its ranks some of the high state officials.[16]

In general, contemporaries of the reform era emphasize the relative poverty of the *shaykhs* and how few among the names from the eighteenth-century *shaykhs* seem to appear in the nineteenth century. This shows how a profession which had been largely passed from father to son was changing. Edward Lane tells in quite vivid detail of the economic straits of the *shaykhs*, which is confirmed by other sources.[17]

The *ʿulamāʾ* were quite successful in making "religious" demands on Muḥammad ʿAlī, that is, demands in which class conflict was not so obvious. One study based on the Turkish archival sources lists a number of cases in which Muḥammad ʿAlī was obliged to eliminate or diminish the power of certain persons who annoyed the *ʿulamāʾ*; cases in which he granted the *ʿulamāʾ* tax concessions or customs exemptions on their goods; and cases in which he facilitated the Pilgrimage, gave money to support poor *shaykhs*, and gave special money to support Turkish *ʿulamāʾ*. Naturally, these were not altruistic gestures; he hoped to gain support by making them. But this fact alone makes it clear that the *ʿulamāʾ* were still a force to be reckoned with and that they could not be easily bypassed.[18]

Another approach to an estimation of the relative strength of the Egyptian middle classes lies in a consideration of the more Sharīʿa-minded Ṣūfī confraternities. It is generally accepted that the government of Muḥammad ʿAlī attempted to dominate the *ṭuruq* as much as possible thru the office of the Shaykh Mashāyikh al-Ṭuruq; nonetheless, the Ṣūfī orders continued somewhat independently.[19] Rapid expansion of different branches and offshoots of the Khalwatīya continued uninterruptedly during the first half of the nineteenth century. Branches of the order reached the Maghrib, the Sudan, and, after the Wahhābī wars, the Ḥijāz. These branches in time became separate orders, clearly independent of Egypt. The paths they followed were the traditional trade routes, and the *zāwiyas* were established in trade centers. There is no doubt that the moving force behind this spread was the merchants, whose conservative religious doctrine had some degree of support from various local rulers.[20] Independent movements led by merchants in Egypt were suppressed ruthlessly.[21]

In Egypt itself, the two national shrine cults which had played a central role in the cultural revival of the eighteenth century, the Khalwatīya Bakrīya and the Sādāt al-Wafāʾīya, exercised a degree of influence in the first half of the nineteenth century, although organizationally they were in a state of decline. In the circles of the Wafāʾīya, the name of Muḥammad Abī Anwār continued to be cherished by the bellelettrists. His name was repeatedly mentioned in their poetry, and the cultural tradition of the Fāṭimids and of Persia was still occasionally referred to in their writings. In the reform period, Wafāʾī members, because of their knowledge of language and literature, gained most of the few important jobs which were open to Egyptians (see below). Through the influence of Ḥasan al-ʿAṭṭār, some worked on the official newspaper, *Al-Waqāʾiʿ al-Miṣrīya*,[22] in the Būlāq Press, and in the correction of translations. At least one of their group did literary translations, Shaykh al-Ṭahṭāwī. However, comparatively little is known, and this is important, about the persons who became Shaykh al-Sijāda and who kept the order functioning. After Muḥammad Abī Anwār, one family dominated the order for three generations, and of these three generations, the grandson seemed to have been the only important personality. Of the first generation, Shaykh Sayyid al-Sādāt, little is recorded; his son was Aḥmad Abū al-Nāṣir b. Sayyid al-Sādāt, known as Abū Iqbāl. The grandson was ʿAbd al-Khāliq al-Sādāt, known as Abūʾl-Futūḥāt, who was born in 1848/1263. ʿAbd al-Khāliq studied in the Amīrīya Madrasa, where Shaykh Muḥammad ʿIyād al-Ṭanṭāwī was *nāẓir*. The subjects which he studied included Turkish, Arabic grammar, handwriting, and arithmetic. He then entered al-Azhar and studied with Ibrāhīm al-Saqqāʾ. The relative breakdown in *silsila* literature, which told of the series of links from the life of one Shaykh al-Sijāda to the next, does not mask the vitality and importance of the Wafāʾīya as an institution, at least during the period of Muḥammad ʿAlī. One can still, however, conclude from the available evidence that the Wafāʾīya existed as a coherently functioning institution of the indigenous middle class, dependent of course on the wider patronage of a society which sympathized with its neoclassical outlook. Lane mentioned that it was customary to find, among the funeral processions of the wealthy, people reciting the Qurʾān and the traditional poem *Burda*, followed by four or more orders, each chanting one of its characteristic prayers. He mentioned in particular the Shādhilīya, the Wafāʾīya, and the Shaʿrāwī. This was in the 1830's.[23]

The older Bakrīya (there was no longer a reform movement) in the first half of the nineteenth century continued to be quite wealthy. A number of new suborders branched away from it and became independent. In Egypt the position of the main order was guaranteed by a special relationship to Muḥammad ʿAlī. He had delegated to members of the order, on a permanent basis, the position of Naqīb al-Ashrāf, charging them with carrying out such annual celebrations as the Mawlid al-Nabī, which honored the Prophet's birthday. Sayyid ʿAlī Efendī al-Bakrī al-Ṣiddīqī became Shaykh al-Sijāda after his father. In 1854–55/1271, he was known to have been on intimate terms with the Khedive Ismaʿīl and urged him to avoid the penetration of foreign capital.[24]

In conclusion, it would seem that the continuity and the relative importance of the Sharīʿa-minded Ṣūfī orders in Egypt and their capacity for growth and expansion out from Egypt, especially along the trade routes, indicate the continuing strength of the middle classes under Muḥammad ʿAlī. Muḥammad ʿAlī may have given bequests, but he is not known to have "promoted" Ṣūfism. The middle class, composed of both merchants and *ʿulamāʾ*, could be co-opted individually by Muḥammad ʿAlī for certain rewards, but the majority could not be moved, despite the offers of honors and presents. This, too, is a clue to their relative strength. The conflict between the two classes carried over into every sphere of life. In religion, the middle classes supported the continuation of *ḥadīth* studies in the context of the Ṣūfī orders. The upper classes had meanwhile turned to *kalām*, and their lives revolved around the new institutions. In the cultural sphere, the conflict took the form of the issue of upper-class reform versus middle-class revival, with a small group seeking to bridge this cleavage.

The Lower Classes

In the absence of any socioeconomic study of the middle classes of Egypt, and with no correct information available on the way in which the local economies of Cairo and Alexandria were changing during the period of Muḥammad ʿAlī, a study of the lower classes is all the more difficult. According to a recent study, the basic monopoly system which characterized the commercial sector was created during the years 1816–1818. The "national" industries, a major employer of the urban lower classes, began with an artisanal form of production, with the government supplying the raw materials and taking the finished product. The office of market inspector, or *muḥtasib*, rose in importance, and some *muḥtasibūn* became known as tyrants. An anecdote is told by Lane about one inspector of cloth named ʿAlī Bey who used to burn artisans who were caught selling their own linen or possessing a loom of their own.[25] The uprooting of the poorer craftsmen who lost this means of supplementing their income facilitated their induction into the state factories. One is in some ways reminded of the enclosure acts in England which helped to create an industrial proletariat. But in Egypt industrial revolution was hampered by the lack of essential raw materials, such as iron and coal, and by the lack of adequate sources of power. Furthermore, the rate of industrialization in Europe at this time was much greater than in Egypt; the pressure of cheap European machine goods prevented a fuller transformation of the lower classes in Egypt. The uprooting which had led either into the armies or into the factories came to a standstill with the decline of these institutions; the traditional modes of production continued. Nevertheless, during the height of the factory system, a situation resembling that of England in the time of the Luddites emerged. The pre-industrial lower classes demonstrated the limits to which traditional governmental coercive devices could be used in a modern work situation.[26] Contemporary observers reported many unexplained explosions and other acts of industrial sabotage. And Lane, for example, noted that the urban crime rate rose noticeably between his two visits in 1820 and 1833.[27]

The application of the corvée to the problems of the creation of an army meant the breaking up of families and the uprooting of many members of society. The army also grew very rapidly from 16,000 in 1821 to 62,150 in 1829, then to 83,000 in 1832, 100,000 in 1833, and finally 157,000 in 1838. Numerous accounts of resistance to conscription are reported, especially of peasants who mutilated themselves. Reports, especially from the countryside, of revolts are mentioned; for example, in Sharqīya province, there were five separate revolts in fifteen years. There was, however, little opportunity for revolts in the army itself. The officer corps, which was highly paid, was ethnically and to a degree linguistically separated from the troops. Thus the officers, whether high or low, were not likely to provide the leadership for any revolt. But in the one important "near mutiny" which followed the failure of the siege of Acre in March 1832, those who were hung included *ʿulamā*ʾ and some Turks.[28]

A number of accounts of the popular Ṣūfī orders which engaged in "radical and dangerous" practices can be found in this period. These orders appear to be the heirs of the Bayyūmīs of the eighteenth century, but they had taken a turn toward even greater extremism than had the Bayyūmīs, reflecting the more oppressive conditions under Muḥammad ʿAlī. The Bayyūmīs themselves were weakened during the reform period, and under the third *khalīfa*, Muḥammad Nāfiʿ, there occurred a split in the organization. The main segment seemed to broaden its base from among the Cairo water carriers to include Bedouins as far away as the Ḥijāz.[29] The main popular orders of the reform period were not those which had been significant in the eighteenth century; they clearly rose in importance during this period. The most important was the Rifāʿīya, a branch of which was called the ʿIlwānīya. They engaged in such practices as thrusting iron spikes through their bodies, eating live coals, and so forth. Members of another branch, the Saʿdīya, were known for their handling of poisonous snakes or riding horseback over their disciples. Some earned or probably supplemented their living by charming snakes out of people's houses. The second main order was the Qādirīya. They were described as being mostly fishermen. The third main order was the Aḥmadīya, the order of Sayyid Aḥmad al-Badawī. This last was centered in Ṭanṭā, in the Delta, although it had connections with the Bayyūmīs, the Shaʿrāwīs, and the Shinnāwīs. Another branch was the Awlād al-Nūḥ; it had young men who paraded with swords, beads, and whips. A third popular order was also centered in the Delta; it was a branch of the Disūqīya called the Burhāmīya. Lane offered the opinion that almost all Ṣūfīs, such as the Burhāmīya, were artisans or farmers, that the majority participated only occasionally, and that only beggars and the poor, that is, those without other occupation, were engaged fulltime.

The practices described above scandalized the *shaykhs* of al-Azhar and the rest of the middle and upper classes, and this led the government to sponsor a more controlled version of the Mawlid al-Nabī. The extreme orientation toward ecstasy and the desire for escape from this life which were acted out symbolically in the rituals of these orders suggest the increasing misery and the growing exploitation of the lower classes. The widening social gap of the late eighteenth century was apparently only a foreshadowing of the far worse conditions which were to come in the reform period. Under such circumstances, one might expect a saint to arise to lead the people. This occurred at least once and with fairly spectacular results. In 1824, Aḥmad Idrīs, a Maghribī merchant, emerged as a *mahdī*, a charismatic leader claiming divine inspiration, and enlisted thousands of Upper Egyptian peasants to join a brief rebellion. Rebellions guided by ideology were, however, very rare. In this the lower-class movements of the eighteenth century and those of the nineteenth century appear to differ. In the nineteenth century, the Ṣūfī orientation mentioned above toward an individual social catharsis predominated over an impulse toward the development of social doctrine, all of which points to the conclusion that, temporarily at least, resistance was not institutionalized in the Nile Valley. The opposite was the case in the hinterlands of Egypt, for example, Libya and the Sudan. To restate the main premises of this discussion of social structure: the view that the dynamics of this period can be understood mainly in terms of intrabureaucratic politics of the elite is challenged by the view that the upper bureaucrats were the political center of a relatively small and coherent ruling class which pitted itself against the indigenous merchant class of Egypt, the backbone of the eighteenth-century middle class. The bureaucracy was a traditional way to escape from dependence on this class; it bypassed it, using foreigners, minorities, and, on the local level, the village *shaykhs*. The middle classes underwent a relative decline; but they survived, as is indicated by the fact that the regime never felt strong enough to "reform" al-Azhar. Al-Azhar, in turn, never felt so seriously threatened as to turn against the ruling power and to side with the people, as a number of *shaykhs* had done in the eighteenth century, when grievances were by no means as great. Numerous expressions of discontent among the *ʿulamāʾ* were of course registered, but they apparently did not lead to any significant protest.

Numerous *ʿulamāʾ*, in fact, devoted themselves to writing conservative tracts in support of the government-sponsored *mawlids*. One is driven to try to find some explanation for middle-class quietism in the vast wealth of the government coming from the sale of cotton. Students could be drawn to the new schools, and *ʿulamāʾ* to the service of the regime, because of the large financial benefits involved. Thus, during the period of its peak, while the government could not transform the nature of the middle class, it could render its resistance harmless by buying off those whom it needed to neutralize. The policy of the regime toward the lower classes was far more brutal. Large-scale military ventures with high costs in human lives eliminated many of the enemies of the new order.

Ḥasan al-ʿAṭṭār and the New Cultural Structure

Al-ʿAṭṭār returned to Egypt in 1815 and quickly acquired renown in al-Azhar as a teacher. ʿAlī Mubārak stated that other *shaykhs* left their teaching to attend his public lectures and that he was particularly noted for his lectures on the *Tafsīr al-Bayḍāwī*. It is said that he astonished his audience by his method of presenting it.[30] The novelty which he represented (which was presumably an instant source of jealousy) was twofold. First was the method of teaching and second was the orientation which he gave to the subjects which he taught. Al-ʿAṭṭār as a teacher was a continuation, probably quite self-consciously so, of al-Zabīdī. Al-Zabīdī had presented texts and the supportive chains of *ḥadīth* evidence in their totality, moving from the recounting of them (*riwāya*) to their analysis (*dirāya*). Al-Zabīdī taught without recourse to formal logic. Al-ʿAṭṭār represented something of an advance in this respect in his application of formal logic in his teaching. His manner of presentation, given the composition of the student body and the orientation of the majority of the *shaykhs* toward the transmitted sciences, was brilliant but provocative. By the end of the 1820's, al-ʿAṭṭār was doing his most serious teaching informally at home, feeling constrained in al-Azhar, where, for reasons which I have already alluded to, he had not influenced the dominant religious orientation.

Al-ʿAṭṭār's public lectures were no doubt an important vehicle through which he established his reputation. While no lists exist of those who studied with him, a number of students have given his name as one of their teachers. There were doubtless a great many such students, if the reports which ʿAlī Mubārak received about his popularity as a teacher were correct. Among the names which have been located was Muḥammad al-Banānī al-Makkī, died 1831/1245. He became a Mālikī *muftī* in Mecca and was the author of a commentary on al-Bukhārī.[31] Al-ʿAṭṭār drew students from Syria as a consequence of his having taught there, and he drew Maghribī students because of his own ethnic background. One Syrian student was Sayyid Qāsim Daqqāq al-Duda, died 1845/1260. He studied with al-ʿAṭṭār around 1827/1242 and subsequently wrote a work on *al-mīqāt*.[32] A second Syrian student who studied with al-ʿAṭṭār shortly after his return to Egypt was Ḥusayn b. Ḥusayn b. Muḥammad al-Dimashqī al-Ḥanafī, died 1832/1247. He was a Ḥanafī *qāḍī* and spent a lifetime involved with different Ṣūfī orders, especially the Khalwatīya. He had been a disciple of Muṣṭafā al-Bakrī al-Ṣiddīqī in his youth and later studied with a Khalīfa of Aḥmad al-Ṣāwī, Shaykh Faṭhallah al-Mālikī.[33] Another student who studied with al-ʿAṭṭār was also known for his involvement in Ṣūfī orders, Yūsuf Badr al-dīn, died 1863/1278. He was a member of the Qādirīya order and at the same time was a student, possibly a disciple, of the Shaykh Ṭarīqat al-Shādhilīya, Bahāʾ al-dīn Muḥammad b. Aḥmad b. Yūsuf b. Aḥmad al-Bahī al-Murshīdī. He also studied with two Egyptian Ṣūfīs who were each Shaykh al-Azhar, al-Sharqāwī and al-Quwaysnī.[34]

These students were the norm. They were drawn from the culture of *ḥadīth* and mysticism of the suppressed middle classes. For them, al-Azhar was a supportive environment which reinforced their social and religious outlook; and their contacts with al-ʿAṭṭār did not alter this fact. In "withdrawing" to concentrate on teaching a handful of students at home, students whom he found receptive, al-ʿAṭṭār accepted this reality. His move in the 1820's foreshadowed the creation of the new schools, such as the school of languages (1836). It was impossible to train students to serve the needs of the new regime in al-Azhar because of the political situation. The students themselves, well trained in rote memorization and possessed of high language ability, could develop quite differently if removed to a setting other than al-Azhar, especially if they came from families without strong ties to the old Cairene middle classes. This accounts in a general way for the number of new names in this period. Al-ʿAṭṭār himself came from such a background, as did his principal students. After withdrawing to his home, al-ʿAṭṭār gave his students two types of instruction. One was the intellectual framework of the elite for those who had the talent and inclination to serve in the new cultural structure. This included, for all students, rational theology; logic; appreciation of a conservative, contemplative mysticism; and philology. For his closest students, he included other fields, such as history, geography, and Islamic science and medicine, transmitting to them a vision of the unity and relevance of Islamic civilization based on very broad scholarly foundations. In addition, al-ʿAṭṭār was able to introduce his students to members of the ruling class. Al-ʿAṭṭār's period of activity, in which he trained and placed his students as Arabic literary editors (from the 1820's to his death in 1835), coincided with the peak years of development of the reform period. The institutions of the later 1830's came after the crest had been reached.

In the context of his tutorials, al-ʿAṭṭār continued his study of Andalusian literature.[35] He used this to enhance his reputation in the Maghrib, following the example of his teacher Muḥammad al-Amīr. Among the literary relationships through which al-ʿAṭṭār sustained his study of Andalusian literature during the 1820's was one with the secretary to the ruler Mulay Sulaymān Mālik al-Maghrib. His name was Abū Ḥāmid al-ʿArabī b. Muḥammad al-Dumnātī al-Fāsī, died 1838/1253. Sometime before 1828, he made a trip to the Arab East and was a student of al-ʿAṭṭār while on his way to make the Pilgrimage, and their relationship continued after al-Dumnātī's return to Morocco.[36] "The great litterateur Sīdī al-ʿArabī al-Dumnātī al-Fāsī, the secretary to the Sultan of the Maghrib. He had sent me a copy of "Kitāb al-Rayḥānī" by Ibn al-Khaṭīb al-Andalūsī and other books. He had come to our land as he was making the Ḥijj. There took place between us a number of discussions and correspondence."[37] He also included a letter from him in which he requested an *ijāza.* He praised al-ʿAṭṭār in his letter for his concern with the scholastic sciences. In al-ʿAṭṭār's reply, he mentioned having taught al-Dumnātī lessons from the text *Al-Shifāʾ* of the Qāḍī ʿIyād in theology, among others. When al-ʿAṭṭār wrote his *Ḥāshiya ʿalā sharḥ al-Khabīṣī* on logic, he apparently sent al-Dumnātī a copy and received ecstatic praise from him in prose and poetry.[38]

Another focus of interest in classical Arabic literature also had a practical application which brought al-ʿAṭṭār into contact with some of the leading figures of the period. This was the prose genre of *al-inshāʾ*, or letter writing of an elegant type, which enjoyed a revival during this period among the bureaucratic elite.[39] Al-ʿAṭṭār dedicated his *Inshāʾ* to Muḥammad ʿAlī. He intended it to be of practical use to the ruling class as a guide for the secretaries and other bureaucrats of the new Jihādīya school, which he also praised. By 1827, the Būlāq Press, perhaps under al-ʿAṭṭār's influence, published a second *Inshāʾ*.[40] Al-ʿAṭṭār also taught *al-inshāʾ* to his students.[41]

Another figure with whom al-ʿAṭṭār came in contact as a result of his concern with language was a Turkish Şeyh ul-Islam, who was also a leading poet. Another was a leading bureaucrat in the government of Muḥammad ʿAlī. Both were interested in modernist reforms and at the same time in the neoclassical revival. Neither studied *ḥadīth.* The Ottoman Qadi to Egypt in the year 1823, and future Şeyh ul-Islam, was Arif Hikmet Bey, who played an important role in the cultural life of Turkey in the first half of the nineteenth century, as a poet and as Şeyh ul-Islam in Istanbul. He was born in 1786/1201 into a prominent family in Istanbul. His father, Ibrahim Ismet (died 1807), was a Naqshbandī Ṣūfī and the author of a number of books. Al-ʿAṭṭār may have met the family when he was in Istanbul, as Arif's father was well known at the time, although I have no evidence of this. Arif began as *muftī* and ended as Şeyh ul-Islam (1845–1854). He was a close friend of Cevdet Pasha but at the same time a critic of certain aspects of Tanzimat education policy. He was a Naqshbandī Ṣūfī, a student, and a good friend of al-ʿAṭṭār. Arif was also a poet, author of a well-known Dīwān.[42]

Another close friend of al-ʿAṭṭār and a leading figure in cultural reform was Abderrahman Sami Pasha, scion of a wealthy Moreate. His father had been a Khalwatī *murshid* and he, like his son, had had a long relationship with Muḥammad ʿAlī. Sami was born in 1795 and initiated into his mystical studies by his father along with another student and close friend, Mustafa Reshid, the future Tanzimat reformer. Sami left Morea in 1821 after the Greek uprisings, and returned during the campaign in 1824 as personal secretary to Ibrāhīm, son of Muḥammad ʿAlī. Thereafter he was named to head *Al-Waqāʾiʿ al-Miṣrīya* and then in 1831 to head the cabinet of Muḥammad ʿAlī, with a promotion to brigadier-general. Sami Bey was also in touch with the Saint-Simonians, and they thought highly of him. (The Saint-Simonians, of course, were something of a mystical movement.) Sami's main writings were in the area of mysticism and *al-ḥikma*.[43]

As a consequence of his friendship with Sami Bey, al-ʿAṭṭār was favorably presented to Muḥammad ʿAlī and received from him his two most important appointments, the editorship of the official gazette (*Al-Waqāʾiʿ al-Miṣrīya*) and then, two years later, the position of Shaykh al-Azhar. What factors sustained the relationship between al-ʿAṭṭār and Sami Bey and induced Sami Bey to help al-ʿAṭṭār cannot be fully known without extensive archival research. However, literary sources are helpful in pointing to a shared intellectual outlook between the two writers, both of whom were interested in science, *al-ḥikma*, and progress à la the Muḥammad ʿAlī regime. Al-ʿAṭṭār, like Sami, wrote several books on *al-ḥikma* during the 1820's (see below). *Al-Waqāʾiʿ al Miṣrīya*, in fact, reflected the interest in an intellectualized mysticism on the part of Sami, al-ʿAṭṭār, and Shihāb al-dīn.[44] The interests which they are known to have had in common make it difficult to sustain the general assumption that the Turkish version of the official gazette was conceived separately or that it was written first and the Arabic version merely followed it. There was, in fact, an underlying unity of outlook among the chief editors of both sections. In addition, most of them probably read Turkish and Arabic with ease. Thus the question of what influenced any particular piece of writing, be it in Turkish or in Arabic, is truly difficult to determine, although it deserves some attention.[45]

The interests which al-ʿAṭṭār shared with Sami Bey in *al-ḥikma*, a field which was devoted to questions of logic, natural science, and metaphysics, are further evidence that his close friends shared an intellectual orientation which differed markedly from that of the majority of his students at al-Azhar. Neoclassicism was the common basis. In sum, the writings of the reformer Sami Bey were philosophical and scientific; the writings of the reformer Arif Hikmet Bey, literary.

A study of al-ʿAṭṭār's career in the 1820's as a teacher has indicated that within al-Azhar he found himself in a situation of relative intellectual isolation. The main conclusion is that his efforts at social mobility within al-Azhar roused the antipathy of his colleagues, who were jealous of his qualifications and his outside connections. Al-ʿAṭṭār's career in the 1820's brought him into increasing contact with other members of the ruling class. In al-ʿAṭṭār's dedication of the *Inshāʾ* to Muḥammad ʿAlī, he praised the latter as the righter of wrong, as being fearless, as having a mighty army, and so on.[46] Al-ʿAṭṭār served, although probably briefly, as a tutor to Ibrāhīm.[47] The first manifestations of opposition to al-ʿAṭṭār—although their origins are not always clear—date from the period when al-ʿAṭṭār was being praised by the Europeans. The two facts, of course, are not unrelated. Matters came to a head after 1830 with his appointment as rector of al-Azhar, to which we now turn.

Al-ʿAṭṭār was appointed on March 19, 1831/4 Shawwāl 1246, following the death of the previous Shaykh al-Azhar, Aḥmad al-Damahūjī. The choice was justified in the official release as if in anticipation of immediate opposition. One point mentioned was that Ḥasan al-ʿAṭṭār was appointed because Ḥasan al-Quwaysnī (another possible candidate for the post) would not accept the position due to his blindness. No particularly distinctive praise was made of al-ʿAṭṭār's qualifications for the position; he was praised merely for his abilities in the rational and the transmitted sciences. The same had been said for his predecessor, who was in fact not distinguished at all. Al-ʿAṭṭār's homosexuality was also commented on (*ḥālu maʿlūm*, his condition is known).[48] The role of the Shaykh al-Azhar during this period remains ill-defined. He was neither the *nāẓir* of vast *awqāf*, as in the eighteenth century, nor a pre-eminent religious bureaucrat, as in the late nineteenth century. He was, as can be shown, involved in bureaucratic (especially administrative and judicial) matters, but these involvements cannot be assessed as long as the inner workings of the bureaucracy have not been properly studied.[49]

Al-ʿAṭṭār's conflict with Ḥasan al-Quwaysnī dated back at least to 1823. Their names are linked as far back as 1820. Al-Quwaysnī was a prominent member of the Bayyūmīya *ṭarīqa*. He was also Shaykh al-Riwāq of the blind, a group of poor men, estimated by Lane to have numbered about three hundred. In 1820, communal tensions reflecting the growing power of the foreign-based commercial sector were aired (although indirectly) in the complaint raised by one of the chief *ʿulamāʾ* of Alexandria, who questioned whether the Jewish butchers slaughtered animals in a manner acceptable to the Qurʾān. The matter could not be settled, and finally it was decided that it should be taken to Cairo, where Shaykh Ḥasan al-ʿAṭṭār and Ḥasan al-Quwaysnī, who were both known for their fairness, would decide the question. Both apparently agreed to dismiss the case.[50] In 1823, however, with the arrival of a potential patron, a personal dimension to their rivalry flared up when both al-ʿAṭṭār and al-Quwaysnī taught Arif Hikmet Bey.

The really bitter antagonisms between al-ʿAṭṭār and al-Quwaysnī, however, developed after al-ʿAṭṭār became Shaykh al-Azhar. He was frequently obstructed in his administrative duties. One example was the complaint that the editors and correctors whom he had appointed for the press did not work: they "exploited their talents in reading and writing"![51] Opposition to al-ʿAṭṭār took a more extreme form later in the same year (1832), when a relative of Ḥasan al-ʿAṭṭār, a *shaykh* named Ibn al-Ḥusayn, was appointed Shaykh Riwāq al-Maghāriba. It seems reasonable to assume that he received the position with the support of al-ʿAṭṭār. According to a not unprejudiced source compiled by a member of his family, a group of "plotters" told lies about al-Ḥusayn to Muḥammad ʿAlī so that Muḥammad ʿAlī ordered him exiled. Al-ʿAṭṭār intervened on his behalf with Muḥammad ʿAlī in order that the latter order an investigation. The plotting *shaykhs* convened in an official meeting place and when the investigator reported the complaint of al-ʿAṭṭār, Shaykh al-Quwaysnī answered it by rejecting it; all the *shaykhs* present supported al-Quwaysnī's testimony, testifying falsely against al-ʿAṭṭār. They thus maligned him so much that al-ʿAṭṭār asked the council (*majlis*) to relieve him of the rectorship of al-Azhar, but the *majlis* refused. On another occasion while al-ʿAṭṭār was rector, there was a meeting of the *shaykhs* at the Citadel to decide on certain matters. A number of them were dissatisfied with al-ʿAṭṭār's view, so they stole his shoes; and one of them, Muṣṭafā al-ʿArūsī, who was later to serve as rector of al-Azhar, told al-ʿAṭṭār's donkey boy to go home, making him think that it was his master's order. When al-ʿAṭṭār wanted to go home, he found himself obliged to go on foot in his stockings to his home in Darb al-Ḥammām. A third reported incident occurred after al-ʿAṭṭār's death in 1835. Al-Quwaysnī, who succeeded al-ʿAṭṭār as Shaykh al-Azhar, declared that the family of al-ʿAṭṭār had no right to the personal effects of the late *shaykh*, because al-ʿAṭṭār's son, Asad, was a minor and his mother was a slave. Shaykh al-Quwaysnī went to al-ʿAṭṭār's home in Darb al-Ḥammām, taking with him a group of persons, and threatened the family, saying they would sell Asad's mother. Thereupon (and afterward on several occasions) they removed a number of books from al-ʿAṭṭār's library, claiming that they had been willed (*mawqūf*) to the Riwāq al-Maghāriba. Of the books which they took on this pretence, some found their way to the *riwāq*, but the majority apparently went to personal libraries. Aḥmad al-Ḥusaynī registered a complaint with Muḥammad ʿAlī to prevent further pillaging, but Muḥammad ʿAlī at that time was in Alexandria; by the time he issued the decree forbidding *ʿulamāʾ* to enter the house, much had already been lost. In his account, al-Ḥusaynī reported that he became personally convinced of the truth of this story when he found among the books in the Riwāq al-Maghāriba, *Kitāb al-umm*, vol. 1, in which there was an inscription, but not in al-ʿAṭṭār's own handwriting. The inscription read, "This book of Shaykh Ḥasan al-ʿAṭṭār is a *waqf*, the place of which is the Riwāq al-Maghāriba." Al-Ḥusaynī observed that, apart from the matter of the handwriting, this was scarcely the style in which such dedications were usually written, as it was devoid of praise or elevated expressions. The writer failed to describe al-ʿAṭṭār with any of the conventional honorific expressions, such as al-ʿAllāma, al-Fahāma, and so on, thereby showing his dislike of al-ʿAṭṭār. Yet another incident related by al-Ḥusaynī involving Shaykh al-Quwaysnī shows the latter's envy of al-ʿAṭṭār in the rational sciences. Al-Quwaysnī, perhaps to show his own brilliance, set out to write a commentary on the *Sullam* in logic without, as he said, using any sources.[52]

The structure of al-ʿAṭṭār's family is difficult to study from the few sources which we have; however, sometimes their scarcity and their silence on these points become topics in themselves. Al-ʿAṭṭār's mother never figured in the discussion of his youth; his "wife" at the pinnacle of his career was a slave. The imbalance in power between the sexes in this marriage must have been very exaggerated. In the eighteenth century, there had been a trend toward manumission of slaves among the middle classes. Is it not possible that al-ʿAṭṭār's continued acceptance of slavery had a bearing on the Aristotelianism for which he was so unusual among the *shaykhs* of his period? Obviously, his homosexuality also played an important role in his attitude toward women. In the only lengthy statement on women of his adult years, there is a scornful rejection of the *imāma* of women. In his rejection of this doctrine, al-ʿAṭṭār makes clear his concept of women as sex objects. It is significant that, whereas his teacher al-Zabīdī had had female students and went into extraordinary mourning on the death of a wife he adored, al-ʿAṭṭār with all his travels never is reported to have had women students. Finally, there is the anecdote recounted by one of al-ʿAṭṭār's Egyptian students of the day when kinsmen of his Turkish wife, a woman who was long since dead, arrived in Cairo, and there ensued a violent argument. If she was a woman of such importance that her kinsmen would come to visit al-ʿAṭṭār in Cairo, what a contrast she must have been to Asad's mother, and how badly al-ʿAṭṭār received this challenge from his deceased wife's family.

Al-ʿAṭṭār in fact suffered greatly during his last few years from the turmoil of bureaucratic in-fighting. In a remarkable piece written shortly before his death on the margin of a manuscript in the field of history belonging to his student al-Ṭahṭāwī, he gave vent to his feelings. This short work took the form of his reflections on the life of a *shaykh* who lived in the tenth century in Damascus. This *shaykh*, having acquired wealth and respect in his life, withdrew from society and devoted himself to building gardens, growing flowers, and the creation of natural beauty. His works had a profound effect on his contemporaries who, according to his biographer, followed his lead and themselves turned to this worthwhile activity. Near the conclusion the historian said that when this man, whose name was Qāsim, died, "a piece of humanity died with him." Al-ʿAṭṭār wrote:

> The historian said in his discussion "when he died"; he was in the tenth century, we are in the thirteenth century and no longer find a use for this expression. Because when people die, they are followed by voracious animals and attacking monsters. If we have relations with them, they will ravish them, they will ravish us; if we stay away from

> them, they slander us. So we have no safety from them. Either we are with them or not with them. I say that may that time be praised which comes to me and makes pleasant the day so that I may sit alone in my chair away from these voracious monsters, who have no humanity in them, neither for this world nor for the one to come. . . . All in all, those whom God Almighty kept far removed from these people, they are the blessed ones, praiseworthy are their lives. Yes, yes, yes, indeed!
>
> I wish that I myself could withdraw and refuse entirely to see mankind, as if I were on top of some tall mountain. For when I became Shaykh al-Azhar, toward the end of my life, I forgot even the scholarship in which I had spent my life, until my eyes finally grew weak. And [when I became] Shaykh al-Azhar, my relations with people were such that they prevented anything worthwhile in either my religious or my secular life. I do not see anything but enemies wearing the clothes of friends. [I see] only arrogant, wily, malicious tricksters who are laying traps for me . . . and my destruction stares me in the eye. O! my God, protect me from those who want to injure me, and stand between them and me. O! my God, with whom I communicate through your beloved Muṣṭafā and his family, save me from their treachery. For I sense that many of those who smile at me would never hesitate if they were given the chance to drink my blood. God is my guardian; for indeed, before I entered this position, I had not known that there were human beings like these. May God protect me from them. [signed, Ḥasan al-ʿAṭṭār] [53]

European contemporaries who were involved in setting up the new institutions praised al-ʿAṭṭār highly, especially in the field of medicine, in which he had worked for many years.[54] Al-ʿAṭṭār's support for the founding of the school of human medicine and his praise for Clot Bey are indicated in his address to the graduating class of the Abū Zaʿbal medical school in 1832.[55] Edward Lane, who was interested in philology and literature, knew al-ʿAṭṭār. He singled al-ʿAṭṭār's *Inshāʾ* out from his other writings for praise.[56]

It would certainly seem that for al-ʿAṭṭār, who was still rooted in Maghribī circles, the creation of the new social class linked to Europe, with the concomitant suppression of the old commercial middle class, was a very painful and trying event in which to participate. For the younger generation, and notably his students, we find no evidence suggesting such a degree of inner turmoil. Most of them were still children during the time of most rapid social change, and they grew up to accept the system which rewarded them. By the 1830's, al-Azhar had, in fact, declined as an intellectual center, and the new schools were gaining prominence. For those with a literary or philological orientation, the position of corrector or editor was a rewarding, if intellectually strenuous, one, very different, of course, from the role of the eighteenth-century poet or litterateur.

How students found their way into the new cultural infrastructure, especially before the creation of the School of Languages in 1835, depended much on their luck in securing patronage, which may explain why most of the main scholars discussed came through al-Azhar and were helped by Ḥasan al-ʿAṭṭār. In 1836, al-ʿAṭṭār's most famous student took over the direction of the newly created School of Languages, in which Frenchmen taught French and *shaykhs* of al-Azhar taught Arabic. The seventy-odd graduates in the first decade of its existence came to be among the most prominent cultural figures of the age of Ismaʿīl. This was ultimately a consequence of the rivalry between England and France over Egyptian cotton. We turn now to an examination of the religious framework of secular culture in the reform period, saving for the two last chapters a detailed study of the developments in the arts and sciences.

Chapter 7
The Revival of Theology and *Kalām*: Hallmarks of the Culture of the State Commercial Sector

This chapter develops the idea proposed earlier that the *ʿulamāʾ* served the modernizing state in Turkey and Egypt by adjusting and adapting the received cultural and religious forms. In particular, the *ʿulamāʾ* turned to Māturīdite theology and other rational sciences which shared a common link to the Aristotelian framework developed under conditions of agrarian feudalism. The task which the *ʿulamāʾ* performed—providing a justification for the policies of the state and defending the state against its enemies—was a traditional task. What makes their activities worthy of note is that they were functioning under modern conditions in the nineteenth century. It is this fact which gives their reintroduction of traditional logic and other subjects a new meaning, a meaning which can only be understood against the backdrop of the modern world market. We do not find the static, antinomic rationalism of the medieval logicians, such as the Muʿtazilī or St. Anselme, who flourished in the settled conditions of a feudal society. Nor is this the rigorous self-contained rationalism of a Descartes reflecting an organic capitalist development impossible except at the center of the world market. One thinks more of Kant, whose thought was rooted in the culture of a semiperipheral region, who combined some of the medieval elements, like antinomies of faith and reason, with his modernist critique of pure reason.

Māturīdism in Egypt is even more eclectic. The precapitalist division of labor clearly affects the level of conceptualization, and this accounts for the retention of the Aristotelian framework; but the uses to which the conceptual framework is put, most notably the exaggerated dependence on arguments by analogy, suggests the new reality of a capitalist mode of distribution which was emerging, notably in its utilitarianist orientation.

I shall pursue the study of Māturīdism in Egypt through the writings of the two principal spokesmen for the reform period, al-ʿAṭṭār and his student al-Ṭahṭāwī. In al-ʿAṭṭār's writings, a Māturīdite theology becomes uncomfortably linked with the study of formal logic and argumentation. Theology was no longer susceptible to a pure logical treatment. Al-ʿAṭṭār was not concerned with questions of the limit of reason so much as its plasticity.

Once reborn, the study of logic, like the analogous study of disciplines ancillary to the study of *ḥadīth* in the eighteenth century, took on a life of its own. It opened the way to a study of physical medicine and the natural sciences, and to a challenge of other fields, such as *al-ḥikma*, which had been part of the eighteenth-century revival. The religious revival in this way resembled the first phase, 1760–1815, in that it exploited a single religious modality: the general development of culture flowing out of it. That the pressures imposed by the market distorted both the balance of religious culture and the course of cultural development should by this time come as no surprise.

To locate the characteristic problems of the age and the way in which they were resolved, I return to the corpus of religious writing. One is immediately struck by the quantity of polemical material which this age produced, both in Turkey and in Egypt, and by the particular concern in the textbooks of logic for the topic of analogy (*qiyās*). While the rebirth of *kalām* explains in a general way the study of the structure of logical argument, it does not clarify the reasons for the great concentration on argument by analogy. I pause here briefly to recapitulate some of what has been said previously. This concentration on analogy was no doubt related to the intellectual drive on the part of the ruling class to understand and adapt numerous aspects of Western science and technology. It is generally accepted that Western science and technology of the early industrial revolution had encouraged an extremely empiricist outlook and that the new classes it produced reflected very little of the classical education of "Oxbridge," an education which, as did the Azharite education, stressed the Aristotelian corpus. However, our concern here is more properly with the modernizing elite on the periphery of the industrial revolution and not with the classes in its heartland. On the periphery, the historical situation was different. The intellectual task of the ruling classes on the periphery was the reception of blueprints which had already been constructed, and the adaptation of these blueprints to local conditions. This situation encouraged neither the empiricism of pure scientific research nor technological development. It encouraged, of necessity, a more deductive approach; argument through analogy was perhaps the method through which existing problems could best be confronted. In the nineteenth century, it will be shown, the students who revived Aristotelian logic were those who supported modern Western science, especially in the period 1815–1837.

It would seem that the arguments used by the higher *ʿulamāʾ* of Turkey who supported the Tanzimat and an analogous although much smaller group in Egypt drew on the logical tradition of India, the stronghold of later Sunnī rationalism, when they needed to use *kalām* as a vehicle of "ideological" defense. The Indian intellectual traditions were already well known, especially in Turkey and Syria, as a consequence of the spreading popularity of the Naqshbandīs and their offshoots. In Turkey, polemics centered around the orthopraxy urged by the Ṭarīqa Muḥammadīya. In Syria and Turkey, the differences between Māturīdite and Ashʿarite theology were disputed—the Naqshbandīs and the members of the elite supported the former. In Egypt, *kalām* was used as a weapon against the pretensions of the Ahl al-Ḥadīth. Sunnī orthodoxy, allying itself with modern science, attacked the overreaching claims of *al-ḥikma*, on the one hand, and mystical theology, on the other. In both Turkey and Egypt, al-ʿAṭṭār was a participant in these conflicts, and he always sided with the ruling class. He was the pre-eminent *mutakallim* of the reform period in Egypt; for this he had had a long period of preparation in Syria and Turkey. In his writings which will be studied here and in the following chapters, the major trends of this important, if short-lived, Aristotelian revival in theology, logic, medicine, and science, are pursued.

Al-ʿAṭṭār and the Theology of the Religious Elite

The Period of Development

If one is to pursue al-ʿAṭṭār's involvement in religious polemic, which inevitably embraces both his studies of logic and theology and the controversies themselves, a schematic overview of his development in *kalām* is necessary. His first phase, as an Ashʿarite, ended early in his stay in Turkey. Thereafter, his study of logic and other rational science drew him toward a Māturīdite position. The most "radical" position which he reached came during the 1830's, when he wrote on *ijtihād* from a Māturīdite outlook.

During his youth, Ḥasan al-ʿAṭṭār had studied a number of basic theological texts with the well-known teachers of his period: two teachers in particular are mentioned, al-Sharqāwī and al-Disūqī.[1] Al-ʿAṭṭār studied theology with ʿAbdullah al-Sharqāwī,[2] receiving two special diplomas and a general diploma on the remainder of his teacher's books. He studied logic and theology with the Mālikī Muḥammad al-Disūqī, who was a *faqīh*, and received an *ijāza* from him, later teaching his work on credo (*ʿaqīda*), "Ḥāshiyat al-Disūqī ʿalā sharḥ al-Sānūsī ʿalā muqadimmat umm al-barāhīn." His theological education continued in Turkey. Details are lacking, for al-ʿAṭṭār merely mentions that he "studied with many of the famous teachers of Turkey."[3]

Al-ʿAṭṭār's first essay and his only Ashʿarite work was the "Tuḥfat gharīb al-waṭan," an attack on the Ṭarīqa Muḥammadīya. "Al-Ṭarīqa al-muḥammadīya" was the title of a book written by Pīr Birkāwī (Birghili Mehmet Efendi), died 1573/981. It also referred to a distinct theological tendency within orthodox Sunnism, focusing on the importance of orthopraxy. The continuous existence of the Ṭarīqa Muḥammadīya over more than three hundred years suggests that its followers—and these were numerous—may have represented a particular social force as well.[4] Europeans in contact with the Orient during the seventeenth, eighteenth, and early nineteenth centuries were quite familiar with the Ṭarīqa Muḥammadīya; many regarded it as the "true Islam."[5] In the period of al-ʿAṭṭār's life, spokesmen for the movement had written a number of books supporting it, thereby attesting to its continued vitality. While it is difficult to determine from scant evidence exactly what it represented in social terms, the points most often made about its strong feelings about coined money and that it did not initially attract the common people seem clear enough.

The sector of society which was most affected by the inflation of the sixteenth century and thereafter was the Turkish merchant community, or those segments of it who confronted the growing entrenchment of the minorities as the dominant commercial class, and those affected by the concomitant erosion of the guild economy. Landholders united with foreign traders were turning Turkey into an exporter of raw materials. One would expect certain ideological convulsions to take place among the merchants who were threatened economically by the new commercial nexus with Europe. As the essay of al-ʿAṭṭār on the Ṭarīqa Muḥammadīya has not been located, we are left with his own brief description of it as a defense of the Ashʿarite doctrine of *kasb* against certain deterministic (*jabrīya*) ideas of Khadimi-Zadeh.[6]

The Beginning of al-ʿAṭṭār's Māturīdite Period

The most important break in al-ʿAṭṭār's thought coincides with his study of rational sciences in Istanbul. It was in Istanbul and Alexandretta that he read widely on medicine, science, logic, and argumentation. These were translated shortly thereafter into religious categories in his subsequent theological essays. The latter took up a range of topics which confronted him in Damascus and later in Cairo. Damascus was the probable point of crystallization.[7]

Al-ʿAṭṭār wrote several essays while on his travels, of which two remain. These deal with natural science and man's freedom. In them he offered a Māturīdite justification for his positions in these fields. One was written in 1813/1228 while he was in Syria and was entitled "Hadhā jawāb shaykh Ḥasan al-ʿAṭṭār ʿan suʾāl Muṣṭafā al-Bidīrī." The essay set out to deal with the point of view of the reformist concerning the Ṭabīʿiyīn (natural scientists) and especially the idea of the latter that the creator of events is nature, with respect to the idea of the ancients that health could be regulated through a regulation of the humours. Al-ʿAṭṭār began by following the Aristotelian physics and Galenic medicine in explaining these views. This included a discussion (folio 12) of several naturalistic ideas of causation, including, surprisingly, the writings of ʿAbd al-Laṭīf al-Baghdādī on the *Qānūnjā* (see below under medicine). Al-ʿAṭṭār concluded his answer to the question on natural scientists by stating (especially on folio 14B) that they were not wrong for being scientists but that they did not adduce a proper account of causation. Al-ʿAṭṭār then referred his readers (folio 16B) to his own work on Dāʾūd al-Anṭākī, reconciling the Greek and theistic systems by stating that in the end God is the first influence or mover. In the conclusion of the essay, he offered a linguistic explanation for the causes of misunderstanding in religion. It is necessary, he said, that discussion be confined to correct technical usages and correct principles.

In another work written during this period, entitled "Risālat al-ʿAṭṭār fī khalq al-afʿāl fīʿilm al-kalām," al-ʿAṭṭār took up the question of the createdness of man's acts.[8] In a third essay linked in part to his studies in the natural sciences, al-ʿAṭṭār discussed the question of whether or not the world was eternal or created.[9] In this and other works, he took a view sympathetic to the natural sciences, defending the study of these fields while rejecting the point at issue. He himself required this shield in order to write his own works on *al-handasa* (geometry, with topics in astronomy and engineering). The fact that one of the commentators in a section on geometry had Shīʿī leanings, and that that could be used against him, led al-ʿAṭṭār to argue that the commentator, Nāṣir al-dīn al-Ṭūsī, did not write the "objectionable" parts of a book, "Al-Tajrīd," as alleged.[10]

Al-ʿAṭṭār's return to Egypt, especially the period immediately after his arrival, provides additional evidence of the development of his Māturīdite doctrinal outlook. This period should be included here, since it is logically separate from his subsequent entrance into the new institutional structure. When al-ʿAṭṭār returned to Egypt, he made an immediate reputation by teaching the "Ṭawāliʿ" of al-Bayḍāwī and the writings of al-Bayḍāwī's student in *kalām*, al-Ījī.[11] Mubārak stated that the "Ṭawāliʿ" was a work which no one had read (i.e., taught) before. While this is not true, it is true that the approach to theology through *kalām* was relatively unknown.[12] Al-ʿAṭṭār's presentation stressed analysis and logic over accumulated knowledge of individual points. We have some idea of his main points because they were incorporated in later writings. On essential points of doctrine, al-ʿAṭṭār sought to define the terms so that some degree of judgment was incumbent upon the believer. For example, in his discussion of ritual impurity (*al-najāsa*), al-ʿAṭṭār stressed the importance of the taste, color, and smell of the water as against the more static notion embodied in the definition of cleanliness as dependent on a fixed quantity of water.[13]

To conclude, al-ʿAṭṭār's conversion to Māturīdism dated from his contact with the Turkish ruling class. In a series of essays reflecting this experience, he began to attempt to find arguments for modern science from within *kalām*.

Al-ʿAṭṭār in Egypt

The entrance of al-ʿAṭṭār to a position of authority within the cultural elite at a time when modern class structure was undermining the independence of the corporate institutions of the Middle Ages explains many of the difficulties which confronted him. This theme has already been pursued on the level of biography; I turn now to a discussion of his later writings, in which there appeared the problems of defending in traditional intellectual categories a regime which no longer could be fully understood through them. Of these later writings, one has been referred to many times, the gloss on the *Jāmiʿ al-jawāmiʿ*. The second is an unknown manuscript on *ijtihād*, which is likewise of great importance for what it reveals about the transformation of thought.

As both these works are on the science of the roots of jurisprudence, *uṣūl al-fiqh*, I shall briefly discuss this subject. Al-ʿAṭṭār did not write extensively on *tafsīr*. His one independent work on *ḥadīth*, or more properly on *muṣṭalaḥ al-ḥadīth*, has not been located, but his views on certain matters in the *sunna* appear in the main work on *uṣūl al-fiqh*. This work also contains a large section on *qiyās*, which is much the same as his several texts on logic (which will be treated below). This leaves his essay on *ijtihād* and a similar but shorter work by his student al-Ṭahṭāwī, also on *ijtihād*. Thus, I concentrate here on *sunna* and *ijtihād*, studying them for the moment in isolation. I begin with al-ʿAṭṭār's discussion of the role of *ḥadīth* in religious thought. In the context in which he wrote in 1830, it can be taken as a manifestation of the emerging class conflict.

One topic which was particularly important to the *ḥadīth* movement was that of the *ṣaḥāba*. A concern with the *ṣaḥāba* may be said to have pervaded the circles of the Sādāt al-Wafāʾīya, but its influence was much wider. Al-ʿAṭṭār rejected the claim that the *ṣaḥāba* were a category of human beings possessed of some special virtue. In so doing, he was of course raising doubts about the validity of eighteenth-century *ḥadīth* study, which dealt heavily with questions of their spiritual status. In another discussion, al-ʿAṭṭār raised the question of how the *ṣaḥāba* were to be defined, a question dealt with only implicitly in the writings of the eighteenth century. He referred to a commentary by al-Māzrī which stated that the most important criterion in identifying the *ṣaḥāba* was whether they attended the sessions of the Prophet as a way of manifesting their adherence to him. Another condition which al-ʿAṭṭār mentioned had been laid down by Saʿīd al-Muṣīb, who said that one could not be among the *ṣaḥāba* unless one had gone on a *ghazwa* (raid) with the Prophet. Al-ʿAṭṭār preferred the first definition over the second because the second would have eliminated several well-known Companions, for example, Jarīr b. ʿAbdullah al-Baljī.[14]

Al-ʿAṭṭār never took seriously the important eighteenth-century contention of the merit of visiting the tombs of the *ṣaḥāba*. He denied that either visitation or knowledge of the special virtue of each individual member of the *ṣaḥāba* had the slightest religious efficacy. He also raised the question of whether the *ṣaḥāba* were accurate in their narration. Al-ʿAṭṭār concluded that the *ṣaḥāba* were all accurate, deducing that all those who have subsequently done research have been content to note whether a *ḥadīth* was *mursal* or not, that is, whether the chain of authorities for a given report went back at least until the second generation. He did caution, however, that one must discount the stories of those who saw the Prophet as babies, such as Ḥasan, Ḥusayn, and ʿAbdullah b. Zubayr. Al-ʿAṭṭār then quoted the opinion of one of the main figures in *kalām*, the Imām al-

Ḥaramayn, who said that we do not examine the reliability of the Companions because they transmitted the Sharīʿa. If it were agreed to permit inquiry over their accuracy, then the Sharīʿa might have to be limited to the generation of the Prophet. But al-ʿAṭṭār was not entirely satisfied with such medieval logic. He returned to al-Māzrī, who stated that not all those who greeted the Prophet once, or visited him, or met him, should be included; but rather, those who had attached themselves to him, whose pride had been subdued by him, who were victorious with him, were likely to be accurate in their narratives. Al-ʿAlāʾī said that al-Māzrī's claim concerning the accuracy of their narration is strange, since many of the famous Companions were known to have been inaccurate, for example, Wāʾil b. Ḥajar, Mālik b. Huwarith, ʿUthmān b. Abī al-ʿĀṣī, and others. Some stayed with him only a short time, others could report only a single *ḥadīth*. For others, the length of their stays among the Arab tribes could not be determined. The majority of the *muḥaddithīn* who spoke of the *ṣaḥāba* referred to those who could speak with understanding.[15]

Al-ʿAṭṭār's statements on the *ṣaḥāba* are also interesting for the psychological analysis presented above. By rejecting the claim of the *ṣaḥāba* in favor of the claims of the *mutakallimīn*, al-ʿAṭṭār was eliminating the role of women as a voice of authority. When al-ʿAṭṭār rejected the criterion of *ghazwa*, it was to defend the reputation of a man and not ʿĀʾisha or some other woman. The defining of a trustworthy knowledge of Muḥammad in terms of whether or not one had attended sessions with him runs against the spirit of authenticity of the eighteenth century. Women had played an important and well-known role in the life of Muḥammad. Is it a coincidence that al-ʿAṭṭār does not write about Muḥammad? Muḥammad's life was a matter of fascination to the writers of the eighteenth century, even to al-ʿAṭṭār's student Ibrāhīm al-Saqqāʾ, who wrote on Muḥammad's wives, and, of course, to his student al-Ṭahṭāwī.

Ijtihād: *Background*

Ijtihād, or the theological imperative to exercise disciplined self-judgment according to certain specified conditions, the last pillar of *uṣūl al-fiqh*, has throughout Islamic history been one of the most important vehicles for inspiring and ratifying social changes. In writings on Egypt, a great deal of attention has been paid to the essay on *ijtihād* by Shaykh Muḥammad ʿAbdu, which was written late in the nineteenth century. It has been generally claimed that he wrote this as a consequence of his association with Jamāl al-dīn al-Afghānī. However, no wider study of *ijtihād* in the Egyptian context has been undertaken, no inquiry into the later development of *uṣūl al-fiqh* has been made; despite the widely recognized participation of certain *shaykhs* in the reform activities of the era of Muḥammad ʿAlī and afterward.

A brief survey of existing books and manuscripts indicates that the revival of the Māturīdite theology among the Naqshbandīs in India in the context of severe social conflicts and the subsequent spread of the order to Turkey and the Arab world in the eighteenth century is generally a more suitable point of departure for the study of *uṣūl al-fiqh* in modern history than Muḥammad ʿAbdu. The writings on *ijtihād* by Shāh Walīʾullah were in fact read and quoted by Egyptian writers, beginning in the eighteenth century, and this continued to be the case into the nineteenth century, as a revived concern with *uṣūl al-fiqh*, especially *sunna*, penetrated Egypt through al-Zabīdī and others. For example, Muḥammad al-Ṣabbān and ʿAbdullah al-Sharqāwī wrote on *uṣūl al-fiqh*. Al-Ṣabbān wrote on a section of the *Jāmiʿ al-jawāmiʿ* of Imām al-Subkī, although for this generation the focus within *uṣūl* was *ḥadīth* not *fiqh*.[16]

An analysis of the *mujtahidīn* who wrote prior to Muḥammad ʿAbdu and of their writings on *ijtihād* presents not only problems of new and undigested material but problems of method as well. It would seem, in considering the new material, that those claiming the right to *ijtihād* may not in fact have been more radical in the content of their thought than those who opposed or attempted to limit *ijtihād*. This can be determined only through a study of their historical circumstances. The same would seem to apply in reverse to those traditionalists who adhered to *taqlīd*.

The *mujtahidīn* of the eighteenth and early nineteenth centuries lived during the initial impact of the Western industrial revolution on their societies. Among the most visible signs of the period were governmental dependence on foreigners and the opposition of local courts to Muslim merchants. Shāh Walīʾullah, a *mujtahid* of India and a major figure in the Naqshbandī Māturīdī reform movement of which I have written, wrote as a defender of the Indian Muslim merchants. The Imām al-Sānūsī, another *mujtahid*, wrote from a situation in North Africa in which the coastal beys were becoming satellites of the Europeans, and then using their newly gained power to try to dominate the commercial economy of the hinterlands.

In Shāh Walīʾullah's "ʿIqd al-jīd fī aḥkām al-ijtihād waʾl-taqlīd," *ijtihād* was presented as a utilitarian and inescapable part of *iftāʾ*, the issuing of legal opinions. The real source of contention in law came not from *mujtahidīn* reaching divergent conclusions but from a persistent clinging to generalities (to universals).[17] In a second work, the *Ḥujja*, Shāh Walīʾullah explicitly dealt with the plight of merchants. In contrast to the utilitarian *ijtihād* of Shāh Walīʾullah was the more eclectic yet more dogmatic *ijtihād* of Imām al-Sānūsī. Utilitarianism, an avoidance of extremes and universal pronouncements, was the logic of the merchant. It could function securely within the confines of a *madhhab* and had merely to struggle with the pretensions of *kalām* to systematization. Imām al-Sānūsī, who came from the hinterlands and nomad regions, did not impose the necessity that one follow a particular *madhhab*; rather, he argued, one could choose a ruling from what was most advantageous.

It was the challenge of Imām al-Sānūsī's arrival in Egypt and his contact with Azhar *shaykhs* which inspired several Azharite writings on the subject of *ijtihād.* I shall follow this controversy closely, as it led to important clarifications of thought in Egypt. When al-Sānūsī arrived in Egypt around 1830, he accused the *shaykhs* of al-Azhar of being indifferent to learning and of being overly attached to Muḥammad ʿAlī. Concerning the exact nature of his relations with the *shaykhs* of al-Azhar, there is relatively little information. According to one account, al-Sānūsī studied with Ḥasan al-ʿAṭṭār and took an *ijāza* from him as well as from some other Azharites. Another account stated that he merely met with al-ʿAṭṭār and discussed various matters with him.[18]

Other ambiguities center around his most bitter opponent in the Azhar, Shaykh Hanīsh, whose motives do not clearly come to light; in addition, it is difficult to tell if the *fatwa* (legal opinion) attacking al-Sānūsī issued by the Muftī of the Mālikīs, al-Būlāqī, was actually issued while al-Sānūsī was there or later.[19] Furthermore, it is difficult to determine which work of al-Sānūsī was being answered by al-ʿAṭṭār and al-Būlāqī. Many of the points in al-ʿAṭṭār's essay appear to be replies to a short essay for which, however, there is no date of original composition.[20]

Al-Sānūsī affirmed that, where matters of law were not clearly resolved by earlier thinkers, judges and *muftīs* had a certain latitude. The main condition which al-Sānūsī laid down was that the opinion given must be grounded in both the Qurʾān and *sunna.* If he so bases his opinion, the *mujtahid* does not err. An additional implication was that, if he finds his opinion in agreement with aspects of *taqlīd*, he is not bound to follow that Imām in other respects. Here Shāh Walīʾullah was more radical, for al-Sānūsī claimed that this did not constitute *taqlīd*. But in other respects, his ideas were similar to those of Shāh Walīʾullah, at least in method. For example, Imām al-Sānūsī asserted the following traditional views: *taqlīd* was contrary to the Qurʾān (the view of Ibn Taymīya), but unlike most *mujtahids*, al-Sānūsī denied that it was necessary to accept one of the four rites even as a point of departure; rather, people were free to seek opinions (hence *ḥadīth*) wherever they were to be found.[21]

The most reasonable hypothesis to explain the extreme opposition of certain *shaykhs* to al-Sānūsī is that the appeal of the latter in Egypt was to groups which were not sympathetic to the Muḥammad ʿAlī regime. This explains why two leading persons, identified with the regime, a Shaykh al-Azhar and a Muftī, should attack him. Since al-Būlāqī and al-ʿAṭṭār were not opponents of Ṣūfism, not opponents in any sense of the radical innovations of the regime, their intense opposition to al-Sānūsī goes beyond methodology and must therefore be attributed to their circumstances.[22] Evidence on these points is very limited, however. One of the charges which al-Būlāqī made, if true, is suggestive: he referred to the majority of the partisans of the *shaykhs* as from the wealthy materialistic class of this world.[23] From this it may be surmised that al-Sānūsī, whose basis was among the merchants and tribesmen of the North African hinterland, might have been trying to win converts among Egyptian merchants and tribesmen. Did al-

Sānūsī try to picture Muḥammad ʿAlī as a dey, allied to a Christian power?

Al-ʿAṭṭār's unknown essay, in addition to being an attack on al-Sānūsī, is the first independent essay on *ijtihād* in Egypt in the nineteenth century.[24] Al-ʿAṭṭār organized his essay as a rejoinder to a question put to him by an African named Muḥammad Ibn Abī Saʿīd al-Kirkāsī al-Ṣanāwī, who was said to have been born in al-Shindī and to reside in al-Shākī. The principal question was whether *taqlīd* is incumbent on the believer, or in what sense does *ijtihād* exist.

Al-ʿAṭṭār's defense of *ijtihād* within the *madhhab* is clearly a *mutakallim*'s defense of the mosque center against the claims of an outsider. *Ijtihād*, he insisted, implied an institutional basis. More significant than the degrees of *ijtihād* was perhaps the reassertion in *uṣūl al-fiqh* of the conflict between Ahl al-Kalām and Ahl al-Ḥadīth. Al-Sānūsī claimed that he performed *ijtihād* on the basis of familiarity with the Qurʾān and *sunna.* Al-ʿAṭṭār showed that a knowledge of the obvious analogy, a part of *kalām*, was also necessary.[25] A further clue to the essentially polemical nature of the distinctions can be found through comparison to yet another work discussing *ijtihād* by the leading Mālikī jurisprudent of the eighteenth century and one of the principal teachers of al-ʿAṭṭār. In a well-known text, Muḥammad al-Amīr wrote of the *mujtahid* not in terms of his mastery of the mechanism of *ijtihād* but in terms of his divine inspiration "which permitted him at the same time to act in the eyes of his contemporaries as one who followed the Sharīʿa."[26]

Finally, there is strong evidence provided in al-ʿAṭṭār's essay of its polemical nature by the frequent recourse to personal invective. He insulted al-Sānūsī in terms of his origins and in terms of the low state of learning in Tripolitania (!?), of which he alleged that al-Sānūsī was a product.[27] He indicated that al-Sānūsī's claim to be a *mujtahid* was based on his mistaken belief that any man with understanding could use the Qurʾān and *ḥadīth*, a conclusion in contradiction to the "corpus of Mālikī learning."[28] Later a similar approach to *ijtihād* was worked out by al-ʿAṭṭār's student al-Ṭahṭāwī in his essay "Al-Qawl al-sadīd fīʾl-ijtihād waʾl-taqlīd."[29] Although there are some points which are not found in al-ʿAṭṭār's essay, the basic concept of the *madhhab*, of the law school as a living chain leading back to one of the four great Imāms, was the same. Within each of the four orthodox schools of law, a hierarchy of different degrees of *ijtihād* within the *madhhab* was established, and here al-Ṭahṭāwī repeats a number of traditional details. He stated, for example, that before the Imām al-Shāfiʿī came, the students of *ḥadīth* were on weak ground vis-à-vis the adherents of *al-raʾy* (self-judgment not based on the Qurʾān or *sunna*) because they lacked the skills of argumentation, but that the Imām al-Shāfiʿī had put *ḥadīth* studies on a firmer basis. Concerning *ijmāʿ*, or consensus, as a method of resolving jurisprudential impasses, al-Ṭahṭāwī, as did al-ʿAṭṭār, related it to the *ijmāʿ* of the four Imāms. Then, following al-ʿAṭṭār, he argued that in matters concerning *ijtihād* the Ẓāhirīs, a fifth school of law which flourished in medieval times, had little to contribute. What was new was a section on the valid reasons for changing one's *madhhab*. Al-Ṭahṭāwī stressed that the only valid reasons were religious and not material ones, such as might be related to employment.[30]

An aspect of the debate on *ijtihād* and *taqlīd* between al-ʿAṭṭār and al-Sānūsī revolved around a series of technical matters which shed further light on their respective concepts of *ijtihād* and more generally on their respective situations. Al-Sānūsī contested the need for prayer during a trip involving the stay of less than four days in a single place and likewise contested the need to fast in Ramaḍān during a voyage. Al-ʿAṭṭār dealt with the subject (on folio 66 of his essay on *ijtihād*) in utilitarian terms, relating the conditions in which prayer might be shortened to the question of the actual length of travel. He was able to find justification for his interpretation from al-Bukhārī and Ibn ʿAbbās. Al-ʿAṭṭār dealt similarly with other modifications which al-Sānūsī permitted. While al-Būlāqī merely observed that, for example, the prolongation of the *rakʿa* (bending of the torso in prayer) was contrary to Mālikī practice, al-ʿAṭṭār spoke of the violation of the symmetric shape of prayer. Al-ʿAṭṭār also dealt with another point which al-Būlāqī did not, namely, the cutting of the lotus tree. The lotus tree had a special place in Islam, and it was mentioned in the Qurʾān, where it is stated that washing with lotus leaves is more beneficial than anything else for the head, that it drives away scurf. The Prophet Muḥammad mentioned using it with regard to the washing of the dead.[31] Al-ʿAṭṭār cited a *ḥadīth* (on folio 68) that "whoever cut down a lotus tree, God will strike his head with fire." He then proceeded to explain the intention which underlay this saying. He stated that these trees tended to grow in the desert and that they were a great boon to wayfarers. In this way, the prohibition against cutting down the lotus is similar to the prohibition against cutting the trees of al-Ḥaramayn, Mecca and Madīna. Al-ʿAṭṭār concluded his argument, based on geography, by accusing al-Sānūsī (folio 71) of being ignorant of the writings of the *mutakallimīn* on such points. Al-ʿAṭṭār took up yet another point of al-Sānūsī's argument which did not appear in al-Būlāqī's work, the pollution of ritual water (*al-najāsa*). Again, al-ʿAṭṭār's approach attempted a balance, and he dismissed al-Sānūsī's view by accusing him of misuse of *ḥadīth* sources.[32]

Al-ʿAṭṭār opposed al-Sānūsī's support of the *imāmate* of women, citing a saying by Muḥammad "that no people will succeed if their affairs are ruled over by women." He further stated that women lack intellect and religion compared with men. Finally, in a rare note of levity, he added that if a woman were the *imām*, and stood in front of the men in prayer, when she made the *rakʿas* and kneeled, the thoughts of the males would stray and they would be overcome with lust (such is human nature), and thus the humbling of oneself in the face of God would be impossible. Another point which al-ʿAṭṭār raised against al-Sānūsī concerned the nature of God's light. Al-Sānūsī had apparently based his arguments on *aḥādīth* of which al-ʿAṭṭār did not approve. Al-ʿAṭṭār began by stating that *ḥadīth* could be used only if handled in a scientific manner, which meant that only those which had been properly preserved should necessarily be accepted. To claim (as al-Sānūsī did?) that God was the best of saints, and that the other saints were created by His divine spark, was a Karmathian doctrine. Al-ʿAṭṭār concluded the essay by stating that, while the danger exists that the mob (the hangers-on around the mosque) will follow anyone, in any case (folio 81) al-Sānūsī was destined to go to Hell. Al-Būlāqī offered a slightly different view, which has been cited above, that al-Sānūsī appealed to the wealthy and the "materialists."[33]

While not enough is given in al-ʿAṭṭār's résumé of al-Sānūsī's ideas, nor is the identification of that text certain enough to know what the differences between the two were on every point, the topics raised—such as travel and the proper organization of prayer, the sex of the *imām*, the cutting of the lotus tree, and the problem of securing ritual water—all seem to be topics of practical concern to the traveling merchants of the caravan who had to fulfill their religious obligations as best they could in whatever circumstances they found themselves. Al-ʿAṭṭār's disagreement with al-Sānūsī over these points reflected the position of the *mutakallim* in an urban scholastic center, as well as the position of a *mutakallim* in the secure material environment of Cairo. Al-ʿAṭṭār could afford to dismiss al-Sānūsī, to "refute" al-Sānūsī by claiming that it was an impossibility that he could be a *mujtahid*.

Ahl al-Kalām and Mysticism

The Writings of al-ʿAṭṭār

The attitude of the new regime toward Ṣūfism was ambivalent. As a coherent vision of reality, it attracted and brought together many of the intellectuals of the Ottoman Empire. Also, the *ṭarīqa* was a refuge within which one could find one's balance. But no one had managed to define a role for Ṣūfism in the new era.

This section deals with the relationship of al-ʿAṭṭār to the mystical confraternities. Al-ʿAṭṭār had lasting contacts with the Ṣūfī *ṭuruq* of his time, during his youth and thereafter, although he himself did not become a *murīd*. He had belonged to the Khalwatīya, as did a number of his Egyptian teachers and associates, and at the same time he had been initiated into the circles of the Sādāt al-Wafāʾīya. The Khalwatīs sought from their disciples a rigorous *tahdhīb*, including *khalwa*. The Wafāʾīya of the late eighteenth century did not require the path, but it was the convention among them to reflect on the spiritual qualities of their Shaykh, Muḥammad Abī Anwār, in their writings. Al-ʿAṭṭār did not comply with the practices of either of the two orders. His period of study of Ṣūfī texts in Damascus was probably more a literary diversion than a period of religiosity. It was his intellectual commitment to science and theology which obliged him to be concerned with mystical religion, for the later development of science and logic in Islamic history was carried on by Ṣūfīs.

Among the most important facts which emerge from al-ʿAṭṭār's relations with the two Egyptian orders is the fact that he could not make the fundamental commitment to be a *murīd*. The alternative of "abandoning" mysticism was not, of course, posed. In this ambience, al-ʿAṭṭār appeared to share the position of many Ṣūfīs, especially Naqshbandīs and Khalwatīs, who identified with the dominant class and adhered to a Sharīʿa-minded theology.

The great appeal of Ṣūfism remained for him cultural, the surrender of the literal to the allegorical, and this was the case in his adult life as it had been in his youth. Al-ʿAṭṭār's attitudes toward mystical thought developed gradually from an ambivalent acceptance to an ambivalent rejection, broadly corresponding to his shift from Ashʿarism to Māturīdism. His mature position in about 1830 was basically that mystical thought was best left to those who understood it.

In 1830, al-ʿAṭṭār's position on the nature of mysticism crystallized, and he attempted to confront the problem of his own relationship to it. Concerning the "principles (*mabādiʾ*) of Ṣūfism," he wrote that Ṣūfism was a "science" with its own principles and objectives, but he acknowledged that it was not like other sciences since it was a resultant of all other fields. Ṣūfism was of two basic sorts: the first was ethics, the second relied on masters, on flashes of revelation. Al-ʿAṭṭār preferred the first, the idea that Ṣūfism was not wearing of wool, weeping, singing, dancing, or wandering as a madman but rather purification without turbidity. "For he who is pure is called Ṣūfī."[34]

These words, drawn from his major work, which was written between 1828 and 1830, show the degree to which a strict Sharīʿa consciousness dominates mystical consciousness. The most that al-ʿAṭṭār would accept was the possibility that God had granted to some what He had withheld from others. Al-ʿAṭṭār did not accept the mystical way as having any exemplary value. For him, the genuineness of religious experiences was directly related to the degree to which it adhered to the Sharīʿa. The formulation of his analysis of Ṣūfism, that is, the concept of the two types of Ṣūfism, the one the antithesis of the other, is derived from *kalām*, not from *taṣawwuf* (mysticism). Al-ʿAṭṭār's interest in mysticism as religion was the scholarly interest of a *mutakallim* in the subject. In Damascus, when he was studying with Shaykh al-Yāfī, he admitted to owning a copy of *Al-Futūḥāt al-makkīya*, but when he attempted to explicate the difference between "*raḥman*" and "*raḥīm*" as describing God's attribute of mercifulness, he did so not from this source but as a problem in philology, which represents a profound shift in the semantic direction.[35]

The "reformulation of mysticism" by al-ʿAṭṭār so that it was subsumed under the Sharīʿa and the appeal of mysticism as a cultural form are characteristic of his period and his social situation. For the intellectuals of the

1830's, knowledge was becoming fragmented and compartmentalized. This was true of Western knowledge and it was reflected in the revival of *kalām*. Holistic speculative thought was not easy in this situation for them. The opposite, however, was true for the downtrodden Ahl al-Ḥadīth, for whom the inward-turning, integrative vision was entirely possible. Most of the important Ṣūfīs of the nineteenth century came from such a background.

The Study of Traditional Logic and the Development of Modern Secular Culture

Heretofore, I have referred to logic a number of times, generally in a slightly pejorative manner. It was described as having been imposed by structural necessities brought about by the industrial revolution, as coexisting uncomfortably with Māturīdite theology, and as having been used as a weapon for ideological purposes. Finally, it was shown performing a rather sophistic refutation of mysticism. There was more to the revival of the logical sciences than this, a point which has often been missed. The revival of the study of classical logic in the nineteenth century was a scholastic endeavor which obviously depended from a technical point of view on what material was accessible. One could argue, however, that the turn to the formal study of logic was part of a general intellectual response to modern conditions, an effort to rise above the process of piecemeal, ad hoc adaptation to situations as they arose, to a more general stance. Al-ʿAṭṭār's writing was central to the tradition of rationalism in Egypt in the nineteenth century.

The history of logic in the Islamic world had been associated largely with the rise and decline of the "Baghdad School" of the tenth century. Thereafter, the study of logic, from a modern European point of view, made very little advance; in the eleventh century, the only important figure was Ibn Sīnā, and after that there was only the brief connection between logic and astronomy in the thirteenth century in the circle of Nāṣir al-dīn al-Ṭūsī. Thereafter, the influence of theology on logical studies was paramount in the writings of such figures as the theologian al-Bayḍāwī and the later *mutakallimīn*, such as ʿAbdullah ibn ʿUmar and al-Dawwānī. The study of logic also became increasingly connected with the study of Arabic grammar, beginning with al-Qazwīnī al-Kātibī, known as the Imām al-Ḥaramayn. The use of logic as an independent tool, à la the Muʿtazilites, was ritualistically denounced in all the elementary books on *kalām*.[36]

In eighteenth-century Egypt, the study of logic was, while not neglected, developed in a fashion suitable to the needs of the *ḥadīth* movement. The principal text by Muḥammad al-Ṣabbān was a very short book which devoted exactly two pages to reasoning by analogy. It actually dealt with topics in *ḥadīth* at greater length.[37] In the beginning of his book, al-Ṣabbān devoted a section to the religious reasons for invoking the names of different caliphs and so on.

The principal revival of logic in Egypt occurred during the reform period and continued throughout the nineteenth century. It centered around three figures, all of whom served as Shaykh al-Azhar: Ḥasan al-ʿAṭṭār, Ḥasan al-Quwaysnī, and Ibrāhīm al-Bājūrī. This discussion will be limited to a treatment of the writings of al-ʿAṭṭār. Al-ʿAṭṭār wrote three works and a number of lesser compositions on logic.[38] The term "revival" of course needs to be used advisedly, as the content of al-ʿAṭṭār's writings in particular has been singularly criticized for its lack of originality. Its importance lies, historically, in the larger alignment of the study of logic with the reformism of Muḥammad ʿAlī. Compared to that of the classical age, writing of logic was weak; there were numerous misunderstandings of technical terms and the emphasis on argument by analogy led to frequent errors.[39] *The Fifth Book of Aristotle*, which dealt with *al-burhān* (proof) and *al-jadal* (argumentation), was poorly presented in al-ʿAṭṭār's period. From the perspective of the study of logic in the classical period, an account of its development in later centuries is perhaps irrelevant. From the point of view of modern history, however, a selective revival of parts of the Aristotelian tradition at the expense of others calls for an investigation.

Al-ʿAṭṭār on Logic

In his first main work, al-ʿAṭṭār attempted to show that logic was an important subject which must be studied. He chose to write a gloss on a text by the Indian Muḥibb Allah al-Bihārī (died 1707/1119) which was particularly concerned with analogy, called "Sullam al-ʿulūm fīʾl-manṭiq."[40] Al-ʿAṭṭār undertook this work after his return from his travels, after he was given the commentary by his friend and student then Qāḍī Arif Hikmet. Through his student, al-ʿAṭṭār became acquainted with the text and with the commentaries which others had written on it, because, as he said, it was unknown in Egypt until his own time. Al-ʿAṭṭār knew some of the rudimentary biographical facts about al-Bihārī. The Qāḍī had come in contact with some of the students of his commentator while he was in Madīna. Al-ʿAṭṭār also states that he knew some of the contemporary literature on the text and mentions the work of a contemporary, Baḥr al-ʿUlūm ʿAbd al-ʿAlī b. Muḥammad Niẓām al-dīn al-Lakhnāwī (died 1810/1225). Al-ʿAṭṭār referred to others but did not mention them by name, nor did he mention his opinion of these various writers. Baḥr al-ʿUlūm, for example, was known to have been a mystic of the school of Muḥī al-dīn ibn al-ʿArabī.[41] Furthermore, al-ʿAṭṭār did not mention the best known commentary of al-Bihārī, a work which Brockelmann called the standard text of logic in India in the eighteenth century, the *Munhīya* of Qāḍī Mubārak.[42]

Al-Bihārī, author of the basic text, dealt extensively in his writings with the use of analogy and even dealt with the use of analogy by the Shīʿīs. However, he favored a Ḥanafī position: what is general (*ʿāmm*) comes from the Qurʾān and *ḥadīth.* The dominant law school, the Shāfiʿīs permitted *al-raʾy.* The Shāfiʿīs limit the absolute (i.e., the general) by analogy, while the Ḥanafīs do not. Concerning the use of *ḥadīth*, al-Bihārī followed the Ḥanafī practice: he would not accept the bearer of *ḥadīth* except after *al-ra*ʾ*y*, while the Shāfiʿīs use *al-ra*ʾ*y* only if the bearer does not have an *isnād* (chains of authorities), or is not supported by another *rāwī*, or if it is known that he is unreliable.[43]

Al-ʿAṭṭār obviously composed this work for an audience which had some doubt about the status of logic as a discipline, and perhaps associated it with Muʿtazilism. On folio 15A, al-ʿAṭṭār includes in his definition of logic such points as that it was not a "divine" science, but neither was it philosophy, a forbidden science. In citing his sources, he mentioned "the gloss of our teacher al-Ṣabbān" and more often the gloss of Shaykh al-Mallāwī. Reference to familiar sources from the *ḥadīth* revival would have had the effect of making his work more acceptable, and this was needed.

A few years later, al-ʿAṭṭār wrote a gloss on the famous *Al-Īsāghūjī* of Athīr al-dīn al-Abharī (died A.D. 1264). It seems probable that al-ʿAṭṭār's interest in this manual was aroused by the fact that so many of the later *mutakallimīn* commented on it. Also, members of al-Abharī's circle, especially Nāṣir al-dīn al-Ṭūsī, were very important to al-ʿAṭṭār's scientific studies.[44] Contemporary observers affirm that the *Īsāghūjī* had a recognized place in the corpus of logic which was studied in the Ottoman Empire, along with other works on the subject of the syllogism, for example, Aristotle's "Alvias."[45]

Al-ʿAṭṭār studied the text of the *Īsāghūjī* through later commentaries, mainly that of Zakariyā al-Anṣārī (1422–1520). Al-Anṣārī was very much a representative of the later medieval trend which fused logic with theology and separated it from science and philosophy.[46] As this was not al-ʿAṭṭār's orientation, it is not surprising to find him rebelling against the views of al-Anṣārī and praising instead the writings of earlier *mutakallimīn* and logicians, such as Mīr Zāhid. In one place, al-ʿAṭṭār argued that al-Anṣārī did not understand what is meant by the term *ʿilm* (science), citing the views of Mīr Zāhid; elsewhere, he rejected the views of his commentator and followed Mīr Zāhid in his discussion of the whole and the part.[47] Criticisms of the well-known work of Zakariyā al-Anṣārī were a part of al-ʿAṭṭār's critique of the study of logic by *ḥadīth* students in the eighteenth century. This was doubtless an easy target, although perhaps sensitive. In the introduction to *Ḥāshiya ʿalā . . . al-Īsāghūjī*, al-ʿAṭṭār stated that he was relying on a gloss on the *Īsāghūjī* by Yūsuf al-Ḥifnāwī. The latter was the brother of the Ṣūfī *shaykh* and not an important scholar in his own right. His short text was a wholly insignificant work.[48] Al-ʿAṭṭār treated it very seriously, however, stating that it was not entirely comprehensible to students and that he had to disagree with some of the author's views. Thereafter, al-ʿAṭṭār switched to a discussion of works which he said were of value in the field of logic. He mentioned such books as the commentary of al-Quṭb al-Rāzī on the text "Al-Maṭāliʿ" (al-Bayḍāwī), al-Rāzī's glosses on the text "Al-Shamsīya" (al-Kātibī), the gloss of al-Taftazānī on the text of "Al-Shamsīya," along with its subcommentaries by Jalāl al-dīn al-Dawwānī and Amīr Abīʾl-Fatḥ (called "Ḥawāshī al-fatḥīya"). These were, of course, some of the major texts in *kalām*.[49] In praising the virtues of these Ahl al-Kalām al-

ʿAṭṭār was preparing to rehabilitate al-Abharī's student al-Ṭūsī, who had to be "salvaged" from the reputation, not only as a Shīʿī, but also as a *mutakallim*.

The last main work on logic which al-ʿAṭṭār undertook was completed in 1825/1240; it was his gloss on the commentary of ʿUbaydullah al-Khabīṣī on the *Tahdhīb*. As in previous works, he referred warmly to the tradition of *kalām*, which he called the way of the *muḥaqqiqīn*, a term reserved for those who took an approach based on reason but within the bounds of the Sharīʿa. These included the works of ʿAbd al-Ḥakīm al-Sīyalkūtī, "Al-Maṭūl," and Mīr Zāhid, "Risālat al-Rāzī fīʾl-taṣawwur waʾl-taṣdīq."[50]

Among the few Arab writers whom al-ʿAṭṭār dignified with the rank of *muḥaqqiq* was Yasīn b. Zayn al-dīn. In nearly every case, however, he referred to Indian writers on *kalām* in preference to later figures from the Arab world. In this work, he attacked Ibn Saʿīd al-Maghribī, who had criticized Shaykh Yasīn.

The gloss on al-Khabīṣī created a reputation for al-ʿAṭṭār both in Egypt and abroad. His Moroccan friend Sīdī al-ʿArabī al-Dumnātī, the court figure, praised it effusively.[51] Perhaps more importantly, this *ḥāshiya* (gloss) became incorporated into the curriculum of Egyptian higher education, as did *Al-Azharīya* in grammar. In his reform of the curriculum of the college of Dār al-ʿUlūm in 1901–1903, Muḥammad ʿAbdu retained the work of al-ʿAṭṭār in logic. In 1911, it was supplemented by the *Risāla* of Sultan Muḥammad for fourth-year students.[52]

Ādāb al-Baḥth *(Argumentation)*

Background

The progress of the study of *ādāb al-baḥth* closely resembled that of logic; for, indeed, it was virtually a branch of logic. It was well known in Turkey in the eighteenth century, but its principal recovery in Egypt came in the early nineteenth century. As was the case with logic, there were a few texts written in al-Azhar in the eighteenth century, for example, by Muḥammad al-Ṣabbān and Aḥmad al-Sijāʿī, but the character of the discipline changed with the growing interest in argument by analogy (*qiyās*). The field likewise owed much to the contributions of the *ʿulamāʾ* of India and to the revival and spread of the Naqshbandīs from India, which was very important in terms of its accessibility. Al-ʿAṭṭār gained a head start in this field, which was little known in Egypt, through his study of it in Damascus.[53] His works became standard texts.

Al-ʿAṭṭār's Writings on Ādāb al-Baḥth

Al-ʿAṭṭār's interests within *ādāb al-baḥth* changed radically, from employing it in religious disputes in Syria to making it serve more secular needs for argument to "reconcile, adjust, and modify." This lends credence to my hypothesis regarding the concern with analogy and the kind of problems which Muḥammad ʿAlī faced. In his first work, written in Egypt in 1795, it is clear that al-ʿAṭṭār was grappling with the contours of the discipline rather than being concerned with its application. There is no emphasis on *qiyās*, although even at this time he was aware of many Indian sources. His reliance on Indian sources anticipates what he later said about the isolated state of the field in Egypt. For example, al-ʿAṭṭār stated in the introduction to his second work: "Muḥammad al-Marʿashī, known as Sajaqli-Zadeh, was the most famous of the later distillers of *ādāb al-baḥth* in his 'Taqrīr al-Qawānīn' and then his 'Risāla walādīya' . . . when al-Zabīdī was in Egypt, no one taught these two books, nor were they known until some troublemakers [*al-afātīn*] came to Egypt from among the established professors."[54] Al-ʿAṭṭār proceeded, after this oblique criticism, to praise the scholars in Turkey who were much more interested in this field. On his return to Egypt, he reported teaching this work to some notables who had not studied it previously. Damascus had been the place where this work was actually completed.

Damascus in the early nineteenth century was an arena in which were debated the merits of the Ṭarīqa Muḥammadīya, the doctrine of the unity of man with God (Waḥdat al-wujūd), and Māturīdism versus Ashʿarism, as well as Wahhābism.[55] It was clearly being in Damascus which created a certain urgency for the study of the discipline for al-ʿAṭṭār. This is manifested in his striving for precision of meaning, through rules which could be understood, rules concerning the generalization of meaning or concerning whether a word was used as a metaphor, as an honorific, or, if not as a metaphor, then in a combination form between the literal and the metaphorical.[56]

In al-ʿAṭṭār's last work on *ādāb al-baḥth*, which was undertaken after he had returned to Egypt, one can see a still further degree of progress in the direction of secular culture and at the same time some basic continuity of the discipline. What was new was the rationale which al-ʿAṭṭār gave for the study of this discipline. He said that it was an "independent discipline," that its rules helped to distinguish the general from the particular, and that it provided rules of argumentation. Al-ʿAṭṭār went on to compare it to logic in that it served many other fields, since no field is free from the conflicts of views which require reconciliation, adjustment, and modification, all of which depend on the syllogism.[57]

What stands out in this work is the concept of the "independent field," a concept which one finds only in al-ʿAṭṭār's last writings. This represents a subtle shift away from the framework implicit in his earlier work, for example, in his revival of Islamic science within the context of *al-ḥikma.* It marks a step toward the acceptance of the intellectual fragmentation of knowledge of the bourgeois era. The loss of the medieval unity is still somewhat implicit in al-ʿAṭṭār's thought; even where he admires the methodology of Western science and praises scientific specialization (see Chapter

5), he does not understand the full implications of the effect of changing conditions on his outlook.

In the transition from corporate structure to class structure, the role of religion itself changed. Gradually, religion ceased to uphold the medieval unity of religion and state, "*dīn wa dawla*," and the unity of all knowledge. Theoretically, it did as before, but fragmentation was increasingly the reality. One may still speak of the religious framework of culture, but without either speaking of religiosity (at least as the eighteenth century knew it) or asking what is meant by framework other than law. Discussing the phase termed "merchant capitalism" in the eighteenth century I spoke of secular culture as a byproduct of religious scholarship; during the reform period, Māturīdite *kalām* was itself molded by logic, which served the juridical needs of the state. Here was a revival of Aristotle, but without the Aristotelian logos or theoretical reason. This left only the rationalism of instrumentality or of practice. The real "logos" was Europe. Between the two was the Māturīdite numen, which held that faith, not pure reason, sanctioned the rationalism of instrumentality. Māturīdite theology became a middle road which connected the ruling class to its own society, on the one hand, and to Europe, on the other, condemning the extremes of both. Māturīdite reformism had arisen in India with the earlier impact of the Portuguese. It reached Egypt and gained in influence from the later eighteenth century as conditions similar to those in India prevailed.

Chapter 8
The Reform Period, 1815–1837, and the Development of Neoclassical Culture: The Study of Language Sciences, Literature, and History

This chapter presents a survey of the main writings of the reform period. These works reflected the dominant rational-deductive orientation discussed in the preceding chapter; furthermore, they were neoclassical in form. During this period, there were also a growing number of works of European inspiration. These were integrated into the dominant framework of thought and were used to fulfill certain concrete needs of the time. This period witnessed a noticeable expansion in the number and variety of works which could be termed secular, although the total production of writings fell precipitously from that of the eighteenth century. However, the progress of secular culture should not be taken as proof of modernity, as it often is in cultural history. More important to the culture of capitalism is utilitarianism, and this, as I have shown, may emerge in religion.

The onslaught against religion in the name of reason or secularism is, we are wrongly led to believe, a main theme of modern Western history. If one looks at all of Europe and chooses representative examples of the culture of different ruling classes, this is certainly not the case.[1] Even in areas in which secularism seems to have progressed the furthest, religion has a defined role. In no instances in the history of capitalism has atheism emerged among the ruling class as the end product of secularism; in fact, in the more highly developed capitalist societies, the contradictions of excessive individualism are projected intensely into religion in which God, no longer the simple watchmaker of early capitalist thought, must perform a more active role in the harmonization of interests.

In England after the first world war a religious revival took place among the ruling class, a literary expression of which can be found in the writings of T. S. Eliot. The return of "religious" conviction was neither an accident nor a transitory phenomenon. With the rise of organized labor in the 1890's and the great disillusionment with the European state system which followed World War I, the ruling class embraced the Church, an ally which it now needed.[2]

On the Continent, too, the course of development of the dialectic between secular and religious culture was grounded in the development of the economy and social structure. In France and Italy, for example, where the ruling class included large commercial as well as industrial sectors, these classes lacked the power for a prolonged period to transform the society as a whole as the English industrial bourgeoisie had done. Thus there arose in these two countries and in other regions (e.g., southern and central Europe) polarities between regions or urban and rural areas. In politics, these polarities expressed themselves with some interruptions from the nineteenth century onward in the form of clerical versus anticlerical disputes. While class conflict entered into these struggles, a main characteristic was the struggle within the ruling class.

On the periphery of the world market, we find the early history of modern secular culture linked as in Europe to the specific course of capitalist development. In Egypt, as in Italy, the history of capitalism was largely bound up with commerce until the later nineteenth century, but with the difference that Egyptian commerce was controlled from abroad. Thus, unlike Italy, where indigenous centers of capital carried forward the process of economic transformation and differentiation, commerce on the periphery was much weaker as an economic force.

Cultural developments during the period between 1815 and 1837 reflect the measure of power and autonomy which Egypt possessed prior to its full integration into the world market. A rational-deductive outlook characterized all fields of inquiry. By the age of Isma'īl, this gave way to more passive, absorptive cultural style *ḥadīth* studies. In the language sciences in the reform period, this was exemplified in the prominence of lexicography, which was developed for the purposes of the translation movement. The rulers needed to find or develop the logical Arabic equivalents of European words and concepts.

Language Sciences

Of the three subjects which are treated in this chapter, the most important for the medieval world was the language sciences. This was because revelation was vested in the Arabic language, which therefore had a special position. The preservation of the Arabic language was a religious obligation. In the Middle Ages, theorization about the nature of the language was permitted but within certain theological limits, as the main spirit was one of transmission. This meant that, particularly with respect to grammar, certain areas of substantive change were virtually closed. In other areas, however, important changes did take place, as in the field of lexicography. While this field produced no figures comparable in stature to al-Zabīdī in the eighteenth century, a group of scholars who entered the field as a by-product of their primary occupation as translators or book editors followed a new direction. This group needed to transfer with speed and accuracy concepts from modern European languages into Arabic and Turkish. Such works had been compiled in the medieval period, especially in pharmacology, with equivalents of terms made available in as many as five or six languages. What was new in this period was not the concern for equivalent terms, but the transfer of a body of concepts into a language which had not been modernized.[3] Lexicography thus came to be an arena for the practice of analogical reason (*qiyās*).

Al-Zabīdī's revival of lexicography, as an outgrowth of his *ḥadīth* study, was carried on and expanded by others who wished to find in the Arabic classical heritage the word or phrase which would convey a modern meaning. The writing of the "universal dictionary" broke down because of the complexity of technical subjects, and a number of more specialized dictionaries were composed. Collective projects were undertaken jointly by Europeans and Egyptians, for example, Don Raphael's Italian and Arabic dictionary. Apart from specialized dictionaries, there was a renewed interest in the structure and organization of existing dictionaries, reflecting the needs of the new users. Fāris Shidyaq attacked the "*qafīya*, or rhyme, order" and called for a strict alphabetical order following the *Mujmal* of Ibn Fāris (died 387). He also argued against the inclusion of proper names and favored a more empirical approach to language. For example, he thought that the lexicographer should go and talk to the tribes and rely on the later Arabic writers as well as the earlier ones. His dictionary, the *Jāsūs*, marked a sharp break with the eighteenth-century lexicographical revival of al-Zabīdī on several main points, although it still lay clearly within the neoclassical tradition. The rejection of *qafīya* order in favor of alphabetical order was not substantively significant and was again rejected as it had been earlier. But what is important is that Shidyaq's work reflected the view that the utility of the language was relative and changeable. While previously there had been an intimate connection with rhyme order and poetry, by the nineteenth century the needs which society imposed on the language scholar were different. Shidyaq's concern with a historical approach to language is important. It showed that his conception of language was linked less to the single event of the revelation of the Qur᾿ān than to its larger historical development. For Shidyaq, the meaning of going to the tribes was different than it had been for al-Zabīdī. For the latter, it was a matter of faith that the reports of the tribes would confirm and clarify the medieval sources. Shidyaq did not believe this a priori. For both, it was an article of faith that the history of the tribes was one and the same, that their language remained pure through lack of contact with "corrupting" influences.

Shidyaq was not the first writer to undertake a criticism of medieval lexicography, but he was the first to do so from a modern, secular perspective. The distinction has led to confusions. Germanus Farḥāt wrote a dictionary at the beginning of the eighteenth century. He followed the *qafīya* order but dropped many of the obscure usages for flowers, rivers, and mountains and omitted the discursive essays found in al-Firūzabādī's *Qāmūs*. This is perhaps the basis for his work's claim to fame. Following the comments of a later editor of this work, one can deduce that the principal consequences of these adaptations was to render Arabic lexicography more suitable for propagating the Catholic faith. The dictionary included numerous biblical references. As a consequence of the secular needs posed by the translation movement, the traditional Arabic lexicography continued to develop. Lane undertook to work within it with the help of Azhar *shaykhs.* The British in India apparently also saw its utility. A notice in *Journal des Savans* mentioned that a copy of the *Qāmūs* "collated with many manuscript copies of this work was corrected for the press by Shaykh Aḥmad b. Muḥammad al-Anṣārī 'Yumuni-Yoosh' Shīrwānī, employed in the College of Fort Williams, Calcutta, 1817 A.D."[4]

In spirit, lexicography reflected the changes which the era had brought for the cultural elite. This elite was now involved in positivist science and was becoming impatient with the state of the language, desiring to organize it to fit modern needs. These feelings were manifested long before the mechanisms to effect the necessary adaptation, such as *al-ishtiqāq* (the deriving of words), were revived. The study of grammar, which had in the eighteenth century been related to the *ḥadīth* movement, became in the nineteenth century, especially in the writings of its leading figure, Ḥasan al-ʿAṭṭār, more closely aligned with logic. The content of Arabic grammar was not challenged by the intellectual reforms of Muḥammad ʿAlī, but the growing utilitarian spirit of the age affected the style of presentation and pedagogy. The movement to reorganize the teaching of grammar and the approach to understanding grammar as a rational science converged in the works of Ḥasan al-ʿAṭṭār. His writings, especially those in grammar, have had a lasting influence in Egypt, virtually to the present generation.

In turning to the writings of al-ʿAṭṭār on grammar between 1815 and 1830 and to the writings of his students, the importance of the neoclassical revival to the creation of a modern secular culture becomes increasingly apparent. Al-ʿAṭṭār began in this period to abandon the methods of teaching and writing which had characterized eighteenth-century Egypt and which he himself had employed earlier in his life. With the reaction to the *ḥadīth* movement, there came a reaction to the approach to all knowledge through the "chain of authority." The *ḥadīth* movement had probably encouraged the writing of glosses (*ḥawāshī*), a genre which had begun to appear in Egypt in the eighteenth century in large numbers, but it perhaps discouraged the production of "independent" works. Paradoxically, this is the period in which one finds the greatest creativity. The later reaction against the *ḥadīth* revival encouraged the tendency to edit classical selections, to compose works not linked in any way to *ijāzāt*, that is, linked to one's teachers, but it did not have time to mature. The reform movement in language sciences among a small group of scholars in the service of Muḥammad ʿAlī naturally did not destroy the former traditions of pedagogy. These were clung to tenaciously by the majority of *ʿulamāʾ* until the early twentieth century. In fact, with the British occupation, one finds the evolution of an even more exaggerated concealment, the *taqrīr*, which is commentary on a gloss.

Al-ʿAṭṭār's participation in editing an anthology was obviously connected with his association with the institution of the Būlāq Press, for the book appeared in 1825/1240 as one of its earliest printed works. This book was entitled *Hadhihi majmūʿa fī ʿilm al-taṣrīf* and contained selections from a number of classical grammatical writers. The principal grammarian was Aḥmad b. ʿAlī b. Masʿūd, who was known for his *Marāḥ al-arwāḥ.*[5]

In al-ʿAṭṭār's other works on grammar, he chose to write on several commentaries at the same time. The spirit in which the gloss was conceived would normally, of course, preclude this. In one gloss dated 1827/1235, five commentaries are mentioned as the basis. In this work,[6] he still continued to employ examples from Arabic poetry, although to a lesser extent than he had in the eighteenth century. Perhaps this was because the independent study of literature had in the post-Napoleonic era become slightly more acceptable again.[7]

Al-ʿAṭṭār was in this regard rather ahead of his era. Even he was not free to avoid the "traditions"; nor could his students pursue the language sciences without reference to the past.[8] Nonetheless, al-ʿAṭṭār's efforts to recover the classical texts, such as those of Masʿūd, which approached grammar through *raʾy*, and his assault on the pedagogy of grammar seen in the perspective of two hundred years still seem quite radical, especially as the morphology of even the contemporary language does not differ notably from that of the classical.[9]

Finally, an influence on the development of philological studies in Egypt which remains unassessed is the role of Orientalists. A body of literature exists which shows the close relationship which existed in the 1830's and 1840's between the correctors and editors, on the one hand, and the Western Orientalists, on the other. The orientation toward rationalism in cultural studies in Egypt may have led some *shaykhs* to become interested in the primitive structuralist theories of language which were being developed in Europe during this period. A simpler explanation, of course, is that numerous Orientalists appeared and needed help with Arabic.[10]

Literature

Literary prose declined with the gradual decline of the *maqāma* form after al-ʿAṭṭār. The principal achievement in this area was in the revival of letter writing, which served an important function as Arabic became the language of government. In poetry, the *waṭanīyāt*, or patriotic themes, marked a development over the earlier expressions found in eighteenth-century lyric poetry. More challenging to the literary utilitarianism of the age was the continuing revival of Andalusian literature, and the imitation of its forms. Perhaps the greatest long-term impact of the Andalusian cultural heritage was in the area of music, where the *muwashshaḥāt* have played a role until the present.

Composition and letter writing had been highly developed in Egypt in Mamlūk times and did not require a great deal of adaptation given the structure of society. Al-ʿAṭṭār had had a number of years of experience with *inshāʾ* dating back to about 1815. In writing the major *inshāʾ*, however, al-

ʿAṭṭār produced an important work which greatly exceeded in scope what might actually have been required.[11] Al-ʿAṭṭār wrote his work for the secretaries of the new Jihādīya school and praised Muḥammad ʿAlī in his introduction. The connection between the creation of the new institutions and the use of this literary form is thus quite clear. The development of the *Inshāʾ* as a manual for writers in government service was different than and more elaborate than the *inshāʾ* of al-Zabīdī and al-Jabartī in the eighteenth century.[12]

Al-ʿAṭṭār's *Inshāʾ* is divided into two parts. The first and longer of the two is devoted to the writing of different types of letters. The second is devoted to the writing of various legal documents (*al-shurūṭ waʾl-sukūk*). Among the justifications for writing this work, which he gives in the introduction, is his concern "for how the ruler and his lieutenant would be communicating." The first section is composed in *sajʿ*, according to the norms of the period; the second part (pp. 100–119) is an instruction manual which is written in ordinary classical prose. Al-ʿAṭṭār introduced this section with the cryptic comment that "traditionally, the *ʿulamāʾ* had considered this to be a separate field and it is a very beneficial one."

Al-ʿAṭṭār was profoundly concerned with the problem of communication, but because of the nature of his audience, he stressed technical, not aesthetic, problems in many of his works. He stated that his own age was characterized by a deterioration in writing and copying and urged the secretaries to be concerned with accuracy. In another work in the same period, he complained of the *shaykh*'s inattention even in their own writings. He stated, again in the *Inshāʾ*, that it was the responsibility of the copyist to give the author's full name, point of origin, tribe, honorific names, and so forth, for on this basis alone could one writer be distinguished from another. He stated that this type of precision was also required in any legal document. Such documents call for a rigorous description.[13]

The renewed dominance of insincere expression in the form of *sajʿ* was a major literary problem for writers of the reform period. In this respect the writers of the *majālis* of the eighteenth century were freer, and this in turn is reflected in the relative decline of *sajʿ* during the later eighteenth century.[14] The important point lies with the nature of patronage. The *Inshāʾ* of al-ʿAṭṭār shows clearly where the patronage was in the period of Muḥammad ʿAlī.

The first section contains examples of how to write letters to kings, rulers, and members of the Ottoman court. The next section contains two examples of letters to the Sharīf of Mecca, then to the Sultan of the Maghrib. The following sections contain letters to high-ranking military officials down to the provincial *amīr*. The section following that contains letters to *qāḍīs*, *ʿulamāʾ*, and *shaykhs*. Finally, letters for different occasions are included. In a society such as Egypt under Muḥammad ʿAlī, which was based on hierarchy, where honor followed from rank, and where patronage and favoritism played an important role, exaggerated expressions of praise and mourning had a legitimate place. When the structure of society was altered somewhat by the enlargement of the middle classes, as was the case in the age of Isma'īl, the characteristic literary needs also changed. Letters of this sort to the monarch and the poetry of the court and its circle continued to be required, but the characteristic mode of communication shifted from vertical to horizontal, and exaggeration of style was no longer necessary. In the major work on *inshā'* of the Isma'īl period, the use of *saj'* was extremely limited.[15]

Changes in the literary needs of the elite, beginning even in the Muḥammad 'Alī era, played a role in the breakdown of the dominance of *saj'*, notably in the translation movement. The movement began with nonspecialists, frequently Levantine translators, who knew European languages. The works of the first translation period were characterized by rhetoric and imprecision. With the return of the Egyptian mission students, *saj'* was abandoned except for the title page, and accuracy became more important.[16] The Andalusian heritage was another influence against *saj'*. Al-Ṭahṭāwī greatly valued this aspect of his education with al-'Aṭṭār and repeated years later fragments of al-'Aṭṭār's favorite poetry, praising him for his life-long devotion to the study of Andalusian literature.[17]

The impact on literature of the cultural links which existed between the Egyptians and the Ottomans remains unstudied. The older view that the Ottomans brought the use of *saj'* to Egypt has been discarded without a new hypothesis to replace it. If we relate language style to social relations, it is not difficult to imagine Levantines and Ottomans in this period using exaggerated forms, while the Egyptian middle class would struggle against it—at least those who had the option of putting up such a struggle. Not surprisingly, Muḥammad 'Alī's secretary of the 1820's, Khayret Efendi, used *saj'* continuously; another Turk whose education had been partly Egyptian, Arif Hikmet used *saj'* somewhat less. Several Egyptian poets used *saj'* when they wrote for Muḥammad 'Alī. Finally, with the arrival of Sami Bey and the rationalization of the institutional structures of the early 1830's, the use of Ottoman itself was said to gain in precision.[18]

The principal literary phenomenon was the decline of the *maqāma* in the first half of the nineteenth century. Some of the reasons have already been given; they broadly correspond to the reasons for the revival of *inshā'* and to *saj'*. Others have been suggested in the fifth and sixth chapters. The struggle to dominate prose pitted a bourgeois realism—in journalism, translation, and literature—against the aristocratic, hierarchic use of language called *saj'*. Each according to the dynamics of the larger society was utilitarian and in a sense rationalist. However, the *maqāma* was subject to struggles not only within the cultural elite, but also between the cultural elite as a whole and the intelligentsia of the suppressed middle classes. *Maqāmāt* continued to be used in the religious education and scholarship of this class as it had more generally been in the eighteenth century. Al-Ḥarīrī was used throughout the century in connection with *ḥadīth* studies. The dependence on the *maqāma* form by this class for didactic purposes boded ill for its evolution into a form intended for upper-class enṭertainment and edification. At the same time, there was a genuine attempt on the part of Ḥasan al-ʿAṭṭār, whose *Maqāma* was studied in Chapter 4, and his student al-Ṭahṭāwī and others to promote the *maqāma* within the framework of bourgeois realism.[19] The ultimate decline of the *maqāma* in this latter sense was a reflection of the growing dependence of the upper classes on Europe by the middle of the century and the increasingly clear identification of the *maqāma* with traditional merchant culture.

The poetry of the reform period presents some of the most extreme examples of exaggerated praise and barren imagery. It was the last age in which the court was the only patron, and it was an age of decline in comparison to the later eighteenth century. The only new development was the *waṭanīya*, or patriotic poem. An examination of the *waṭanīya* as literature, apart from the theme itself, does not yield much that is new. Praise of the country, or more correctly of the dynasty, could be found in the eighteenth century. The imagery and technique of the early *waṭanīyāt* added little to what was available; there is no new development of feeling. It is said that the *waṭanīya* was a response by al-Ṭahṭāwī to Europe. Actually, it began with al-ʿAṭṭār and his pupil Shihāb ad-dīn.[20] Al-Ṭahṭāwī contributed very little until later in his life.

The poetry of the reform period employed the most mechanical application of *sajʿ* to a range of themes, European and medieval Arabic. Shihāb ad-dīn revealed in his *Dīwān*, as did his contemporary ʿAlī Darwīsh in his, in startling depth the deadening life in a bureaucratic environment.[21] Yet Shihāb ad-dīn was steeped in literary culture, classical and modern. The best reading of his poems in *sajʿ* on the English government and in praise of European consuls would be that on some level he intended exaggeration to convey mockery.

For al-ʿAṭṭār, in the later part of his life, literature was something he regarded with nostalgia. Neoclassicism was becoming dry and intellectualized. It had lost the feeling of his youthful *Maqāma*. While he still preferred the Arabic popular poetry *zaghal* and *muwashshaḥāt* to other forms, his writings were theoretical arguments, virtually an outgrowth of his work in logic.[22] Where earlier, Al-ʿAṭṭār spoke of moonlit nights and cups of wine, when he wrote in the 1820's about *Kitāb al-musāmarāt* and *Turjumān al-ashwāq*, he approached these erotic and mystical works as a theoretician of aesthetics.[23] These became the springboard to an attack on the neo-Pythagorean ideas of the Ikhwān al-Ṣafāʾ (brethren of purity). They had claimed that the study of music demonstrates that the world conforms to arithmetical and geometrical relations. Al-ʿAṭṭār rejected this, claiming that the science of music is a separate discipline. The principal justification which al-ʿAṭṭār gave for this claim was that music had its own distinct sphere of practical application. Music, he said, almost quoting Ibn al-ʿArabī, was useful for swaying man's soul, which meant that it can be used to encourage him to do tiring physical labor and to encourage those who participate in war (although money is needed for these also). Al-ʿAṭṭār offered a warning that music has stirred up wars and passions.[24]

While the Ikhwān themselves were not in the least acceptable to the *ʿulamāʾ* of al-Azhar, the general idea of music as integrated into a larger intellectual whole was a broad common denominator which could unite the conservative religious studies in *ʿilm al-qawāfa* (science of rhyme) with those of the mystics' use of music in the *dhikr.* What distinguished al-ʿAṭṭār's position, and this was a revolutionary one, is the advocacy of the position that music should break free from any larger whole. Al-ʿAṭṭār's rejection of the Ikhwānian theory of music in favor of the idea of music as an independent art form was still far from *l'art pour l'art.* It may have been evolving in that direction, but in the 1820's it was still almost a production of logic. Music was discussed as an analogy to various other practical arts which had their domain. Still his teaching of literature in the privacy of his home and his sustaining of the freer forms of poetry like the *muwashshaḥa* were in the long run of great importance to the development of literature in Egypt. Shihāb ad-dīn's famous compilation of *muwashshaḥāt,* which influenced the music from the age of Ismaʿīl on, had its origins in al-ʿAṭṭār's work.

History and Geography

In the writings of al-ʿAṭṭār and al-Ṭahṭāwī, history and geography drew their inspiration from Islamic rationalism to confront the positions which had been advanced by the writers of the previous generation. Al-ʿAṭṭār, basing himself on Ibn Khaldūn, dealt with the ʿAlid tradition and its interpretation of the caliphate as well as its views on the Battle of Badr. Al-Ṭahṭāwī, who studied with al-ʿAṭṭār, based his own geographical and historical work on Abūʾl-Fidāʾ. He made his *riḥla* into a polemic for reform.

Al-ʿAṭṭār wrote a major work in the field of history based on the methodology of Ibn Khaldūn. In so doing, he transformed a traditional religious topic of veneration into a basis for rationalist-cum-secular argument. It is clear, from the title, that it was partly Ottoman inspired.[25] The subject is one which had often been raised in previous works, the sequence of legitimate caliphs and the justification for the rule of the family of ʿUthmān as the legitimate successor to the earlier caliphate. What is unusual in this period is the degree to which Māturīdism relied on naturalistic causality, while of course opposing *falsafa.* This is shown in the concept of *ʿaṣabīya* (group loyalty, or solidarity) which is invoked in this essay to explain the success of certain caliphs. The style of writing is a clear modern prose with no *sajʿ*, a fact as striking as the content itself.

The first topic in this book is the Khilāfa, the caliphate. It was al-ʿAṭṭār's intention to explain the special role of the Quraysh, the Meccan tribe from which the Prophet arose, and at the same time to reject certain Shīʿī ideas on the *imāma.* The first source which al-ʿAṭṭār quotes is Abū Bakr al-Bāqillānī, but the second is Ibn Khaldūn. Ibn Khaldūn, al-ʿAṭṭār stated, said that the Prophet mentioned the Quraysh, not because of some special blessing, but to accomplish certain objectives, notably the general welfare (*al-maṣlaḥa*). Their designation, Ibn Khaldūn concluded, was related to their widely agreed upon virtues, among which was social solidarity (*al-ʿaṣabīya*), which granted them a certain freedom from internal feuds.

In his discussion of the Rāshidūn period, the Battle of Badr was one of several topics which al-ʿAṭṭār discussed. It was dealt with without *ḥadīth* sources and without commentary on the *shuhadāʾ*, or martyrs. The main problem which al-ʿAṭṭār dealt with in the Rāshidūn section was the reason for the breakdown of the original *ʿaṣabīya*, which led to the feuds and permitted the rise of the Ummayads. Al-ʿAṭṭār found the division of loyalties between ʿAlī and Muʿāwiya explicable in terms of geographical differences (Syria vs. other regions), tribal loyalties (the opposition of the tribes from Rabīʿ and Yaman to ʿAlī), and occupational loyalties (support for ʿAlī from the military), but that the decisive factor was the *ʿaṣabīya* of the Syrian troops who had been through the experience of the conquest. He gave precedence to this over the weakening of ʿAlī's forces by the desertion of the Khawārij.[26]

With the rise of Muʿāwiya, al-ʿAṭṭār's mild ʿAlid sympathies, gathered perhaps from his Wafāʾīya background, emerge: "The crowd accepted the designation of Muʿāwiya in the middle of the year 41, at which point the people had forgotten prophecy and had forgotten miracles and sided with solidarity and military triumph. Thus the Banū Umayya and Muʿāwiya were appointed by their victory over the Muḍar and the other Arabs on their great day."[27]

Al-ʿAṭṭār's treatment of ʿAbbāsid history (folios 15–24) is largely a discussion of the development of Shīʿism with some references to the Zaydīs and the Rāfidīs, not to be expected, given his overall theme of the Khilāfa. At the same time, it was his intention to refute the Shīʿī account of Muḥammad's deathbed designation of ʿAlī, which many of the Ahl al-Bayt accepted. In his argument, he turned to *ḥadīth*, citing ʿĀʾisha's rejection of this account. Al-ʿAṭṭār gives his view in the beginning of the discussion: "It should be known that the basis of this dynasty was that the Ahl al-Bayt, following the death of the Prophet, saw themselves as being the rightful heirs to rule and not the tribe of Quraysh."[28]

Al-ʿAṭṭār denied the claims of ʿAlī but argued also against the claim that the subsequent dynasties, ʿAbbāsid and Fāṭimid, lacked ʿAlid roots. The defect of the ʿAbbāsid state was that its rulers, one after the other, permitted it to grow weaker until it was conquered by the Mongols. In contrast, the Ottomans maintained their strength.

In his discussion of the special virtues (*manāqib*) of the Ottomans, al-ʿAṭṭār stated that the role of reunifying the Sunnī world was reserved for them. This world had so disintegrated (note the opposite of *ʿaṣabīya*) into small units that the village *shaykhs* grew ignorant of their religion. Among the special virtues of the House of ʿUthmān was the conquest of Constantinople, which had been attempted repeatedly since Ummayad times. Al-ʿAṭṭār concluded the essay with a series of ambiguous comments, perhaps reflecting the intentional ambiguity of one who is writing under certain constraints. "Among the special virtues of this state was also that it protected the pale of Islam. But after a while Islam became strangely weak, a piece of whiteness surrounded by the blackness of its enemies. It was as if God had absented himself, leaving it to face the most severe troubles."[29] Al-ʿAṭṭār was not in a position, as was al-Ṭahṭāwī, to initiate the long discussion in Arabic writing on the strength of the West.

One might note the effect of al-ʿAṭṭār's use of Ibn Khaldūn on the traditional eighteenth-century account of the Battle of Badr and the special virtues of its heroes. The Badrīyīn are transformed by Al-ʿAṭṭār into an abstract collective force, characterized by a certain social solidarity, which ran all through Sunnī history. In the eighteenth-century accounts, the Badrīyīn had been studied one by one, that is, as individual moral examples. The emphasis on the use of logic and analysis is clear throughout, even though the author does not entirely eschew the use of *ḥadīth* sources. It would seem to be the first integrated work of Arab historical analysis in modern times. Unlike the great work of al-Jabartī, it is not compartmentalized but pursues a central theme and argument to the end.

One topic which it treated was a matter of special concern to al-ʿAṭṭār: Shīʿism. His principal source for his studies on natural science was an Imāmite, Nāṣir al-dīn al-Ṭūsī. In his work on *al-handasa*, which will be discussed in Chapter 9 and elsewhere, al-ʿAṭṭār attempted to defend the views expressed in al-Ṭūsī's book *Matn al-tajrīd*. Another concern was to moderate the exaggerated claims of the *ṣaḥāba* movement in Egypt. His essay apparently attempted to accomplish both tasks.[30]

Al-ʿAṭṭār's use of Ibn Khaldūn's general conceptual framework was not limited to the above work, but can be found in another work on tribal history. In this work on the tribes of Egypt, al-Maqrīzī had discussed the Awlād al-Muqaddam, who lived between Greater ʿAqaba and Alexandria,[31] and their various subdivisions. He suggested that they might have originated from the Ghaṭafān in Arabia. Al-ʿAṭṭār, commenting on this particular discussion, stated, "Now [in the 1820's] their genealogy has become mixed," meaning that they are no longer distinctly Bedouins but have become mixed with other elements of the society. Some, he said (referring to al-Maqrīzī's subdivisions) no longer existed; others had joined the ranks of the Egyptian *fallāḥīn*. This meant that only some of the Bedouin tribes have actually remained in a state of purity, and even those which have remained pure have become ignorant of their lineage and are no longer interested in it. Al-ʿAṭṭār is grappling here with the problem that Ibn Khaldūn posed of the Bedouin as an absolutely separate element in society, who entered civilization only under certain conditions.[32] Ibn Khaldūn's theory of history was clearly on the mind of al-Ṭahṭāwī when he read Montesquieu, whose work he found to be very similar to the *Muqaddima*. He referred to Montesquieu as the Ibn Khaldūn of the West.[33]

The study of Islamic works on geography and history had first been revived in Turkey in the late eighteenth century in connection with the needs of the military. A number of Western works were translated into Turkish at that time as well. A number of these works were later reprinted at Būlāq during the Muḥammad ʿAlī period, some in Turkish and some in Arabic, and for the same reason. In general, as Lane stated, the knowledge of physical geography among the Egyptians was very low, owing in part to the lack of maps.[34] Al-ʿAṭṭār and al-Ṭahṭāwī were among the main students of geography in Egypt, and they had had contact with the Turkish studies in these fields. For both of them, however, the factor of personal travel, more than that of military reform, informed their interest in geography. Al-ʿAṭṭār wrote in the introduction to the Būlāq edition of the *Takhlīṣ*, in praise of the book, that it should make any reasonable man seek to travel from country to country until he arrived at certain knowledge. The importance of the *Takhlīṣ*, he stated, lay in the fact that there was no other work in Arabic on the history of Paris.[35]

As in the case of history and literature, al-Ṭahṭāwī had received training in the rationalist tradition of classical geography from al-ʿAṭṭār, who had read with him the classical texts and had written explanatory notes in the margins. Al-Ṭahṭāwī is the witness to this, and it is confirmed by literary evidence.[36] He obviously relied on these works which he studied with al-ʿAṭṭār. "Kitāb taqwīm al-buldān" formed the basis of one section of his own work, *Bidāyat al-qudamāʾ* (1838).[37] The other sources which he used were European. In turning to these marginal notes to read the comments of al-ʿAṭṭār, one finds an example of a rational-deductive approach (à la Abūʾl-Fidāʾ) adjusting to European positivism. Abūʾl-Fidāʾ had mentioned Germany, which, he stated, was an unknown region. Al-ʿAṭṭār commented that this may have been the case for the Greeks, "but in our time we know it east and west," from knowledge which the Greeks did not possess. On the same page he translates *farāsikh* into miles and refers to information on the size of the earth and the height of some mountains.[38]

Al-ʿAṭṭār made some other comments which reveal his familiarity with the Westernized Turkish geographical tradition. In a discussion of the West Indies (al-Hind al-Gharbīya), he referred in particular to a work entitled "Yeni dunya" (New World), which was apparently an atlas and a history book. His reaction to it, however, was rather reserved. He concluded that the theory of seven continents was still compatible with the "fundamental" division of north and south.[39]

The influence of Abūʾl-Fidāʾ on al-ʿAṭṭār and al-Ṭahṭāwī was greater in geography than in astronomy. Al-ʿAṭṭār remarked that the astronomical data found in the "Kitāb taqwīm al-buldān" were now contained in works on *ʿilm al-hayʾa*, although he did not absolutely reject the traditional unity of these fields. Similarly, when al-Ṭahṭāwī discussed European geographical writing, he called it *ʿilm al-hayʾa al-dunyawī*, or *hayʾa* of this world, implying that he judged it in terms of the "Kitāb taqwīm."[40]

The same held true of al-Ṭahṭāwī's astronomical discussions in the *Takhlīṣ*, but by 1835 he had turned against Ptolemaic astronomy. For example, in the *Takhlīṣ* he wrote, concerning map making in Paris, that a similar operation could be found in Ptolemy. Where European theories diverged, he expressed some doubts, for example, on the rotation of the earth. "When it is morning in Paris, it is noon in Cairo."[41]

Al-Ṭahṭāwī broke decisively with the Ptolemaic view in a work on *ʿilm al-hayʾa* (that is, geography and astronomy) which was completed in 1835, in which he translated portions of geography books on Europe and the rest of the world, concluding with a section on astronomy. His source for the latter was Isaac Newton, and he made no effort to reconcile contradictory traditions.[42]

Despite the Islamic intellectual formation of al-Ṭahṭāwī, the *Takhlīṣ* was poorly received among conservatives in al-Azhar and elsewhere. This is not surprising. Lane recorded an observation on October 27, 1834, of a conversation in a bookstore where it was described as "his voyage from Alexandria to Marseilles; how he got drunk on board the ship and was tied to the mast and flogged; that he ate pork in the land of infidelity and obstinacy, and that it is a most excellent meat; how he was delighted with the French girls, and how superior they were in charms to the women of Egypt; and having qualified himself, by every accomplishment for an eminent place in Hell, returned to his native country."[43]

In this brief, brilliant anecdote, Lane evokes the latent social conflict between the ruling class and the suppressed middle class. Al-Ṭahṭāwī had written a *riḥla*; he had, in fact, abandoned the structure and style of the familiar pietistic *riḥla* in all but name, in favor of the secular, geographical studies favored by the Ottoman ruling class. In the view of one student, what attracted him most was the genre favored by seventeenth- and eighteenth-century Ottoman diplomats who, having traveled to Europe, sat down to write about their experiences.[44]

The Integration of Egypt into the World Market and the Development of Modern Culture: A Brief Sketch

The third phase in the development of modern culture in Egypt can be conveniently dated from the generation after the Land Law of 1837, during the age of Ismaʿīl in the mid-1860's, the period characterized by the integration of Egypt into the world market. The age of Ismaʿīl witnessed the creation of a new historical formation and the growth of a bourgeois society based on landownership and trade. This class was composed largely of Europeans, members of minorities, and Turks, but it also included a steadily growing number of Egyptian Muslims. The Europeans and minorities were representatives of the international trading community which controlled the Egyptian economy and dominated Egyptian politics. The Turks and Egyptians served mainly in the bureaucracy, the court, or the educational system. Underneath this class was the much larger local middle class composed primarily of Egyptian merchants and artisans and, in the 1860's, rural notables.[45] This class manifested its power in cultural expression and in the continuing opposition to "reform" on the part of al-Azhar.

In cultural fields, the changed historical context, one of economic dependence of not only the monarchy but also the rest of the ruling class on Europe, found expression in a fragmented, assimilative approach to knowledge, whether European or Islamic. Māturīdite theology was now expressed predominantly in *ḥadīth* studies by the leading reformers, who continued to support neoclassicism. As in the Muḥammad ʿAlī period, the works in various fields which were based on religious modalities were no longer an outgrowth of "religious" research, for example, in *ḥadīth* chains. This syncretic empiricism was now dissociated from *ḥadīth* studies and was dominated by a secular content. The expansion of the fragmented secular sphere caused a sense of dislocation, and this feeling of dislocation led the young Muḥammad ʿAbdu to write his *Risālat al-tawḥīd*.

The main writers of this period were Shaykh Ḥusayn al-Marṣafī in language sciences, the prose writer Ibrāhīm al-Muwayliḥī, the poet Sāmī al-Bārūdī, ʿAlī Mubārak in history, and al-Ṭahṭāwī. All these writers contributed formally to educational and cultural reform; all opposed the *kalām* of the Muḥammad ʿAlī period; all tended in varying degrees toward the nascent positivism now embodied again in *ḥadīth* studies, although this development was blocked by the imposition of Aristotelianism in aesthetics.

This chapter showed the continuation of neoclassicism as the dominant form of Egyptian culture, embodied in the writings of Ḥasan al-ʿAṭṭār and his students. Neoclassicism's originality lay in the scholarship which unearthed appropriate models for an agrarian age and in the creative imitation of these models. The task of the scholars who served in the editorial and journalistic positions of the reform era was one of critically appropriating the fruits of the eighteenth-century revival while turning away from its cultural ethos, its aesthetics, and its logic. The task of appropriation was inescapable because the early nineteenth century also marked a continuation toward the development of a modern culture, a culture of capitalism. The rising critical consciousness of the eighteenth century, the early utilitarianism, and the sentiments of patriotism found a more or less direct continuation in the reform period. Despite the structural change from a more inductive to a more deductive basis for religious thought, positivism was becoming more and more clearly the epistemological foundation of upper-class intellectual life. Conflicts in language reform likewise had their eighteenth-century antecedents. The middle-class interest in realism, whether in the writing of *maqāmāt* or in the technical translations, had important precedents in the work of the *majālis*. The struggle against the agrarian monarchical flattery of *sajʿ* was actually more advanced in the eighteenth century than in the Muḥammad ʿAlī period, which was a period of general cultural decline. In the final chapter we shall conclude our discussion of neoclassicism by surveying the sciences in which its development was totally thwarted by a more precipitous transition to bourgeois culture, rendering it irrelevant far earlier than in cultural fields.

Chapter 9
The World Market as a Limiting Factor in the Development of Neoclassicism: The Case of Science and Medicine

In the first phase of its revival, neoclassicism was the dominant expression of an economically powerful sector of the economy. It served the function of rationalization and legitimization of the Mamlūk–rich merchant ruling class's orientation in the broadest sense. In the second phase, neoclassicism had a more limited role. It served to legitimize the ruling class by creating an approach to history, language, literature, and science to fit its needs. Neoclassicism in this phase was the product of a small number of religious and literary figures who were themselves part of but marginal to the ruling structure which they sought to legitimize. They were among the worst paid, and their skills were not highly respected. The reasons for this derived not from ethnicity, but rather from the structure of the world market and the development of the internal dynamics. The dominant class was sufficiently strong not to require neoclassicism in science as an ideological foil. This class, following Western tutelage and being interested in distancing itself from both the Mamlūks and the eighteenth-century Egyptian scholars, repudiated its immediate ancestry as decadent and as responsible for the present backwardness of society. It followed that they too saw Islam's true glory now to be in the distant past; but, in contrast to figures like al-ʿAṭṭār, they had less interest in the study of the past to find what was useful in it.

In accepting Western technology, this class came increasingly to accept the West's evaluation of all aspects of its history. Thus, there were limits to the role which was defined for neoclassicism, far more than there had been during the previous period. The effect of al-ʿAṭṭār's extraordinary rediscovery of Ibn al-Nafīs on the Egyptians trained as doctors can only be imagined. Perhaps it stirred romantic feelings, perhaps a sense of ambivalence.

Did the collapse of neoclassicism which accompanied the change in the structure of the ruling class signify a break in the continuity of Egyptian cultural history? Did the abrupt political changes brought about by the Muḥammad ʿAlī regime have their counterpart in a sudden break in cultural continuity? This was not the case. Cultural life did not, of course, depend totally on the state. The individual scholars who lived in this transitional age provided continuity through their work. But, first, the state itself depended on a complex religious and juridical framework, just as it operated within a given level of technology. Even in an era dominated by *kalām*, it was necessary for scholars to teach *ḥadīth* and to maintain competence in it, not only for polemical reasons but also for liturgical and scholarly requirements. In addition, there was the question of the structural relationship of the ʿ*ulamāʾ* to the dominant class. In all three eras which we deal with here, the ʿ*ulamāʾ* lived from the patronage of the wealthy, but their relationship to the ruling class was a marginal one. This was true even of those who were favored by the regime. It is natural that they retained, if not an actual independence, at least a range of values and concerns which were potentially in conflict with the regime. This had a bearing on cultural continuity. Second, given the less than homogeneous character of the ruling class, the activities of the state were far from being a clear reflection of any group. Those working in cultural fields certainly were in no position to challenge the policies of the state, but in small ways—as in the choice of certain books to be translated or printed at Būlāq, or in the decision of al-ʿAṭṭār to continue teaching Andalusian literature—the existence of the cultural structure allowed both a dominant orientation and several subordinate, divergent trends. The intervening complexity of the cultural structure itself thus helped to overcome the chasm left by a switch from a revival based on *ḥadīth* studies in the eighteenth century to one based in *kalām* in the nineteenth century.

In contrast to fields which developed more directly out of religious studies, medicine and sciences had also to justify their existence in European terms. The expansion of the world market required a level of technique which only existed in Europe. What Europe needed was encouraged. It is not too strong to say that in science and medicine Islamic emulation of European science was suppressed, even if it emanated from the intellectual elite.

The "suppression" of neoclassicism in science and medicine deserves clarification. The writings which we discuss below are important documents from the perspective of the history of science and culture. They are still unpublished, although they were written by Ḥasan al-ʿAṭṭār, who was in favor in the regime and had some measure of power. Politically they were consistent with the main trends of thought which the regime was following. In fact, they were major intellectual labors, especially his main work in medicine and the work in geometry. Yet they were not published and there is no indication that a struggle occurred in which al-ʿAṭṭār's writings were suppressed, in a formal sense.

Cultural production was, as the result of the state-owned printing facilities, a matter of policy. The publication of neoclassical works in medicine would be ingratiating to the suppressed merchant artisanal milieu; it might even be taken as a sign of weakness. It might not be understood by the Europeans.

In Morocco, a student of the new medical school in Egypt did publish such a work, but the situation of the reform movement in early nineteenth-century Morocco was much more precarious than it was in Egypt. It should not be argued that these writings would not have been of any scientific use. In eighteenth-century Istanbul even Europeans had acknowledged the utility of classical Islamic science, at least as elementary textbooks. Doctors coming to Egypt throughout the Muḥammad ʿAlī period were interested in the indigenous knowledge. While Europeans might not accept Islamic science as a replacement for their own textbooks, classical texts could have found a place in the curriculum.

If a residual classicism, exemplified in medicine by the tradition of Ibn Sīnā, could be tolerated, why could not a neoclassical critique of Ibn Sīnā be tolerated in a period when clearly the hold of Ibn Sīnā was waning? Were the later generations of Ottoman doctors ignorant of Western clinical medicine? A survey of the printed sources for this period suggests the opposite. The Ottoman Muslim medical elite was always aware of trends in the West through translations of leading works. In al-ʿAṭṭār's period, doctors of different nationalities met regularly in the Istanbul hospitals. A more probable explanation for the continuing influence of Ibn Sīnā was the cultural formation of the medical profession in this period. The vast majority were Ṣūfīs, members of the Sharīʿa-minded orders like the Naqshbandīs, who drew their clientele from the upper classes.

From the renaissance to the late eighteenth century, doctors of the Near East could accommodate the findings of physical medicine in Ibn Sīnā's framework. With the decisive transformation in the West which Michel Foucault termed the rise of clinical medicine—or what we have termed in a more general sense positivism—arose a crisis in metaphysics. This crisis is reflected in the arguments over medical procedure among Europeans and between Europeans and among Middle Easterners. Arguments concerning medical procedure were thus very much reflected by one's relation to the industrial revolution.

The question which I posed concerning the rejection of neoclassicism cannot be answered in terms of differences existing in the field of medicine between Istanbul and Cairo. Until the middle of the eighteenth century, the ruling Turkish military group relied on classical physical medicine and were probably less aware of the West than the ruling class in Istanbul. In the middle of the eighteenth century there were two significant changes. The influx of European refugees, some of whom became Mamlūks, mercenaries, or merchant adventurers, included a number of doctors. Of these several were quite reputable; several others were not. One killed his patients as a favor to his chief patron. With the rise of this new group of doctors, there ceased to be Mamlūk patronage in physical medicine for Muslim Egyptians. This was noticeable by 1770, when several hospitals virtually fell into disuse. Therefore, Egyptian medical work turned from physical medicine to spiritual medicine; often this took the form of group therapy under the aegis of the leading Ṣūfī *shaykhs*.

The change in the social composition of the profession of physical medicine did not have the dramatic effects which one might expect. The same was not true in the area of military technology. There Western advisors played an important and transformative role from the eighteenth century onward. From a medical standpoint, European progress was less certain: the Napoleonic invasion of Egypt was a disaster. Of the 24,000 soldiers who evacuated Egypt, it is estimated that 2,400 already had ophthalmia or were blind. Even the savants came to respect "folk remedies," as they were known, and actively solicited advice in areas like veterinary medicine, following the impressive show of the Mamlūk cavalry.

Al-ʿAṭṭār stands at something of a distance from these events, having passed a number of years in Turkey where he studied medicine. In Turkey he learned the Ibn Sīnā tradition which had been available before his time in Egypt, a tradition which one could call the classicist tradition. In addition he came in contact with other traditions of physical medicine, Islamic and Western, which contradicted Ibn Sīnā, and he saw their utility. But neither he nor even the European doctors in Egypt in his lifetime totally abandoned Ibn Sīnā. What was taking place was the transformation within a part of the ruling class which was shifting from a physical medicine based in religious metaphysics to one rooted in a secular positivism. The opposition of the suppressed middle classes to all the sciences, as manifested in their opposition to quarantine, an opposition defended by logic, continued through the Muḥammad ʿAlī period.

Since the sixteenth century, when syphilis reached the Ottoman Empire from Europe, Istanbul was a center of medicine which remained in contact with the West. This is manifested in the series of translations from European languages into Turkish. In the contacts between Jewish, Armenian, and Turkish doctors, a direct link with Europe was sustained. Turkish doctors who reached high positions in the Ottoman Empire were frequently reformers. They often belonged to the Naqshbandī and Khalwatī Ṣūfī orders. They traveled to Istanbul for their education, as many did from Damascus in the eighteenth century. In the provincial capitals of the empire, the medical establishments were much smaller than in Istanbul. Prior to the middle of the eighteenth century, the minorities are not mentioned in medical history of Ottoman Cairo; but with the commercial revival, the Mamlūks switched to Greeks and Jews exclusively, and permitted the Muslim hospitals, Māristān al-Manṣūrī, to decline. The last Egyptian writings on anatomy in the eighteenth century date from mid-century.

The sudden growth of European influence in physical medicine was not the result of European success in dealing with the age-old local ailments. Eye diseases which plagued Egypt had their traditional remedies and these were used by European and Muslim alike through the Napoleonic period until the 1820's. Napoleon's doctors tried desperately to stop the spread of blindness from bienorrheal ophthalmia with dry collyria (*kuhl* and *shishm*). Europeans in Egypt were equally confused about what response to take to the plague. The chief doctor, Clot Bey, opposed the theory of contagion, but Muḥammad ʿAlī, concerned for his army and his family's welfare, advocated it. It is interesting that one of the textbooks used in the Medical School of Clot Bey should quote Ibn Sīnā.

With the expulsion of Egyptians from physical medicine, it is not surprising to find that the great achievements of Egyptians in the eighteenth century were in the area of spiritual medicine, particularly areas which resemble forms of group therapy. Middle Eastern concern with dream interpretation, with music, with water treatments, and with lasting relationships between healer and healed was not recognized by nineteenth-century Western Europeans as science. This was a period when Western psychology was particularly sterile. The talismanic significance of ritual, the giving and receiving of names, the dialectical interpenetration of the well and the sick would have to await an observer like Jung.

The traditions of travel and study permitted the Ottomans to sustain an intellectual division of labor. Those Egyptians like Ḥasan al-Jabartī or Muḥammad ibn ʿArafa al-Disūqī who wanted rational sciences traveled to Istanbul or elsewhere. In the early nineteenth century this was continued by Ḥasan al-ʿAṭṭār. Al-ʿAṭṭār's work catches not merely the corrections integrated into the traditional corpus of Galen and Ibn Sīnā but also the breakdown of the traditional structure under the blows of positivism, as evidenced in the empirical study of anatomy.[1]

Ḥasan al-ʿAṭṭār's "Sharḥ Nuzha"*: A Turning Point in the History of Arabic Medical Writing*

Ḥasan al-ʿAṭṭār wrote his main book on medicine in Syria in 1814. It was the most important work on medicine in the Arab world in the early nineteenth century and is perhaps the first work by an Arab to discuss the modern study of anatomy.[2] It preceded the systematic study of the Turk Shani Zadeh by some six years and the "official" beginning of modern medical history in his own country by ten years or more. The form of the work was to a large extent dictated by the literary and pedagogical style of the era. It was a commentary on a text by al-Anṭākī. Al-ʿAṭṭār's commentary occupies more than four hundred pages and covers an enormous range of subjects. It is also a major document of neoclassicism.

The "Nuzha," the shortest of Dāʾūd al-Anṭākī's three main works on medicine, and probably the least known, is an essay containing material for which "the well-informed will need no further elongation." The principal source was Ibn Sīnā, who is referred to numerous times as simply "our *shaykh.*" Certain occult sciences not in the *Qānūn* are also discussed; for example, the first main topic treated by al-Anṭākī was the Three Kingdoms of Nature.[3] Unlike the *Tadhkara*, which was in the tradition of the medical formulary of Ibn al-Bayṭār, the "Nuzha" was, al-ʿAṭṭār pointed out, a mixture and, furthermore, an uncritical one. Dāʾūd al-Anṭākī was a student of *ḥadīth*, as his medicine shows.[4]

Al-ʿAṭṭār chose not to take on the *Tadhkara* directly; rather, he chose another of al-Anṭākī's works. For, as he said, the *Tadhkara* of Dāʾūd was the fundamental work on medicine (*ʿumda wa imām*), at least among the *ʿulamāʾ*.[5] He claims that he had been prepared to accept the evaluation until he read some of the predecessors of Dāʾūd al-Anṭākī in medicine and *al-ḥikma.* Their writings showed that Dāʾūd's were very confused and in fact had little value at all. Concerning the *Tadhkara* itself, there is little that is worthwhile, except simple remedies and some treatments which he copied from the books of the ancients. His account of the humours in the introduction, based on mystical sources, is "worthless"; his decision to include in the introduction information on *al-handasa* and *al-hay'a* is "not according to the practice of doctors." However, "the times" were not suitable for a real onslaught on al-Anṭākī.[6]

Perhaps what is most remarkable about al-ʿAṭṭār's critique is the sources which he himself used, sources which were thought to have been lost to later Arabic medicine. These included the "Sharḥ al-qānūn" of Ibn al-Nafīs (died 1288) and the "Sharḥ qānūnjā" of ʿAbd al-Laṭīf al-Baghdādī. In the former work, Ibn al-Nafīs sets out a theory of the lesser, or pulmonary, circulation of the blood, contradicting Ibn Sīnā and anticipating Harvey. With a couple of minor exceptions, this theory has not been found in other books, leading me, in the light of "Sharḥ nuzha," to revise my understanding of the role of anatomy in Arab medical education.[7]

The main work in which Ibn al-Nafīs expressed his ideas on the circulation of the blood was "Sharḥ al-qānūn," the relevant portions of which were assembled in a derivative work called "Sharḥ tashrīḥ al-qānūn." This has led to some confusion because his other work, "Sharḥ mū'jaz al-qānūn," sometimes called "Sharḥ mukhtaṣar," does not contain this material. In "Sharḥ al-qānūn," Ibn al-Nafīs wrote: "When the blood has been refined in the right ventricle, it needs be that it pass to the left ventricle, where the vital spirit is generated. But between these two there exists no passageway, for the substance of the heart there is solid and there exists neither a visible passage, as some writers have thought, nor an invisible passage which will permit the flow of blood as Galen believed. But on the contrary, the pores of the heart are shut, and its substance there is thick. But this blood, after being refined, must of necessity pass along the pulmonary artery into the lung."[8]

Al-ʿAṭṭār obviously read some passage such as this, but he misunderstood the author's intent. He appears to have thought that Ibn al-Nafīs denied the above contention. "This is the view of al-Qurashī [Ibn al-Nafīs], and it is incorrect, for the heart has two internal ventricles only, one of which is filled with blood, and it is on the right side. The other is filled with vital spirit [*rūḥ*] and it is on the left side. There is absolutely no passageway between the two, nor does the blood penetrate into the side of the spirit, and thereby correct its essence. Dissection makes a lie of what they have said [al-ʿAṭṭār concludes with a contrast between the heart in larger and smaller animals]."[9]

Despite this curious involution of the ideas of Ibn al-Nafīs, it is obvious enough that the tradition of Ibn al-Nafīs was known in Turkey in the circles of the Hakimbashi where al-ʿAṭṭār studied. This information alone justifies a new study of the tradition of Ibn al-Nafīs. Such a study would surely revise the prevailing image of the dominance of Ibn Sīnā. It might also add something to our knowledge of the curious Western figure Michael Servetus, the unexplained forerunner of Harvey. Another example of al-ʿAṭṭār's familiarity with the history of Islamic medicine is his use of al-Rāzī to justify dissection. Like Ibn al-Nafīs, al-Rāzī represented a critique of the Ibn Sīnian tradition of medicine. Al-Rāzī represented the development of an empirical approach, an experimental method in science and medicine, and opposition to the purely deductive approach or to the search for integration through symbolic meaning.[10]

In later years, when al-ʿAṭṭār was securely part of the upper class, he did not need to veil his opinions. In 1830 he wrote that, while Ibn Sīnā was the great doctor of the theory of medicine, al-Rāzī was the great practitioner. The distinction was itself significant, especially because of his linking practice to dissection, and his obvious preference for practice as opposed to theory. "He was Muḥammad al-Ṭabīb [the physician] al-Rāzī, who preceded Ibn Sīnā, and a biography of him was written by the author of the *Ṭabaqāt al-aṭibbā*ʾ. Al-Rāzī wrote many books, some of which can still be found in our country, and some of which I have read. I found that he had done extensive work on treatment, in contrast to Ibn Sīnā. Ibn Sīnā's skill was in theory and not in practice. Perhaps that was because he did not personally engage very much in practice, as the rest of the doctors did, because he was involved in affairs of state and held many positions. He encountered many miseries, making his writings unique as he composed them in flight or in hiding or moving from one place to another."[11]

This was written in the secure context of the Muḥammad ʿAlī era. But the same thought underlay his comments in "Sharḥ nuzha" (1813), because al-Anṭākī was no more than a continuator of Ibn Sīnā in many respects. In "Sharḥ nuzha," al-ʿAṭṭār stressed how important was the knowledge of empirical anatomy for diagnosis in internal medicine, as well as was knowledge of the essential nature of each organ and its function.[12] Al-ʿAṭṭār also stressed the importance of experimentation and mentioned several experiments, including his own failure to keep a servant boy alive. In the preceding folio, he said that in the past Muslim doctors explained the climax of an illness as God's will, or they claimed that it depended on the moon and stars. Al-ʿAṭṭār stated that he witnessed an experiment tending to disprove the latter.[13] In rehabilitating the more empirical tradition of science and medicine, al-ʿAṭṭār made yet another attack on the Ahl al-Ḥadīth by showing that what was meant by "Arab medicine" did not mean Arab in any narrow sense but included all those who worked in the Arab lands, especially at the time of the ʿAbbāsid Caliphate, who received the tradition of Greek medicine translated into Arabic.[14] Finally, al-ʿAṭṭār relied on his own experience, implying that this was surer than what he had read in the earlier books.

Al-ʿAṭṭār offered in particular some opinions based on his travels as to the healthfulness of living in the wind, or in a moist place, or at a high altitude. He likewise made a number of comparisons of different climates and related them to public baths in Syria, Istanbul, and Cairo.[15] Al-ʿAṭṭār also showed some knowledge of Egypt which he must have acquired in his youth, for example, of folk habits of the *rīf* (countryside of Egypt) and of the people of Rashīd and the Delta, and of the different climatic regions of Egypt.[16] A last area of criticism which al-ʿAṭṭār began in the "Sharḥ nuzha" was his attack on the tradition of *al-ḥikma* for its vagueness and inaccuracy.

I now return to the question of the "circumstances" which made it ill-advised for al-ʿAṭṭār to undertake an attack on al-Anṭākī and, more generally, what were al-ʿAṭṭār's accomplishments in medicine prior to his return to Egypt. The commentary on al-Anṭākī reflected part of the steadily evolving elite transformation as it was emerging in medicine and science in the Ottoman Empire. Al-ʿAṭṭār's position when he wrote "Tuḥfat gharīb al-waṭan" and when he wrote the "Sharḥ nuzha" was that of an *ʿālim* seeking the patronage of the ruling class. "Sharḥ nuzha" was an attack on the Ahl al-Ḥadīth. Dāʾūd al-Anṭākī, like Nūr al-dīn al-Ashmūnī in grammar, was a symbol in this sense of a contemporary reality rather than simply a figure from the past.

The criticism of Ibn Sīnā was more implicit than explicit. It sufficed for al-ʿAṭṭār to show an apparent harmony of outlook among Ibn al-Nafīs, al-Rāzī, and the European medicine with which he came in contact. While he was prepared to admit that Ibn Sīnā made mistakes in detail which attention to dissection would have prevented, it was impossible for him, given the historical context of rationalism within which he was functioning, to abandon his belief in the validity of a rational-deductive approach to the understanding of medicine. In the second phase of the neoclassical revival, al-ʿAṭṭār was prepared to demonstrate more and more mistakes in the writings of Ibn Sīnā, but he was indisposed to break with the philosophical orientation which caused these errors.[17]

Al-ʿAṭṭār and the Recovery of the Tradition of ʿIlm al-Hayʾa

Between the sixteenth and the eighteenth centuries, both Turkey and Egypt engaged in a range of scientific activities according to their needs. Turkish science in particular is known for its influence on work in Europe in areas like mathematics. Napoleon charged four of his scientists to examine the mills in Egypt.

By the eighteenth century, the contacts were much more numerous, but the Ottoman contribution in science and technology was of less importance. In eighteenth-century Egypt, the changing policy of the Mamlūks affected Egyptian scientists as it had Egyptian doctors. Several *ʿulamāʾ* who were denied patronage in the physical sciences turned to a revival of *al-ḥikma*, distinguishing themselves from the dominant concern with *al-mīqāt*. The revival of *al-ḥikma*, particularly one part of it, *ʿilm al-hayʾa*, was important to nineteenth-century writers like al-ʿAṭṭār who sought to arrive at a positivist philosophy of science through indigenous lines of thought. The background to al-ʿAṭṭār's writings included two types of writings, one on the meaning of scientific terminology and the other concerned with the sorting of different types of matter.

Al-ʿAṭṭār's Critique of the Study of al-Ḥikma *in the Eighteenth Century*

During the reform period, al-ʿAṭṭār carried on an intellectual campaign to defend the legitimacy of science in the eyes of the *ʿulamāʾ* and to attract the attention of the ruling class to the Islamic tradition of science.[18] In this campaign, he defended *al-ḥikma* against those who attacked its rationalist inclinations. Thereafter, he criticized it from the vantage point of positivist science.

Some people, said al-ʿAṭṭār, probably referring to the Ahl al-Ḥadīth of his own day, say that

> unrestricted investigation, or plunging, into *al-ḥikma* is risky and thus forbidden, but this is only partially true because researchers in *al-ḥikma* who are expert in Qurʾān and *sunna* strengthen their understanding thereby . . . because they have a pious means to answer those with false doctrines and to refute misguided beliefs. *Al-ḥikma* provides a source of knowledge of the technical vocabulary which the later *ʿulamāʾ* in *ʿilm al-kalām* invented [or at least thought to be new]. No one has said that this [last] was forbidden, and perhaps it is even among the religious obligations. . . . The first thing in this field which man may profit from in this discipline is the capacity to make a suitable reply and thereby to make the truth triumph. For this reason, later scholars like Fakhr al-dīn al-Rāzī, Ḥujjat al-Islām al-Ghazzālī and others of the innumerable geniuses and distinguished scholars have carried on their research in *al-ḥikma*. As for those with stupid minds, simple thoughts, and naïve natures, such as would lack the sciences of the sacred law which should guide research, . . . *al-ḥikma* is forbidden to him. . . . We say that research in it is similar to research in logic. There is no doubt that one who seeks to resolve such problems would be working on important matters of the greatest seriousness and benefit, as in the Shaykh al-ʿIqlīmī's commentary on "Al-Jāmiʿ al-Ṣaghīr." . . . Indeed , a certain number of eminent persons of the later period, such as the Imām Ibn al-Ṣalāḥ, al-Nawawī, and others, who were also poets, forbade the sciences of *al-ḥikma*, even in the purely logical aspects. Another group which investigated the matter concluded that adherence to one of these two positions obliges censure of the other. We might add by way of interpretation that "he who raises the cloth, removes the secrets, makes clear the right path."[19]

Having established a fundamental legitimacy for the existence of the field (largely in terms of its relationship to logic) and having dealt with certain linguistic considerations which were, of course, not central to the study of *al-ḥikma* itself, al-ʿAṭṭār proceeded to criticize it more or less for the same reasons for which he praised it, that is, that *al-ḥikma* is composed of many aspects, some of which are useful to the well informed but others are misguided. Al-ʿAṭṭār never dealt with the proposition that *al-ḥikma* rested on a higher unity than the sum of its parts. He dealt with it only in terms of merits of its various parts.

Al-ḥikma, he said, was traditionally divided into three general categories: *al-ṭabīʿyāt*, *al-riyāḍīyāt*, and *al-ilahīyāt*. He thought that research on *al-ilahīyāt*, subjects such as the attributes and existence of God, was impossible. Much of the research performed in *al-riyāḍīyāt* likewise dealt with imaginary subjects (*umūr mawhūma*), such as the domain of the stars (*al-dawāʾir al-fālakīya*) and the theory of numbers (*ʿadd*). Furthermore, research on *al-riyāḍīyāt*, he claimed, had not served the needs of the community; AlʿAṭṭār cited in particular its inability to predict the times of eclipses. He said that this had had a bad effect on the Muslim community and on the maintenance of the Divine command. Such problems, he concluded, are rightly the province of *al-handasa*.[20] His criticism of the study of *riyāḍīyāt* in *al-ḥikma* was pursued further in his major work on *uṣūl al-dīn*, which was published in 1830.

> And I say, concerning the subject of the vacuum and other branches of the physical sciences, that their investigation will uncover strange secrets; this is necessary in the fields of mechanics, gravity (*jarr al-athqāl*), and force (*ḥayl*) and for other unfamiliar inventions. Recently books have been translated into Arabic containing numerous matters of great precision. I read some of these, deducing that they were based on application of the principles of geometry (*al-handasa*) and the physical sciences, both on the level of theory and on the level of practice. . . . In these books, one finds discussed military technology and fire-throwing apparatus, which is explained systematically, until the field becomes a separate discipline, possessing its own subdivisions. He who pursues the reading of these unusual books will learn a great deal about sound science, the study of which is essential to the completion of one's education.[21]

That this passage was located in a work on the religious sciences by the Shaykh al-Azhar underscores the fact that the regime's outlook opposed heretical and "misguided" orientation, even in science, which could be linked implicitly to *ḥadīth* studies and possibly to heterodox mystical theology. The idea of "separate disciplines," as opposed to mere subdivisions, shows the influence of Western positivism.

In his study of medicine, al-ʿAṭṭār had a forthright criticism of the role of *al-ḥikma*. He clearly preferred the tradition of the "doctors" to the tradition of the "*ḥukamāʾ*" in medicine. He ridiculed dream interpretation, saying that it was entirely based on surmise and varied from one doctor to another.[22] He also dismissed the contribution of astrology (*raml* and *zāʾirjā*) to medicine. In his most important book on *al-ḥikma*, the *Ḥāshiya ʿalā sharḥ al-Balīdī* (1818/1234), al-Aṭṭār discussed problems in the field of astronomy. It was his intention to criticize certain claims made by Ibn Sīnā which were unverified. In doing so, he drew on the Safavid writer Bahāʾ al-dīn al-ʿĀmilī. Al-ʿAṭṭār stated that there was no proof for the existence of the ninth starless heaven of Ibn Sīnā, according to al-ʿĀmilī.[23] Following this is al-ʿĀmilī's criticism of Ibn Sīnā on another point: Al-ʿĀmilī stated on the subject of the rotation of the stars that, contrary to Ibn Sīnā, most do not go from east to west.

In addition to the writings of al-ʿAṭṭār on *al-ḥikma*, there were also the writings of his colleague and friend Sami Bey, some of which appeared in the editorials of *Al-Waqāʾiʿ al-Miṣrīya*, which he was editing. His intention in writing on *al-ḥikma* appeared to be to defend it as a spiritually unifying force. He wrote an autobiographical fragment in one issue in which he mentioned the mystical education of his youth.[24]

Al-ʿAṭṭār and the Revival of ʿIlm al-Hayʾa

Al-ʿAṭṭār's principal aim in rejecting *al-ḥikma* was not the destruction of *al-ḥikma* per se but the discovery of an approach to science which would bring satisfactory results. This he finally found in the field of *ʿilm al-hayʾa*, although he was not fully able to keep separate its two orientations: the one in astronomy, the other in mystical philosophy. The most accessible of the two was mystical philosophy, which had ultimately originated in the *Rasāʾil* of the Ikhwān al-Ṣafāʾ. It was, however, the field of *ʿilm al-hayʾa* as an empirically based science that basically interested al-ʿAṭṭār.[25] Al-ʿAṭṭār's confusions in this field arose as a result of his introduction to it through the writings of Bahāʾ al-dīn al-ʿĀmilī. Al-ʿĀmilī represented a mixture of both traditions, but more so than not he was a spiritual descendant of the Ikhwān al-Ṣafāʾ.[26]

Al-ʿAṭṭār's main work on natural science represented an effort to clarify the relationship between the astronomy represented by Qāḍī Zadeh and Nāṣir al-dīn al-Ṭūsī, on the one hand, and of al-ʿĀmilī, on the other: the tradition of astronomy which was studied in the astronomical observatories of postclassical Islam as opposed to astronomy through philosophy. The work was begun before al-ʿAṭṭār left Cairo, but most of it was written in Turkey, and it was completed in 1831/1237 after his return to Cairo.[27] The text, with the commentary of Qādī Zadeh, was traditionally widely read in connection with the study of *al-mīqāt*, which required a knowledge of the fundamental principles of Euclidian geometry.

Al-ʿAṭṭār's intentions in writing this work were apparently quite similar to his intentions in writing the "Sharḥ nuzha" in medicine. One can see, in his choice of a basic text in the natural sciences of the Ahl al-Ḥadīth, elements of class conflict, theological struggle, and conflict within the confines of secular knowledge itself. Neoclassicism was a weapon which undermined the traditional authorities and pointed to a reconciliation between earlier Islamic sources and contemporary Western science.

It is thus not surprising to find in this book extended coverage of empiricism and rationalism in Islamic science, for example, in its description of the school of Qāḍī Zadeh at the astronomical observatory, which obviously impressed al-ʿAṭṭār. He recounted in detail the life of Qāḍī Zadeh, including material on his quarrels with al-Jurjānī and on his life in Samarqand. One can tell from his gloss that this was clearly the model for *ʿilm al-hayʾa* which he had in mind, for he began his work with it and devoted much of his space to such figures as Nāṣir al-dīn al-Ṭūsī, who was also a representative of this tradition. He even presented a theological defense of Nāṣir al-dīn al-Ṭūsī, who held "Shīʿite" views. Al-ʿAṭṭār claimed that al-Ṭūsī's work on al-Imāma, which expressed a Rāfidite point of view, was written not by Nāṣir al-dīn himself, but by one of his associates after his death.[28]

Al-ʿAṭṭār was apparently seriously misled by al-ʿĀmilī (or by other writers) in his effort to trace the Euclidian tradition of geometry in Islam and to dissociate the one side of the Pythagorean heritage in the theory of numbers from the others.[29] The problem arose in an acute form in spherical geometry (*ʿilm al-manāẓir*), where, following al-ʿĀmilī, he mentioned finding a useful essay based on Euclid.[30] Spherical geometry, however, underlay both the empirical work of the observatories in the compilation of star charts and the cosmological ideas of the Persian tradition, based on the *Rasāʾil* of the Ikhwān al-Ṣafāʾ. Al-ʿAṭṭār could not maintain the distinction, as one can tell from his discussion of the "throne and the chair."[31]

The influence of al-ʿĀmilī on al-ʿAṭṭār in plane geometry was probably less significant.[32] In number theory, al-ʿAṭṭār found reason to attack al-ʿĀmilī's dependence on the *rasāʾil* of the Ikhwān. He said of their theory that their definition of number was composed of two parts: the theoretical and the practical. The theoretical is available only to certain people (*al-khawāṣṣ*), while the practical was no more than everyday mathematics.[33] Herein lay the contradiction. Al-ʿAṭṭār rejected both the mathematical and the geometrical bases of al-ʿĀmilī's theory, but he accepted the cosmological ideas which were derived from this tradition at the expense of the more empirically minded tradition of Qāḍī Zadeh. If *ʿilm al-hayʾa* was to mean science in the positivist sense, it had to reject the entire tradition based on the writings of the Ikhwān.[34] Why did this confusion exist? Was it due to the influence of the Wafāʾīya and their reliance on Bahāʾ al-dīn al-ʿĀmilī? Areas of ambiguity seem to be the necessary consequences of joining mystical theology with positivist science.

Toward a Sociology of Knowledge Based on the Structure of the Market

Writings on Egypt tend to stress the neat and orderly transfer of modern knowledge to Egypt that took place when Egyptian students went to study in Europe during the period of Muḥammad ʿAlī. Writings on Europe in the same period speak of the intellectual disarray, the theoretical ferment, rather than the existence of a well-defined body of knowledge. Why is none of this reflected among the returning students? Eric Hobsbawm has written of Europe in the 1830's: "Few except mathematicians will appreciate the profundity of the innovation brought into science by the theory of the functions of complex variables. . . , of the theory of groups, . . . or of vectors. . . . But even the layman can grasp the bearing of the revolution by which Lobachevsky of Russia (1826–29) and Bolyai of Hungary (1831) overthrew that most permanent of intellectual certainties, Euclid's geometry."[35] French mathematicians began to deal with the concept of irrational numbers. Yet during this period no such revolution was transported to Egypt or Turkey.

Theoretical ferment was unlikely in the context of a state commercial sector resisting the pull of the West. Unlike the situation in England and France, the cognitive system which prevailed on the periphery did not grant primacy to scientific knowledge but, as in the nascent capitalist societies of early modern Europe, cognitive primacy was shared between philosophical and technical knowledge. In England in the nineteenth century, scientific and technical knowledge remained largely independent of one another, while in Egypt they were fused. In Egypt, philosophical knowledge had not yet "disintegrated" into scientific knowledge, as it had by this time in England. Unlike the nascent capitalist regimes of early modern Europe, state capitalist regimes on the periphery of the modern world market, such as Egypt, Turkey, and later (to a degree) Japan, were characterized by a dominance of the rational and the conceptual over the empirical and at the same time were obliged, in the process of importing knowledge from the West, to make empirical adjustments at every phase to fit their concrete situation.[36]

In contrast to culture at the center of the world market, culture at the periphery during the early industrial revolution was characterized by a prolonged period of neoclassicism. Neoclassicism was a two-edged sword. While it was used by the ruling class to counteract the culture of the traditional middle class, it could also undermine the intellectual justification of the ruling class by threatening to break through the artificial dichotomy of (in this case) Muslim versus Christian civilization. Where a strongly entrenched compradorial bourgeoisie could dispense with neoclassicism as a serious enterprise, it would do so—but neoclassicism would re-emerge when the power of that class waned. In fields in which indigenous scholarship was indispensable, it was transformed to fit the needs of nation building. Hobsbawm said of eastern and northern Europe in the early nineteenth century that, "in hitherto unawakened nations, the historian, the lexicographer, and the folksong collector were often the very founders of national consciousness." This point can be extended to cover Egypt as well.[37]

Chapter 10
Conclusion

From its inception modern capitalism depended on an international division of labor. To remove a population from farming and turn it to production at a time when the home markets were small and undeveloped one needed a world system structured to consume the products produced and to feed the workers in the new industries. What has been obscured in the conceptualization of history is the role of the periphery, the struggle of its merchants and manufacturers to maximize the opportunities that were open to them and were integral to the total process of industrial development. This study covers a period in that struggle and studies in some detail one country of the periphery. Between 1760 and 1840, Egypt attempted to retain control over her trade and not be restricted to production and consumption. It is not surprising that in merchant and government bureaucratic circles there developed in this period an indigenous "modernism" in Islamic thought stabilizing the economic situation prevailing in Egypt. The discovery of this Islamic cultural evolution in the economic context outlined above forces a reconstruction of knowledge. The common premise of no modern non-Western thought which does not ultimately derive from the West must be abandoned. The study of social struggle and cultural development in individual countries of the periphery like Egypt clearly affects the character of the overall development of the modern world.

In the first chapter an effort was made to reconstruct a picture of what eighteenth-century Egypt must have been. The body of information at our disposal has in the past led writers to conclude that this was a period of barbarism and anarchy.

In place of this traditional picture of Mamlūk Egypt as one of barbarism and incessant military strife, I found a widening section of the most productive farmland of the Egyptian delta being turned over to the production of export commodities destined for Europe. This change was accompanied by a penetration of moneylenders and monetary relations. In the city of Cairo equally important changes took place. The gradual growth of modern products available to the elite from Europe led to a generalized shift in their patronage. Large segments of the artisanate became underemployed by the end of the eighteenth century and as a result were turned into day labor. This change was one of the most important, as it brought to an end the guild structure which had characterized the medieval society.

Finally, the chapter addresses itself to the fusion of the commercial middle strata with the Mamlūk political elite, which took place throughout the later eighteenth century. Mamlūks became sleeping partners in trade and in the sale of agricultural produce to Europe as this was the new source of wealth. To accomplish this there was a breakdown in the traditional elite political structure of the Mamlūk house. Numerous Mamlūks were abandoned, that is, manumitted by their former lords as an expense.

In the place of Mamlūk warriors, the *beys* relied on mercenaries trained in the use of firearms. These they armed with European military and naval technology. The year 1760 is a useful point of departure to see this process in Egypt because the reform-minded ruler ʿAlī Bey abandoned local Muslim medical, scientific, and commercial expertise, while turning to that of Mediterranean minorities. The study of rivalry and struggle commenced at this point, when the Egyptian intelligentsia and commercial elite perceived their power and influence in society deteriorating. The chapter concludes with some comments on the breakdown of the guilds, a development which led to much of the urban violence commented on in the well-known travel books of the time. In subsequent chapters dealing with the renewal of Ṣūfī orders, it became possible for the first time to show that, confronted with competition, the merchants attempted to squeeze the artisans. As a result of this, the artisans showed growing signs of turbulence. As a way of stabilizing the situation, the Azhar and other official mosque centers permitted their leading members to promote religious revival among the masses. This is never stated in so many words (and one would not expect it to be), but taken together, the comments of al-Jabartī about the lower classes and the writings of all the orthodox *shaykhs* about lower-class religious expression indicate that this is what the *ʿulamāʾ* were attempting. The type of Ṣūfism which existed in the eighteenth century was abandoned when these centers of production were themselves abandoned in the early nineteenth century.

The second chapter commences with a discussion of eighteenth-century intellectual life, which is integral to the discussion of political economy in the first chapter. By contrasting the existing legal writings for the eighteenth-century period, 1760–1790, with the period 1790–1840, I discovered that a single modality of argumentation and a single root of jurisprudence dominated each period. For the period in which merchant capital predominated, the modality of logic was induction, which was rooted in *ḥadīth*; for the period of state commercial dominance, systematic theology rooted in deductive logic enjoyed a rebirth. The fact that these changes took place purely in the logical structure of thought and not in the ideas presented meant that, in the domain of social theory, modern ideas (e.g., utilitarianism and realism) show a significant measure of continuity in their development from one period to the next, while many of the thematic expressions of these ideas (e.g., the Battle of Badr) are quite short-lived. Utilitarianism was the basis of argument in *ḥadīth* studies, which were carried on inductively according to the rules of evaluation. Utilitarianism and realism, which I take to be the dominant expressions of classical capitalism, were carried forward attached to a universalist Aristotelian logic in the subsequent period. Thus, once again the theory of reflection comes under attack. Change in the organization of work does not lead automatically to change in culture or in ideology, only to the restructuring of the form of argument. The incidence of trade-related statements is minimal, perhaps the number of metaphors in which mosques are compared to place of trade is somewhat greater, but they would not lead to a satisfactory explanation of a wider range of themes. The best way to approach the subject of the Ṣūfī revival of the eighteenth century is one in which the totality of culture within the life of the socioeconomic formation is seen as a complex structure, so that culture production can be seen at once as part of the processes of integration and reproduction of the formation (the historicist moment) and only contingently as a part of a continuum of elite culture which has its own internal logic(s). The discovery that a single modality of legal reasoning underlies a particular social formation led us to discover that the same corpus of medieval learning was subject to appropriation and re-appropriation in different ways. This was borne out in the material presented in the third chapter and thereafter.

The development of secular culture was found to buttress *ḥadīth* studies in the eighteenth century and to buttress or at least parallel studies of *kalām* in the period between 1790 and 1840. Studies in language, literature, and history supported points of contention directly affecting *ḥadīth* and indirectly affecting the way in which the classical language could be approached and understood. These studies thereby contributed to the ongoing struggle of the *muḥaddithīn*, who engaged in them with the popular orders and regime enemies. It is thus not surprising to find the same type of logic underlying the works of religious and secular culture, but what is even more striking is that, whereas in the modern industrial West of which Weber and Lukács write, secular culture emerges as a separate genre with the rise of the middle class, in the countries of the Mediterranean this is less common. It seems probable that, both in the early phases of capitalist transformation, as studied here, and in the later phase of retarded or periphery capitalist formation, the dominant genre would continue to be works of religion and culture in which the domain of the sacral interpenetrates with that of human control. Often the Western scholar influenced by his or her own model of development will look for the production of independent works of secular culture, such as histories or novels, thereby eschewing theology books with traditional-sounding titles. Such shortsightedness has impoverished the study of Egyptian, Greek, and Syrian Christian culture. If the larger framework of my study is correct, then the Greek religious manuscripts of Egypt and the other writings of the churches of the Syrian Christians of the eighteenth century must contain evidence in the area of theology of the momentous changes which the respective communities were undergoing. Embedded in these writings one would expect elements of secular culture to appear unexpectedly in the midst of discussions of scripture. In fact it would not be surprising if there was a general mystical revival accompanying the commercial struggles of the late eighteenth century around the Mediterranean. At least this seems to be the case among Jews and Muslims in Algiers.

The principal features of the cultural revival discussed in the third chapter are that it took the form of a neoclassical revival of Islamic culture and that it increasingly emphasized utilitarian resolutions of problems, which permitted critical thought to dominate over the authoritative dispensations of the earlier Ottoman period. Taken as a whole, this sustains the thesis of Maxime Rodinson that Islamic theology had roots in the culture of capitalism. It serves as a critique of the view of the study of modern Islamic law which perceives a dichotomy between an Islamic sector of personal status and a public sector of Western derivation. This dichotomy is not the result of some inherent deficiency, but a product of colonial arrangements. Arrangements, one might note, in which Islam is used to oppress women. The development of neoclassicism in the later eighteenth century led increasingly to experimentation. Where the *Maqāmāt* of al-Ḥarīrī initially served linguistic and philological needs of the revival because of al-Ḥarīrī's own familiarity with pre-Islamic culture, the *maqāma* begins to emerge in the late eighteenth century as a prose piece of its time. A number of *maqāmāt* are recorded as having been written in the eighteenth century, a few have been located. The *Maqāma* of Ḥasan al-ʿAṭṭār discussed in Chapter 4 and presented in an appendix contains features of the classical novel, notably plot and characterization. In this short autobiographical piece there is a noticeable realism.

The third chapter surveys the neoclassical revival in the area of philology and history. In philology, it is discovered that the half-dozen subdisciplines mentioned in classical accounts of philological education do not sustain equal prominence within the structure of any particular period. In the eighteenth century, lexicography experienced a rebirth and dominated all other branches. In the later seventeenth and mid-nineteenth centuries, style dominated, while in the eighteenth century, a consideration of style was minimal. Lexicography was of course linked to *ḥadīth* studies. One great production established the historical development of the meaning of words as certified by chains of scholars. This book, the *Tāj al-ʿarūs* of the Ṣūfī Muḥaddith al-Zabīdī, continues to serve in Arabic as the O.E.D. does in English. Not surprisingly, it was unpopular in the age of Muḥammad ʿAlī. In that period the reassertion of logic led to an emphasis in lexicography on the structure of logically possible meanings (*al-naḥt* and *al-ishtiqāq*).

In the study of eighteenth-century historical writings several larger assertions about the nature of culture in this period are sustained: notably, the idea of the interpenetration of the religious and the secular and their idea of the role of culture, as a product of a class in a condition of struggle. The principal discovery concerning the historical writing of the late eighteenth century is the focus on the subject of the Battle of Badr. In no previous period in Islamic history has the Battle of Badr been singled out for such individualized study. Also unique was the particular tack of claiming that the number of Muḥammad's supporters was exaggerated, thereby demonstrating that the Prophet of God wrested a victory against even greater odds than previously imagined. These writings, uniformly a part of the *ḥadīth* writing and research of the period, are found to be reflective of a mood of struggle among the Muslim merchants in the face of the European-minority alliance. The works on the Battle of Badr are with the writings of the Protestant merchants studied by Lucien Goldmann in their confrontation with French Absolutism in *The Hidden God: A Study of Tragic Vision in the "Pensées" of Pascal and the Tragedies of Racine.*

The third chapter concludes with an effort to interpret the best-known writing of the period, the *ʿAjāʾib* of al-Jabartī. Al-Jabartī unwittingly has contributed to the mystification of his work's significance by his lament on the lack of historical sources. In reading this work of great erudition, modern students have found it to be the product of an accidental genius working in a Dark Age, a man whose thinking came to fruition by the coming of the West. An examination of the work (or of the statements of the author as to its purpose) does not sustain the view of Western influence. Episodes of contact with the French are recorded, but the methodology and structuring of the work show the novelty of fusing two types of indigenous historical consciousness in one work. It is thus scarcely the production of a genius in a vacuum. The first type of history is the chronicle format, identified with the dominance of the older landed system of the Ottomans; the second type is the pietistic biography of the commercial middle classes, the *tarjama* of the *shaykhs.* This latter type is actually the more important as it is in this section that al-Jabartī argues his political views, that the *ʿulamāʾ* have the right to take over with the collapse of the Mamlūk Bayt. The fusion of the economic and political elites during the late eighteenth century also underlines the fusion of genres in al-Jabartī's writing and it is for this reason that al-Jabartī was not attracted to the more traditional chronicles at his disposal, some of which I also discussed.

The fourth and fifth chapters deal with the life of al-ʿAṭṭār, a figure of importance as a link between the culture of the eighteenth century and its continuation in the reform period of Muḥammad ʿAlī. These chapters also suggest a resolution to some general problems of the study of culture and cultural change which affect the peripheral regions of the world market. In the earlier studies of the development of culture based on England or other parts of western Europe (except for Ireland), the social struggle which led to the victory of capitalism and the rise of the middle class was carried on as an open struggle of social forces on the scene. This struggle was reflected in the approach to the history of the culture. One could speak of the "seeds of contradiction," or of "the working out of contradictions," or of the logic of the inevitable development of one social form to another, in culture as in society. Much of Russian and American writing concerning modernization supposes a path of development where phases one could choose follow each other. However, numerous studies now exist contradicting this trend (coming from different persuasions). This study is one of these. There still remains the problem of discussing change in a general way, specifically the movement from one social formation to another. The hypothesis developed here is termed the regional division of labor in culture. The elite in Egypt in the early nineteenth century was reconstituted in response to the pressure of world market forces, through access to the reform culture of Istanbul. The travel of al-ʿAṭṭār should not be seen as that of an isolated individual but as part of the mechanism of socialization and resocialization, involving travel and study abroad. The meaning which I attach to the travel of al-ʿAṭṭār follows from the discovery of the fact that the later Islamic societies rooted themselves in a single modality of law and logic and did not (or could not) permit the adumbration of contradictory tendencies in their midst, as one would have found in a comparable study of England. As a hypothesis the idea that foreign travel serves as a mechanism of resocialization would seem to deserve further development, given the continuing relation between foreign education and elite transformation within a capitalist framework up to the present time.

The documentation presented is of two sorts: biographical and sociological. Al-ʿAṭṭār is shown to be blocked from realizing intellectually and socially the type of development which could have been expected in the preceding decades. This appeared to solidify his resolve to study those subjects not available in his own environment. His travel abroad takes him to two very different centers of learning which appear to have had a long and complex relation through early modern history. In Istanbul, al-ʿAṭṭār finds a structure of culture which has long been aware of trends in the West and which represented a pinnacle of the study of rational sciences. Al-ʿAṭṭār imbibes this culture and returns home to be a leading reformer in the new Muḥammad ʿAlī reform era.

On the sociological level, it is suggested that Cairo, Istanbul, and Damascus represented different sets of class relations in the eighteenth century and that from these relations arose different epistemologies in the ruling-class cultures. Istanbul was seen as progressing toward latifundia. The polarity between landlord/bureaucrat and peasant was seen as the foundation for the dominant Aristotelian character of thought: rationalist and systematic. Struggles over surplus between the regional and central authorities do not appear to affect this. Damascus, a traditional center of holistic mystical thought, was an industrial, commercial city. The dependence of the entire population on the fate of the long-distance trade and on predictable relations with Bedouins precludes the possibility that vertical cleavages could impose themselves as they did in Cairo and Istanbul. Among the discoveries of this study was that modern positivist science and medicine taught in Istanbul often shocked intellectuals accustomed to a holistic approach to knowledge. They would follow up an Istanbul period with a period of reintegrative study in Damascus. Thus, al-ʿAṭṭār's effort to synthesize the findings of modern medicine into an Avicennian framework in 1814 was probably not uncommon, especially from what we know of the biographies of a number of Syrian and Turkish science students. This would perhaps be the case in Germany or Russia as well. It was al-ʿAṭṭār's effort to confront the problem of the circulation of the blood which brings him to read Ibn al-Nafīs, alerting us to a discovery for the field of later Islamic medical history that Ibn al-Nafīs' theory—a forerunner of or, conceivably, an influence indirectly on Harvey—was never entirely lost during the era of Avicennian dominance.

The return of al-ʿAṭṭār to Egypt (Chapter 6) makes clear that intellectual integration is no longer a necessary part of resocialization. The findings in this study are that it might in fact be an obstacle. The higher military officers and technocrats in alliance with foreign merchants carried out policies in Egypt in intellectual as well as physical isolation from the masses who were being manipulated. It was the lower bureaucrats, primarily Egyptians, who bore the brunt of reconciling their society to the changes taking place. This was an elite function but never one which could interfere with what was actually being done. Neoclassicism in language, literature, and history served the new ends but in science and medicine it did not, because it would reopen a path of mobility for socially discontented Egyptian Muslims by legitimizing their heritage. Thus the two major neoclassical works of al-ʿAṭṭār, the one in medicine and the other in elementary science, remain in the library of al-Azhar as forgotten manuscripts. A few copies of the scientific works of his close friend the Syrian Muḥammad al-ʿAṭṭār are to be found in Cairo, Damascus, and Istanbul, dating from a period of Turkish reform. However, further clarification is needed as to the role of Azhar culture within the context of the changed ruling-class orientation. This study poses the Azhar as pre-eminently the institution of the submerged middle class of the eighteenth century, in conflict with the new ruling class. This follows from a study of the lives of the different Shaykhs al-Azhar, apart from al-ʿAṭṭār. It is also based on the sympathy of the Azharites for the Wahhābī enemy of Muḥammad ʿAlī. It might possibly be demonstrated that, given the small size of the new elite, not merely the bureaucratic formation, but the Azhar as well, served as a buffer between itself and the masses, served therefore as a necessary part of the social and economic cycle. This point is raised since the development of a theory must account for the rapid even frenetic creation of, and abandonment of, institutions as a feature of ruling-class activity on the periphery (in Egypt from Muḥammad ʿAlī), while institutional reform is commoner in the industrial heartland.

In Chapter 7, we picked up the study of the development of law as theology as it evolved in the writings of al-ʿAṭṭār from the late eighteenth century. Al-ʿAṭṭār's first studies in logic in the 1790's point to his frustrations with the dominant culture of *ḥadīth* studies. First he passed through an Ashʿarite polemic phase, then more self-confidently he moved to Māturīdism, in which the role of reason is asserted as more determinative. His major work, completed in Egypt shortly before his accession to the position of Shaykh al-Azhar in 1831, was the most important systematic theology of the reform period. It was a two-volume gloss on a traditional text in *uṣūl al-dīn* (the roots of jurisprudence). It contained a discussion of the fruits of modern science and it employed in a number of areas a naturalist causality.

Chapter 7 brings out the way in which continuity is maintained in the shift from *ḥadīth* and inductive logic to *fiqh* and deductive logic. Utilitarianism is shown in the later works of al-ʿAṭṭār to flow from the expansion of the role of argument of analogy, by which a flexible response to change could be achieved.

A feature of culture during the reform period was that it became disjointed from religion and law in certain ways. It was still neoclassical and it flowed from the general Aristotelian orientation. The models from the past were thus entirely different than they had been in the eighteenth century. This trajectory, superficially similar to that of the West, in fact owes its existence to the structure of society on the periphery. The conclusion of this chapter is that the models chosen in history, language, and literature were congruent with but not necessarily a product of research in theology, for example, Ibn Khaldūn. Some of the productions, such as a revival of *al-inshāʾ* (composition writing), clearly came from the new needs of the clerks of the bureaucracy.

Another clear effect of the vertical structure of bureaucratic life was the deterioration of poetry which became patently more insincere and high-flung. The free development of prose or musical composition seems to have been discouraged. Al-ʿAṭṭār, as is shown in another autobiographical fragment, never reconciled himself to all the changes. He hated bureaucratic relationships and missed the broader cultural environment which had existed in Egypt in his youth. The study of the well-known student al-Ṭahṭāwī in contrast to al-ʿAṭṭār in chapters 7, 8, and 9 completes the discussion of transition. The study of al-Ṭahṭāwī's major and minor writings led to the discovery that most of what is regarded as European influence came from his association with al-ʿAṭṭār. So he himself proclaims in his two major books, and this is substantiated by comparing the types of concerns, the choice of sources, the categories of thought of al-ʿAṭṭār and al-Ṭahṭāwī in the later 1820's and earlier 1830's. This necessarily revises sharply the view of al-Ṭahṭāwī as an innovator bringing back ideas from France. One need only know that he read Ibn Khaldūn with al-ʿAṭṭār, possibly even the work of al-ʿAṭṭār in which the latter used Ibn Khaldūn as a model to understand how he could find Montesquieu to be the Ibn Khaldūn of the West, to regard Lord Chesterfield's *Letters to his Son* as *maqāmāt*, to prefer republicanism to absolute monarchy. Al-Ṭahṭāwī's social background alone would explain why he would appreciate the virtues of the *dīwān* system of the eighteenth century, a form of republicanism, especially for merchants like his father, and the total disruption brought about by the bureaucracy of Muḥammad ʿAlī. His taste in science in Paris was quite Islamic; he liked observatories, which al-ʿAṭṭār had pointed out in his scientific writings were central to later Islamic science. But there are differences between the generations of al-ʿAṭṭār and his students which perhaps contribute to the discussion of our larger problem of transition. The students of al-ʿAṭṭār continued the neoclassicism, but having lacked a contact with the more broadly creative and less-regimented life of the eighteenth century, they greeted life in the reform period with a certain optimism in the unfolding progress of humanity. Al-ʿAṭṭār did not. It would be interesting to pursue the thoughts of these students through the period in which the reform bureaucracy itself was destroyed and progress, in the sense they understood it, came to an end. Al-Ṭanṭāwī went to Russia, al-Ṭahṭāwī was in the Sudan, others were also scattered.

I began chapter nine by making an important distinction between creation and use of a given idea or technique, in order to suggest that Egypt, like much of the periphery of the world market, could not support a social structure that could create new technology, although the ruling class was aware of what existed and could selectively integrate those aspects which were politically possible, given class balances. This meant that the introduction of the printing press was much more difficult than European luxury products. The introduction of Western technology would and did involve a capacity to destroy the artisanate. Connected to the idea of use, and an awareness of relative utility, is the idea of the choice of the most advantageous source. Such calculations by the Mamlūks in the eighteenth century led them to abandon Muslim doctors and medical institutions in favor of those of Mediterranean minorities, with whom they had important economic relations as well. From a purely medical or scientific point of view, this was not rational on several counts. They were not acquiring anything new, particularly in medicine. The main medical developments were in England and Holland. Only later, when an Egyptian ruler, Muḥammad ʿAlī, had direct dealings with the industrial world of northwest Europe did one find that the technical advisors from these regions predominated.

The main contribution of chapter nine was to indicate the role of Islamic neoclassical thought in the rise of positivism in Egypt. The main conclusion reached was that in the sciences this route was bypassed in favor of a straight adoption of Western European books, despite the existence of impressive contributions from the neoclassical movement which could provide a congruent set of assumptions for modern scientific development and which, in some cases, like Ibn al-Nafīs, contained knowledge deemed correct by modern science. In Turkey indigenous writings continued to serve, but in Egypt the most important of these writings, the two surveyed in this chapter, remained in manuscript form. Ḥasan al-ʿAṭṭār's *Ḥāshiya ʿalā Sharḥ Qāḍī Zadeh* expressed the need of breaking down wholes into explainable parts, of testing propositions, and of relying on experiment over authority. In his *Sharḥ Nuzha*, the critique from within the Avicennian tradition, both of its accuracy on given points and of its soundness methodologically, is quite developed. These findings have a certain novelty, as scholastic writing is routinely dismissed by scholars as too narrow or rigid to convey modern thought. Hopefully, the fact that the Arabic route to positivism (at least in a number of fields) involved neoclassicism will stimulate a renewed interest in these writings, not just in the Arab lands but also in similar Mediterranean societies like Italy or Spain which have a huge heritage of scholastic literature as well.

Specifically, in chapter nine, I placed the decline of indigenous Egyptian participation in physical medicine and natural science in the eighteenth and early nineteenth centuries in a historical context. To do this I had to take sides in favor of an externalist type of explanation as opposed to an internalist one. In some fields, the application of political economy to technical knowledge is quite familiar. Unfortunately, this is not the case in the field of history of science and medicine, especially with regard to Arabic and Islamic studies. The balance here has always been on the side of the internalists, those who study development from within the problems generated by the discipline. First, the paradigm of Golden Age and decline, which has been adopted in the history of Islamic science and medicine and which has been clung to tenaciously, has nothing to say about the Islamic writings of the later centuries except that they are derivative of earlier ones. Second, the paradigm necessarily implies that the coming of the West was the principal watershed of modern times. Earlier, I had argued that, historically, Europeans were continuously in the Middle East and that their ideas were as varied as, and in fact identical with, those held by Middle Easterners. This should come as no surprise to readers of Michel Foucault or others who have traced the long slow rise of positivism to a position of dominance in French thought in the nineteenth century.

For the researcher of the future, the turn toward metaphysics and *al-ḥikma* in Egyptian eighteenth-century writings, which resulted from the writers' loss of patronage, should be seen as a challenging new subject. In chapter nine, this subject is cut short for the sake of developing fully the notion of neoclassicism. If, however, one pursued the writings of Aḥmad al-Sijāʿī or Aḥmad al-Damanhūrī and compared them to the scholars of Padua, a center of deductive medicine in Italy, or to the German medical schools of the nineteenth century which read Ibn Sīnā, a social analysis of the opposition to positivism could be produced.

Finally, the ninth chapter returns us to the claim made at the outset of this book, which is that underlying the writing of Middle Eastern history there have been long-term problems of proper conceptualization. As a hypothesis for why this should be the case, I offer the suggestion that the field is caught up with extraneous issues over which it has no control, for example, Western self-definition, as in propositions like the rise of the West or the coming of the West. Such ruling propositions show where the center of gravity of the discipline lies. *Islamic Roots of Capitalism*, as the title suggests, has as its central preoccupation the Western-centered structure of the discipline of history, notably the shackles this imposes on the development of the history of non-European peoples. From the perspective of Arab society this is a colonialist approach which only has room for Arabs as passive recipients of the West. Specialists in Middle East history have sometimes played into this by concentrating on various political elites in the Arab world who were weak at home and who very much relied on Western European support from their trading partners. These fit the stereotype. The decolonialization of history for Western scholars, including myself, is a slow process. The very context which most of us take for granted, the strong state, is at issue. Our research based in the Arab or Ottoman state archives often serves to confirm our general picture of the world. As a result, women, who are half of any population, and groups who have avoided state dominance or whom the state administers indirectly, drop out of the picture. If one turns to the commercial sector, either Arab or that of the Mediterranean minorities functioning in Arab lands, one finds quite a different picture. The commercial sector was and is competing and struggling with Western Europe to wrest every possible gain out of the ongoing economic flow of world capitalism. If one looks at the large masses of peasants, tribes, and workers, again one finds it is their struggle which in large measure accounts for the rulers' weaknesses. The Arab world has made anything but a passive response to the pressures exerted by the world market through the local rulers. Of course Arab and Islamic lands did not produce systems on the periphery of the world market resembling in shape or in culture or in coercive technique what emerged in England. However, they did participate crucially in the development of the modern world through the international division of labor with its well-known unequal trade relations, before, during, and after the colonial period. Thus, logically, Islamic culture played a part in the main phases of modern world history. To allow, as is usually done, a watershed in world history like the industrial revolution of the eighteenth century to be constituted as a local event in English or French history is thus a regression to colonial history writing. A study of Egypt at the time of Shaykh Ḥasan al-ʿAṭṭār necessarily demonstrates these points.

Appendix I
The *Maqāmat al-ʿAṭṭār*

Various profligate wine-drinking people told me of how the French disturbed people on Tuesday and frightened many of them from the streets, gasping as they ran.

I went out of my house in confusion, not knowing what direction or what street to take; I was expecting my own destruction. But although I was afraid and unsettled, I did not restrain myself until as if by an unalterable fate I was drawn to al-Azbakīya, which is the residence of the wealthy. I was feeling a mixture of foreboding and yet desire, a feeling of venturesomeness. Thus, when I arrived, I fled back; then, steadying myself, I forced myself to think a second, which resulted in there coming to me a conclusion which gave me a feeling of peace and security—which was that the people of this area [al-Azbakīya] were a peaceful people and that many of them had been mingling without any fights occurring and with neither bad consequences nor awkwardness.

And I had heard from knowledgeable people who had traveled in different countries that these people were not cruel except to those who make war on them, and that some of them knew obscure fields of learning. They are informed about them and make experiments which appeal to them. Their hearts are filled with a love for philosophy, and they cherish what they acquire from its books. They esteem intellectual labor and reflection, and they seek out those who have knowledge of it and they would have the deepest conversations with them.[1]

Beside the house in which he lived there were youths. These youths stood out like suns, vibrating and swaying like bridegrooms; their faces were veiled with beauty and they were tall and handsome like arrows. Their hair was like a banner which an army of lovers would follow, an army vibrating passionately with love. And I stared at them, gazing passionately, seeking that they come. Then I stopped staring at their beauty to praise their figures, and they became aware of what glances I was pouring on them, so that the group came right up to me and began to greet me. A youth from among them made me look at a book and we began talking; and I found his Arabic to be free from ungrammatical usages and from barren phraseology and other defects. After that, he began to tell me about some of the classical books of our famous writers, mentioning that he possessed various books and notebooks; then he began to enumerate and characterize them until he mentioned the "Tadhkara" of al-Ṭūsī and the "Shifāʾ," which he called *Al-Shifāʾ al-sharīf*. And this astonishing fact confused me, made me dizzy—but what increased my astonishment even more was his love for literature. . . . He told me that he had translated from Arabic into his own language and that this piece [a piece of poetry which he recited to al-ʿAṭṭār] he had decided to memorize. . . . A passion stirred in me which I had not felt for a long time. And a passion for literature which had once grown stronger, then weaker, was now revived. I sat up all night in dreamy meditation like one giddy with love, for no sleep came to me—so I decided to concentrate on writing some verses of poetry, and they are:

> One of the French is a gazelle, the beauty of his eyelids has a strong effect on the one who loves him
> He appeared in dark clothes and I thought that they were alive
> He is a garden of beauty, we must help him. . . .[2]

I met him in the afternoon of that day while he was with his youthful compatriots—all of them preoccupied with obscure areas of learning—some of them were versed even in intricate matters in the field of literature, to which they showed devotion. When I arrived at the session, they were beginning to let flow the wine, but observing the intensity of my disapproval, they let me look at books, large and small, books some of which I had never seen before, some of which [I knew to be] famous—and all either in the physical sciences or in literature. They put me at my liberty with their astronomical and engineering equipment, then they discussed with me various matters in these fields, writing down what I said. Then they sought from me a clarification of some of the verses of the *Burda*. After that they showed me some verses of poetry which were not compatible and asked me to explain to them their obvious meanings and their hidden meanings.

Someone told me that in their country they have a copy of the *Dīwān of the Seven Muʿallaqāt*, and that they have some collections of poetry in their language that stir the spirit. And they continued to ask me to explain linguistic terms, comparing my answers to what was written in a precious book written along the lines of *Al-Jumhara*, containing Arabic expressions and their translation into French. After that I wrote for them some verses explaining the meaning of various words. Among these were two verses which I had composed previously, at a time when I was at my best:

> Give me a chance, that I may describe to you how arrows fill my heart
> Arrows which shed my blood—and bloodshed is forbidden
> And then I will make any sin permissible!

To this I added two verses of a new poem which inspiration granted me, containing some words of their language. I gave it extemporaneously, and I do not want anyone to make an analysis of it.

> Among the French there is a branch on which beauty has sprouted of various kinds—and he has a face like a new moon.

From inside the night of his clothes shines forth the pearls of his smile,
which flows out like forbidden wine.
His looks had the same effect on my heart as old wine
O heart! Have patience! For love once more shall rekindle your spirit
But to know him has become impossible,
For he has no pity on my passions. . . .

This poetry transported them with joy, astonishing them no end. They began to praise me for it, praising me to excess. Then they urged me to live with them, making me realize that this was a real request which they meant. But I kept putting off giving an answer and kept it a secret for lack of authorization, knowing that if I had gone ahead with this matter, rebukes and hostility would have awaited me as well as the scorn of society. Thus I returned to my senses and made my decision. May God forgive me for what I have done.[3]

Appendix II
Al-ʿAṭṭār's Itinerary from 1802 to 1810

The interpretation presented in Chapter 6, relying on al-ʿAṭṭār's own writings, is quite at odds with the biography of Mubārak and al-Ḥusaynī. In this appendix, the questions of whether he visited Albania and whether he visited Syria more than once are discussed in greater detail.

Precise information about al-ʿAṭṭār's travels and associates is, as has been previously stated, difficult to find before the period in Damascus from 1810 to 1815. Concerning his departure from Egypt, al-ʿAṭṭār wrote: "I finished the rough draft of this gloss at the end of Dhū'l-Qaʿda in the year 1217 [approximately March 20, 1802], at which time I was in the fort at Damietta on my way out of Egypt to Turkey; and this rough draft stayed with me until I returned from Turkey to Syria in 1225; when the French came, I left Egypt, taking this rough draft and some of my books. I stayed in the Ottoman [Rumīya] lands a long time; then I went to Damascus in Rabīʿ al-Awwal 1225 [April 14, 1810]."[1]

If one supposes that the long stay in Damascus occupied the last five years which al-ʿAṭṭār spent abroad, there are still problems related to the first eight years, from 1802 to 1810. Al-ʿAṭṭār himself is not always clear. He stated: "I began my writing on this [book] when I was in Cairo, Egypt; then I traveled to Constantinople and wrote some of it, then I transferred to Alexandretta and wrote some more . . ."[2] If one understands this as an exact description of the sequence of events, we can locate a part of the time during which he was in Alexandretta from a reference in another of his writings, from the year 1807/1222. "Ḥasan al-Miṣrī thus ends his marginal comments, agreeing that the day of completion was on a Friday in Shaʿbān of the year 1222 [October 1807], signing his name Ḥasan b. Muḥammad al-ʿAṭṭār al-Azharī al-Shāfiʿī al Miṣrī al-Khalwatī. I was in the city of Alexandretta when this was done on my trip out of Egypt."[3] Elsewhere in the same work, we learn that, due to the inaccuracies in his work, it was actually completed not in Alexandretta itself but on the shores of the Black Sea at a place called Bayqūdh in a fortress called Yūdūdh. This would suggest that the date given may have been approximately a departure date. On the same page, he indicates that Alexandretta represented a busy period in his life, that he was teaching nearly every day in the mosque: a group of ten soldiers until they were taken off to battle, then some law clerks, and later a man who wanted to read a grammar book with al-ʿAṭṭār and chose ʿAbd al-Qāhir al-Jurjānī's commentary called "Dalāʾil al-iʿjāz innā li khaṣāʾiṣ" on the work of ʿIṣām.

Thus, if we imagine that al-ʿAṭṭār left Alexandretta in 1807/1222 and that he had given a number of lessons over a period of time, we may postulate that he was in Alexandretta at least during 1806–1807/1221–1222.[4] If he had given us a clearer idea of how much he accomplished in Alexandretta, the period might be considerably extended. He might have gone there as early as 1805. We know from al-Ḥusaynī that he wrote a "part" of his book on geometry while there. In the field of argumentation (*ādāb al-baḥth*), he had been reading various commentaries in Turkey (i.e., in Istanbul), but found none that were to his satisfaction until he arrived in Alexandretta. However, al-ʿAṭṭār stated that "when I went to Damascus, I became occupied with reading that book with some brighter students; I found it to be a strenuous matter."[5] The stay in Damascus which he refers to followed, but not necessarily directly followed, his stay in Alexandretta. From this one could understand either that he traveled to Damascus at a later date or that he visited Alexandretta a second time on his way out of Turkey. The first is the more likely. The only real problem here is what he meant by "I was in the city of Alexandretta [in 1807] on my way out of Egypt." This could be taken to support Mubārak's account, except that all the dated evidence from Syria is for the later period, and the Syrian sources virtually deny the existence of such a stay, as did al-ʿAṭṭār's own words in his work on *Al-Azharīya.*

The second major problem is whether or not al-ʿAṭṭār went to Scutari in Albania; or whether this "Scutari" was Ushkudar, a part of Istanbul known in English as Scutari and in Arabic as Ashkūdrā. Al-Ḥusaynī and Mubārak both based their information on al-ʿAṭṭār's son or on other relatives who claimed that he went to Albania, married there, had a son, and that both his wife and his son died. This would suggest a stay in Scutari of more than a year. Both sources also claim that he wrote at least two works while there, the "Ḥāshiya ʿalā natāʾij al-afkār" and the "Tuḥfa"[6] An examination of the first work, however, proves that it was written in Alexandretta. Alexandretta is on the extreme southeast edge of Turkey, a point very distant from Albania. One might note that in yet another writing al-ʿAṭṭār was fairly specific about his travels. This was a diploma given to a Syrian student, in which he listed his travels as "Turkish, Syrian, and Ḥijāzī." In this, he did not mention Albania.[7] Another piece of evidence adduced concerning his alleged travels to Albania was that one of his wife's relatives was said to have come from Albania to sit in his circle in the Azhar years later when he was a teacher there. According to this anecdote, which was told by one of his students, Ibrāhīm al-Saqqāʾ, they spoke in Turkish, and when the man left, al-ʿAṭṭār had his mind on killing.[8] It may well have been that he married an Albanian woman, and that one of her relatives came to Cairo. However, one might note that the Albanians generally spoke Illyrian rather than Turkish, and that, since there was a state of open warfare between the

Turks and ʿAlī Bey of Yanina, contact between the two was on the whole probably limited. It certainly does not seem likely that al-ʿAṭṭār went to Albania. But if he did, the strongest evidence to support such a claim has been overlooked. This is a comment on the writing of his "Tuḥfa" which appeared in his major work on theology, which was written between 1828 and 1830. Here he stated that while he was writing the "Tuḥfa," he was in "Rūmīlī." One meaning of this term (if it was not a misprint) is the Ottoman administrative district of Rumelia (as opposed to Anatolia), that is, on the European side of the Bosphorus. Scutari of Istanbul is on the Asiatic side. However, since no one has seen the "Tuḥfa," there is no textual evidence of where it was written. Perhaps it was simply written in the European part of Istanbul where al-ʿAṭṭār may have been staying. This view is supported by the claim which al-ʿAṭṭār made in the same sentence, that when he finished it he took it immediately to the Şeyh ul-Islam, who wrote down his praise of it. The difficulty of coming from Scutari in Albania to Istanbul to see the Şeyh ul-Islam would almost seem to preclude this—quite apart from the special wartime circumstances.

ʿAlī Mubārak may have been misled about the travels of al-ʿAṭṭār by a copy of Muḥammad al-ʿAṭṭār's commentary on anatomy, the "Sharḥ ʿalā manẓūmat al-ʿAṭṭār." This source states that Ḥasan al-ʿAṭṭār composed his grammar text on the work of al-Birkāwī in the city of "Skandirīya al-Arnāʾud."[9] Muḥammad al-ʿAṭṭār is the earliest source for the "Albanian trip"; al-Ḥusaynī and Mubārak had read him. This particular copy was autographed by Ḥasan al-ʿAṭṭār, and he also wrote some comments on the text. Whether he had read the introduction (with the biography) cannot be ascertained. The printed text of the grammar book, however, as was stated above, denies this account, and cites Alexandretta as the place where it was written. The only conclusion which we can otherwise draw is that "al-Arnāʾud," generally understood to mean Albania, might have meant "Turkey" to the Syrian Muḥammad al-ʿAṭṭār. Since "Skandarīya," a version of the Arabic word for Alexandria and the Turkish word for Alexandretta, cannot be made to fit the geography of Albania, this is a possibility.[10]

While it would be difficult to prove that al-ʿAṭṭār did not visit Albania, it can be proved from al-ʿAṭṭār's writings that he was very familiar with the intellectual life in Scutari in Turkey during the early years of the nineteenth century. Scutari in Turkey, traditionally a terminus of the caravan routes from Persia (the Tabriz route) and Armenia, was also a Ṣūfī cultural center. There was an important Mevlevi *tekke* next to one of the several great cemeteries which contained the tombs of numerous saints.[11] In the eighteenth century, it had been for several decades an important center for the diffusion of Western science in the Ottoman empire. In 1734, a school of geometry had been founded in Scutari with a corps of mathematicians under Sulayman Bonneval, the son of Aḥmad Bonneval. The first professor of geometry at this school was Muhammad Saʿid Mufti Zadeh of Beyshehir (in Asia Minor) who was also the inventor of an instrument for artillerymen consisting of a quadrant and two arcs.[12] At the end of the eighteenth century, at the time of Selim, there were advances in military engineering, and Scutari was an important center for these developments. In the 1790's, Selim, who was concentrating on his land army, set up fortifications at Levend-Tchiflik and Scutari in Turkey. These centers had cannoneers and bombardiers drilled by Europeans. The commanding officer for the latter was a Scotsman named Campbell, alias Inglis-Mustafa.[13] The setting up of a printing press in Scutari was closely related to the needs of the army. Among the earliest works of the press were a number of texts and translations to be used by the Turkish officers.

However, as was the case with many of the early printing presses in the Middle East, the range of subjects included gradually widened, reflecting the cultural and religious orientations of the period. Such was the case with the press at Scutari. In 1802 and then again in 1804, it published the *Ṭarīqa muḥammadīya*, as well as al-Birkāwī's work on Arabic grammar, *Iẓhār al-asrār.* A second author whose works appeared was Nāṣir al-dīn al-Ṭūsī, author of *Kitāb Iqlīdīs fīʾl-handasa.*[14]

Al-ʿAṭṭār would seem to have had some degree of familiarity with this press and its publications, because in the same year in which the Scutari press was publishing these works, we find him studying and commenting on them. Al-ʿAṭṭār wrote a grammatical essay commenting on al-Birkāwī's grammar text, which was identified above as having been finished in Alexandria in 1807. He wrote an essay attacking the *Ṭarīqa muḥammadīya*, which he called the "Tuḥfa." He also wrote a commentary on a work by al-Ṭūsī.

Both Ḥasan al-ʿAṭṭār and Muḥammad al-ʿAṭṭār wrote or commented on "Riyāḍīyāt" and "al-Ṭabīʿāt" while they were in Istanbul, as has been mentioned above. Indeed, it is borne out that both men worked on texts on solid geometry and wrote on classical texts of military engineering. While we possess no accurate list of the writing which was undertaken in these fields by either person, it was clearly substantial. As al-ʿAṭṭār's interest in medicine formed a distinct part of his work during his stay in Istanbul, and as we understand that his writings in the natural sciences, together with his two works on al-Birkāwī, were done between 1802 and 1806 in Istanbul and Scutari, this material was being made available there at that time; the study of medicine came later.

The evidence is all circumstantial, but it is substantial. The existence of the press in Scutari and the interest in military engineering, on the one hand, and remoteness and relative backwardness of Scutari in Albania, on the other, make it seem much more reasonable that al-ʿAṭṭār chose to stay in Scutari in Turkey.[15] Of the books which al-ʿAṭṭār was supposed to have written while in Albania, the one which was located was actually written elsewhere. Because of the existence of the press and its publications, it seems much more natural that it was written in Ushkudar than in Scutari, Albania. Finally, the other essay which is alleged to have been written in Albania, entitled "Risāla fīʾl-farq bayn al-imkān waʾl-lā-imkān" (which has been lost), appears to be a study in *al-ḥikma*, which he studied in Istanbul.

We conclude, therefore, that we have no persuasive evidence that al-ʿAṭṭār acutally did go to Albania, nor even any logical reason for him to have traveled there, whereas all the activities which are recorded for him during his alleged stay in Albania appear to fit into the events of the time in the Istanbul-Scutari area in Turkey.

Appendix III
The Writings of Ḥasan al-ʿAṭṭār

Sciences of the Sharīʿa

1. "Risāla fīʾl-basmala waʾl-ḥamdala" (*tafsīr*). Manuscript. Dār al-Kutub, Cairo. 353 Tafsīr, Taymūr. 11 folios. Copy made in 1863/1280 in Damascus by an Algerian, Aḥmad b. Muḥammad al-Balīdī.
2. "Al-Taqayyud waʾl-īḍāḥ li mā uṭliq wa ughliq min kitāb bi-Ibn al-Ṣalāḥ fī ʿulūm al-ḥadīth" (*muṣṭalaḥ al-ḥadīth*). Manuscript. Dār al-Kutub, Cairo. Manuscript 25337. 107 folios. Edited by al-ʿAṭṭār, 1818/1234.
3. "Ḥāshiyat al-ʿAṭṭār ʿalā matn al-nukhba fī uṣūl al-ḥadīth" (*muṣṭalaḥ al-ḥadīth*). Unlocated.

   Cited by ʿAbd al-Ghanī Ḥasan, *Ḥasan al-ʿAṭṭār*, pp. 84–85; al-Ḥusaynī, "Sharḥ al-umm al-musammā bi murshid al-anām li birr umm al-imām," p. 38. One basic text is the *Nukhba* of Ibn Ḥajar (Brockelmann, *Geschichte der Arabischen Litteratur*, GAL 2, p. 68; in No. 4, II, 189, al-ʿAṭṭār cited in a section on *ḥadīth* criticism "my Shaykh Shihāb"), possibly referring to Shihāb al-dīn Ibn Ḥajar. See Chap. 7, n. 14, indicating the influence of Ibn Ṣalāḥ.
4. *Ḥāshiyat al-ʿAṭṭār ʿalā sharḥ Jalāl al-dīn al-Maḥallī ʿalā jāmiʿ al-jawāmiʿ li ʿAbd al-Wahhāb al-Subkī*. 2 vols. Cairo: Muṣṭafā al-Ḥalabī, n.d.

   Original date of composition is 1828–1830 (Brockelmann, *Geschichte der Arabischen Litteratur* GAL 2, p. 89). This is the most important piece of systematic thought written during the reform period.
5. "Risāla fī ḥall lughz baʿḍ al-ʿulamāʾ min Latbalun" [*sic*]. Unlocated. Cited by al-Ḥusaynī, "Sharḥ al-umm al-musammā bi murshid al-anām li birr umm al-imām," p. 39.

   Undoubtedly a work on *ʿilm al-kalām* written between 1802 and 1810. *Latbalun* could be a copying error for al-Tebelen, the South Albanian town of Tepelene. Al-ʿAṭṭār also stated that a group of Bulgarian *ʿulamāʾ* had come to him over a problem in *ʿilm al-kalām* concerning the attributes of God, a problem over which there was a conflict in their area. Al-ʿAṭṭār stated that he wrote an essay for them basing it on Fakhr al-dīn al-Rāzī, also citing the *Sharḥ al-Muʿallim* of Ibn al-Tilmansī, which attacked the Muʿtazilī position. See No. 4, II, 457.

6. "Tuḥfat gharīb al-waṭan fī taḥqīq naṣr al-Shaykh Ibn al-Ḥasan al-Ash'arī" (*kalām*). Unlocated.
   Can also be dated from the stay in Turkey, since al-'Aṭṭār stated that he took it to the Şeyh ul-Islam Arab Zadeh, who wrote in praise of it. Al-'Aṭṭār identified this work as an attack on *Al-Ṭarīqa al-muḥammadīya* of Pir Birghili, and especially the commentary on it of Khadimi Zadeh. Al-'Aṭṭār stated that he defended the Ash'arī position. See No. 4, II, 523–524; al-Ḥusaynī, "Sharḥ al-umm al-musammā bi murshid al-anām li birr umm al-imām," p. 38.
7. "Risālat al-tadmīr 'alā Izmīr" (*kalām*?). Unlocated.
   Al-Ḥusaynī, "Sharḥ al-umm al-musammā bi murshid al-anām li birr umm al-imām," p. 38, stated that al-'Aṭṭār wrote this while in Izmir, Turkey (probably in 1806–1807). It is mentioned in conjunction with other essays on *kalām* which he was studying at this point.
8. "Hadhā jawāb Shaykh Ḥasan al-'Aṭṭār 'an su'āl al-faqīr Muṣṭafā al-Bidīrī." Manuscript. Dār al-Kutub, Cairo. 1171 Kalām. 18 folios.
   This deals with the materialist views of creation in Islamic and pre-Islamic philosophy. Dated August 1813/Sha'bān 1228.
9. "Risālat al-'Aṭṭār fī 'ilm al-kalām." Manuscript. Dār al-Kutub, Cairo. B25816. 15 folios.
   This is the same as "Risālat al-'Aṭṭār fī khalq al-af'āl fī 'ilm al-kalām," manuscript (al-Azhar, Cairo, 22985 Kalām [2344], folios 52–60). The difference is that the Dār al-Kutub copy has extended marginal comments by Shaykh 'Alī al-Mīlī, and some marginal comments by al-'Aṭṭār. This work was written, according to al-'Aṭṭār, to correct mistakes in the *Kubrā* of al-Sānūsī, in 1813/1228.
10. "Risāla tata'alliq bi mawḍū' 'ilm al-kalām." Manuscript. Dār al-Kutub, Cairo. Kalām, dated 1813/1228.
   An essay on the utility of the rational sciences, based on the contention that one can approach every problem scientifically.
11. "Jawāb al-'Aṭṭār 'an su'āl jā' 'alayhi min Ustādh al-Shaykh al-Thu'aylīb." Manuscript. Dār al-Kutub, Cairo. 1172 Kalām, dated 1814/1230. 30 folios.
   See also al-Ḥusaynī, "Sharḥ al-umm al-musammā bi murshid al-anām li birr umm al-imām," p. 41, who states that this was one of two essays of importance on *'ilm al-kalām* which became known only posthumously through copies made by al-'Aṭṭār's student Muḥammad al-Khuḍarī al-Dimyāṭī.
12. "Jawāb al-'Aṭṭār 'an su'āl jā' 'alayhi min Shaykh al-Faḍḍālī." Unlocated.
   Cited by al-Ḥusaynī, "Sharḥ al-umm al-musammā bi murshid al-anām li birr umm al-imām," p. 4, who states that this was the second of two essays referred to in No. 11, and that it dealt with the differences among the Ahl al-Sunna, al-Mu'tazila, and al-Ghaybiyīn. On the back of this essay, presumably the first copy, Shaykh al-Faḍḍālī was said to have written in praise of al-'Aṭṭār's answers to these two

questions, saying that he gave answers which very few people could have given. The date and title are not known precisely.

13. "Risālat al-ʿAllāma Ḥasan al-ʿAṭṭār fīʾl-ijtihād." Manuscript. Dār al-Kutub, Cairo. 323 Majāmīʿ, Taymūr, folios 45–81. Copied in 1841/1264 by ʿAlī b. Futūḥ.

   From internal evidence, the date of composition was probably around 1832, but on the first folio it is stated that it was written in 1844/1260, which was after al-ʿAṭṭār's death. The essay is an attack on the Ṣūfī Shaykh al-Sānūsī, who was a student or acquaintance of al-ʿAṭṭār when he came to al-Azhar around 1832.

14. "Hadhān masʾālatān min arbaʿīn al-masāʾil allatī ṣannafahā al-Imām Fakhr al-dīn al-Rāzī fī ʿilm al-kalām." Manuscript. Dār al-Kutub, Cairo. 122 Kalām, Majāmīʿ, Taymūr, pp. 271–326.

   This bears the signature ex libris Ḥasan al-ʿAṭṭār and underlinings in the text, apparently in the same ink.

Philosophy and *al-Ḥikma*

15. "Ḥāshiyat al-ʿAṭṭār ʿalā sharḥ Sharīf al-Ḥusaynī ʿalā hidāyat al-ḥikma li Athīr al-dīn al-Abharī." Unlocated.

   Incomplete as of 1828. This is cited in No. 4, I, 31. See al-Ṣabbān's work on the same or a related text. Al-Jabartī, *ʿAjāʾib al-āthār fīʾl-tarājim waʾl-akhbār*, II, 237.

16. "Qalāʾid al-durr fīʾl-maqālāt al-ʿashar." Manuscript. Dār al-Kutub, Cairo. 340 al-Ḥikma wa al-falsafa.

   This is the same as "Sharḥ al-ʿAṭṭār ʿalā al-Sijāʿī fīʾl-ḥikma" (or ". . . ʿalā manẓūmat al-Sijāʿī"). The work of Aḥmad al-Sijāʿī was "Naẓm al-ʿashar fīʾl-ḥikma." The date of al-ʿAṭṭār's work is 1804/1219. Brockelmann, *Geschichte der Arabischen Literatur*, S2, p. 256, cites another copy, Bayrūt 393, which has not been seen.

17. "Risāla fīʾl farq bayn al-imkān waʾl-lā-imkān." Unlocated.

   Al-Ḥusaynī, "Sharḥ al-umm al-musammā bi murshid al-anām li birr umm al-imām," p. 38, states that this was composed in Albania. The argument which has been presented in the text of this thesis is that al-ʿAṭṭār never went to Albania, which makes it more likely that he wrote this while in Turkey, i.e., before 1810.

18. *Ḥāshiyat al-ʿAṭṭār ʿalā maqālāt al-Sayyid al-Balīdī*, written in 1818/1234 (al-Ḥikma). Cairo: al-Maṭbaʿa al-Khayrīya, 1911/1329.

   The first of three works in which al-ʿAṭṭār moved to introduce elements of modern scientific thought into Egypt.

19. *Ḥāshiyat al-ʿAṭṭār (al-kubrā) ʿalā sharḥ al-Sijāʿī ʿalā al-maqālāt*, written in 1818/1234. Cairo: al-Maṭbaʿa al-Khayrīya, 1911/1329.

   This is a full-length book written after his work on al-Balīdī and intended as a completion of it.

20. *Ḥāshiyat al-ʿAṭṭār (al-ṣughrā) ʿalā sharḥ al-Sijāʿī alā al-maqālāt.* Cairo: al-Maṭbaʿa al-Khayrīya, 1911/1329.
Composed in 1826/1242 and based on the writings of his teacher Muḥammad al-Disūqī.
21. "Tafsīr maqālāt Arisṭū li Ibn al-Farrāj ʿAbdullah b. al-Jīb." Manuscript. Dār al-Kutub, Cairo. M-1 Falsafa. Not located.
Al-ʿAṭṭār made corrections ("Taṣḥīḥ al-ʿAṭṭār") in 1827/1243.

Natural Science and Technology

22. "Sharḥ al-ʿAṭṭār ʿalā risālat tashrīḥ al-aflāk fī ʿilm al-hayʾa." Unlocated.
The commentary or gloss is on the text of Bahāʾ al-dīn al-ʿĀmilī (dated after 1818/1234). See No. 18, pp. 178, 221.
23. "Ḥāshiyat al-ʿAṭṭār ʿalā Ḥāshiyat Ibn al-Fatḥ (Muḥammad b. al-Hādī b. Naṣr b. Saʿīd al-Ḥusnī al-ʿIraqī, al-musammā bi Tāj al-Saʿīdī, ʿalā sharḥ taʾsīs al-ashkāl li Mūsā b. Muḥammad al-maʿrūf bi Qāḍī Zadeh al-Rūmī ʿalā ashkāl al-taʾsīs li Shams al-dīn al-Samarqandī)," completed 1821/1237. Manuscript. Dār al-Kutub, Cairo. 219 Khidīwī, Riyāḍīyāt, Majāmīʿ, folios 41–100. The copyist was ʿAbd al-Khāliq Sulaymān al-Burhīmī.
This is a major work of Egyptian neoclassicism in science.
24. "Kitāb īḍāḥ al-Murādī bi sharḥ hidāyat al-rāmī li Muḥīy al-dīn b. Taqī al-dīn al-Sulṭān al-Dimashqī." Closing few pages written by Ḥasan al-ʿAṭṭār. Unlocated. Dār al-Kutub, Cairo. Funūn al-ḥarbīya.
25. "Risāla fī kifāyat al-ʿamal biʾl asṭurlāb waʾl-muqanṭar waʾl-mujīb waʾl-basāʾiṭ" (*al-mīqāt*). Unlocated.
Cited in Mubārak, *Khiṭaṭ*, IV, 30–31, but not in earlier sources. This leads to the deduction that it was written after 1815.
26. "Ḥāshiyat Faṣīḥ al-dīn li Muḥammad al-Niẓāmī ʿalā sharḥ Qāḍī Zadeh al-Rūmī," written in 1473/878, dedicated to al-Amīr ʿAlī Shāh al-Wazīr. Manuscript. Dār al-Kutub, Cairo. 58 Riyāḍīyāt. Unlocated.
This has the writing of Ḥasan al-ʿAṭṭār on it.
27. Theodosius, *Kitāb al-Ukar.*
An Arabic translation of the *Spherica* begun by Qusṭāʾ b. Lūqā and completed by another hand. This manuscript is an eighteenth-century copy with an autograph ex libris Ḥasan al-ʿAṭṭār. Listed in Leon Nemoy, "Arabic Manuscripts in the Yale University Library," *Transactions of the Connecticut Academy of Arts and Sciences* 60 (1956): 158, item 1495.
28. "Risāla fīʾl-raml waʾl-zāʾirjā." Unlocated.
Al-ʿAṭṭār might have approached this subject either from *kalām* or from science. It is cited only by Mubārak, *Khiṭaṭ*, IV, 40, and hence was probably written after 1815.

Logic and *Ādāb al-Baḥth*

29. "Ḥāshiyat al-ʿAṭṭār ʿalā sharḥ Muḥibbullah al-Bihārī ʿalā sullam al-Akhḍarī," written in 1819/1235. Manuscript. Dār al-Kutub, Cairo. 4 Manṭiq, Ādāb al-Baḥth, Ḥalīm. 111 folios. Copy dated 1820/1236. Marginal comments on folio 111 are by Naṣr al-Ḥurīnī and are dated 1269.

    The manuscript does not identify the commentary by name, which creates some ambiguity. The information is provided in No. 31. Likewise, a copy of *Sharḥ sullam al-ʿulūm* by al-Bihārī (Dār al-Kutub, Cairo. 88 Manṭiq, Khidīwī, printed in 1861/1278). Al-Bihārī also wrote "Ḥāshiya ʿalā sharḥ Mullā Ḥasan ʿalā sullam al-ʿulūm" (Al-Azhar, Cairo. Manuscript 48727, 1230 al-Imbābī). In the text cited he refers only to al-Mallāwī, leaving it unclear which text the gloss was written on.

30. *Ḥāshiyat al-ʿAṭṭār ʿalā sharḥ Shaykh al-Islām Zakariyā al-Anṣārī ʿalā matn Īsāghūjī liʾl-Abharī*, written 1820/1236. Cairo: al-Maṭbaʿa al-ʿilmīya, 1908/1327.

31. "Ḥāshiya [or Sharḥ] al-ʿAllāma ʿAbd al-Ghaffār ʿalā al-fawāʾid al-ḍiyāʾīya." Unlocated.

    Cited in No. 29, p. 24, in which al-ʿAṭṭār stated that he discussed "*al-dalāla waʾl-lafẓ*" and that he had obtained some good insights in his marginal comments. Written before 1820/1236.

32. *Ḥāshiyat al-ʿAṭṭār ʿalā sharḥ ʿUbaydullah al-Khabīṣī ʿalā tadhhīb al-manṭiq al-shāfī liʾl-Taftazānī*, dated 1824/1240. Cairo: al-Maṭbaʿa al-Azharīya, 1927/1346.

33. "Ḥāshiyat ʿAbd al-Ḥakīm al-Sīyalkūtī ʿalā Ḥāshiyat ʿAlī b. Muḥammad al-maʿrūf bi-l-Sayyid al-Sharīf al-Jurjānī ʿalā sharḥ Quṭb al-dīn Muḥammad al-Rāzī, al-musammā bi lawāmiʿ al-asrār fī sharḥ maṭāliʿ al-anwār." Manuscript. Al-Azhar, Cairo. 48736 al-Manṭiq, 1239 al-Imbābī.

    On the selection on logic of "Kitāb Maṭāliʿ al-Anwār," by Qāḍī Sirāj al-dīn b. Aḥmad, known as al-Urmāwī (died 1283/682). Al-ʿAṭṭār wrote extensive comments on the margins, mainly in the first 60 folios of the total of 198. He signed his name and dated it 1828/1242. (The text reads 1142, but this is clearly an error.)

34. "Taqrīrāt al-ʿAṭṭār ʿalā ḥāshiyat ʿAbd al-Ḥakīm al-Sīyalkūtī ʿalā sharḥ Quṭb al-Rāzī ʿalā al-māshīya." Manuscript. Dār al-Kutub, Cairo. 556 al-Manṭiq, Ādāb al-Baḥth, 6 folios. Undated, but probably written after 1815.

35. "Risālat hal al-Māhīya majʿūla ām lā." Unlocated.

    This is an essay on logic dealing in part with *qiyās*. It is cited in No. 28, folio 69B, which was completed in 1819/1235.

36. "Ḥāshiyat al-ʿAṭṭār ʿalā sharḥ ʿalā al-risāla al-waladīya li Muḥammad al-Marʿashī," 1795. Manuscript. Al-Azhar, Cairo. 36484 (147), folios 29–80.

37. "Ḥāshiyat al-ʿAṭṭār ʿalā sharḥ al-Bahnasī ʿalā al-risāla al-walādīya li Muḥammad al-Marʿashī," 1811. Manuscript. Al-Azhar, Cairo. 14484, 400 Majāmīʿ, folios 71B–98A.
38. "Ḥāshiyat al-ʿAṭṭār ʿalā sharḥ Mullā Ḥanafī ʿalā ādāb al-baḥth li ʿAḍud," 1826/1242. Manuscript. Al-Azhar, Cairo. 36484 (147), pp. 1–28.
The "Sharḥ" is by Muḥammad al-Tibrīzī, known as Mullā Ḥanafī (died 1494), in "Al-Risāla al-ʿAḍudīya fī ādāb al-baḥth waʾl-munāẓara," written by ʿAḍud al-dīn al-Ījī (died 1355).

Language Sciences

39. "Manẓūma fī ʿilm al-naḥw" (grammar), dated 1787/1202. Manuscript. Dār al-Kutub, Cairo. 449 Grammar, majāmīʿ, folios 114–117.
French edition is entitled *Pétit traité de grammaire arabe en vers*, translated by J. Sicard. Algiers: Imprimerie Orientale Pierre Fontana et Cie., 1898.
40. "Ḥāshiyat al-ʿAṭṭār ʿalā sharḥ Khālid al-Azharī ʿalā al-ājurrūmiya li Abū ʿAbdullah b. Ajurrūm," 1792/1207 [?]. Manuscript. Dār al-Kutub, Cairo. H4876. 9 folios. Copied by ʿAbd al-Majīd al-Jizrī in 1792/1207.
41. "Risāla tataʿalliq bi khatm sharḥ al-Azharī ʿalā al-ājurrūmiya." Unlocated.
Al-Ḥusaynī, "Sharḥ al-umm al-musammā bi murshid al-anām li birr umm al-imām," p. 59, dates this between 1810 and 1815.
42. "Ḥāshiyat al-ʿAṭṭār ʿalā sharḥ Khālid al-Azharī al-musammā bi mawāṣil al-ṭullāb ilā qawāʾid al-iʿrāb li Ibn Hishām," 1794/1209. Manuscript. Dār al-Kutub, Cairo. H6416. 228 pages.
This is one of several grammar works from the eighteenth century which were used into the twentieth century.
43. *Ḥāshiyat al-ʿAṭṭār ʿalā sharḥ Khālid al-Azharī ʿalā matnihi al-muqaddima al-azharīya fī ʿilm al-ʿarabīya* (grammar), 1802/1217. Cairo: al-Maṭbaʿa al-Adabīya, 1901/1319.
44. "Ḥāshiyat al-ʿAṭṭār ʿalā sharḥ Muṣṭafā b. Ḥamza al-Aṭrūlī [*sic*] al-musamma bi natāʾij al-afkār fī sharḥ iẓhār ʿalā iẓhār al-asrār li Muḥammad Pīr al-Birghīlī," 1805. Manuscript. Dār al-Kutub, Cairo. 212 Qawala, Grammar.
Note that the name of the commentator is variously spelled; see Brockelmann, *Geschichte der Arabischen Litteratur*, GAL 2, p. 441, who wrote "Aṭalizade" but "Ataly" in ibid., S2, p. 656.
45. "Ḥāshiyat al-ʿAṭṭār ʿalā lāmiyat al-afʿāl li Ibn Mālik." Manuscript. Al-Azhar, Cairo. 8756 (119). Copied in 1820/1236 by Muṣṭafā Suwaylim. A second copy of the manuscript is Dār al-Kutub, Cairo, 9 Ṣarf; the latter has been misplaced.
Presumably the author of the commentary was also Ibn Mālik,

but this has not been confirmed. This copy is 78 pages long.

46. Aḥmad b. ʿAlī b. Masʿūd. [*Hadhihi*] *majmūʿa fī ʿilm al-taṣrīf mushtamil sitta kutub.* Cairo: Būlāq Press, 1825.
 Introduction by Ḥasan al-ʿAṭṭār.
47. "Al-Farq bayn al-jāmʿ wa ism al-jāmʿ wa ism al-jins al-jamāʿī waʾl-fardī" (n.d.). Manuscript. Dār al-Kutub, Cairo. 1294 Grammar. One folio. Co-authored with Shaykh Muṣṭafā al-Badrī al-Dimyāṭī, probably after 1815.
48. "Qaṣīda fīʾl-naḥw min baḥr al-taʾwīl." Unlocated.
 Al-Ḥusaynī, "Sharḥ al-umm al-musammā bi murshid al-anām li birr umm al-imām," p. 39, states that this gives examples of *ghazal* poetry and that it begins, "Bi ḥamdak yā mawlāya ibdāʾ fī amrī."
49. "Manẓūma fīʾl-farq bayn 'ām' al-muttaṣila waʾl-munqaṭiʿa." Unlocated.
 Cited by al-Ḥusaynī, "Sharḥ al-umm al-musammā bi murshid al-anām li birr umm al-imām," p. 39.
50. "Hidāyat al-anām li 'ām' atā min al-aḥkām." Manuscript. Dār al-Kutub, Cairo. 601 Grammar. Unlocated.
 Cited by Brockelmann, *Geschichte der Arabischen Litteratur,* S2, p. 720. Copied by ʿAbd al-Fattāḥ al-Sayyid Muḥammad al-Dimyāṭī.
51. "Ḥāshiyat al-mughnī fīʾl-naḥw." Unlocated.
 Presumably a gloss on the text of Ibn Hishām called "Mughnī al-labīb ʿan kutub al-aʿārīb." The commentator is not known, but was perhaps Jalāl al-dīn al-Suyūṭī. See al-Bayṭār, *Ḥilyat al-bāshir,* I, 492.
52. "Ḥāshiyat al-ʿAṭṭār ʿalā al-samarqandīya fī ʿilm al-bayān [*or* fīʾl-istiʿāra]," 1797/1212. Manuscript. Dār al-Kutub, Cairo. H5255.
 The basic text is called "Farāʾid al-fawāʾid [*or* al-ʿawāʾid] li taḥqīq maʿanī al-istiʿāra" and was written by Abūʾl-Qāsim al-Laythī al-Samarqandī (died 1483). The name of the commentator is not given.
53. *Ḥāshiyat al-ʿAṭṭār ʿalā al-samarqandīya fī ʿilm al-bayān.* Cairo: al-Wahhābīya Press, n.d.
 An enlargement of the same work as No. 52. Written in 1815.
54. "Ḥāshiyat al-ʿAṭṭār ʿalā sharḥ ʿIṣām al-dīn al-Isfarāʿinī b. ʿArabshāh ʿalā risāla waḍʿīya al-ʿaḍudīya li ʿAḍud al-dīn al-Ījī." Manuscript. Al-Azhar, Cairo. 131 ʿIlm al-waḍʿ, al-Imbābī, folios 123–194. Copy dated 1861/1278.
 Probably written before 1815. Al-ʿAṭṭār referred to it (in folio 123A) as "*taqayyudāt.*" This precedes No. 57, which was his last work on this text.
55. "Ḥāshiyat al-Khiṭāʾī (Niẓām al-dīn ʿUthmān) ʿala sharḥ al-mukhtaṣar li Saʿd al-dīn al-Taftazānī ʿalā talkhīṣ al-miftāḥ li Jalāl al-dīn al-Qazwīnī." Manuscript. Dār al-Kutub, Cairo. 13M al-Balāgha.
 The catalog cites that there are marginal comments on this copy by al-ʿAṭṭār; this was not easy to determine.
56. "Ḥāshiyat ʿalā taʿrīb al-risāla al-fārsīya fīʾl-bayān li ʿIṣām al-dīn al-

Isfarā'inī al-musammā bi risālat 'Iṣām al-dīn." Unlocated.
Cited by Muḥammad al-'Aṭṭār, "Sharḥ 'alā manẓūmat al-'Aṭṭār," folio 2B.

57. "Ḥāshiyat al-'Aṭṭār 'alā sharḥ 'Iṣām 'alā al-risāla al-'aḍudīya." Manuscript. Aḥmadī Mosque, Ṭanṭā. 8 (558). 16 folios. Dated 1814–1815.
On folio 16 al-'Aṭṭār states that he was "approaching Egypt" when he wrote this.

History and Geography

58. "Risāla fī taḥqīq al-khilāfa al-islāmīya wa manāqib al-khilāfa al-'Uthmānīya." Manuscript. Dār al-Kutub, Cairo. 380 Maktaba Zakīya, n.d. 36 folios.
This is a major work of neoclassical scholarship. It marks the earliest Egyptian attempt to employ the model of Ibn Khaldūn.

59. Taqī al-dīn al-Maqrīzī. *Al-Bayān wa'l-ārāb 'an mā bi arḍ Miṣr min al-a'rāb.* Cairo: 'Alām al-Kutub, 1961.
There are comments by Ḥasan al-'Aṭṭār on the margins, which are drawn from the manuscript Dār al-Kutub, Cairo, 1150 Tārīkh, preserved by the editor, 'Abd al-Majīd 'Ābidīn. See especially pp. 9–10, 73.

60. Abū'l-Fidā'. "Kitāb taqwīm al-buldān." Manuscript. Maktaba Baladīya, Sūhāj. 13 al-Jughrāfīya.
With marginal comments by al-'Aṭṭār which are dated 1833. This manuscript came from the library of al-Ṭahṭāwī, who studied it with al-'Aṭṭār. See al-Ṭahṭāwī, *Manāhij*, p. 375.

61. Muḥammad b. 'Abd al-Raḥman al-Sakhāwī. "Al-Ḍaw' al-lāmi' li ahl al-qarn al-tāsi'." Manuscript. Dār al-Kutub, Cairo. 675 Tārīkh.
Inscription by al-Zabīdī, 'Abd al-Raḥman al-Jabartī, and Ḥasan al-'Aṭṭār, who stated that he had read this book.

62. Muḥammad b. Ibrāhīm, known as Ibn al-Ḥanbalī. "Durr al-ḥabb fī tārīkh a'yān Ḥalab." 2 vols. Manuscript. Maktaba Baladīya, Sūhāj. 60 al-Tārīkh.
Extensive marginal comments by al-'Aṭṭār in II, folio 10.

63. Ṣalāḥ al-dīn al-ma'rūf bi-Ibn Shākir al-Kutubī al-Ḥalabī. "'Uyūn al-tawārīkh." Manuscript. Dār al-Kutub, Cairo.
Bears the signature of al-'Aṭṭār.

Medicine

64. "Manẓūmat al-'Aṭṭār fī 'ilm al-tashrīḥ." Manuscript. Al-Azhar, Cairo. 508 Abāẓa. 49 folios. Dated 1808/1223. Unlocated.
Marginal comments by al-'Aṭṭār are dated 1813/1228.

65. "Sharḥ al-Qānūnjā li'l-Jaghmīnī." Unlocated.

Cited by al-Ḥusaynī, "Sharḥ al-umm al-musammā bi murshid al-anām li birr umm al-imām," p. 38, as work which al-ʿAṭṭār began but did not complete in Damascus.

66. "Sharḥ al-ʿAṭṭār al-musammā bi rāḥat al-abdān ʿalā nuzhat al-adhhān fī ʿilm al-ṭibb," 1813/1228. Manuscript. Al-Azhar, Cairo. 3434 Riwāq al-Maghāriba. 251 folios.

A prodigious work of neoclassicism in medicine, including a major critique of Ibn Sīnā's findings in anatomy.

67. "Nubdha fī ʿilm al-jirāḥa li taʿrīf akl al-fūl biʾl-qaṭʿ waʾl-khaṭṭ." Unlocated.

Cited in Mubārak, *Khiṭaṭ*, IV, 39, and supposedly written in Damascus.

68. "Maqāla li taʿrīf al-baṭṭ." Unlocated.

Cited in Mubārak, *Khiṭaṭ*, IV, 39. On lancing of ulcers.

69. "Maqāla li taʿrīf al-faṣd." Unlocated.

Cited in Mubārak, *Khiṭaṭ*, IV, 39. On bloodletting.

70. "Maqāla li taʿrīf ḥāl al-kayy." Unlocated.

Cited in Mubārak, *Khiṭaṭ*, IV, 39. On cauterization.

71. "Juzʾ ʿalā sharḥ al-mubarrad." Unlocated.

Cited in Mubārak, *Khiṭaṭ*, IV, 39. Al-ʿAṭṭār stated that in this book he discussed the difficulty of pulse taking with a *qaṭṭ*. This problem was also discussed in No. 64, which was written in Damascus.

72. "Ḥawāshī al-ʿAṭṭār ʿalā sharḥ al-manẓūma al-ṭibbīya li Baḥrāq al-Ḥaḍramī." Unlocated.

Cited in No. 30, pp. 102, 106, 172. Dating from 1820/1236 or earlier. On a question in anatomy. Probably the commentator was Jamāl al-dīn Muḥammad b. ʿUmar Baḥrāq al-Yamanī al-Ḥaḍramī, died 1524/930, known for his "Sharḥ al-kifāya fīʾl-ṭibb" (Brockelmann, *Geschichte der Arabischen Litteratur*, S2, p. 554). The only work located entitled "Kifāya fīʾl-ṭibb" was by Masīḥ b. Ḥakīm al-Dimashqī (Brockelmann, *Geschichte der Arabischen Litteratur*, S2, p. 1029).

73. Amīn al-dawla b. al-Faraj B. Yaʿqub b. Ishāq al-maʿruf bi-Ibn al-Qiff. "Al-Uṣūl fī sharḥ al-fuṣūl li kitāb al-fuṣūl li Buqrāṭ." Manuscript. Dār al-Kutub, Cairo. 4 Ṭibb, a copy dating from 1712/1124.

Marginalia and signature of Ḥasan al-ʿAṭṭār on the last folio. In No. 64, he noted having used Ibn al-Qiff as a source.

74. Sulaymān al-maʿrūf bi Ibn Juljul. *Ṭabaqāt al-aṭibbāʾ waʾl-ḥukamāʾ*. Unlocated.

Al-ʿAṭṭār is said by al-Ṭahṭāwī to have written marginal notes in a copy of this work. See al-Ṭahṭāwī, *Manāhij*, p. 376.

Literature

75. Shihāb al-dīn al-Khafājī. *Rayḥānat al-alibbāʾ wa nuzhat ḥayāh al-dunyā* [also called *Rayḥānat al-adab*]. Leningrad: University of

Leningrad Manuscript 733. With al-ʿAṭṭār's signature.

Cited in Kratchkowski, *Ḥayat Muḥammad ʿIyād al-Ṭanṭāwī*, p. 145. The text was published in Cairo by Būlāq in 1856 and was edited by one of al-ʿAṭṭār's associates, Ibrāhīm al-Disūqī. See al-Shūrbajī, *Qāʾima bi awāʾil al-maṭbūʿāt al-ʿarabīya al-maḥfūẓa bi Dār al-Kutub*, p. 170.

76. "Maqāma fī dhukūl al-Faransāwiyīn liʾl-diyār al-Miṣrīya." Manuscript. Dār al-Kutub, Cairo. 7574 al-Adab.

Approximate date of composition, 1800–1801/1216–1217. A short autobiographical work, an important forerunner of modern literary realism.

77. *Hadhā nakhb dīwān al-fātin al-adīb . . . Ibrāhīm b. Sahl al-Isrāʾilī al-Andalūsī al-Ishbīlī.* Cairo: Maṭbaʿat ʿAbd al-Ghanī Fikrī, 1862/1279. Manuscript version is Dār al-Kutub, Cairo. 222 al-Adab.

Introduction and conclusion and selection of poems by Ḥasan al-ʿAṭṭār. Dated 1229/1814. Al-ʿAṭṭār's editing of this *dīwān* marks a reaction against poetic formalism.

78. "Dīwān al-ʿAṭṭār." Unlocated.

Said to have been lost in Damascus in or before 1815 (al-Ḥusaynī, "Sharḥ al-umm al-musammā bi murshid al-anām li birr umm al-imām," p. 39). Al-ʿAṭṭār is quoted as saying that he lost it in Damascus with some baggage, that it was 80 folios in length. See *Rawḍat al-madāris al-miṣrīya* 1, no. 18 (1869/1287): 36–37. The loss of this work makes it very difficult to study al-ʿAṭṭār as a literary figure. Many old books cite one or two lines of his. He himself quotes his poetry in small pieces in virtually every work he wrote. The largest collection, No. 81, unfortunately represents the conventional poetry that he wrote for the court.

79. "Risāla jumiʿa fīhā baʿḍ muqaṭṭaʿāt shiʿrīya fī funūn mukhtalifa." Unlocated.

Cited by al-Ḥusaynī, "Sharḥ al-umm al-musammā bi murshid al-anām li birr umm al-imām," p. 39.

80. Ismaʿīl al-Khashshāb. *Dīwān al-Khashshāb.* Edited by Ḥasan al-ʿAṭṭār. Istanbul: Maṭbaʿat al-Jawāʾib, 1882/1300.

Compiled around 1815 on the death of his friend al-Khashshāb.

81. *Al-Inshāʾ*. Cairo: Maḥmūd Tawfīq, 1936.

An early edition is Cairo: Būlāq Press, 1835/1250. The date of the first edition or of the original composition is not known (Salāma, *Enseignement islamique en l'Egypte*, p. 199). Another old copy which was located is Dār al-Kutub, Cairo, 25 al-Adab. This was published by Būlāq in 1859. It was edited by a *shaykh* known himself to have written in prosody, Shaykh Muḥammad al-ʿUdwī.

Miscellany

82. "Mukhāṭaba wa mujāwaba bayn al-adīb al-Shaykh Muṣṭafā Bakrī al-Saʿātī . . . wa Shaykh Ḥasan al-ʿAṭṭār," *Rawḍat al-madāris al-miṣrīya* 1, no. 18 (1869/1287): 25–32; no. 19, pp. 24–28; see also nos. 18 and 19 passim.
83. *Ijāza* to Abū Ḥāmid al-ʿArabī b. Muḥammad al-Dumnātī al-Fāsī (died 1837/1253).
    Summarized in al-Kattānī, *Fihris al-fahāris*, II, 469, in which it is stated that the original could be found in a manuscript, which was not located, entitled "Fahrasat Ibn Ḥāmid al-Dumnātī."
84. *Ijāza* in medicine to ʿAbd al-Qādir al-Khulāṣī (died 1839/1255).
    Cited in al-Maʿlūf, *Al-Usra al-ʿarabīya al-mushthara*, p. 19. It was located in the deceased author's family library in Baʿlabakk, where it remained until at least 1973, when it was allegedly sold.
85. *Ijāza* to Arif Hikmet Bey.
    Cited *in extenso* by Shihāb al-dīn al-Alūsī, "Al-Ṣādiḥ bi shahīq al-nujūm ʿalā afnān tarjamat Shaykh al-Islām wa walī al-niʿam" (al-Azhar, Cairo, manuscript, 7221 Tārīkh, Abāẓa). This work is an important source on the life of Arif by a well-known ʿIraqī reformer.
86. Letters to ʿAbd al-Raḥman al-Jabartī, 1798–1800, in al-Jabartī, *Maẓhar al-taqdīs fī dhahāb dawlat al-Faransīs*, pp. 14, 382, and passim. Idem, *ʿAjāʾib*, III, 163–64.
87. Praise of the Madanīya Ṣūfī order (a branch of the Shādhilīya), in Muḥammad Ẓāfir al-Madanī, *Al-Nūr al-sāṭīʾ waʾl-burhān al-qāṭiʿ* (Cairo, 1883/1301), p. 43.
88. Address to the Abū Zaʿbal medical school graduating class of 1834, in Clot Bey, *Mémoires de Clot Bey*, edited by Gaston Wiet (Cairo: Imprimerie de l'Institut Français d'Archaeologie Orientale, 1949), pp. 130–131.
89. *Ijāza* to Ḥasan al-Bayṭār (ca. 1815).
    See ʿAbd al-Razzāq al-Bayṭār, *Ḥilyat al-bāshir fī tārīkh al-qarn al-thālith ʿashar*, II, 489–492.
90. Minor poetry in al-Jabartī, *ʿAjāʾib*, III, 44, 97, 114, 307; IV, 28, 232–233, 239, 240; Mubārak, *Khiṭaṭ*, IV, 38–40; No. 4, I, 8, 214, 249, 316, 326, 446; II, 195, 247, 255, 332, 448, 453, 466, 506, 510, 513, 514, 527, 552; No. 31, pp. 19, 25, 62; No. 33, p. 215; Ṭaha Ḥusayn and others (eds.), *Muqtaṭafāt min kutub al-adab al-ʿarabī* (Cairo, n.d.) I, 246, II, 246; al-Ṭahṭāwī, *Takhlīṣ*, p. 53.
91. Unlocated correspondence: letter to Muṣṭafā al-Bakrī in *Rawḍat al-madāris al-miṣrīya*. Cited by ʿAbd al-Ghanī Ḥasan, *Ḥasan al-ʿAṭṭār*, pp. 58–59.
92. Bureaucratic communications: These are extensive. Bureaucratic communications exist for the last ten years of al-ʿAṭṭār's lifetime and are located in the National Archives (Dār al-Wathāʾiq al-Qawmīya)

of Egypt, which I was not able to secure permission to use. Some of these communications are summarized in *Al-Waqāʾiʿ al-Miṣrīya* and in Sāmī, *Taqwīm al-Nīl.* A study of the bureaucratic structure based on these archives could greatly increase our understanding of the ruling class of Egypt during this period, and would also add much to what is known of individual persons.

93. Introduction: *Taqrīẓ al-ʿAṭṭār ʿan Takhlīṣ al-ibrīz liʾl-Ṭahṭāwī.* Cairo: Būlāq, 1850. Title page.

Notes

1. The Social and Economic History of Egypt, 1760–1815

1. The coffee trade and its impact on Egypt are not studied here. The reader may wish to consult André Raymond (*Artisans et commerçants au Caire au XVIIIième siècle*, I, 157–175).
2. Douglas C. North and Robert Paul Thomas, *The Rise of the Western World*; and Naʿīm Zakī Fahmī, *Ṭuruq al-tijāra al-duwalīya wa maḥaṭṭātuhā bayn al-sharq waʾl-gharb.*
3. E. J. Hobsbawm, "The Crisis of the Seventeenth Century," in *Crisis in Europe*, ed. Trevor Ashton, pp. 55–56.
4. Ibid.
5. Henry Dodwell, *The Founder of Modern Egypt*, pp. 3–6.
6. James Capper, *Observations on the Passage to India through Egypt*, p. xvii.
7. Alfred C. Wood, *A History of the Levant Company*, p. 165 and passim.
8. Barrington Moore, Jr., *The Social Origins of Dictatorship and Democracy*, pp. 45, 108–110, and passim.
9. This movement contrasts sharply with the enclosures movement in England, which was contemporaneous with it. Moore suggests (ibid., p. 48) that this may have been related to the fact that French viniculture did not require enclosures.
10. Ibid., pp. 45, 53–55.
11. Ibid., p. 75.
12. Ibid., pp. 75, 80, 89, 103.
13. R. R. Palmer, *Twelve Who Ruled*, pp. 235–236. Also note the comment on the shortage of gunpowder during this period. This is also commented upon by French travelers to Egypt, and Napoleon commented on it (see Georges Rudé, *The Crowd in the French Revolution*, chap. 11).
14. P. Masson, *La Histoire du commerce Français dans le Levant au XVIII*[e] *siècle*, p. 479; French food insufficiency and high cost of imports discussed in *L'Ankylose de l-économie Meditérranéene au XVIIIième et au début du XIXième siècle: Le rôle de l'agriculture*, ed. L. Bergeron; Ruggiero Romano, *Commerce et prix du blé à Marseilles au XVIIIième siècle*, pp. 20–21.
15. John W. Livingston, "ʿAlī Bey al-Kabīr and the Jews," *Middle East Studies* 7 (May 1971): 221–229. Customs receipts increased for the government when the Syrians took over (see Raymond, *Artisans et commerçants au Caire*, I, 11, 486).
16. Masson, *La Histoire du commerce Français*, pp. 595–596; Raymond, *Artisans et commerçants au Caire*, I, 174.
17. Masson, *La Histoire du commerce Français*, p. 602.
18. The source is Jean-Baptiste Trécourt (*Mémoires sur l'Egypte 1791*, ed. Gaston Wiet). The author was a French consul in Egypt.
19. Ibid., p. 25.
20. Ibid., pp. 26 n. 6, 92. For a more comprehensive discussion of the diet of the lower

classes, see Edward W. Lane, *The Manners and Customs of the Modern Egyptians*, p. 198, where he states that the lower classes ate mainly bread made of millet or maize, plus milk and cheese, but that rice and meat were too expensive for them (pp. 581, 589). Lane adds that the cost of wheat was four times that of rice. He also adds that this apparently poor diet is belied by the apparently healthy physique of the lower classes. Unlike Lane, Trécourt (*Mémoires sur l'Egypte 1791*) seems to have had little firsthand knowledge of the lower classes.

21. Trécourt, *Mémoires sur l'Egypte 1791*, p. 27. The writer cannot of course make clear the relationship between fluctuating prices and monopolies. He was perhaps aware of profiteering in grain by the *beys*, a practice quite common in France as well.
22. Ibid., pp. 51–55. Trécourt, like other writers, contrasted it to the trade in rice which, while clandestine, was very considerable (p. 89). Like other writers, he also commented on the weakness of the Egyptian defenses (p. 29). Trécourt referred to yet another product on which the French became increasingly dependent after 1789. This was natron salt, which was used in a number of soap factories in Marseilles and in making gunpowder (p. 25). Raymond (*Artisans et commerçants au Caire*, I, 186) stated that Damietta was the only source of rice for the Ottomans as well and that they continued to take the great bulk of what was produced.
23. Palmer, *Twelve Who Ruled*, p. 227.
24. G. A. Olivier, *Voyage dans l'empire Othman*, II, 166. Writing in 1795, he stressed French dependence categorically.
25. François Charles-Roux, *Les Origines de l'expedition de l'Egypte*, p. 262. This writer is typical in his portrayal of the rapacious activities of the *beys* in the 1790's, ignoring what must have been for them a major economic problem following the decision of the Convention and the British contraband decree.
26. Ibid., pp. 275, 323–325.
27. Raymond, *Artisans et commerçants au Caire*, I, 814–815.
28. Ashin Das Gupta, "Trade and Politics in the Eighteenth Century in India," in *Islam and the Trade of Asia*, ed. D. S. Richards, pp. 190–191; see also Helen Rivlin, *The Agricultural Policy of Muhammad ʿAlī in Egypt.*
29. John W. Livingston, "The Rise of Shaykh al-balad ʿAlī Bey al-Kabīr: A Study of the Accuracy of the Chronicle of al-Jabartī," *Bulletin of the School of Oriental and African Studies* 33 (1970): 283–294; Stanford Shaw, *Ottoman Egypt in the Age of the French Revolution*, pp. 241–278.
30. Lusignan, *A History of the Revolt of Ali Bey against the Ottoman Porte*, pp. 20–31. See also Chapter 3 under "History."
31. Shaw, *Ottoman Egypt*, p. 144.
32. Ibid., pp. 77–81. Shaw presents one account of the Suez customs according to which it had been controlled by the Mamlūks since 1713, and another according to which the governor controlled it throughout the eighteenth century.
33. Stanford Shaw, *The Financial and Administrative Organization of and Development of Ottoman Egypt, 1517–1798*, pp. 297–300.
34. Ibid., pp. 316–337.
35. Shaw, *Ottoman Egypt*, p. 144.
36. Masson, *La Histoire du commerce Français*, p. 33.
37. Shaw, *Ottoman Egypt*, pp. 110–111. The illegal *awqāf* had the effect of handing

down possession of land within families without going through the bureaucratic procedures upon the death of the owner, and undoubtedly constituted, especially in the Delta, the first step toward the development of private property in land.

38. Ibid., p. 83.
39. Shaw, *Financial and Administrative Organization*, p. 194; see also his *Ottoman Egypt*, pp. 73, 91–92. Raymond, *Artisans et commerçants au Caire*, II, 729, gives evidence of some Janissary assimilation into Egyptian society.
40. Shaw, *Ottoman Egypt*, p. 94.
41. Ibid., pp. 95 nn. 92–102, 137 n. 2.
42. Ibid., pp. 137–138 n. 3.
43. Raymond, *Artisans et commerçants au Caire*, I, 103, discusses fighting between the *beys* for control of grain in Upper Egypt in 1788.
44. P. M. Holt, "Al-Jabartī's Introduction to the History of Ottoman Egypt," *Bulletin of the School for Oriental and African Studies* 25 (1962): 38–52.
45. David Ayalon, "Studies in al-Jabartī, I: Notes on the Transformation of Mamlūk Society in Egypt under the Ottomans," *Journal of the Economic and Social History of the Orient* 3 (1960): 148–174, 275–325, esp. pp. 157–160.
46. Ibid., p. 290, suggests two factors: intermarriage within a Mamlūk household and reliance on mercenaries to do the fighting. Perhaps the use of mercenaries did save Mamlūk lives, but in the long run the decline of the household as a warrior unit, which was its basic raison d'être, combined with the new economic incentives to trade on an individual basis undermined the Mamlūk system.
47. The latter point is argued in Derek Hopwood, *The Russian Presence in Syria and Palestine, 1843–1914*, pp. 11–12.
48. Masson, *La Histoire du commerce Français*, p. 580. But despite these claims, the French had much closer relations. In 1786, when the Ottomans invaded Egypt and temporarily expelled Murād and Ibrāhīm, several French merchants who were owed large sums of money went bankrupt. The Russians were never this deeply involved.
49. L. P. Choiseul-Gouffier, *La France en l'Orient sous Louis XVI*, p. 121; Masson, *La Histoire du commerce Français*, p. 311.
50. Masson, *La Histoire du commerce Français*, p. 570. For Russian influence among the *beys* a little earlier, see Lusignan, *A History of the Revolt of Ali Bey.*
51. Ayalon, "Studies in al-Jabartī, I," p. 278; on Africans, see p. 315.
52. Gabriel Guémard, *Adventuriers Mamluk de l'Egypte*, pp. 1–43. This will be discussed in the section on the Napoleonic period.
53. E. R. J. Owen, *Cotton and the Egyptian Economy, 1820–1914*, p. 15. A main obstacle to tax collection was that the government actually received only about 20 percent of the taxes raised.
54. A. G. Politis, *L'Hellènisme et l'Egypte moderne*, I, 92–94.
55. Jean Savant, *Les Mamelouks de Napoleon*, p. 31.
56. Guémard, *Aventuriers Mamluk de l'Egypte*, p. 22 and passim.
57. Citizen Andréossy, "Extract of a Report . . . Relative to the Manufacture of the Saltpetre and Gunpowder of the Country," in *Memoirs Relative to Egypt*, pp. 39, 42–43; "n.b. We have entered into a few of the details relative to the fabrication of gunpowder, the object of which was entirely foreign to the programme, merely for the purpose of painting the barbarous physiognomy of the

arts, among a people who have attained the last stage of degeneracy" (p. 44).

58. Gabriel Guémard, *Une Ouevre française: Les réformes en l'Egypté d'Ali-Bey El-Kebir à Mehemet ʿAli 1760–1848*, pp. 63–64.

59. Ayalon, "Studies in al-Jabartī, I" p. 302.

60. Palmer, *Twelve Who Ruled*, p. 237. The French weaponry which Egypt imported was made at St. Etienne.

61. André Raymond, "Essai de geographie des quartiers de residence aristocratique au Caire au XVIIIième siècle," *Journal of the Economic and Social History of the Orient* 6 (1963): 58–103, esp. p. 79.

62. G. Douin, "Le Carosse de Mohamed Bey," *Bulletin de l'Institut de l'Egypte* 8 (1926): 168–169. It would seem that his honorific name came not from this specific occasion but from his general love of luxurious tents and harnesses.

63. G. Guémard, "De l'Armement et de l'équipement des Mamelouks," *Bulletin de l'Institut de l'Egypte* 8 (1926): 8, 10, 12.

64. V. J. Parry, "Djarīd," *Encyclopedia of Islam*, 2d ed., I, 532. How they paid for their new expenses deserves a separate study which has never even been attempted. Clearly, many Mamlūks invested in trade, as one can tell from the names on the *wikālas* listed by ʿAlī Mubārak in *Al-Khiṭaṭ al-tawfīqīya al-jadīda*, II, 25; or from a *waqfīya* studied by Afaf Lutfi al-Sayyid Marsot ("A Socio-Economic Sketch of the ʿUlamāʾ of the Eighteenth Century," in *Colloque Internationale sur l'Histoire du Caire*, pp. 313–321), discussing M. Effendī al-Bakrī (died 1779), who the author discovers is drawing military wages and at the same time is employed in the coffee trade.

65. Raymond, *Artisans et commerçants au Caire*, II, 401. Raymond gives the information that after 1776 more than one-third of the rich merchants were foreigners, elsewhere stating that they had monopolies in important export items, such as senna (pp. 622–623). Raymond also indicates a growing difference for such families as Dou or Borelly-Reboul in the rate of profit on investment in Egypt as compared to rates of profit in Europe. In these ways Egypt anticipates by a century a number of the key aspects of the model of Samir Amin (*Accumulation on a World Scale*, I, 102–103; II, 379) as characteristic of "mature" underdevelopment. On intermarriage see Raymond, *Artisans et commerçants au Caire*, II, 414–415, 684.

66. Raymond, *Artisans et commerçants au Caire*, II, 412, 414–415, 578–582.

67. Ibid., I, 194; II, 461–462.

68. Ibid., I, 291–300.

69. Ibid. II, 406–407; I, 212, 232, 236. On capitalist as opposed to "feudalist" mentality of a merchant with regard to farm labor, see II, 722. There were objective forces propelling those who could afford to invest in land to do so as urban rent on shops was declining after 1789, and the Ḥilw made changes in proprietors complicated (see I, 268–270).

70. Ibid., I, 175, 299–300.

71. Terence Walz, "The Trade between Egypt and Bilād As-Sūdān" (doctoral dissertation), shows the rising price of household slaves in the late eighteenth century.

72. Raymond, *Artisans et commerçants au Caire*, II, 406–412.

73. ʿAbd al-Raḥman ʿA. ʿAbd al-Raḥīm, "Dirāsa nuṣṣīya liʾl-kitāb hazz al-quhūf fī sharḥ qaṣīdat Abī Shadūf," *Al-Majalla al-Miṣrīya liʾl-Dirāsāt al-Tārīkhīya* 20 (1973): 287–316. Stanford Shaw, "Landholding and Land Tax Revenues in Ottoman Egypt," in *Political and Social Change in Modern Egypt*, ed. P. M. Holt, pp. 91–103.

74. ʿAbd al-Raḥman ʿA. ʿabd al-Raḥīm (*Al-Rīf al-Miṣrī fīʾl-qarn al-thāmin ʿashar*) deals with rural industry and commerce, which served as outlets for urban capital.
75. Raymond, *Artisans et commerçants au Caire*, II, 421–423, 426–427.
76. Marsot, "A Socio-Economic Sketch of the ʿUlamāʾ," pp. 313–321; Shaw, *Ottoman Egypt*, p. 98. Raymond (*Artisans et commerçants au Caire*, II, 421–423) stresses that the direct ties of the *ʿulamāʾ* were in most cases to the lower merchants.
77. Marsot, "A Socio-Economic Sketch of the ʿUlamāʾ," pp. 4–8. The *shaykhs* of many Ṣūfī orders had close connections to guilds, especially among the poor (Raymond, *Artisans et commerçants au Caire*, II, 437, 439, 441).
78. André Raymond, "Tunisiens et Maghrebins au Caire au dix-huitième siècle," *Les Cahiers de Tunisie* 7 (1959): 336–371, see esp. p. 360. In his study of the Maghribī community, Professor Raymond found a close connection between the commercial and religious professions.
79. George Baldwin, *Memorial Relating to the Trade in Slaves*, p. 2. Baldwin evaluated the Sudanese trade at about the same value, while the Meccan trade he put at 3 million pounds and the Syrian trade at 50,000 pounds. The trade to Mecca, however, is not easily separable from the ventures of several communities, so that this figure is a little confusing.
80. Raymond, "Tunisiens et Maghrebins au Caire," pp. 353–354.
81. John Burckhardt, *Arabic Proverbs, or the Manners and Customs of the Modern Egyptians*, p. 183. This book was compiled in 1817, at which time the author found that the elite of the Maghribī community was intact and that the expression "the word of a Maghāriba (*kilma maghribīya*)" was used as an expression for commercial honesty, a trait for which they were known.
82. Raymond, *Artisans et commerçants au Caire*, II, 383, 386.
83. Ibid., I, 283ff, 238–239.
84. Ibid., II, 379; I, 215.
85. André Raymond, "Problèmes urbains et urbainisme au Caire aux XVIIième et XVIIIième siècles," in *Colloque Internationale sur l'Histoire du Caire*, pp. 353–373. This excluded the port of Būlāq, which was always maintained.
86. Ibid., p. 13.
87. Raymond, *Artisans et commerçants au Caire*, II, 512, 566, 558. The best evidence for the breakdown of the guild is the breakdown of the *futuwwa*, or corporate identity, the last document of *futuwwa* being found was dated 1733 (ibid., II, 529–543). The role of Coptic artisan in Muslim guilds could have been only a minor factor (ibid., II, 459, 526).
88. Ibid., II, 546, 565–566.
89. André Raymond, "Quartiers et mouvements populaires au Caire au XVIII siècle," in *Political and Social Change in Modern Egypt*, ed. P. M. Holt, pp. 104–116, esp. pp. 110–111.
90. Ibid., pp. 107–108; André Raymond, "Deux leaders populaires au Caire à la fin du XVIIIè et au début du XIX siècle," *La Nouvelle Revue du Caire* 1 (1975): 281–298. For the appeal of the Bayyūmīs to lower-class elements, highwaymen in particular among its adherents, and also water carriers, see W. A. S. Khālidī, "Bayyūmīya," *Encyclopedia of Islam*, 2d ed, I, 1151–1152. The middle class disapproved of their wild and ecstatic *dhikr*.
91. Raymond, "Quartiers et mouvements populaires au Caire," p. 115.
92. Raymond, "Problèmes urbains et urbainisme au Caire," p. 19.

93. Maxime Rodinson, *Islam et capitalisme*, pp. 68–69. There were 2,000 textile workers in al-Maḥalla al-Kubrā, 600 in Banī Swaif, and 250 in Qīna (Owen, *Cotton and the Egyptian Economy*, pp. 12–13).
94. Citizen Girard, "Remarks on the Management and the Produce of the Land in the Province of Damietta," in *Memoirs Relative to Egypt*, I, 393–417; Olivier, *Voyage dans l'empire Othman*, II, 167; Amīn, *Accumulation on a World Scale*, I, 149–150.
95. Shaw, *Ottoman Egypt*, pp. 142–143.
96. Khalīl Shaybūb, *ʿAbd al-Raḥman al-Jabartī*, pp. 10–11.
97. ʿAbd al-Razzāq al-Bayṭār, *Ḥilyat al-bāshir fī tārīkh al-qarn al-thālith ʿashar*, see esp. I, 534.
98. Masson, *La Histoire du commerce Français*, p. 597.
99. Politis, *L'Hellènisme et l'Egypte moderne*, I, 99; Masson, *La Histoire du commerce Français*, p. 604.
100. Masson, *La Histoire du commerce Français*, pp. 467, 597. The presence of a Syrian Christian customs official in Damietta doubtless helped the French.
101. J. Heyworth-Dunne, *Introduction to the History of Education in Modern Egypt*, pp. 22, 249; Afaf Lutfi al-Sayyid Marsot, "The Political and Economic Functions of the ʿUlamāʾ in the 18th Century," *Journal of the Economic and Social History of the Orient* 16 (1973): 154.
102. Heyworth-Dunne, *History of Education in Modern Egypt*, pp. 88, 333.
103. Rivlin, *Agricultural Policy of Muḥammad ʿAlī*, pp. 7–9.
104. Politis, *L'Hellènisme et l'Egypte moderne*, I, 127.
105. *Copies of Original Letters from the Army of General Bonaparte in Egypt*, p. 7.
106. Ibid., p. 100; Politis, *L'Hellènisme et l'Egypte moderne*, I, 127.
107. Politis, *L'Hellènisme et l'Egypte moderne*, I, 142.
108. Guémard, *Une Ouevre française*, pp. 69–72.
109. Savant, *Les Mamelouks de Napoleon*, pp. 41, 52–54.
110. Matti Moosa, "Napoleon's Islamic Policy in Egypt," *Islamic Quarterly* 9 (1965): 103–116, esp. p. 111 n. 2.
111. Terence Walz, "Notes on the Organization of the African Trade in Cairo, 1800–1850," *Annales Islamologiques* 11 (1972): 266, 269–270. The author stresses that the Dārfūr caravan brought a wide range of African products, including feathers and ivory, and not merely slaves. Shaw (*Ottoman Egypt*, p. 156) states that there was a decline in the profitability of the slave trade during the occupation, but it must have been in more than only slaves. This would seem to be a way in which the occupation, in trying to side with the middle class, actually disrupted it.
112. Shaw, *Ottoman Egypt*, p. 156.
113. M. Abir, "The 'Arab Rebellion' of Amīr Ghālib of Mecca, 1788–1813," *Middle East Studies* 5 (1972): 191–194. Amīr Ghālib, it turned out, was willing to accept French subsidies in return for the loss of trade, and even sent Napoleon supplies so that he could turn his main attention to the Wahhābī threat.
114. Some of the Mamlūks did return, after their wives paid out large sums in ransom called "safeguard." The French raised some 490,000 pounds in this way, but there is no indication that returning Mamlūks could get their claims to the land validated. See Ibrāhīm El-Mouelhy, "L'Enregistrement de la propriété en Egypte durant l'occupation française," *Bulletin de l'Institut de l'Egypte* 30 (1949): 199.

115. Ibid., p. 208.
116. Rivlin, *Agricultural Policy of Muḥammad ʿAlī*, pp. 40–41.
117. Owen, *Cotton and the Egyptian Economy*, p. 14. This failure must have been all the more bitter to the French because, even in the short time during which the savants worked in Egypt, they discovered a number of new commercial possibilities which enhanced the attractiveness of the idea of staying. Berthollet and Descotils proved that henna, which was a profitable export item for Egypt, would be profitable as well for the coloration of wool. An improvement in the refining of local sugar would make sugar export very profitable. See Olivier, *Voyage dans l'empire Othman*, II, 171–173.
118. Guémard, *Aventuriers Mamluk de l'Egypte*, p. 37. See also Omar Toussoun, "La Fin des Mamelouks," *Bulletin de l'Institut de l'Egypte* 15 (1933): 187–205, esp. p. 189, where travelers' reports are quoted on the number of Mamlūks seen in Egypt during this period who were of German, Catalan, Sicilian, and Italian origin, who had converted to Islam and served various houses. Toussoun also mentioned that with the withdrawal of the English army in 1807 a number of English prisoners also became Mamlūks.
119. Rivlin, *Agricultural Policy of Muḥammad ʿAlī*, chap. 2.
120. Owen, *Cotton and the Egyptian Economy*, pp. 17–19. Particularly active in the development of Muḥammad ʿAlī's trading policy were the Greeks. The Greeks created Muḥammad ʿAlī's merchant marine (1809–1811) as they had Murād Bey's before him. Some of these Greeks had known Muḥammad ʿAlī from his youth in Cavalla, for example, the former tobacco merchants, the Tossizza brothers, who later served him in Egypt in diverse capacities. Among others who served Muḥammad ʿAlī were Athanasious Lasulli and Jean Anastasios. Muḥammad ʿAlī protected the Greek community during the Greek War of Independence, when the Ottomans ordered him to exterminate the Greeks in Greece. In fact, he permitted the Greek independence movement to function in Cairo and Alexandria. See Politis, *L'Hellènisme et l'Egypte moderne*, I, 168.
121. John Burckhardt, *Notes on Bedouins and Wahabys*, pp. 344–345.
122. Ernest Missett to the Foreign Office, Cairo (January 12, 1814), British Foreign Office (FO 24/5). The same source had earlier detected the possibility of an alliance between the Wahhābīs and the Mamlūks; Missett to the Foreign Office (March 25, 1812), British Foreign Office (FO 24/4); John Burckhardt, *Travels in Arabia*, p. 261.
123. Lane, *Manners and Customs of the Modern Egyptians*, p. 340.
124. Owen, *Cotton and the Egyptian Economy*, p. 20. A contemporary source commented that, of the eight hundred deserters of the French army who had converted to Islam, he could count in 1818 no more than eighty. The rest had been cut down by wars and the plague. They complained of being in arrears in their pay. Their leader, ʿAbdullah of Toulouse, had recently died, and the second man, Salīm of Avignon, was dying (Count de Forbin, *Travels in Egypt, Being a Continuation of Travels in the Holy Land*, p. 15). One suspects that their more clever compatriots had by this time left the ranks of the Mamlūks to enter trade or service in the bureaucracy of the new army. Those who attempted to regain control of their land after the abolition of the *iltizām* system generally lost out.
125. Anwar Abdel-Malek, *Idéologie et renaissance nationale de l'Egypte moderne*,

pp. 232–234; Ṣāliḥ Mursī, "Thawrat al-ʿumyān," *Al-Hilāl* 78 (1970): 76–84.

126. ʿAbd al-Raḥman al-Jabartī, *ʿAjāʾib al-āthār fīʾl-tarājim waʾl-akhbār*, IV, 161. Reference courtesy of Professor Afaf Marsot.

127. Rivlin, *Agricultural Policy of Muḥammad ʿAlī*, pp. 54, 56.

2. *The Religious Framework of the Eighteenth-Century Revival*

1. A seminal work on the role of structures such as these at the dawn of modern capitalism is James L. Peacock, "Mystics and Merchants in Fourteenth Century Germany: A Speculative Reconstruction of Their Psychological Bond and Its Implications for Social Change," *Journal for the Scientific Study of Religions* 8 (1969): 47–59.
2. S. Moreh, "The Sociological Role of the Ṣūfī Shaykh in Eighteenth-Century Egypt" (doctoral dissertation), pp. 398–399.
3. Ernst Bannerth, "La Khalwatiyya en Egypte," *Mèlanges Institut Dominicains Etudes Orientales* 8 (1964–1966): 10.
4. The Wafāʾīya also had a branch in Aleppo, although to what extent it recognized the authority of Muḥammad Abī Anwār in Egypt is not known (see al-Bayṭār, *Ḥilyat al-bāshir fī tārīkh al-qarn al-thālith ʿashar*, III, 1553–1555).
5. On the different branches of the Khalwatīya, see B. G. Martin, "A Short History of the Khalwatīya Order of the Derviches," in *Scholars, Saints and Sufis*, ed. Nikki R. Keddie, pp. 275–307.
6. The main source is Tawfīq al-Bakrī, *Bayt al-Sādāt*. An article based on this source is N. C.-D., "L'Aristocratie réligieuse en Egypte," *Révue du Monde Musulmane* 2 (1908): 241–283.
7. Muḥammad Sayyid al-Kilānī, *Al-Adab al-Miṣrī fī ẓill al-ḥukm al-ʿuthmānī*, pp. 144–145.
8. Al-Bayṭār, *Ḥilyat al-bāshir fī tārīkh al-qarn al-thālith ʿashar*, I, 97–98.
9. Al-Bakrī, *Bayt al-Sādāt*, p. 16; al-Kilānī, *Al-Adab al-miṣrī fī ẓill al-ḥukm al-ʿuthmanī*, p. 145.
10. Shaw, *The Financial and Administrative Organization*, p. 139; C.-D., "L'Aristocratie réligieuse en Egypte," p. 263. The same source lists numerous other properties which he either inherited or acquired in some other way, which included agricultural lands, urban real estate, and a palace at Azbakīya (p. 269). Additional information was supplied by a distant relative of Muḥammad Abī Anwār, a lawyer named Ḥāmid ʿAbd al-Ḥamīd al-Hakāʿ, who possesses copies of court records from the Maḥkāma al-Sharīʿa confirming the information in this article.
11. Al-Kilānī, *Al-Adab al-miṣrī fī ẓill al-ḥukm al-ʿuthmānī*, pp. 135–172 and passim. Al-Bakrī (*Bayt al-Sādāt*, p. 3) cites a poem by the Sultan Selim mentioning the connection of the Wafāʾ family with Ahl al-Bayt.
12. Al-ʿĀmilī was known in several fields (see Carl Brockelmann, *Geschichte der Arabischen Litteratur*, II, 357; S1, p. 114; S2, p. 595). Fuat Sezgin (*Geschichte des Arabischen Schriftums*, I, 527, 546) states that he wrote a commentary in three parts on Imāmī Shīʿi *fiqh* as well as essays in science and literature. He also wrote on the theme of Ahl al-Bayt.
13. Another work on Ahl al-Bayt by a Ṣūfī contemporary stated that the author had heard warnings that it is necessary for the Muslims to seek the blessings of the Ahl al-Bayt, citing the fact that the Prophet visited Zaynab's tomb when she

died (Aḥmad al-Sijāʿī, "Al-Ruwwād al-naḍīra fī mā yataʿalliq biʾl-bayt al-bashīr al-nadhīr").

14. The chief collection was made by a disciple, al-Ḥasan al-Badrī al-ʿAwaḍ, in "Al-Lawāʾiḥ al-anwārīya."

15. Al-Kilānī, *Al-Adab al-miṣrī fī ẓill al-ḥukm al-ʿuthmānī*, pp. 159–160. Ibn al-Hānī was an important literary source of al-ʿAṭṭār (see Chapter 4). Al-Sādāt was likewise referred to by various writers, according to al-Kilānī, with expressions of highest praise, "*rūḥ al-dahr*" and "*qurrat ʿayn al-dīn.*"

16. Al-Kilānī, *Al-Adab al-miṣrī fī ẓill al-ḥukm al-ʿuthmānī*, pp. 163, 169.

17. Ignace Goldziher, *Muhammadan Studies*, ed. S. M. Stern, II, 290, esp. pp. 255–344 n. 2.

18. An early example exists by a famous Shaykh al-Azhar in his work on the *ṣaḥāba* dated 1741/1154 (see Chapter 4 on tomb visiting in Egypt, miracles, and spirits rising from the tomb, ʿAbdullah al-Shubrāwī, *al-Itḥāf bi ḥubb al-ashrāf*).

19. C.-D., "L'Aristocratie réligieuse en Egypte," especially pp. 263, 268; al-Jabartī (*ʿAjāʾib al-āthār fīʾl-tarājim waʾl-akhbār*, II, 227) gives his death as 1206 and not 1205. The book by al-Ṣabbān referred to in the text is not identified.

20. Al-Jabartī, *ʿAjāʾib al-āthār fīʾl-tarājim waʾl-akhbār*, II, 227; ʿAlī Mubārak, *Al-Khiṭaṭ al-Tawfīqīya al-jadīda*, VIII, 109–110; ʿAbd al-Hāʾī al-Kattānī, *Fihris al-fahāris wa āthbāt wa muʿjim al-maʿājim waʾl-mashīkhāt waʾl-musalsalāt*, II, 109–110; Brockelmann, *Geschichte der Arabischen Litteratur*, GAL 11, p. 288.

21. Muḥammad al-Ṣabbān, *Kitāb isʿāf al-rāghibīn fī sīrat al-muṣṭafā wa faḍāʾil ahl al-bayt*. On the margin of this book is published another work entitled *Nūr al-abṣār fī manāqib al-bayt al-nabī al-mukhtār* by Sayyid al-Shiblānjī. This last work is an especially good source on al-Zabīdī.

22. Al-Ṣabbān, *Kitāb isʿāf al-rāghibīn fī sīrat al-Muṣṭafā wa faḍāʾil ahl al-bayt*, p. 1.

23. Shaybūb, *ʿAbd al-Raḥman al-Jabartī*, pp. 34–42. Al-Jabartī had a *kunya* (it was Abūʾl-ʿAẓim) from the Wafāʾīya, as did his brother. Another student of al-Ṣabbān, Ḥasan al-ʿAṭṭār, was known as Abūʾl-Saʿādāt. The most appropriate name was reserved for al-Zabīdī, Al-Sayyid Abūʾl-Anwār b. Wafāʾ bi-Ibn al-Fāyiḍ (see al-Kilānī, *Al-Adab al-miṣrī fī ẓill al-ḥukm al-ʿuthmānī*, p. 287).

24. Al-Kilānī, *Al-Adab al-miṣrī fī ẓill al-ḥukm al-ʿuthmānī*, pp. 153, 169–170.

25. Ibid., pp. 97, 129, 131. The smaller Khalwatīya-Dimirdāshīya branch was not part of the Bakrīya reform movement.

26. Hans Joachim Kissling, "Aus der Geschichte der Chalvetijje-Ordens," *Zeitschrift der Deutsches Morgenlander Gesellschaft* 103 (1953): Table 2, p. 282; Bannerth ("La Khalwatiyya en Egypte") claimed that the Sammānīya derived from al-Ḥifnāwī and not al-Bakrī, and that they were located in the eastern Sudan. He likewise found a long list of those who became Khalwatīs (cf. al-Jabartī, *ʿAjāʾib al-āthār fīʾl-tarājim waʾl-akhbār*, I, 298–299) under al-Ḥifnāwī. Kissling ("Aus der Geschichte der Chalvetijje-Ordens") states that al-Ḥifnāwī had only two main disciples, Aḥmad al-Dardīr and Maḥmūd al-Kurdī, and that the others were followers of these.

27. Al-Jabartī, *ʿAjāʾib al-āthār fīʾl-tarājim waʾl-akhbār*, I, 291. Courtesy of Professor A. Marsot.

28. The view that the line of al-Kurdī led only to the Tijānīya is contradicted by al-Bayṭār, *Ḥilyat al-bāshir fī tārīkh al-qarn al-thālith ʿashar*, III, 1415, where the example is given of Muḥammad al-Saqqāṭ al-Maghribī al-Khalwatī, died 1794/1209. In Cairo, he went to his teacher's *murshid*, al-Kurdī. Al-Kurdī revealed to

him his future mission from revelations received in dream form. See B. G. Martin, "Notes sur l'origine de la ṭarīqa des Tijānīya et sur les début d'al-Ḥājj ʿUmar," *Révue des Etudes Islamiques* 37 (1969): 267–290.

29. Abūʾl-Wafāʾ al-Ghunaymī al-Taftazānī, "Al-Ṭuruq al-ṣūfīya fī Miṣr," *Majallat Kullīyat al-Ādāb* 25 (1963): 66.

30. M. Ghayth, "Shaykh al-Azhar fīʾl-qarn al-thāmin ʿashar," in *Al-Majalla al-tārīkhīya al-miṣrīya*, pp. 272–282; al-Jabartī, *ʿAjāʾib al-āthār fīʾl-tarājim waʾl-akhbār*, III, 192; IV, 170–173; V, 159–166.

31. Al-Bayṭār (*Ḥilyat al-bāshir fī tārīkh al-qarn al-thālith ʿashar*, III, 1558–1559) gave the life of al-Sayyid Muṣṭafā al-Damanhūrī al-Shāfiʿī al-Miṣrī al-Azharī, died 1798/1213. He was deeply interested in the study of history and had read (parts of?) the *Sulūk* and the *Khiṭaṭ* of al-Maqrīzī, the *Tārīkh al-ʿaynī* of al-Sakhāwī, and others. Al-Sharqāwī himself studied history.

32. Ibid., II, 1088, for his student Shaykh ʿAlī al-Ḥiṣāwī al-Shāfiʿī (died 1816/1231). In Chapter 7 the religious texts which he taught al-ʿAṭṭār will be discussed.

33. Al-Bayṭār, *Ḥilyat al-bāshir fī tārīkh al-qarn al-thālith ʿashar*, II, 1068–1070, from the life of ʿAlī b. Muḥammad al-Qināwī al-Miṣrī al-Shāfiʿī al-Khalwatī, who died after 1785/1200. It is probable that the *dhikr* used the colloquial language along with classical Arabic, as well as music.

34. ʿAlī b. Maḥmūd al-Khalwatī (*Hadha minḥat al-majīd ʿalā sayf al-murīd*, p. 56) and al-Bayṭār (*Ḥilyat al-bāshir fī tārīkh al-qarn al-thālith ʿashar*, III, 1411) give an account of perhaps the only real recluse of the late eighteenth century in Egypt. This man was said to have left his house only twenty-one times in his life.

35. Muṣṭafā Yūsuf Salām al-Shādhilī, *Jawāhir al-iṭṭilāʿ wa durr al-intifāʿ ʿalā matn Ibn Shajāʿ* contains a number of al-Bayyūmī's essays on the margin and following the main text.

36. ʿAlī al-Bayyūmī, *Al-Muntakhab*, copied by Ibn Shabha, in Salām, *Jawāhir al-iṭṭilāʿ wa durr al-intifāʿ ʿalā matn Ibn Shajāʿ*, pp. 3–147 (margin), which deals with differences between the four rites, an unusual topic in this period. See esp. p. 70.

37. Al-Bayṭār, *Ḥilyat al-bāshir fī tārīkh al-qarn al-thālith ʿashar*, III, 1545–1552. Whether he was related to the Khalwatī *shaykh* Aḥmad b. Muḥammad al-Ṣāwī (died 1825/1241) could not be determined. The son Muṣṭafā had some relationship with al-Azhar, according to the same biography. He moved to the Ḥusaynīya quarter to study with Shaykh ʿĪsā al-Barmāwī. The Ṣūfī al-Ṣāwī died in Mecca, there being some indication that his order, the al-Ṣāwīya, spread there as a consequence of the Wahhābīs' defeat.

38. Salām, *Jawāhir al-iṭṭilāʿ wa durr al-intifāʿ ʿalā matn Ibn Shajāʿ*, pp. 177–234 (margin), esp. pp. 177–178, 182.

39. Ibid., p. 202.

40. Ibid., pp. 204–205.

41. Moreh, "The Sociological Role of the Ṣūfī Shaykh in Eighteenth-Century Egypt," p. 389, citing al-Jabartī (*ʿAjāʾib al-āthār fīʾl-tarājim waʾl-akhbār*, IV, 128); al-Taftazānī ("Al-Ṭuruq al-ṣūfīya fī Miṣr," *Majallat Kullīyat al-Ādab* 25 [1963]: 64) arrived at the conclusion that the radical Ṣūfī orders spread to Egypt only in Ottoman times and that they were distinct from the popular orders which came with the first Mamlūk era.

42. Rodinson, *Islam et capitalisme*, pp. 33–34 and passim.

43. Ibid., p. 35.

44. Muḥammad Murtaḍā al-Zabīdī, *Tāj al-ʿarūs min sharḥ jawāhir al-qāmūs*, VII, 294.
45. Ibid., I, 455–456.
46. Al-Zabīdī, *Itḥāf al-sādāt al-muttiqīn bi sharḥ asrār iḥyāʾ ʿulūm al-dīn*, V, 417. This is discussed by Hellmitt Ritter in "Ein arabisches Handbuch der Handelswissenschaft," *Der Islam* 7 (1919): 32; Rodinson, *Islam et capitalisme*, p. 124. Al-Zabīdī taught the *Sunan* of al-Dārimī among which it is cited that the sincere merchant will be among the prophets on the Day of Judgment (Rodinson, *Islam et capitalisme*, pp. 33, 256 n. 17). Al-Ghazzālī was attacked by Ibn al-Jawzī for his use of suspect *ḥadīth*. The *Itḥāf* of al-Zabīdī was especially devoted to the study of al-Ghazzālī's *ḥadīth* (cf. Goldziher, *Muhammadan Studies*, II, 146).
47. Al-Ghazzālī, *Iḥyāʾ ʿulūm al-dīn*, II, 48ff, cited in Neffening, "Tidjāra," *Encyclopedia of Islam*, 1st ed., III, 747–751.
48. ʿAbdullah al-Sharqāwī, *Fatḥ al-mubdī bi sharḥ mukhtaṣar al-Zabīdī*, II, 176. This appeared in the chapter on selling. The key phrase was "al-iktisāb lā yunāfī al-tawakkul" (profit-making does not negate personal piety). This is in contradiction to the view which holds that *al-tawakkul* is an obstacle to commercial practices.
49. Ibid., II, 214. This appeared in a chapter on agriculture. The resort to a naturalistic explanation was novel. One is tempted to see it as the view of a man who was deeply involved in urban commercial affairs and at the same time a *multazim*.
50. Muṣṭafā al-Bakrī, *Risāla fī rudd ʿalā manʿ al-ziyāra li qubūr al-anbiyāʾ waʾl-awliyāʾ* ("Al-Bakrī's essay in reply to the objection to visiting the tombs of the prophets and saints"), pp. 310–316.
51. Ibid., pp. 312–313. Al-Bakrī acknowledged that he himself frequently visited tombs and that he had heard that ʿAbd al-Ghanī al-Nābulusī had told people that visiting tombs might lead to the revelation of future events. That this had actually happened to Sīdī Ḥasan al-Rāʿī, who learned that he was going to be ordered to leave his village, is adduced; al-Bakrī also mentioned (*Risālat al-Bakrī fī rudd ʿalā manʿ al-ziyāra li qubūr al-anbiyāʾ waʾl-awliyāʾ*, pp. 310–316) that, according to a *ḥadīth*, God's pardon could be obtained only by visiting the tombs of one's parents on Friday and reciting the Sūrat al-Yasīn.
52. ʿAbdullah al-Majīd b. al-ʿĀrif billah Shaykh ʿAlī al-ʿUdwī, "Hadhihi risālat al-tabshīr fī faḍl man banī masjidān aw farrasha biʾl-ḥaṣīr," folio 2A. The author then cited a *ḥadīth* on putting candles in the wall of a mosque. The *ḥadīth* said that he who lightens a mosque will have God's light fall on him. Then he cited a similar *ḥadīth* regarding the rewards which will come to those who put cloth on the tombs (folio 7A).
53. Moreh ("The Sociological Role of the Ṣūfī Shaykh in Eighteenth-Century Egypt," pp. 181–183) observed that there was a rather close relationship between *iftāʾ* and Ṣūfī *shaykhs* in the eighteenth century. He cites a number of examples. He also claims that a number of works in *fiqh* were written by eighteenth-century Ṣūfīs. This seems eminently sound.
54. Al-Jabartī, *ʿAjāʾib al-āthār fīʾl-tarājim waʾl-akhbār*, IV, 233–235. A later *muftī* of the Mālikīs collected al-Amīr's decisions in *Khatmat al-majmūʿ liʾl-Shaykh al-Amīr*. There is also a *Fatāwī al-Shaykh al-Amīr*.
55. Al-Bayṭār, *Ḥilyat al-bāshir fī tārīkh al-qarn al-thālith ʿashar*, III, 1564–1565. Aḥmad al-ʿArūsī was made a Qāḍī during the time of Napoleon. He had some connections to the Syrian *riwāq* in the past and was a close friend of Ḥasan al-Jabartī.
56. Statistics will be presented. They are based on the manuscript holdings of the

mosque library of al-Azhar: Abū'l-Wafā' al-Marāghī, *Fihris al-kutub al-mawjūda bi'l-maktaba al-Azharīya ilā 1952/1371.*

57. Ibid., I, 439–458.
58. Ibid., I, 399–406, 561–563, 557–559.
59. Brockelmann, *Geschichte der Arabischen Litteratur*, S2, pp. 415–424, listed some five *shaykhs* (including members of the Wafā'īya and Khalwatīya) who wrote in *ḥadīth*, comprising a dozen works in all, but there is no extensive commentary on these. In contrast to these is *Munẓūmat al-bayqūnīya*, by Shaykh ʿUmar b. Muḥammad b. Fattūḥ al-Bayqūnī, died 1669/1082.
60. Brockelmann, *Geschichte der Arabischen Litteratur*, S2, p. 419.
61. *Sharḥ Sīdī al-Zurqānī ʿalā al-manẓūma al-musammā bi'l-bayqūnīya fī muṣṭalaḥ al-ḥadīth*, published with the major eighteenth-century gloss in the margin by ʿAṭīya al-Ajhūrī.
62. Al-Kilānī, *Al-Adab al-Miṣrī fī ẓill al-ḥukm al-ʿuthmānī*, p. 125; al-Zabīdī, *Tāj al-ʿarūs min sharḥ Jawāhir al-qāmūs*, VII, 380. He stated in connection with *ḥadīth* studies that he had received more than four hundred *ijāzas* (special and general) in Ḥaramayn, Yaman, Egypt, and Jerusalem. One study of his life located more of his manuscripts and established the identity of his *ḥadīth* teachers in Zabīd: in al-Zabīdī, "Tarwiḥ al-qulūb fī dhikr al-mulūk banī Ayyūb," ed. Ṣalāḥ al-dīn al-Munajjid. He wrote this work on *insāb* (genealogy) after his first period in Cairo, 1773/1187.
63. See a heretofore unknown manuscript, "Samā' li ʿallāmat ʿAbd al-Raḥman b. Ḥasan al-Jabartī ʿalā al-ʿallāma Muḥammad Murtaḍā al-Ḥusaynī" (1780/1194), one folio. Ḥasan al-Jabartī also studied with him. Shaybūb, *ʿAbd al-Raḥman al-Jabartī*, p. 39.
64. One might note that four different copies of the *Ṣaḥīḥ al-Bukhārī*, dating from between 1775/1189 and 1780/1195, carry his signature.
65. Al-Zabīdī, "Ijāza Mustafa Efendi al-Qaysuri."
66. Al-Zabīdī, "Sanad al-Zabīdī bi ḥadīth al-raḥma al-musalsal bi'l-awwalīya thalāthīyāt al-Bukhārī."
67. Shaybūb, *ʿAbd al-Raḥman al-Jabartī*, p. 41.
68. Al-Zabīdī, "Ijāza ilā Mustafa Efendi al-Shahīr bi Bek Zadeh." This student also read other works on *ḥadīth* with al-Zabīdī, such as *Al-Jāmiʿ al-ṣaḥīḥ*. Other students included Mustafa Bey al-Iskandarani, Ayyub Bey al-Daftardar, and his great patron, Muḥammad Pasha ʿIzzat, who gave him wealth in 1777/1191.
69. This *shaykh* received an *ijāza* from al-Zabīdī on the *Thabat al-Nakhlī* known as *Bughyat al-ṭālibīn li bay'at al-masā'iḥ al-muʿtamidīn*. Al-Zabīdī, *Ḥikmat al-ishrāq ilā kuttāb al-āfāq*, ed. ʿAbd al-Salām Hārūn, pp. 49–98.
70. Al-Zabīdī, "Ijāza ilā Muḥammad Ṣādiq . . . bi samāʿihi ʿalayhi al-ḥadīth al-awwal min kitāb al-aḥādīth al-thamānīya al-muntakhaba min nawādir al-usūl al-ʿālīya," by Imām Ibn al-Ḍiyā' ʿAlī b. Ibrāhīm b. Aḥmad al-Buljī al-Shāfiʿī, dated 1776/1190.
71. Al-Zabīdī, "Ijāza ilā Muḥammad b. Yūsuf al-firqi al-Zakī," 1780/1195. Another *ijāza* is appended to this to an unnamed student in geography, history, and the *Aḥādīth Manṣūr b. Aḥmad*, which he also studied by the method of *al-musalsal bi'l-awwalīya.*
72. Al-Zabīdī, "Samāʿ li'l-ʿallāma Yūsuf b. Aḥmad al-ʿAqqād al-Dimashqī," 1780/1195.
73. Shaybūb (*ʿAbd al-Raḥman al-Jabartī*, p. 41) mentions that they studied standard works, such as the *Shamā'il*, the *Amālī*, and the *Ṣaḥīḥ al-Bukhārī.* These

students are also mentioned by another source: al-Zabīdī, *Ḥikmat al-ishrāq*, p. 55. These students also studied lexicography with him. Another student who was probably an Egyptian was ʿAlī b. ʿAbdullah b. Aḥmad (*ijāza* from al-Zabīdī dated 1775/1189).

74. Shaybūb, *ʿAbd al-Raḥman al-Jabartī*, p. 39. See also al-Marāghī, *Fihris al-kutub al-mawjūda biʾl-maktaba al-azharīya*, I, 441, 454, 452, for a number of unidentified *ijāzas* of al-Zabīdī in *ḥadīth*. For example, see the *Ṣaḥīḥ* of al-Bukhārī. Rosetta had its own *ḥadīth* scholars, such as Shaykh Aḥmad al-Khuḍarī, with whom ʿAbd al-Raḥman al-Jabartī studied when he visited Rosetta around 1775 (Shaybūb, *ʿAbd al-Raḥman al-Jabartī*, pp. 35–36). It would be interesting to see if *ḥadīth* studies were colored by local problems in the towns of the Delta during this period.

75. Shaybūb, *ʿAbd al-Raḥman al-Jabartī*, p. 39; al-Zabīdī (*Tāj al-ʿarūs min sharḥ Jawāhir al-Qāmūs*, VII, 380) cites an example of such a work (it could not be located), *Al-Mirqāt al-ʿuliyā fī sharḥ al-ḥadīth al-musalsal biʾl-awwalīya*, which he described as a presentation of *aḥādīth* with their complete chains and all their conditions.

76. Al-Zabīdī, *Ḥikmat al-ishrāq*, pp. 54–55.

77. A discussion of these works follows in the appropriate sections of the next chapter. One of his works in *ḥadīth* is "Manẓūmat al-Ṣabbān fī ḍabṭ asmāʾ rijāl ṣaḥīḥayn al-Imāmī al-Bukhārī wa Muslim wa al-Muwāṭṭāʾ," folios 46–62.

78. Ibid., folio 1B; an article on Islamic evaluation of *ḥadīth* is forthcoming.

79. Al-Jabartī, *ʿAjāʾib al-āthār fīʾl-tarājim waʾl-akhbār*, I, 291. He stated that al-Ḥifnāwī had more than fifty students. Among the works in *ḥadīth* which he wrote (but which could not be located) was his *Ḥāshiya ʿalā sharḥ al-ʿAzīzī liʾl-jāmiʿ al-ṣaghīr*. His teaching of *ḥadīth* was also characterized by concern for unbroken chains.

80. Aḥmad al-Dardīr, "Fatḥ al-qadīr fī aḥādīth al-bashīr," folio 1B. In 8B he refers to an earlier work in *ḥadīth* on *asānīd* which he wrote (not identified).

81. Al-Sharqāwī, *Fatḥ al-mubdī*, I, 2.

3. The Cultural Revival of the Late Eighteenth Century

1. J. Heyworth-Dunne, "Arabic Literature in Egypt in the Eighteenth Century with Some Reference to the Poetry and the Poets," *Bulletin of the School of Oriental and African Studies* 9 (1937–1939): 675–689.

2. *Al-Fawāʾiḥ al-jinānīya* is Dār al-Kutub 1487 Al-Adab. See ibid., p. 683. Al-Idkāwī had a wide range of literary friends and associates. There was a litterateur who knew three languages, a parodist, and a musician.

3. Ibid., p. 684, dismisses the Wafāʾīya on the basis of their small size. The best analysis to date is al-Kilānī, *Al-Adab al-miṣrī fī ẓill al-ḥukm al-ʿuthmānī*.

4. Al-Jabartī, *ʿAjāʾib al-āthār fīʾl-tarājim waʾl-akhbār*, II, 111, 114–115. Although Amīr had come from a family of *multazimīn* in Upper Egypt, he was still an outsider in Cairo. Here we see an example of a conflict which carries on through the early nineteenth century, as in the al-ʿAṭṭār–Sānūsī conflict Chapters 5–7. Even in the earlier *Al-Fawāʾiḥ al-jinānīya* there was a *muwashshaḥa* opposing an Andalusian model of Ibn al-Khaṭīb. Muḥammad ʿAbd al-Ghanī Ḥasan claims that a similar opposition to Andalusian forms is found in the Fāṭimid period (see *Ḥasan al-ʿAṭṭār*, p. 68).

5. Al-Jabartī, *ʿAjāʾib al-āthār fīʾl-tarājim waʾl-akhbār*, II, 184–187. Qāsim and al-ʿAwḍī had wide literary contacts. Qāsim was a close friend of the literary figure Shaykh Amīr al-Zurqānī. He also met with a preacher at Ḥusayn mosque and a poet from al-Manṣūra.
6. Ibid., I, 265–283; II, 186–187; ʿUmar Riḍa Kahhāla (*Muʿjam al-muʾallifīn wa tarājim al-ʿarabīya*, IX, 318) lists three works, one a *maqāma*.
7. Ismaʿīl al-Khashshāb, *Dīwān al-Khashshāb*, edited by his friend Ḥasan al-ʿAṭṭār. It included the *taknīya*: al-Sayyid al-Sharīf Abūʾl-Ḥasan.
8. Ibid., pp. 353–363. Shaybūb (*ʿAbd al-Raḥman al-Jabartī*, p. 42) cites a poem in praise of his teacher al-Zabīdī (pp. 364–365), one in praise of his friend al-Jabartī (p. 374), and one in praise of another teacher, Muḥammad al-Amīr.
9. Charles Pellat, "Al-Ḥarīrī," *Encyclopedia of Islam*, 2d ed., III, 121–122; Brockelmann, "Maḳāma," *Encyclopedia of Islam*, 1st ed., III, 161–164.
10. Al-Khafājī wrote on al-Ḥarīrī's *Durrat al-ghawwāṣ fī awhām al-khawāṣṣ*, which dealt with incorrect usages of certain expressions. Al-Khafājī disputed a number of al-Ḥarīrī's assertions. See Pellat, "Al-Ḥarīrī," and Brockelmann, *Geschichte der Arabischen Litteratur*, S2, p. 487. For the life of al-Khafājī, see al-Kilānī, *Al-Adab al-miṣrī fī ẓill al-ḥukm al-ʿuthmānī*, pp. 276–280.
11. Heyworth-Dunne, *Introduction to the History of Education in Modern Egypt*, pp. 76–77.
12. Al-Jabartī, *ʿAjāʾib al-āthār fīʾl-tarājim waʾl-akhbār*, I, 159.
13. Ibid., I, 179. This is of some interest, because the *beys* were reputed to have a negligible knowledge of Arabic.
14. Ibid., II, 35.
15. Ibid., II, 57.
16. Ibid., II, 96. Mulla Darwish died in 1784/1199.
17. Ibid., II, 96–97.
18. Al-Zabīdī, *Ḥikmat al-ishrāq ilā kuttāb al-āfāq*, p. 55; al-Shiblānjī, *Nūr al-abṣār fī manāqib al-bayt al-nabī al-Mukhtār*, p. 174; al-Kattānī, *Fihris al-fahāris wa āthbāt wa muʿjam al-maʿājim waʾl-mashikhhāt waʾl-musalsalāt*, I, 398–413.
19. Al-Zabīdī, *Risālat nashʾat al-irtiyāḥ fī ḥaqīqat al-maysir waʾl-qidāḥ*, ed. Carlo von Landberg, in *Primeurs Arabes*, I. There is an essay explaining why certain pre-Islamic games were forbidden (pp. 39–55).
20. Al-Zabīdī, *Ḥikmat al-ishrāq ilā kuttāb al-āfāq*, introduction, p. 60.
21. Al-Zabīdī, "Tuḥfat al-qamāʿīl fī madīḥ Shaykh al-ʿArab Ismaʿīl." This genealogical study of a Hawwāra chief reflected many of al-Zabīdī's interests; Brockelmann, "Maḳāma," *Geschichte der Arabischen Litteratur*, III, 161–164.
22. Pierre Cachia (*Ṭaha Ḥusayn: His Place in the Egyptian Literary Renaissance*, p. 5) comments that Aḥmad al-Dardīr wrote heavy, repetitive *maqāmāt* with a characteristic use of *tashṭīr* and *takhmīs*, in which quotes from al-Ḥarīrī and other classics were "diluted" through inserts of his own. Brockelmann ("Maḳāma," *Geschichte der Arabischen Litteratur*, III, 161–164) distinguished between the decadence of the eighteenth century and the revival of the *maqāma* in the nineteenth century with al-Yazījī.
23. Al-Sijāʿī made it clear that the choice of this model by a Jewish poet was made for its eloquence in Arabic. Al-ʿAṭṭār also edited a work by a poet of Jewish origin, but found it necessary to append a theological justification for doing so. His period was much less liberal in certain aspects.

24. Ibn Khaldūn, *The Muqaddimah*, ed. Franz Rosenthal, III, 330. Al-Zabīdī taught the work of al-Thaʿālibī (Brockelmann, *Geschichte der Arabischen Litteratur*, S1, p. 499).
25. Jaroslav Stetkevych, *The Modern Arabic Literary Language*. This book disputes the existence of such a dichotomy (chap. 1). The author demonstrates that, for example, the Baṣra school, including such figures as ʿUthmān b. al-Jinnī, relied in a formative period on the use of analogy. Stetkevych shows, however, that the most extensive use of analogy has been in recent times. This is so, he says, because Arabic culture developed more organically in the Middle Ages than it could in modern times.
26. Zayn al-dīn al-Rāzī, *Mukhtār al-Ṣiḥāḥ* (1760/1358), a version of the *Ṣiḥāḥ al-Jawharī* of Ismaʿīl b. Ḥāmid al-Jawharī (died 1099/393). See al-Marāghī, *Fihris al-kutub al-mawjūda biʾl-maktaba al-azharīya*, IV, 31, in the section called "Al-lugha."
27. Muḥammad b. al-Ṭīb al-Fāsī, "Iḍāt al-rāmūs wa ifāḍat al-nāmūs ʿalā iddiʿāʾ al-qāmūs," a commentary on al-Firūzabādī (3 vols.). The next scholar to comment on this text was al-Zabīdī.
28. Ibid., I, folio 1a.
29. Ibid., I, folios 7a–8b; on al-Shirāzī's (al-Firūzabādī's) use of *ḥadīth* (19a).
30. ʿAbdullah ʿAbd al-Fattāh Darwīsh, "Al-Khalīl Ibn Aḥmad and the Evolution of Arabic Lexicography" (doctoral dissertation). This study and others treat al-Zabīdī as the last of the traditional writers of dictionaries on the basis of the organization he follows and on the basis that his work is a commentary and not an "independent" work. However, in the printed edition of the *Tāj*, referred to above, an index of the location of the letters in the beginning of the first volume makes it very convenient even for the "modern" reader to use. The difference is actually rather small, whether one starts with the first radical or the last. The actual significance of this system lies more in the shift of dictionaries away from the needs of poets.
31. Al-Zabīdī, *Ḥikmat al-ishrāq ilā kuttāb al-āfāq*, introduction, p. 56.
32. L. Kopf, "Religious Influences on Mediaeval Arabic Philology," *Studia Islamica* 5 (1956): 49–50. Cf. Muḥammad al-Amīr, *Ḥāshiyat al-Amīr ʿalā sharḥ al-azharīya*, p. 7.
33. Lane, *Arabic-English Lexicon*, p. xviii, especially the *Lisan al-ʿarab* of Ibn al-Manzur.
34. Anwar Chejne, *The Arabic Language*, p. 45.
35. Ḥasan al-Quwaydār (died 1848/1262), a student of language with Ḥasan al-ʿAṭṭār, wrote a work in lexicography called "Taqrīrāt Quwaydār ʿalā manẓūmatihi fī muthallathāt al-musammā bi nīl al-ʿarab fī muthallathāt al-ʿarab."
36. Not all *shaykhs* of al-Azhar followed the main texts, but this was the basis of the teaching program. For an exception, see Ḥasan al-Jabartī, "Sharḥ Ḥasan al-Jabartī ʿalā risālat al-shurūṭ allatī allafahā ʿAbbās Efendī fīʾl-shurūṭ waʾl-ajzāʾ," folios 13–27, 1758/1172.
37. Muḥammad al-Ṣabbān, *Ḥāshiyat al-Ṣabbān ʿalā sharḥ al-Ashmūnī ʿalā alfīyat Ibn Mālik*. This was written in 1779/1193; see I, 2. Throughout this work al-Ṣabbān's general concern with language through *ḥadīth* studies appears.
38. Prior to this there was only one Egyptian, Aḥmad al-Mallāwī in 1753/1146. Before al-Mallāwī, there had been the Indian Naqshbandī ʿAbd al-Ḥikīm al-Siyālkūtī (died 1656/1067); Mullā Ḥasan Chalabi al-Fanarı (died 1480/885); Mīr Dājān

(Ḥabībullah al-Shirāzī, died 1555/993). Paradoxically, these writers are increasingly important as rationalist sources in the nineteenth century (see below, Chapters 6–7).

39. Muḥammad ʿArafa al-Disūqī, "Ḥāshiyat al-Disūqī ʿalā sharḥ Saʿd al-dīn al-Taftazānī ʿalā matn al-talkhīṣ" (2 vols.), dated 1795/1210. Al-Disūqī attributed his learning in part to his teacher ʿAlī al-ʿIdwī.

40. Muḥammad al-Ḥifnāwī, "Ḥāshiyat al-Ḥifnāwī ʿalā sharḥ Abī Laythīal-Samarqandī ʿalā al-risāla al-waḍʿīya al-ʿaḍudīya," folios 83–123 (1761/1175), folio 83B.

41. The main work was only forty pages long and was written in 1769/1183 by Muḥammad al-Ṣabbān ("Sharḥ al-Ṣabbān ʿalā manẓūmatihi fīʾl-ʿurūḍ al-musammā al-kifāya al-shāfīya fī ʿilmay al-ʿurūḍ waʾl qafīya"). There are also minor essays by al-Shubrāwī and al-Sijāʿī. Of these works those of al-Shubrāwī deserve some attention because he alone had a simplified and clear style.

42. Amīr Ahmad al-Dimirdash Katkhuda al-Azab, "Kitāb al-durra al-muṣānaʾ fī akhbār al-kināna fī akhbār min mā waqaʿa fī dawlat al-mamālīk min al-sanājiq waʾl-dawla wa ʿawāʾidihim waʾl-bāshā" (2 vols.), I, 1, dated 1754/1168.

43. Ibid., I, 180–182, 188, 304. For his visit to the Imām al-Shāfiʿī, see II, 556.

44. Ibid., I, 38, 131, 187.

45. Al-Ḥājj Muṣṭafā al-Ḥajj Ibrāhīm, "Tārīkh waqāʾiʿ Miṣr al-Qāhira," 1739/1152. The author introduces himself as a follower of the late Hasan al-Azab al-Dimirdashi.

46. Ismaʿīl al-Khashshāb, *Khulāṣat mā yurād min akhbār al-amīr Murād* (18 Muḥarram 1215/May 1801), cited by Brockelmann, *Geschichte der Arabischen Litteratur*, S2, p. 720. See below, Chapter 4; al-Khashshāb, "Tadhkara li ahl al-baṣāʾir waʾl-abṣār maʿa wajh al-ikhtiṣār"; also ʿAbdullah al-Sharqāwī, *Tuḥfat al-nāẓirīn fī man wālī Miṣr fī wilāyat al-Salāṭīn* (1892/1310).

47. Brockelmann (*Geschichte der Arabischen Litteratur*) neither lists these works for the most part, nor gives Badr as a genre; Peacock, "Mystics and Merchants in Fourteenth Century Germany," p. 48.

48. Muḥammad al-Ṣabbān, "Manzūmat asmāʾ ahl Badr" (1757/1171), pp. 361–369.

49. Muṣṭafā al-Banānī, "Hadhihi al-kitāb rawḍat al-ṭālibīn li asmāʾ al-ṣaḥāba al-Badrīyīn" (1791/1206).

50. ʿAbdullah al-Shubrāwī, *Hadhihi kitāb sharḥ al-ṣadr bi ghazwāt Badr.* For original, see Brockelmann, *Geschichte der Arabischen Litteratur*, GAL 2, p. 282.

51. Muḥammad b. Sālim al-Ḥifnāwī, *Al-Thamāra al-bahīya fīʾl-ṣaḥāba al-badrīya*, pp. 15–16.

52. Ibid., p. 35. Another writer (one of his disciples) appeared to have reservations about this elevation of the Badrīyīn (or the way the Wafāʾīya elevated the *ṣaḥāba* who were buried in Egypt). ʿAbdullah al-Sharqāwī (*Fatḥ al-mubdī*, III, 113) states that, while the *shuhadāʾ* of the Battle of Badr are dead, and the dead cannot hear, God has granted a life to these martyrs.

53. Jamāl al-dīn al-Shayyāl, *Al-Ḥarakāt al-iṣlaḥīya wa marākiz al-thaqāfa*, I, 96–103.

54. Al-Kattānī, *Fihris al-fahāris wa āthbāt wa muʿjam al-maʿājim waʾl-mashāykhāt waʾl-musalsalāt*, I, 104–105.

55. Al-Zabīdī, "Al-ʿIqd al-mukallal biʾl-jawhar al-thamīn fī ṭuruq al-ılbās waʾl-dhıkr waʾl-talqīn" and "Safīnat al-najāh muḥtawiya ʿalā bidaʿa muzjah min al-fawāʾid al-muntaqaḥ."

56. This contrasts with the standard view which dissociates his work from the allegedly barren period in which he lived. It is commonly believed that the coming of the French deepened (modernized?) his understanding of history.

57. Al-Jabartī, *ʿAjāʾib al-āthār fīʾl-tarājim waʾl-akhbār*, I, 3. The "fusion" of different trends can be seen even in the wording of al-Jabartī's title: *ʿAjāʾib al-āthār fīʾl-tarājim waʾl-akhbār*. "Tarājim" is deliberately used as a counterweight to "akhbār." Compare to the work of al-Zabīdī's student previously mentioned, the Algerian Abū Raʾs al-Naṣīrī (died 1822), author of *ʿAjāʾib al-Asfār wa laṭāʾif al-Akhbār*.
58. Al-Jabartī, *ʿAjāʾib al-āthār fīʾl-tarājim waʾl-akhbār*, I, 3.
59. Ibid. Al-Jabartī's allegiance to the chronological tradition of historical writing on the whole outweighs this commitment, although the reader of the chronological sections will find that the author included many items because of their moral value, and would draw a moral lesson from others. The indictment of his own generation concerning their neglect of history should be understood in this sense.
60. Ibid., I, 5.
61. Ibid., I, 4–5; a common view that al-Jabartī was unique is dismissed by reference to a similar historical work composed by a Tunisian contemporary of his who studied in al-Azhar but seemingly not with al-Zabīdī (Ahmed Abdesselem, *Les historiens tunisiens des XVIIè, XVIIIè, et XIX siècles*, p. 273).
62. Al-Jabartī, *ʿAjāʾib al-āthār fīʾl-tarājim waʾl-akhbār*, I, 10–12. The idea that justice can be maintained by a non-Muslim government, while not unprecedented in medieval political thought, was not common.
63. Anouar Abdel-Malek (*Idéologie et renaissance nationale de l'Egypte moderne*, p. 200 and passim) argues persuasively from the text his case in favor of al-Jabartī's technical ability as a historian. This is in contrast to Richard Verdery's attempt to "test" al-Jabartī against contemporary European sources, which he considered to be more accurate on some preconceived basis.

4. The Decline of the Eighteenth-Century Cultural Revival

1. ʿAlī Mubārak, *Al-Khiṭaṭ al-tawfīqīya al-jadīda*, IV, 38. No information concerning Asad (including information on whether or not he was al-ʿAṭṭār's only son) could be located. Ibid., XVI, 72, stated that al-ʿAṭṭār came from the village of Minyā al-ʿAṭṭār. This is highly unlikely. For al-ʿAṭṭār's later life, the main source is Aḥmad al-Ḥusaynī, "Sharḥ al-umm al-musammā bi murshid al-anām li birr umm al-imām."
2. This work is referred to under various titles, for example, "Manẓūma fī ʿilm al-naḥw," folios 114–117, and as *Pétit traité de grammaire arabe en vers*, trans. J. Sicard (App. III, no. 39). See pp. 22, 30 for a comment on the fact that he wrote it in two days. How did the French in Algeria come to know about it a century later? Was this the first translation? We do know that al-ʿAṭṭār's student Ḥasan al-Quwaydār wrote a commentary on this little work. It is entitled "Sharḥ Shaykh Ḥasan al-Quwaydār ʿalā manẓūmat al-ʿAṭṭār fīʾl-naḥw" and is cited by ʿUmar al-Disūqī in *Fīʾl-adab al-ḥadīth*, I, 40.
3. Al-Jabartī, *ʿAjāʾib al-āthār fīʾl-tarājim waʾl-akhbār*, I, 177; II, 160, 169, 170.
4. Shaybūb, *ʿAbd al-Raḥman al-Jabartī*, p. 63.
5. Ibid., p. 58. Earlier, perhaps around 1778, al-Jabartī was given the name Abūʾl-ʿAẓim during the Mawlid al-Nabī.
6. Jamāl al-dīn al-Shayyāl, *A History of Egyptian Historiography in the Nineteenth Century*, p. 112.

7. See Chapter 3.
8. Shaybūb, *ʿAbd al-Raḥman al-Jabartī*, p. 3.
9. Ibid., p. 9.
10. Shayyāl, *A History of Egyptian Historiography*, p. 112; al-Jabartī, *ʿAjāʾib al-āthār fīʾl-tarājim waʾl-akhbār*, IV, 28 (contains al-ʿAṭṭār's poetry); Georges Douin, "L'ambassade d'Elfi Bey à Londres Octobre–Decembre 1803," *Bulletin de l'Institut de l'Egypte* 2 (1925): 100; Shaybūb, *ʿAbd al-Raḥman al-Jabartī*, p. 100 (on al-Jabartī).
11. This work served as the obvious but unacknowledged source for the essay by Delaporte called "Abrégé chronologique de l'histoire des Mamlouks d'Egypte," in *Déscription de l'Egypte—Etat Moderne*, II (part 1), 165 ff. This is drawn quite literally from al-Khashshāb, "Khulāṣat mā yurād min akhbār al-Amīr Murād." For a comment see P. Holt (ed.), *Political and Social Change in Modern Egypt*, p. 12.
12. Al-Jabartī realigned the *miḥrāb* of Jāmiʿ Abū Ḥuraira Mosque in Giza. He stressed that in doing this, he relied on his father's books (Shaybūb, *ʿAbd al-Raḥman al-Jabartī*, p. 11).
13. Al-Jabartī, *Maẓhar al-taqdīs fī dhahāb dawlat al-faransīs*, pp. 14, 382; al-Jabartī used some poetry and letters which al-ʿAṭṭār wrote in 1798 in Asyūṭ. Al-Jabartī's book was quickly recognized in Turkey, and this may have facilitated al-ʿAṭṭār's travels and intellectual contacts there. The *Maẓhar* was completed in 1801/1216 and was translated in 1810/1225 by Mulla ul-Fadil ul-Sayyid Ahmed Efendi Asim. Another interpretation concerning the writing of this book can be found in a dissertation which asserts that it was a work written to fend off criticism for the author's contacts with the French in the Dīwān. See Richard Verdery, "ʿAbd al-Raḥman al-Jabartī as a Source for the Early History of Muḥammad ʿAlī, 1807–1821" (doctoral dissertation), p. 12.
14. Peacock, "Mystics and Merchants in Fourteenth Century Germany"; M. Foucault, *Madness and Civilization: A History of Insanity in the Age of Reason.*
15. Shaybūb, *ʿAbd al-Raḥman al-Jabartī*, pp. 63–65; Mubārak, *Al-Khiṭaṭ al-tawfīqīya al-jadīda*, IV, 38.
16. "Ḥāshiyat al-ʿAṭṭār ʿalā sharḥ Shaykh Khālid al-Azharī" called "Muwāṣil al-ṭullāb ilā qawāʾid al-iʿrāb li ʿAbdullah b. Hishām al-Anṣārī" (dated 1794/1209, App. III, no. 42). Al-ʿAṭṭār did not directly mention the commentary composed by Muḥammad al-Amīr, although we may deduce it through his frequent references to "my *shaykh*," for example, on pp. 89, 92, 103. On p. 100 he mentions "Shaykunā al-awwalī," which would seem to refer to his old teacher or perhaps his first teacher, al-Amīr.
17. On a text called "Al-Samarqandīya" in rhetoric by Abūʾl-Qāsim b. Abī Bakr al-Laythī al-Samarqandī (died 1493). Brockelmann, *Geschichte der Arabischen Litteratur*, GAL II, p. 194.
18. Al-ʿAṭṭār, "Ḥāshiyat al-ʿAṭṭār ʿalā sharḥ Shaykh Khālid al-Azharī," pp. 4–5.
19. Ibid., p. 5; for comparison see Helmut Ritter (ed.), *Asrār al-balāgha (The Mysteries of Eloquence of ʿAbd al-Qāhir al-Jurjānī)*, esp. pp. 1–20.
20. Al-ʿAṭṭār, "Hadhihi al-risāla ʿalā Shaykh Khālid al-Azharī al-Jirjāwī fī sharḥ al-ājurrūmiya" (App. III, no. 41).
21. A minor example of an effort to make these distinctions arose (see folio 1B-2A) concerning the grammatical point of the "wa" of exception. This, al-ʿAṭṭār indicates, al-Azharī confused with a similar problem in *ʿilm al-bayān.* Al-ʿAṭṭār cites as his sources the glosses of ʿAbd al-Ḥakīm on *Al-Mutawakkil*

and *Al-Khayyālī*, works on *kalām*. A large number of other errors also are pointed out.

22. This was a commentary on the work known as *Al-Azharīya* by Khālid al-Azharī. Al-ʿAṭṭār's gloss served as a basic text in grammar study in the nineteenth and twentieth centuries (Heyworth-Dunne, *History of Education in Modern Egypt*, p. 58).
23. Al-ʿAṭṭār, *Ḥāshiya ʿalā sharḥ Shaykh Khālid ʿalā al-azharīya*, p. 21 (App. III, no. 43). In some other cases, al-ʿAṭṭār was dissatisfied with the system of classification which al-Azharī used; for example, see pp. 21, 23, and 27, esp. p. 29, where he stressed that classification is meant to be a utilitarian device.
24. Al-ʿAṭṭār's teacher wrote *Ḥāshiyat al-Amīr ʿalā sharḥ al-azharīya* (1869/1286), praised Khālid al-Azharī's *Commentary on al-Ājurrūmiya*.
25. This point is not free from controversy, because Mubārak states (*Al-Khiṭaṭ al-tawfīqīya al-jadīda*, IV, 38) that al-ʿAṭṭār deferred beginning his teaching in order to study certain other fields. Al-ʿAṭṭār himself stated in his *Ḥāshiya ʿalā sharḥ Shaykh Khālid ʿalā al-azharīya* (p. 2) that he was teaching it in al-Azhar when the French came. I naturally prefer to follow al-ʿAṭṭār's own text and date his teaching from the 1790's.
26. Al-ʿAṭṭār, *Ḥāshiya ʿalā sharḥ Shaykh Khālid ʿalā al-azharīya*, p. 119.
27. Al-ʿAṭṭār, "Risāla . . . ʿalā . . . al-ājurrūmiya." On folios 2A and 2B, he attacked al-Sānūsī and defended al-Ashʿarī. This was a main point for some Khalwatī Ṣūfīs. On 2A he asserted that he was familiar with the glosses of the *Mukhtaṣar al-Sānūsī fīʾl-manṭiq* (see Heyworth-Dunne, *History of Education in Modern Egypt*, p. 61) which criticized al-Ashʿarī.
28. Al-Amīr, *Ḥāshiya ʿalā sharḥ matn mughnī al-labīb*, p. 34, for biographical information on Andalusian literary sources; idem, *Ḥashīya ʿalā sharḥ ʿAbd al-Salām li jawharat al-tawḥīd liʾl-Laqānī*, pp. 53, 55, on the *Riḥla* of Sīdī ʿAbdullah al-ʿAyyashī.
29. Al-Khashshāb, *Dīwān al-Khashshāb*, p. 345; al-Shayyāl, *Al-Ḥarakāt al-iṣlāḥīya wa marākiz al-thaqāfa*, II, 112; ʿAbd al-Jawwād Ramaḍan, "Bayn al-ʿAṭṭār waʾl-Khashshāb min udabāʾ al-qarn al-tāsiʿ ʿashar," *Majallat al-Azhar* 19 (1948), see esp. part 2 (Ṣafar, pp. 139–144) and part 3 (Rabīʿ al-Awwil, pp. 220–225).
30. ʿAbd al-Ghanī Ḥasan, *Ḥasan al-ʿAṭṭār*, pp. 58–59, mentions the opposition of Ismaʿīl al-Ṭuhūrī al-Miṣrī al-Musīqī (died 1797/1212) to the *muwashshaḥāt* of Lisān al-dīn b. al-Khaṭīb.
31. Al-ʿAṭṭār, *Hadhā . . . dīwān . . . Ibrāhīm b. Sahl* (App. III, no. 77).
32. See Chapter 3.
33. Al-ʿAṭṭār, *Hadhā . . . dīwān . . . Ibrāhīm b. Sahl*, pp. 2–3. This suggests that the original was a manuscript copy, somewhat different from the printed copy, which has no such marginalia.
34. Ibid., p. 51. We might note before proceeding that al-ʿAṭṭār had discussed al-Shalūbīn as early as the 1790's, suggesting that he may also have known his work at this time. See al-ʿAṭṭār, *Ḥāshiya ʿalā sharḥ . . . ʿalā al-azharīya*, p. 118.
35. Al-ʿAṭṭār, *Hadhā . . . dīwān . . . Ibrāhīm b. Sahl*, pp. 52–55.
36. Ibid., pp. 54–55.
37. Al-ʿAṭṭār, "Ḥāshiya ʿalā sharḥ ʿalā al-samarqandīya," pp. 17–18 (App. III, no. 52).
38. Al-ʿAṭṭār, "Ḥāshiya ʿalā sharḥ ʿalā qawāʾid," p. 22, dating from 1794–95/1209.
39. Al-ʿAṭṭār, *Ḥāshiya ʿalā sharḥ . . . ʿalā al-azharīya*, p. 119.

40. The new appointee, Shaykh Shāmil Aḥmad b. Ramaḍān b. Su'ūd al-Ṭarābulsī (al-Jabartī, *'Ajā'ib al-āthār fī'l-tarājim wa'l-akhbār*, III, 114).
41. One might note that al-'Aṭṭār rarely used the word *mawlāna* in his books, except for certain major Ṣūfī *shaykhs*, for example, Mawlāna Jalāl al-dīn al-Rūmī.
42. Ḥasan, *Ḥasan al-'Aṭṭār*, pp. 91–92. Muḥammad al-Kilānī consecrated an entire book to the poems praising al-Azbakīya: *Fī rubū' al-Azbakīya: Dirāsa adabīya, tārīkhīya, ijtimā'īya.*
43. Freely translated from the French: Are you for love? Willowy creature of Turkish stock, with moonlike visage composed of pearls, black eyes, pink cheeks, mouth whose nectar-flavored saliva has the sweetness of perfume (Al-'Aṭṭār, *Pétit traité*, p. 22; here somewhat suppressed by the French translator).
44. Al-'Aṭṭār, *Al-Inshā'*, pp. 84–86 (App. III, no. 81).
45. Ibid., p. 78.
46. Al-Jabartī, *'Ajā'ib al-āthār fī'l-tarājim wa'l-akhbār*, III, 109; Mubārak, *Al-Khiṭaṭ al-tawfīqīya al-jadīda*, IX, 163; al-'Aṭṭār, *Al-Inshā'*, p. 67; al-Jabartī, *Maẓhar al-taqdīs*, pp. 237–240.
47. Shaybūb, *'Abd al-Raḥman al-Jabartī*, p. 70.
48. Moosa, "Napoleon's Islamic Policy in Egypt," p. 115 n. 1; al-Jabartī, *'Ajā'ib al-āthār fī'l-tarājim wa'l-akhbār*, III, 44.
49. These statements should be contrasted with those of 'Abdullah al-Sharqāwī, Shaykh al-Azhar and one of al-'Aṭṭār's teachers, and also with those of al-Jabartī, his friend. In *Tuḥfat al-nāẓirīn*, published in Cairo in 1864, al-Sharqāwī echoed the earlier firman of Sultan Selim III against the French Revolution: "As regards the state of the French, they follow the naturalist philosophy and adhere to the judgment of reason. . . . to them the Prophets Muhammad, Jesus, and Moses were wise men and canonical laws attributed to them are tantamount to . . . statute" (pp. 65–66). Al-Jabartī, in "Muddat dukhūl al-faransīs bi Miṣr," wrote that "the French are neither Christian, Muslim, nor Jew; that which is written of their doctrines is that they do not hold to any religion nor do they agree with any religious community; rather, every one of them follows a religion which he invents by his reason." Al-Jabartī elsewhere accused them of being antireligious materialists. See Leon Zolondek, "The French Revolution in Arabic Literature in the Nineteenth Century," *Muslim World* 57 (1967): 204–205. Zolondek was citing al-Sharqāwī, *Tuḥfat al-nāẓirīn*, pp. 64–65, and al-Jabartī, "Muddat dukhūl al-faransīs bi Miṣr," folio 5, and *Maẓhar al-taqdīs*, pp. 41–42. These quotations, as Zolondek points out, should be seen as written in self-defense against charges of their having co-operated with the French, and thus may be a slight exaggeration of their authors' views; nonetheless, if compared to the above as a *mea culpa*, one can easily see how far removed al-'Aṭṭār had become from the "official" Azhar milieu.
50. Al-'Aṭṭār, *Ḥāshiyat al-'Aṭṭār 'alā sharḥ 'alā al-azharīya*, p. 2.
51. Ibid., p. 125. One might point out that the French were defeated in the year 1801 and that most had left already to be replaced by the British before al-'Aṭṭār himself left.

5. Turkey and Syria in the Early Nineteenth Century

1. Alessio Bombaci, *Histoire de la litterature turque*, pp. 310–312.
2. Constantine Volney, *Voyage en l'Egypte et en Syrie*, p. 386 n. 7; Niyazi Berkes,

The Development of Secularism in Turkey, Chap. 1 and passim.

3. Rodinson, *Islam et Capitalisme*, pp. 135–136; Halil Inalcik, "Ḥarīr," *Encyclopedia of Islam*, 2d ed., III, 209–220, esp. p. 218.
4. M. A. Ubicini, *Letters on Turkey*, II, 339–344. This is quoted in Charles Issawi, *The Economic History of the Middle East, 1800–1914*, p. 43.
5. Uriel Heyd, "The Ottoman Ulema and Westernization in the Time of Selim III and Mahmud II," in *Studies in Islamic History and Civilization*, pp. 77–78. Heyd also cited such examples of corruption as refusal by the wealthy *ʿulamāʾ* to submit their gold and silver objects to the mint in compliance with the law. Outsiders managed to rise to high position through their political connections, for example, Cherkes Khalil, a slave boy and favorite of the Sultan Mahmud II, rose to become Shaykh ul-Islam (p. 81). The link of another Shaykh al-Islam, Velizade Mehmed Emin, to Sultan Selim was also quite clear (p. 80).
6. Berkes, *Development of Secularism in Turkey*, pp. 82–83.
7. T.-X. Bianchi, "Récueil de Fetvas," *Journal Asiatique* 1st ser., 2 (1822): 3–16.
8. John Kingsley Birge, *The Bektashi Order of Dervishes*, pp. 77–78.
9. Wadīʿ ʿAbdullah Qasṭūn, *Al-Afrānj fī Ḥalab fīʾl-qarn al-thāmin ʿashar*, pp. 39–55, 197.
10. Robert Haddad, *Syrian Christians in Muslim Society*, pp. 47, 51, 60–61.
11. Albert Hourani, "The Syrians of Egypt in the Eighteenth and Nineteenth Centuries," in *Colloque Internationale sur l'Histoire du Caire.* The role of the Syrian Christians in Syria is not well known. In Egypt in the time of Muḥammad ʿAlī, such figures as ʿAnḥūrī, Faraʿūn, Sakākinī, and Nīqūlā Musābikī played important roles in cultural development.
12. ʿAbd al-Raḥīm, *Al-Dawla al suʿūdīya al-ūlā*, pp. 202–210.
13. Das Gupta, "Trade and Politics in the Eighteenth Century in India," pp. 181, 195; Abir, "The 'Arab Rebellion' of Amīr Ghālib of Mecca, 1788–1813."
14. Henri Guys, *Esquisse de l'état politique et commerciale de la Syrie*, p. 152. The author, in explaining the steady decline in direct French-Syrian trade between 1775 and 1846, attributed it to the direct European penetration of Persia which cut out the Syrian position as middle man.
15. The intellectual division of labor in the Ottoman Empire will be discussed in a forthcoming article.
16. This route is suggested by his student Muḥammad al-ʿAṭṭār, who wrote a short biographical note, "Sharḥ al-ʿAṭṭār ʿalā manẓūmat Ḥasan al-ʿAṭṭār fīʾl-tashrīḥ," folio 49B, dated 1808/1223.
17. Ḥasan al-ʿAṭṭār, "Ḥāshiyat al-ʿAṭṭār ʿalā sharḥ Qādī Zadeh ʿalā taʾsīs al-ashkāl," folio 100B, dated 1821/1237 (App. III, no. 23).
18. Ḥasan al-ʿAṭṭār, "Ḥāshiyat al-ʿAṭṭār ʿalā natāʾij al-afkār fīʾl-naḥw," dated 1805/1222, p. 407 (App. III, no. 44).
19. Ibid., pp. 252, 406. See also al-ʿAṭṭār, "Rāḥat al-abdān bi sharḥ nuzhat al-adhhān al-Anṭākī," folio 250B, dated 1813/1228 (App. III, n. 66); idem, *Ḥāshiya ʿalā sharḥ jāmiʿ al-jawāmiʿ*, II, 150 (App. III, n. 4), which states that he was in Istanbul twice.
20. Al-ʿAṭṭār, *Al-Inshāʾ*, pp. 67–68, praised the Turkish grammar of Hafid Efendi and stated that he studied and learned composition from it. He may have met its author.
21. In ibid., pp. 58–60, al-ʿAṭṭār wrote, in a section on praise, "Praise for a book which the Şeyh ul-Islam Ataullah Efendi composed in which he refuted the beliefs of the people of falsehoods (qawm al-mubaṭilīn)." In this praise, he referred to the Şeyh ul-Islam's light as conquering the land of the enemy. Another reference

is made to the soldiers who will disperse the darkness of night; and finally the use of the word "*yarudd bi*" in al-ʿAṭṭār's title points to a work directed against the Wahhābis by the Şeyh ul-Islam called "Sharḥ ʿalā risālat Qāḍī Makka min sanat 1210 ruddan ʿalā jamāʿat ʿAbd al-ʿAzīz al-Wahhābī ṣāḥib al-Darʿīya wa ibṭāl ʿaqāʾidihim," listed in Dār al-Kutub, 101 Majāmīʿ, al-Tawḥīd. The repetition of words in the title and in the *inshāʾ* is clear enough. See Kahhāla, *Muʿjam al-Muʾallifīn wa tarājim al-ʿarabīya*, X, 292. Al-Baghdādī (*Hidāyat al-ʿārifīn asmāʾ al-muʾallifīn āthār al-muṣannifīn*, II, 356), in his account of the Şeyh ul-Islam, stated that he wrote "Sharḥ ʿalā al-risāla al-ruddīya ʿalā al-ṭāʾifa al-Wahhābīya." There are no grounds for doubting that this is the same work as the one listed in Dār al-Kutub.

22. Berkes, *Development of Secularism in Turkey*, pp. 82–83; Heyd, "Ottoman Ulema and Westernization."
23. Al-ʿAṭṭār, *Ḥāshiyā ʿalā sharḥ jāmiʿ al-jawāmiʿ*, II, 524. In this work, al-ʿAṭṭār identified the figure as Şeyh ul-Islam Arab-Zadeh. This was no doubt Arabzade Mehmed Arif Efendi, who actually rose to the position Şeyh ul-Islam for a brief period in 1808. This supplied courtesy of Professor Rifaat Abou el-Hajj.
24. Al-ʿAṭṭār himself referred to "two stays": "I went there [Istanbul] twice . . . and I saw there books which exist nowhere else" (ibid., II, 150). On his stay with the Hakimbashi and his contact with European doctors, see idem, "Sharḥ al-ʿAṭṭār al-musammā bi rāḥat al-abdān ʿalā nuzhat al-adhhān," which will be discussed in Chapter 9.
25. Muḥammad al-ʿAṭṭār, "Sharḥ al-ʿAṭṭār ʿalā manẓūmat al-ʿAṭṭār fīʾl-tashrīḥ." Writing later than Ḥasan al-ʿAṭṭār, Muḥammad al-ʿAṭṭār criticized the accuracy of Ibn Sīnā, in particular chap. 4 of *Al-Qānūn*, on bones (folio 8A0), but he does not abandon Ibn Sīnā (see folio 37A). It is interesting to read al-ʿAṭṭār's marginal notes, written later to correct his earlier views. On the margin of this copy, he later inserted a comment by al-Qurashī (Ibn al-Nafīs), a writer who had not been known to him when he began, who was in disagreement with Ibn Sīnā (folio 6A).
26. Al-ʿAṭṭār, "Sharḥ al-ʿAṭṭār al-musammā bi rāḥat al-abdān ʿalā nuzhat al-adhhān," folios 70–71.
27. Ibid., folio 5. Muhammad Tayyib Gokbilgin, "Hekim Bashi," *Encyclopedia of Islam*, 2d ed., III, 339–340; also known in Arabic as Raʾīs al-Aṭibbāʾ, he was.a high medical functionary who appointed even foreign doctors. In the eighteenth century, it is claimed that his position was weakened by the Āghā of the Dār al-Saʿāda.
28. Al-ʿAṭṭār, "Sharḥ al-ʿAṭṭār al-musammā bi rāḥat al-abdān ʿalā nuzhat al-adhhān," folio 163A. He also wrote that the majority of the doctors of his time were ignorant of the pulse because they did not meet with it in their training (folio 173B).
29. T.-X. Bianchi, *Notice sur une ouvrage d'anatomie et de médecin*, p. 4.
30. Al-ʿAṭṭār, "Sharḥ al-ʿAṭṭār al-musammā bi rāḥat al-abdān ʿalā nuzhat al-adhhān," folio 5A. This is not to be confused with two other *madrasas* in Damascus, al-Badrīya (see Mubārak, *Al-Khiṭaṭ al-tawfīqīya al-jadīda*, IV, 38) or al-Badhrāʾīya (see al-Shaṭṭī, *Rawḍ al-bashar fī aʿyān Dimashq fīʾl-qarn al-thālith ʿashar*, pp. 245, 257).
31. Al-ʿAṭṭār, "Ḥāshiyat al-ʿAṭṭār ʿalā sharḥ Muḥammad Efendī al-Bahnisī," folio 97A (App. III, no. 37).
32. Mubārak (*Al-Khiṭaṭ al-tawfiqīya al-jadīda*, IV, 39) appeared to have access to

some sources of precise information on these points. His claim that the Naqīb al-Ashrāf was removed from power and then returned to his position is supported by al-ʿAṭṭār's poetry (see *Al-Inshāʾ*, pp. 71–73). The chief error in the account of Mubārak is the claim that he stayed extensively in Damascus on the way out of Egypt in 1802. Al-ʿAṭṭār stated (see *Ḥāshiyat al-ʿAṭṭār ʿalā sharḥ al azharīya*, 1810/1225, folio 2) that he fled directly from Egypt to Turkey. What Mubārak reported of the Syrian period all came later. The quotation from the *Walādīya* should be understood only in this sense, that is, "After my return to Damascus."

33. Al-Jabartī, *ʿAjāʾib al-āthār fīʾl-tarājim waʾl-akhbār*, III, 266, 276; IV, 51, 65; Henri Pérès, "L'Institut de l'Egypte et l'oeuvre de Bonaparte jugés par deux historiens Arabes contemporains," *Arabica* 4 (1957): 113–130, esp. pp. 113–115; Mubārak, *Al-Khiṭaṭ al-tawfīqīya al-jadīda*, XV, 44–45.
34. Mubārak (*Al-Khiṭaṭ al-tawfīqīya al-jadīda*, IV, 39–40) included al-ʿAṭṭār's poem on Damascus. He interjected a comment on some writings of his which are nowhere else referred to.
35. Al-Shaṭṭī, *Rawḍ al-bashar fī aʿyān Dimashq fīʾl-qarn al-thālith ʿashar*, pp. 223–224; Aḥmad Taymūr (ed.), *Aʿlām al-fikr al-islāmī fīʾl-ʿaṣr al-ḥadīth*, pp. 222–223.
36. Khayr al-dīn al-Ziriklī, *Al-Aʿlām*, III, 194; al-Shaṭṭī, *Rawḍ al-bashar fī aʿyān Dimashq fīʾl-qarn al-thālith ʿashar*, pp. 67–69; al-Bayṭār, *Ḥilyat al-bāshir fī tārīkh al-qarn al-thālith ʿashar*, I, 463–474; II, 667. Other students who studied these subjects with al-ʿAṭṭār at the same time included ʿAbdullah al-Kurdī and Ṣāliḥ al-Zajjāj.
37. Muḥammad al-ʿAṭṭār may have brought them together, since al-Yāfī knew Muḥammad al-ʿAṭṭār; al-Yāfī's "Jawāb ʿalā suʾāl min shaykh Muḥammad al-ʿAṭṭār." Al-ʿAṭṭār, *Ḥāshiya ʿalā sharḥ alā jāmiʿ al-jawāmiʿ*, II, 524; al-Ziriklī, *Al-Aʿlām*, X, 162. On al-Yāfī, who died in 1818/1233, see Kahhāla, *Muʿjam al-muʾallifīn wa tarājim al-ʿarabīya*, VII, 318; Brockelmann, *Geschichte der Arabischen Litteratur*, S2, p. 741; al-Shaṭṭī, *Rawḍ al-bashar fī aʿyān Dimashq fīʾl-qarn al-thālith ʿashar*, pp. 185–187.
38. On al-Ḥimṣī, see al-Bayṭār, *Ḥilyat al-bāshir fī tārīkh al-qarn al-thālith ʿashar*, III, 1521–1525. On al-Mujtāhid, see ibid., II, 131–132; al-Shaṭṭī, *Rawḍ al-bashar fī aʿyān Dimashq fīʾl-qarn al-thālith ʿashar*, p. 187; or a work in praise of the Madānīya (a branch of the Shādhilīya) written by Ḥasan al-ʿAṭṭār. See Muḥammad Ẓāfir al-Madanī, *Al-Nūr al-sāṭiʿ waʾl-burhān al-qāṭiʿ*, p. 43.
39. Al-Bayṭār, *Ḥilyat al-bāshir fī tārīkh al-qarn al-thālith ʿashar*, II, 716.
40. Al-ʿAṭṭār, *Ḥāshiya ʿalā sharḥ ʿalā jāmiʿ al-jawāmiʿ*, II, 398, 405–406. His tone should be contrasted with that of his teacher, Muḥammad al-Amīr, who was also a student of Ibn al-ʿArabī, for example, on the feeling of separation from God according to Ibn al-ʿArabī (al-Amīr, *Ḥāshiyat al-Amīr ʿalā al-jawhara*, p. 102). Al-Amīr also quoted the *Futūḥāt makkīya*. Al-ʿAṭṭār was prepared to accept certain ideas even on the souls of plants and animals from him because these ideas did not deviate from a strict Sharīʿa position.
41. Usāma ʿĀnūtī, *Al-Ḥarakat al-adabīya fīʾl-Shām fīʾl-qarn al-thāmin ʿashar*, pp. 150–151.
42. Al-Bayṭār, *Ḥilyat al-bāshir fī tārīkh al-qarn al-thālith ʿashar*, I, 32; ʿAbd al-Qādir al-Khulāṣī. See ʿĪsā Iskandar al-Maʿlūf, *Al-Usra al-ʿarabīya al-mushthara biʾl-ṭibb al-ʿarabīya wa ashhara al-makhṭūṭāt al-ṭibbīya al-ʿarabīya*, p. 19.

43. By the eighteenth century Aleppo had a highly developed European community, with its own doctors. They were concerned with the plague and quarantine. Qasṭūn, *Al-Afrānj fī Ḥalab fī'l-qarn al-thāmin 'ashar*, p. 33 and passim, mentions its French surgeons.
44. Al-Ma'lūf, *Al-Usra al-'arabīya al-mushthara bi'l-ṭibb al-'arabīya wa ashhara al-makhṭūṭāt al-ṭibbīya al-'arabīya*, p. 19. Until 1973 it was in the family library of the deceased author in Ba'labakk (or Zahlé), when it was allegedly sold.

6. *The Muḥammad 'Alī Period, 1815–1837*

1. Owen, *Cotton and the Egyptian Economy*, p. 20, mentions government financing of rice production and the Upper Egyptian sugar production. In 1816, a majority of crops grown in the Delta were likewise taken over. Muḥammad 'Alī made the sale of agricultural produce to merchants a crime.
2. Gabriel Baer, "Urbanization in Egypt, 1820–1907," in *The Beginnings of Modernization in the Middle East in the Nineteenth Century*, ed. W. R. Polk and R. L. Chambers, p. 158.
3. Guémard, *Une Oeuvre française*, pp. 102–103.
4. The Chamber had been formed in 1826 and was headed by Boghos Bey. Its structure reflected where power lay in the commercial sector. In Alexandria in 1826, the Chamber was composed of two Europeans and seven indigenous merchants; and in Cairo, of two Turks, three Egyptians, two Maghāriba, two Levantine Greeks, two Greek Schismatics, two Armenians, and two Jews. By 1836 the Greeks, especially in Alexandria, had registered a very considerable gain. The number of their houses rose from sixteen in 1822 to forty-four in 1836. In the secondary ports of Egypt, the Greeks began to dominate the scene (Politis, *L'Hellènisme et l'Egypte moderne*, I, 233, 239).
5. Abdel-Malek, *Idéologie et renaissance nationale de l'Egypte moderne*, p. 263, presents the contrary view; see, however, Rivlin, *Agricultural Policy of Muhammad 'Alī*, pp. 174–176, which gives many references for the study of the depressed condition of the indigenous middle classes. Elsewhere, Rivlin stated that in 1831 a number of merchants were rounded up for conscription while at a fair (ibid., p. 203). The exception to this was the small group of wealthy merchants who were generally identified as being in the long-distance trade. This group had skills which Muḥammad 'Alī desired to incorporate into his bureaucracy.
6. Rā'ūf 'Abbās Ḥāmid, *Al-Niẓām al-ijtimā'ī fī Miṣr fī ẓill al-milkīya al-zirā'īya al-kabīra, 1837–1914*, esp. pp. 47, 56, 62. See his quotation from al-Ṭahṭāwī (p. 29) to the effect that those Egyptians who oppose the policy of giving land to foreigners are stupid for not appreciating the beneficial role played by those foreigners. Al-Ṭahṭāwī was one of the government's spokesmen.
7. It is clear that in Cairo the Maghāriba had separate *wakīls* for different regions within the Maghrib who were responsible to the Dīwān Khidīwī (*Al-Waqā'i' al-Miṣrīya*, no. 175 [July 3, 1830/14 Muḥarram 1246]).
8. Barker to Palmerston, Alexandria, July 20, 1833, British Foreign Office series 142, vol. 6.
9. Burckhardt, *Travels in Arabia*, pp. 15–16, 17, 38–39. No date is given on when Muḥammad 'Alī was "strong."

10. Walz, "The Trade between Egypt and Bilād As-Sūdān," pp. 412ff, shows numerous regulations imposed by Muḥammad ʿAlī of a fiscal nature, weakening the *wikāla*'s autonomy while at the same time permitting the entree of European merchants into the most profitable trade. The government took over for itself one lucrative commodity, slaves, yet another blow to merchant capital.
11. Afaf Marsot, "The Role of the ʿUlamāʾ in Egypt during the Early Nineteenth Century," in *Social Change in Modern Egypt*, ed. P. M. Holt, p. 278.
12. Al-ʿAṭṭār, *Ḥāshiya ʿalā sharḥ jāmiʿ al-jawāmiʿ*, II, 527, confirms this view. He stated that many *ʿulamāʾ* engaged in trade (this was written in 1830) while they should rather abstain and minimize their wants. He cited the book of Raghib Pasha, defending trade (*Dharīʿat al-takassub*), but he also stated that he felt the Ṣūfīs were exploiting the people, taking from them, and that God obliged man to earn a living.
13. Dār al-Wathāʾiq, Daftar al-Awāmir, no. 11, p. 11, item 65. Courtesy Professor Afaf Marsot.
14. Marsot, "The Role of the ʿUlamāʾ through the Nineteenth Century," conference paper, American University in Cairo–Columbia University Conference, 1968. Unpaginated original located in the Center for Arabic Studies Library of the American University in Cairo. Here the author was able to make use of the Bakrī family papers. Her interpretation was that al-Azhar in the time of al-Bājūrī regained some of its previous autonomy.
15. Heyworth-Dunne, *History of Education in Modern Egypt*, pp. 133–134, 150, 160, 333. Henri Rusi, the son of a tannery owner in Rosetta, played an important role in the new bureaucracy.
16. Ibrahim Salama, *Bibliographie analytique et critique*, p. 110, cited an event in 1830 in which Muḥammad ʿAlī dedicated the library of *kuttāb* to "the spirit of the Prophet and his companions, and of the jurisconsults of Islam and of Shāh Muḥammad Bahāʾ al-dīn al-Naqshbandī . . ." In another case, Muḥammad ʿAlī was reported to wish his son Saʿīd Bey to be in science like Saʿd al-dīn al-Taftazānī and in morality like Muḥīy al-dīn b. al-ʿArabī (ibid., p. 91).
17. Lane, *Manners and Customs of the Modern Egyptians*, pp. 218–219; Baer, "Social Change in Egypt," p. 147; *Al-Waqāʾiʿ al-Miṣrīya* (January 10, 1831/15 Ṣafar 1246) reports a complaint from rural people (*ahālī al-aqālīm*) that Muḥammad ʿAlī was confiscating food sent to the students at al-Azhar if this exceeded a certain amount.
18. Salāma, *Bibliographie analytique et critique*, pp. 98–100. The willingness of the Qāḍī to receive bribes should not be discounted; it is an indication of disenfranchised power. Lane, *Manners and Customs of the Modern Egyptians*, pp. 115–118; al-ʿAṭṭār, *Ḥāshiyat al-ʿAṭṭār ʿalā sharḥ jāmiʿ al-jawāmiʿ*, II, 187. Al-ʿAṭṭār stated that *rashwa* (bribery) was becoming a commonplace; this was written in 1830.
19. A. Le Chatelier, *Les Confréries musulmanes du Hedjaz*, pp. 3–4 and passim; Shaw, *Ottoman Egypt*, pp. 103–104. But in one case, that of the Sānūsīya, who were critics of Muḥammad ʿAlī (see Chapter 7), their representative, Ibrāhīm al-Rashīdī, was rejected by al-Azhar; presumably those *zāwiyas* opened in Egypt were not effectively administered by the government (Le Chatelier, *Les Confréries musulmanes du Hedjaz*).
20. Le Chatelier, *Les Confréries musulmanes du Hedjaz*, p. 521 and passim; Octave Depont and X. Capolani, *Les Confréries religieuses musulmanes*, pp. 378–382, for North Africa; John Spencer Trimingham, *Sufi Orders in Islam*, pp. 79–80.

More recently, on the Tījānīya and their contacts through Ḥājj ʿUmar with Khalwatīs of al-Azhar, see Martin, "Notes sur l'origine de la ṭarīqa des Tījānīya et sur le début d'al-Ḥājj ʿUmar," p. 282.

21. Movement of Aḥmad Idrīs in 1824; cf. Arthur Robinson, "The Conquest of the Sudan by the Wālī of Egypt, Muḥammad ʿAlī Pāshā," *Journal of the African Society* (1926): 49–50.

22. In the absence of archival studies of institutions, the evidence of continuity is literary:

1. Ḥasan al-ʿAṭṭār. In the later writings of Ḥasan al-ʿAṭṭār, there are continuing references to the Safavid scientist, poet, and mystic Bahāʾ al-dīn al-ʿĀmilī, so important to the Wafāʾīya. In a work written in 1814, he doubted the veracity of an astrological tale which al-ʿĀmilī had recounted ("Sharḥ al-ʿAṭṭār al-musammā bi rāḥat al-abdān ʿalā nuzhat al-adhhān," folio 28). In a later work written about 1822, al-ʿAṭṭār referred in a discussion of architectural problems to a problem raised in al-ʿĀmilī's *Al-Kashkūl* about a piece of land containing a tree of unknown height ("Ḥāshiya ʿalā sharḥ taʾsīs al-ashkāl," folio 99A). In his *Al-Inshāʾ*, written in the early 1820's, al-ʿAṭṭār included a model of a letter to be addressed to a Ṣūfī *shaykh* drawn from *Al-Kashkūl*. Elsewhere in the section on letters of praise, a range of expressions are used which were familiar in Wafāʾīya circles in the praises of Abī Anwār al-Sādāt, for example, "apex of his age" (*dhurwat ṭūrihi*), "the source of its light" (*majāl nūrihi*), "and its visibility" (*wa ẓuhūrihi*), etc. (*Al-Inshāʾ*, pp. 84–87). In a work which was finished in 1830, al-ʿAṭṭār again drew on the traditions of the Wafāʾīya in his explanation of unity of witness, *waḥdat al-shuhūd*, citing ʿAlī b. Wafāʾ (*Ḥāshiya ʿalā sharḥ jāmiʿ al-jawāmiʿ*, II, 517–518); for other poetry by him see pp. 453, 358.

2. Al-Ṭahṭāwī, al-ʿAṭṭār's most famous student, was initiated into the Wafāʾīya and given the name Abūʾl-ʿAẓim by Abī Anwār. He subsequently wrote two works on mysticism, one of which was on the theme of Ahl al-Bayt, and the second a commentary on a mystical poem. He also taught *ḥadīth* and, as his biographer pointed out, he taught it analytically as al-Zabīdī had done. See Ṣāliḥ al-Majdī, *Ḥilyat al-zamān bi manāqib khādim al-waṭan, sīrat Rifāʿa Rāfiʿī al-Ṭahṭāwī*, pp. 17, 18, 28, 29.

3. Muḥammad Shihāb al-dīn, al-ʿAṭṭār's protege in the *Waqāʾiʿ al-Miṣrīya*, wrote many poems praising Muḥammad Abī Anwār and his successor, Sayyid Aḥmad (*Dīwān Muḥammad Shihāb al-dīn*, pp. 115–116, 138, and passim).

4. Ibrāhīm al-Saqqāʾ, a student of literature of al-ʿAṭṭār, was a poet and employee in various government positions. As a teacher in the government school (Madrasa Amīrīya), he was singled out in Wafāʾī sources as the teacher of the son of the Shaykh al-Sijāda (al-Bakrī, *Bayt al-Sādāt*, p. 9). He was also a continuator of eighteenth-century studies in *ḥadīth*, writing two works on history. One was on the theme of Ahl al-Bayt, "Al-Ruwwād al-nadīr fī mā yataʿalliq biʾl-bayt al-bashīr al-nadhīr" (Dār al-Kutub, 430 Majāmīʿ, folios 33–41), and the other is on the subject of the wives of the Prophet, "Risālat al-Saqqāʾ" (al-Azhar, 2163 Tārīkh). Muḥammad ʿIyād al-Ṭanṭāwī also studied literature with al-ʿAṭṭār. He wrote "Ḥāshiyat al-Ṭanṭāwī ʿalā sharḥ al-Saqqāʾ ʿalā manẓūmat al-Sayyid Muḥammad Bulīha al-musammā bi dhalika al-sharḥ bi ʾl-tuḥfa al-sanīya fīʾl-ʿaqāʾid al-sunnīya." See Aḥmad Taymūr, "Al-Shaykh Muḥammad ʿIyād al-Ṭanṭāwī," *Majallat al-Majmaʿ al-ʿIlmī al-ʿArabī* 4

(1924): 387–391, esp. p. 388. Whether or not al-Ṭanṭāwī was formally a Ṣūfī has not been determined.

5. Abū Wafā᾽ Naṣr al-Ḥūrīnī, an editor in the Amīrīya Press, was known for his works in the science of language and for his studies on *ḥadīth.* Both he and his son were Ṣūfīs. See ʿUmar Ṭūsūn, *Al-Baʿthāt al-ʿilmīya fī ʿahd Muḥammad ʿAlī*, pp. 174, 346.

23. Lane, *Manners and Customs of the Modern Egyptians*, p. 522.

24. Al-Bakrī, *Bayt al-Ṣiddīq*, p. 41 and passim. This was in the period in which many glosses appeared on the text *Mawlid al-Muṣṭafā*, for example, that of Ibrāhīm al-Bājūrī, Ḥasan al-Abṭāḥ, Aḥmad Fasharah, and Muḥammad b. ʿUthmān al-Dimyāṭī (listed under history and *ḥadīth* in the Dār al-Kutub MSS catalogue). See also by Muḥammad ʿAlī al-Jirjāwī, Muḥammad al-Amīr al-Ṣaghīr, ʿAlī b. ʿAbd al-Ḥaqq al-Ḥujjājī al-Mālikī, etc. Clearly this related to the needs of the period. Lane, *Manners and Customs of the Modern Egyptians*, p. 473, describes al-Bakrī's carrying out these responsibilities. These studies are of course written in the tradition of eighteenth-century *ḥadīth* studies.

25. Abdel-Malek, *Idéologie et renaissance nationale de l'Egypte moderne*, pp. 28–30; Lane, *Manners and Customs of the Modern Egyptians*, pp. 127–128; Rivlin, *Agricultural Policy of Muḥammad ʿAlī*, p. 191.

26. N. Tomiche, "La Situation des artisans et pétit commerçants en l'Egypte de la fin du XVIIIième siècle jusqu'au milieu du XIX," *Studia Islamica* 12 (1960): 79–94. The parallel to Turkey in Chapter 5 is probably more apt.

27. Lane, *Manners and Customs of the Modern Egyptians*, p. 202; Guémard, *Une Oeuvre française.*

28. Rivlin, *Agricultural Policy of Muḥammad ʿAlī in Egypt*, p. 201.

29. Trimingham, *Sufi Orders in Islam*, pp. 79–80. Perhaps the split came when the son of ʿAlī al-Bayyūmī, Muḥammad, joined the Khalwatīya. See Ismaʿīl ʿAbdullah al-Maghribī, *Kitāb nūr al-waḍʿ fī manāqib wa karāmāt ʿumdat al-awlīyā᾽*, pp. 157–158; a doctor named Muḥammad Nāfiʿ is mentioned in al-Shayyāl, *Tārīkh al-tarjama wa᾽l-ḥarakat al-thaqāfīya fī ʿaṣr Muḥammad ʿAlī*, p. 102. If this were the same man, it would suggest that the order had a new class orientation. Another eighteenth-century lower-class order retained an attenuated existence during the Muḥammad ʿAlī period. This was the ʿĪsawīya, whose members continued to be nearly all Maghāriba. They held irregular *dhikrs.* Among the main figures was Ḥājj Muḥammad al-Salāwī, former lamp lighter in the Mawlid of al-Ḥasanayn. He was renowned as a famous fire and glass eater. Lane observed a *dhikr* and stated that "there was no regularity in their dancing; but each seemed to be performing the antics of a madman; now moving his body up and down, then using strange gesticulations with his arms, next jumping, and sometimes screaming . . ." (Lane, *Manners and Customs of the Modern Egyptians*, pp. 465–466).

30. Mubārak, *Al-Khiṭaṭ al-tawfīqīya al-jadīda*, IV, 40.

31. Al-Kattānī, *Fihris al-fahāris wa āthbāt wa muʿjam al-maʿājim wa᾽l-mashīkhāt waʿl-musalsalāt*, I, 163–164. He is probably the person known as Sīdī al-Makkī, of Maghribī origin.

32. Al-Shaṭṭī, *Rawḍ al-bashar fī aʿyān Dimashq fī᾽l-qarn al-thālith ʿashar*, p. 197. See also p. 205 for his biography of his teacher Muḥammad al-Ayyūbī al-Raḥmātī.

33. Al-Bayṭār, *Ḥilyat al-bāshir fī tārīkh al-qarn al-thālith ʿashar*, I, 535.

34. Al-Kattānī, *Fihris al-fahāris wa āthbāt wa muʿjam al-maʿājim waʾl-mashīkhāt waʾl-musalsalāt*, II, 454–457.
35. For his Andalusian influence on al-Ṭanṭāwī, cf. Ignatius Kratchkowski, *Ḥayat Muḥammad ʿIyād al-Ṭanṭāwī*, p. 145; on Shihāb al-Dīn, cf. Abdel-Malek, *Idéologie et renaissance nationale de l'Egypte moderne*, pp. 302–303, and Taymūr, *Aʿlām al-fikr al-islāmī fīʾl-ʿaṣr al-ḥadīth*, pp. 342–346; on Yūsuf Badr al-Dīn al-Murrākishī, cf. al-Shaṭṭī, *Rawḍ al-bashar fī aʿyān Dimashq fīʾl-qarn al-thālith ʿashar*, pp. 262–264.
36. Abū ʾl-Qāsim al-Zayyātī, *Al-Turjamāna al-kubrā*, p. 561; ʿAbd al-Salām b. Suʿūd, *Dalīl muʾarrikh al-Maghrib al-aqṣāʾ*, p. 331, entry 1424. The book of Ibn al-Khaṭīb has already been mentioned as arousing the enmity of Egyptian litterateurs! Thanks to Ms. Evelyn Early for conducting an interview for me with a very learned scholar of Fez, Morocco, Shaykh ʿAbd al-Qādir al-Zammāma. I would also like to thank Shaykh al-Zammāma for his subsequent help (in 1971–72) through a series of letters in which he gave me what information could be found on this subject.
37. Al-ʿAṭṭār, *Al-Inshāʾ*, pp. 48–49.
38. Ibid., pp. 62–66; idem, *Ḥāshiya ʿalā sharḥ al-Khabīṣī*, pp. 2–3 (App. III, no. 32).
39. Al-ʿAṭṭār's exchange of letters with the court litterateur of Muḥammad ʿAlī, Khayret Efendi, is preserved. Khayret Efendi's *Inshāʾ* was called *Riyāḍ al-kutabāʾ wa ḥiyāḍ al-udabāʾ* (Cairo: Būlāq, 1875/1292); al-ʿAṭṭār, *Al-Inshāʾ*, pp. 61–62; Aziz Efendi, *Inshāʾ* (Alexandria, 1832/1249), not located.
40. By Marāʿī al Muqaddisī al-Ḥanbalī (Cairo: Dār al-Kutub 34 al-Adab).
41. One of his students wrote a criticism of his *Inshāʾ*: Ḥasan al-Quwaydār, "Zuhūr al-nabāt fīʾl-inshāʾ waʾl-murāsalāt" (unlocated manuscript, mentioned by Muḥammad ʿAbd al-Ghanī Ḥasan, *Ḥasan al-ʿAṭṭār*, p. 27).
42. Al-ʿAṭṭār, *Al-Inshāʾ*, pp. 56–58; al-Baghdādī, *Hidāyat al-ʿārifīn asmāʾ al-muʾallifīn āthār al-muṣannifīn*, I, 188; F. Abdullah, "Arif Hikmet Bey," *Encyclopedia of Islam*, 2d ed., I, 564–568. The latter source states that Arif's brother was Ataullah Efendi, whom al-ʿAṭṭār apparently had met in Istanbul (however, the same source states that this was denied by Cevdet Pasha). On Arif's library, which he gave to Madīna, see the catalog called "Fihris kutubkhānat Arif Hikmet Bek biʾl-Madīna al-munawwara wa Miṣr; Fihris kutubkhānat al-Sulṭān Maḥmūd biʾl-Madīna ayyadan," compiled by an unknown hand in 1879/1297 (Dār al-Kutub, Cairo, 36 ʿilm al-maktabāt). For a list of books which he studied with al-ʿAṭṭār, see Shaykh Aḥmad b. ʿAbdullah al-Yās, who wrote an *ijāza* for him in 1820/1236 (Dār al-Kutub, Cairo, 230, ijāza, Talʿat). Among other reformers with whom he was in active contact was the Tunisian Ibn Abī al-Ḍiyaf; cf. Abdesselem, *Les Historiens tunisiens*, p. 113.
43. For the principal biography of Sami Bey, see Dény, "Quatre lettres de Mehmet Ali de l'Egypte," in *Mélanges offerts à Wm. Marçais*, pp. 125–146, esp. pp. 140–146; Claude Henri Saint-Simon and Enfantin, *Oeuvres de Saint-Simon et d'Enfantin*, vol. 28, correspondence dated June 12, 1834, from Enfantin to Lambert; *Al-Waqāʾiʿ al-Miṣrīya*, for example, no. 40 (July 30, 1829/23 Muḥarram 1245); no. 202 (October 23, 1836/7 Jumadā al-Ulā 1246); no. 388 (June 3, 1832/3 Muḥarram 1248).
44. An editorial in *Al-Waqāʾiʿ al-Miṣrīya* on *al-ḥikma* and ʿAbd al-Qādir al-Kilānī (al-Jilānī?) argues for the distinction between *al-ḥikma* of this world and divine *ḥikma*. This article appeared in both the Turkish and the Arabic versions at the time of Sami Bey (*Al-Waqāʾiʿ al-Miṣrīya*, no. 37 [May 13, 1829/8 Dhūʾl-

Qa'da 1244]). In another essay, Sami praised *al-ḥikma* and the study of it, referring to the Ṣūfism of his youth and to his studies in calligraphy (ibid., no. 43 [June 3, 1829/end of Dhū'l-Qa'da 1244]).

45. The studies of the newspaper never consider its intellectual basis. They make the Arabic and Turkish versions seem water-tight language compartments. See Reinaud, "De la gazette arabe et turque imprimée en l'Egypte," *Journal Asiatique* 1st ser., 8 (1831): 240. Reinaud states that the Arabic version followed the Turkish version, which was more detailed. Abūl-Futūḥ al-Riḍwān, *Tārīkh maṭba'at Būlāq*, p. 269, states that al-'Aṭṭār, Fāris Shidyaq, and Shihāb al-dīn were the first group of Arabic editors of the Arabic "copy" (!) of the paper. Ibrāhīm 'Abduh, *Tārīkh al-Waqā'i' al-Miṣrīya*, pp. 33–34, doubts if there were a separate section before Shihāb al-Dīn and claims that he found no documents to support such a claim. This may well be correct in that the group may have been very closely knit in the beginning.

46. Al-'Aṭṭār, *Al-Inshā'*, p. 3.

47. Laverne Kuhnke, "Resistance and Response to Modernization: Preventive Medicine and Social Control in Egypt, 1825–1850" (doctoral dissertation), p. 115.

48. *Al-Waqā'i' al-Miṣrīya*, no. 47 (August 29, 1829); no. 186 (April 4, 1831/20 Shawwāl 1246); Mubārak, *Al-Khiṭaṭ al-tawfīqīya al-jadīda*, IV, 40.

49. An administrative case involving Shaykh al-Azhar and two Bedouin *shaykhs* is discussed in *Al-Waqā'i' al-Miṣrīya*, no. 534 (July 3, 1833/23 Ṣafar 1249); another case, involving inheritance and criminal activity, in ibid., no. 319 (November 23, 1831/16 Jumādā al-Akhīra 1247); administration in a criminal case, ibid., no. 323 (December 3, 1831/26 Jumādā al-Ākhira 1247). All the work on the Muḥammad 'Alī period since J. Dény, *Le Sommaire des archives turques au Caire*, has mentioned the consultative assemblies in which the Shaykh al-Azhar participated, but on the whole little of it is very substantive. Dodwell, *Founder of Modern Egypt*, p. 205, discusses the higher council formed in 1834 to deal with matters regarding the Sharī'a and trade! Lane, *Manners and Customs of the Modern Egyptians*, pp. 121–122.

50. Ḥasan, *Ḥasan al-'Aṭṭār*, p. 40; Lane, *Manners and Customs of the Modern Egyptians*, pp. 299–300. Lane reported that when al-Quwaysnī became Shaykh al-Riwāq of the blind, his first act was to have all the members of the *riwāq* flogged. But they retaliated by flogging him and forced him to leave the office (ibid., pp. 217–218). A poet quoted by Mubārak makes the interesting point that al-Quwaysnī kept his Ṣūfī affiliation secret (*Al-Khiṭaṭ al-tawfīqīya al-jadīda*, XIV, 141–142) and that he adhered to the Sharī'a in public, that is, in the Azhar. Finally, despite the various works in logic which al-Quwaysnī cites, one can judge from his intellectual autobiography that he was much more a product of the *ḥadīth* movement of the eighteenth century than a student of the rational sciences. See his "Sanad al-Quwaysnī" (Dār al-Kutub, Cairo, 23126B), in which he mentions his work on the *Ṣaḥīḥ al-Bukhārī* with Muḥammad al-Ḥifnī and 'Abdullah al-Sharqāwī.

51. *Al-Waqā'i' al-Miṣrīya*, no. 378 (May 1, 1832/end of Dhū'l-Qa'da 1247); another case involved an apparent struggle between al-'Aṭṭār and a proofreader of medical books, Shaykh Muḥammad al-Ḥarāwī. The latter opposed al-'Aṭṭār's choice of proofreaders for the Abū Za'bal Medical School (ibid., no. 408 [July 24, 1832/25 Ṣafar 1248]). See Aḥmad 'Izzat 'Abd al-Karīm, *Tārīkh al-ta'līm fī 'aṣr Muḥammad 'Alī*, pp. 258, 289, 290; also al-Shayyāl, *Tārīkh al-tarjama wa-l-ḥarakat al-thaqāfīya fī 'aṣr Muḥammad 'Alī*, pp. 175–177.

52. Al-Ḥusaynī, "Sharḥ al-umm al-musammā bi murshid al-anām li birr umm al-imām," p. 40; al-Quwaysnī (Ḥasan Ibn Darwīsh) wrote at least two works on logic, and on one, his commentary on the *Sullam*, a gloss was written by Muṣṭafā al-Būlāqī (Dār al-Kutub, Cairo, 120 Manṭiq, Taymūr). Al-Quwaysnī had a second work on the same text of al-Akhḍarī called "Mukhtaṣar sharḥ sullam" (Al-Azhar, Cairo, 34253 Ḥalīm 820).
53. Muḥammad b. Ibrāhīm, known as Ibn al-Ḥanbalī (died 976), "Durr al-ḥubb fī tārīkh aʿyān Ḥalab" (Sūhāj, Egypt, Maktaba Baladīya 60 Tārīkh), II, folio 2, contains the *hāmish* (marginal note) of Ḥasan al-ʿAṭṭār. The bulk of this library consists of the library of al-Ṭahṭāwī. I wish to thank Professor Ḥasan al-Ḥabashī of ʿAyn Shams University, Department of History, who gave me this completely unknown source. The exact death date of al-ʿAṭṭār is not known. Muḥammad ʿAlī appointed his successor on February 18, 1835/19 Shawwāl 1250 (Amīn Sāmī, *Taqwīm al-Nīl*, II, 424).
54. [Dr.] P. N. Hamont, *L'Egypte sous Mehmet Ali*, II, 90–91, mentioned al-ʿAṭṭār's support of anatomical dissection (discussed in full in the section on medicine in Chapter 8) and stated that al-ʿAṭṭār advocated the teaching of hygiene, i.e., preventive medicine (ibid., II, 392–393). Al-ʿAṭṭār had, in fact, since the 1820's supported Hamont's idea of founding a school of veterinary medicine. See Heyworth-Dunne, *History of Education in Modern Egypt*, p. 82.
55. Clot Bey, *Mémoires de Clot Bey*, pp. 130–131 (App. III, no. 88). One should note that al-ʿAṭṭār singled out for special praise his students, the correctors.
56. Lane, *Manners and Customs of the Modern Egyptians*, pp. 196–197. Lane was under the impression that al-Quwaysnī was the most famous *shaykh* in Egypt.

7. *The Revival of Theology and* Kalām

1. Abū al-Thanāʾ Shihāb al-dīn Maḥmūd al-Alūsī, "Al-Ṣādiḥ bi shahīq al-nujūm ʿalā afnān tarjamat Shaykh al-Islām wa Walī al-Niʿam," folio 25 and passim, for a full list.
2. Ibid., e.g., the *Fatḥ al-mubdī bi sharḥ mukhtaṣar al-Zabīdī* . . . (a work on *ḥadīth* which has been previously cited); "Ḥāshiyat al-Sharqāwī ʿalā sharḥ Hudhudā ʿalā umm burhān al-Sānūsī" (*fiqh*).
3. Al-Bayṭār, *Ḥilyat al-bāshir fī tārīkh al-qarn al-thālith ʿashar*, II, 489–492, from an *ijāza* of al-ʿAṭṭār to a Syrian student around 1815. The student studied religious subjects with him (Ḥasan al-Bayṭār). Only al-Alūsī gives a list of works which al-ʿAṭṭār taught (see above), and he listed only the texts taught to the Qāḍī Arif Hikmet Bey.
4. Pīr Birkāwī (Birghili Mehmet Efendi), died 1573/981, author of "Al-Ṭarīqa al-muḥammadīya," was a Bayrāmī Ṣūfī and a zealous preacher of the *sunna.*
5. Article on the Ṭarīqa Muḥammadīya forthcoming.
6. Al-ʿAṭṭār, *Ḥāshiya ʿalā sharḥ jāmiʿ al-jawāmiʿ*, II, 523–524. Al-ʿAṭṭār's sources on *al-jabrīya* included Shāh Walīʾullah al-Naqshbandī's *Ḥujjat allah al-bāligha* (ibid., II, 454). This being a later work, it relied on Māturīdite sources, as well.
7. Dār al-Kutub, Cairo, 1171 ʿIlm al-kalām.
8. This was written in 1813/1228; sometimes called "Risālat al-ʿAṭṭār fī ʿilm al-kalām" (App. III, no 9). Another way of dating this piece is through his opening line. Al-ʿAṭṭār began this essay with a virtual paraphrase of the wording of Ibn

al-ʿArabī in the opening of *Al-futūḥāt al-makkīya*: "Subḥāna man awjada al-ashiyāʾ bi qudratihi min al-ʿadam ilā al-wujūd." He was, of course, reading Ibn al-ʿArabī in this period (see below, under the discussion on mysticism).

9. Al-ʿAṭṭār, "Hadhā jawāb al-ʿAṭṭār ʿan suʾāl jāʾ ʿalayhi min al-Shaykh al-Thuʿāylib," 1815/1230, folio 2A (App. III, no. 11), citing Sayyid al-Jurjānī, "Ḥāshiya ʿalā sharḥ ḥikmat al-ʿayn." On folio 7 he cited the views of Fakhr al-dīn al-Rāzī.
10. Al-ʿAṭṭār, "Ḥāshiyat al-ʿAṭṭār ʿalā sharḥ taʾsīs al-ashkāl," folios 76–77.
11. F. E. Peters, *Aristotle and the Arabs*, pp. 203–207. Al-Ījī was known for his book, the *Mawāqif fī ilm al-kalām*, for which the most famous commentary was that by al-Jurjānī.
12. Mubārak, *Al-Khiṭaṭ al-tawfīqīya al-jadīda*, IV, 40. But in the late eighteenth century, al-Sayyid al-Balīdī taught Aḥmad al-ʿArūsī the *Tafsīr of al-Bayḍāwī* in the Ashrāfīya *madrasa* (Bayṭār, *Ḥilyat al-bāshir fī tārīkh al-qarn al-thālith ʿashar*, I, 171). Aḥmad al-Dardīr wrote a commentary on an essay on al-Bayḍāwī written by Turkish Qāḍī and dated 1782/1197.
13. For the section on impurity see his comments on the "Sharḥ al-Badikhshī on al-Bayḍāwī" (al-ʿAṭṭār, *Ḥāshiya alā sharḥ jāmiʿ al-jawāmiʿ*, II, 33).
14. Al-ʿAṭṭār, *Ḥāshiya ʿalā sharḥ jāmiʿ al-jawāmiʿ*, II, 197, 200. Al-ʿAṭṭār relied on the *Muqaddima* of Ibn al-Ṣalāḥ, a text on *ʿilm muṣṭalaḥ al-ḥadīth.* His familiarity with this author can be traced back to his Damascus period when he wrote a gloss on *Nukhba fī ʿuṣūl al-ḥadīth* (App. III, no. 3).
15. Al-ʿAṭṭār, *Ḥāshiya ʿalā sharḥ jāmiʿ al-jawāmiʿ*, II, 200. Al-ʿAṭṭār may have received a certain amount of criticism of the *ṣaḥāba* from his Khalwatī teachers, who did not concentrate on them to the same degree as the Wafāʾīya (al-Sharqāwī, *Fatḥ al-mubdī bi sharḥ mukhtaṣar al-Zabīdī*, III, 71).
16. Forthcoming article on *ijtihād* will attempt to examine, with some new material, the conception of the closing of the gates of *ijtihād.*
17. Dāʾūd Rahbar, "Shāh Walīʾullah and Ijtihād: A Translation of Selected Passages from his ʿIqd al-Jīd fī Aḥkām al-Ijtihād waʾl-Taqlīd," *Muslim World* 45 (1955): 348.
18. Al-Kattānī, *Fihris al-fahāris wa āthbāt wa muʿjam al-maʿājim waʾl-mashīkhāt waʾl musalsalāt*, II, 374–381.
19. It can be estimated that al-ʿAṭṭār and al-Sānūsī met in Cairo between 1830 and 1832. Al-ʿAṭṭār died in 1835/1250. A signed manuscript by the Muftī reads "Risāla liʾl-ʿallāma Muṣṭafā al-Būlāqī fīʾl-ḥukm ʿalā al-Shaykh al-Sānūsī wa ṭarīqatihi," 1847/1264.
20. Muḥammad al-Sānūsī, *Shifāʾ al-ṣadr bi ārāʾ al-masāʾil al-ʿashar*, pp. 3–4.
21. Nicola A. Ziadeh, *Sanūsīya: A Study of the Revivalist Movement in Islam*, p. 81.
22. Muṣṭafā al-Būlāqī was a *muftī* of the Mālikīs. He was a Khalwatī Ṣūfī who entered the *ṭarīqa* under the tutelage of a Khalīfa of Aḥmad al-Dardīr named Ṣāliḥ al-Sibāʿī. He studied the rational sciences and, like Ḥasan al-ʿAṭṭār, became interested in modern natural sciences. He was a close friend of some of the first Egyptian technocrats, such as Maḥmūd Bey al-Fālakī and Salāma Pasha. He even composed essays on mathematics and the use of instruments in the natural sciences (Mubārak, *Al-Khiṭaṭ al-tawfīqīya al-jadīda*, IX, 33–34; Ziadeh, *Sanūsīya*, p. 38).
23. Ziadeh, *Sanūsīya*, pp. 43–44.
24. Al-ʿAṭṭār, "Risālat al-ʿAṭṭār fīʾl-ijtihād waʾl-taqlīd," no composition date given (App. III, no. 13).
25. Al-Zabīdī, who opposed the use of *raʾy* and *qiyās*, stood in the background. For a

view of *ijtihād* based on *ḥadīth*, see "ʿUqūd al-jawāhir fī adilla madhhab al-Imām Abū Ḥanīfa," I, 14; also his *Tāj al-ʿarūs min sharḥ jawāhir al-qāmūs*, II, 330, where he limits *ijtihād* to Qurʾān and *sunna*, somewhat as al-Sānūsī did.

26. Al-Amīr, *Ḥāshiya ʿalā sharḥ ʿAbd al-Salām ʿalā al-jawhara*, pp. 37, 86.
27. Muḥammad Fūʾād Shukrī, *Al-Sānūsīya, dīn wa dawla*, showed that al-Sānūsī was exceedingly energetic in the pursuit of knowledge and traveled widely in order to obtain it.
28. The main source al-ʿAṭṭār cited in this work was a Mālikī work by Shihāb al-dīn Ibn al-ʿAbbās Aḥmad b. Idrīs al-Maʿrūf biʾl-Qarafī al-Mālikī, died 684. This work is called "Sharḥ tanqīḥ al-fuṣūl fīʾl-uṣūl." Al-ʿAṭṭār's choice of a Cairo Mālikī *faqīh* was obviously a part of the polemic.
29. *Rawḍat al-madāris al-miṣrīya* 1, no. 7 (1865/1282): 7–24 (App. III, no. 82). Al-ʿAṭṭār mentioned another student of *uṣūl al-fiqh* named Burhān al-dīn (unidentified) (*Ḥāshiyat ʿalā sharḥ jāmiʿ al-jawāmiʿ*, I, 268).
30. *Rawḍat al-madāris al-miṣrīya*, p. 25. His source in this essay was a work entitled "Al-Iqtiṣād fī marātib al-ijtihād," by Muḥammad ʿAbd al-Raḥman al-Bakrī al-Ṣiddīqī.
31. Cyril Elgood, "Medicine of the Prophet," *Osiris* 14 (1962): 50.
32. H. Laoust, *Contribution à une étude de la methodologie canonique de Taqī al-dīn Aḥmad b. Taymīya*, pp. 16–23. Al-ʿAṭṭār followed the two-qills theory of the Shāfiʿīs. The same dispute or a similar one involved other Maghāriba in Cairo, as was noted in the case of Muḥammad al-Amīr.
33. Ziadeh, *Sānūsīya*, pp. 43–44. Al-ʿAṭṭār's essay dealt with points which al-Būlāqī did not treat, a *takmila* on al-Būlāqī's attack?
34. Al-ʿAṭṭār, *Ḥāshiya ʿalā sharḥ jāmiʿ al-jawāmiʿ*, II, 513–515.
35. Al-ʿAṭṭār, "Nubdha yasīra fī baʿḍ mā yataʿalliq biʾl-basmala waʾl-ḥamd," folio 8B; standard title is "Risāla fīʾl-basmala waʾl-ḥamdala." Here he opposed Ibn al-ʿArabī and preferred the Muḥaqqiqīn, such as Saʿd al-dīn al-Taftazānī.
36. Nicholas Rescher, *The Development of Arabic Logic*, pp. 46–47, 77–78.
37. Al-Ṣabbān, *Ḥāshiyat al-Ṣabbaṇ ʿalā Mallāwī (al-sharḥ al-ṣaghīr) ʿalā al-sullam al-muraunaq liʾl-Akhḍarī*, pp. 143–144; written 1766/1180. See also Aḥmad al-Damanhūrī, "Iyḍāḥ al-mubham min maʿāni al-sullam."
38. See bibliography of al-ʿAṭṭār's writings, Appendix III.
39. ʿAlī Sāmī al-Nashshār, *Manāhij al-baḥth ʿinda mufakkirī al-Islām wa naqd al-Muslimīn liʾl-manṭiq al-Arisṭū*, p. 21, and Ibrahim Madkour, *L'Organon d'Aristote dans le monde arabe*, p. 248 and passim, give a critique of al-ʿAṭṭār from the perspective of classical logic. Al-ʿAṭṭār was the student of Muḥammad al-Disūqī, an *ʿālim* who, like al-ʿAṭṭār, had traveled abroad to study science and returned to be a *faqīh*. Al-Jabartī, *ʿAjāʾib al-āthār fīʾl-tarājim al-akhbār*, IV, 232; al-ʿAṭṭār, *Ḥāshiya ʿalā sharḥ jāmiʿ al-jawāmiʿ*, I, 2.
40. For al-Bihārī, see Brockelmann, *Geschichte der Arabischen Litteratur*, S2, p. 622. He was known as a *faqīh*, an *uṣūlī*, and a logician.
41. Al-ʿAṭṭār, *Ḥāshiya ʿalā sharḥ al-Khabīṣī*, p. 220. For Baḥr al-ʿulūm, see Muḥammad Shāfiʿī, *Encyclopedia of Islam*, 2d ed., I, 936–937; see Jamāl al-dīn al-Afghānī, "Ḥāshiyat al-Afghānī ʿalā sharḥ al-Lakhnāwī ʿalā sullam al-ʿulūm li Muḥibbullah al-Bihārī," 1875/1292.
42. Brockelmann, *Geschichte der Arabischen Litteratur*, S2, pp. 622, 624. Brockelmann does not list any glosses on it in Turkey or the Arab world.
43. ʿAbd al-Ḥāʾī Fakhr al-dīn al-Ḥasanī, *Nuzhat al-khawāṭir wa bahjat al-masāmiʿ waʾl-nawāẓir*, VI, 250–252.

44. Rescher, *Development of Arabic Logic*, p. 197; Madkour, *L'Organon d'Aristote dans le monde arabe*, pp. 32–33. Edwin Calverley, "Al-Abharī's Īsāghūjī fī'l-Manṭiq," in *MacDonald Presentation Volume* (Princeton: Princeton University Press, 1933), pp. 75–85; Brockelmann, "Al-Abharī," *Encyclopedia of Islam*, 2d ed., I, 98–99; Peters, *Aristotle and the Arabs*, pp. 79–87.
45. Abbé Toderini, *De la litterature des Turcs*, I, 70.
46. Rescher, *Development of Arabic Logic*, pp. 233–234.
47. Al-ʿAṭṭār, *Ḥāshiya ʿalā sharḥ al-Īsāghūjī*, pp. 24, 40, 46 (App. III, no. 30).
48. Al-Ḥifnāwī, *Ḥāshiyat al-Ḥifnāwī ʿalā sharḥ ʿalā al-Īsāghūjī*, dated 1757/1171.
49. Al-ʿAṭṭār, *Ḥāshiya ʿalā sharḥ ʿalā al-Īsāghūjī*, pp. 2–3.
50. Al-ʿAṭṭār, *Ḥāshiya ʿalā sharḥ al-Khabīṣī ʿalā al-tahdhīb*, pp. 18–19, 21. Concerning the work of Mīr Zāhid, he said that it mentioned everything one could wish in the course of the author's investigation. Al-ʿAṭṭār then went so far as to lament the lack of contact with the *ʿulamāʾ* of India, whom he contrasted favorably with those of Egypt (ibid., p. 120). Elsewhere, he affirmed the absolute superiority of Indian *ʿulamāʾ* in logic over the Azharīs (*Ḥāshiya ʿalā sharḥ jāmiʿ al-jawāmiʿ*, II, 531–532). He frequently commented on the Azharīs' lack of originality (ibid., II, 247, 455). In criticizing the Azharīs in this manner, he was showing his loyalty to the dominant class.
51. This was written at a time of recentralization in Moroccan history.
52. Al-ʿAṭṭār, *Al-Inshāʾ*, p. 50; Ibrahim Salama, *Enseignement islamique en l'Egypte*, p. 250; al-ʿAṭṭār's student al-Ṭahṭāwī had a similar preoccupation with syllogism and analogy (*Takhlīṣ al-ibrīz fī talkhīṣ Bārīz*, pp. 291–292).
53. Toderini, *De la litterature des Turcs*, I, 71; al-Ṣabbān's work was *Ḥāshiya ʿalā sharḥ Mullā Ḥanafī ʿalā al-ādāb al-ʿaḍudīya*.
54. Al-ʿAṭṭār, "Ḥāshiya ʿalā sharḥ al-Bahnisī . . . ," folios 71B–72A; al-Ḥusaynī, "Sharḥ al-umm al-musammā bi murshid al-anām li birr umm al-imām," p. 39.
55. Laoust, *Contribution á une étude de la methodologie canonique de Taqī al-dīn Aḥmad b. Taimīya*, p. 8; idem, *Essai sur les doctrines sociales et politiques de Taqī al-dīn Aḥmad b. Taimīya*, pp. 514–523. The Wahhābīs held a distinct view in their denial of the use of *qiyās* in *fiqh*. In this they differed from the main Ḥanbalī tradition.
56. Al-ʿAṭṭār, "Ḥāshiya ʿalā sharḥ al-Bahnisī . . . ," folio 81A.
57. Al-ʿAṭṭār, "Ḥāshiyat al-ʿAṭṭār ʿalā sharḥ Mullā Ḥanafī," folio 3 (App. III, no. 38). Some suggestion of the Wahhābī problem can be found on folio 27B, where al-ʿAṭṭār stressed that the Ḥanbalīs were like the Ashʿarīs in being among the first to accept the use of *qiyās*. The Wahhābīs, as stated above, deviated from Ḥanbalī tradition on this point.

8. The Reform Period, 1815–1837, and the Development of Neoclassical Culture

1. Muḥammad al-Bahī, *Al-ʿIlmānīya waʾl-Islām bayn al-fikr waʾl-taṭbīq*, p. 40. Most works on modernization fail to see this. The model is "*the* West" and "is secular"; e.g., Berkes, *Development of Secularism in Turkey*, stresses the role of Tanzimat technicalism as a background for the Young Turks, passing lightly over the role of the Bektashiya and other mystical groups in the same process, as it has no ready analogue in modern Western history.
2. Lucien Goldmann, *The Philosophy of the Enlightenment*, pp. 62, 53–65 passim; Bryan Wilson, *Religion in Secular Society*, a sociological study of the Church

of England in the twentieth century; Eric Hobsbawm, *The Age of Revolution*, pp. 133, 219–220.

3. Abdel-Malek, *Idéologie et renaissance nationale de l'Egypte moderne*, pp. 135–136; M. Levey, *The Medical Formulary of al-Samarqandī*; a later example of such a dictionary is Fabre, "Kitāb al-shudhhūr al-dhahabīya fī'l-alfāẓ al-ṭibbīya" (1851), a collective work on medicine.
4. De Sacy, "Notice . . . ," *Journal des Savans*, 1817, p. 726. When Lane arrived in Cairo, he was able to buy a copy of *Tāj al-ʿarūs*, copied by Naṣr al-Ḥurīnī (Lane, *Arabic-English Lexicon*, I, v). He later worked closely with one of al-Zabīdī's students, Muḥammad al-Ṭanṭāwī (see below).
5. Aḥmad b. ʿAlī al-Masʿūd, *[Hadhihi] majmūʿa fī ʿilm al-taṣrīf*, ed. Ḥasan al-ʿAṭṭār (App. III, no. 46). Al-ʿAṭṭār made certain corrections which appeared on p. 3.
6. Al-ʿAṭṭār, "Ḥāshiyat al-ʿAṭṭār ʿalā lāmīyat al-afʿāl li Ibn Mālik" (copy dated 1820/1236) (App. III, no. 45). The original text by Ibn Mālik (died 672) is al-Azhar, Cairo, 119 ʿIlm al-ṣarf. The commentators included a later Turkish writer, al-Mullā Bahāʾ Statmīr (Sanfar?) Bek. A second example is "Ḥāshiyat al-ʿAṭṭār ʿalā sharḥ ʿIṣām ʿalā al-risāla al-ʿaḍudīya" (Aḥmadī Mosque, Ṭanṭā, 8/558), dated approximately 1815 (App. III, no. 57).
7. Al-ʿAṭṭār, "Ḥāshiya ʿalā lāmīyat al-afʿāl li Ibn Mālik," quotes from the *Dīwān* of Ibn Sahl al-Andalūsī, which he had edited around 1814.
8. See al-ʿAṭṭār and Muṣṭafā al-Badrī al-Dimyāṭī, "Al-Farq bayn al-jamʿ wa ism al-jamʿ wa ism al-jins al-jamāʿī waʾl-fardī" (Dār al-Kutub, Cairo, 1294 Naḥw, n.d.). This was written in *sajʿ*, probably at the request of some influential person who wanted this as an ornament. A specialist in the Arabic language, known to have been alive in 1876/1293, named Muṣṭafā al-Badrī al-Dimyāṭī al-Shāfiʿī can be found in ʿUmar Riḍā Kahhāla, *Muʿjam al-muʾallifīn wa tarājīm al-ʿarabīya*, XII, 244. He is listed in this source as having written a work bearing this title. The work was no doubt composed after 1815.
9. Abdel-Malek, *Idéologie et renaissance nationale de l'Egypte moderne*, p. 330, citing Hans Wehr.
10. Jamāl al-dīn al-Shayyāl, "The First Cultural Contacts between Egypt and the West in the Nineteenth Century," conference paper, American University in Cairo–Columbia University Seminar, July–August 1965.
11. Al-ʿAṭṭār, *Al-Inshāʾ*; Salama, *Enseignement Islamique en l'Egypte*, p. 199; al-Jabartī, *ʿAjāʾib al-āthār fī-l-tarājim wa-l-akhbār*, IV, 232. Several others were also published.
12. Al-Zabīdī, "Taḥqīq al-Waṣāʾil li Maʿrifat al-mukātabāt waʾl-rasāʾil."
13. Al-ʿAṭṭār, *Al-Inshāʾ*, pp. 101–102.
14. Al-Kilānī, *Al-Adab al-miṣri fī ẓill al-ḥukm al-ʿUthmānī*, pp. 172–190.
15. Al-Marṣafī, *Al-Waṣīla al-adabīya*, II, 576–703.
16. Abdel-Malek, *Idéologie et renaissance nationale de l'Egypte moderne*, pp. 136–137.
17. Al-ʿAṭṭār, *Ḥāshiya ʿalā sharḥ jāmiʿ al-jawāmiʿ*, II, 513, on attempting to understand the mystical tradition of Ibn al-ʿArabī, cited by al-Ṭahṭāwī in *Takhlīṣ al-ibrīz fī talkhīṣ Bārīz*, p. 57; al-Ṭahṭāwī continued al-ʿAṭṭār's interest in Ibn Sahl, e.g., *Takhlīṣ*, pp. 101, 282–284; on the literary interview between al-Saʿātī (a student of ʿAbd al-Raḥman al-Jabartī) and al-ʿAṭṭār, see al-Ṭahṭāwī, *Rawḍat al-madāris al-miṣrīya*, 1 (1869/1287), no. 18, p. 35; no. 19, p. 34.
18. Dény, "Quatre Lettres de Mehmet Ali de l'Egypte," pp. 126–127; Khayret Efendi, *Riyāḍ al-kutabāʾ wa ḥiyāḍ al-udabāʾ*, pp. 312–313.

19. Al-Ṭahṭāwī, *Takhlīṣ al-ibrīz fī talkhīṣ Bārīz*, pp. 129–131, discusses al-Ḥarīrī studies in Europe, and his debt to al-ʿAṭṭār. Among the *maqāmāt* of interest to him were Chesterfield's *Letters*, Montesquieu's *Persian Letters*, and other modern writers, showing of course what he took the *maqāma* to be. For letter writing as a forerunner of the novel, e.g., *Clarissa*, see Ian Watt, *The Rise of the Novel*, chap. 1. Al-ʿAṭṭār had literary discussions with Lebanese *maqāma* writer Buṭrus Karāma (Ḥasan, *Ḥasan al-ʿAṭṭār*, pp. 31–33).
20. ʿAbd al-Raḥman al-Rāfiʿī, *Shuʿarāʾ al-waṭanīya, tarājimuhum wa shiʿruhum al-waṭanī*, begins with al-Ṭahṭāwī. For al-ʿAṭṭār, see Ṭaha Ḥusayn and others (eds.), *Muqtaṭafāt min kutub al-adab al-ʿarabī*, I, 246; II, 246 (App. III, no. 90).
21. *Dīwān Muḥammad Shihāb al-dīn*, he praised Ibrāhīm on his return from Syria, pp. 35–36. ʿAlī Efendī al-Darwīsh, *Al-Ishʿār bi ḥamīd al-ashʿār*.
22. Al-ʿAṭṭār, *Ḥāshiya ʿalā sharḥ al-Khabīṣī*, p. 215. The best sources for the range of his poetic readings in the later part of his life are (*1*) *Ḥāshiya ʿalā sharḥ jāmiʿ al-jawāmiʿ*, I, 8, 214, 249, 316, 326, 446; II, 195, 552, 247, 255, 332, 448, 453, 466, 506, 510, 513, 514, 527, and (*2*) *Ḥāshiya ʿalā sharḥ al-Īsāghūjī*, pp. 19, 25, 62.
23. Rom Landau, *The Philosophy of Ibn al-ʿArabī*, pp. 85–86. Al-ʿAṭṭār cited the *Kitāb al-musamārāt* in his *Inshāʾ*, p. 95. He was praised for his knowledge of Ibn al-ʿArabī in general and especially his knowledge of the literary work *Turjumān al-ashwāq*. See Khayret Efendi, *Riyāḍ al-kutubāʾ wa ḥiyāḍ al-udabāʾ*, pp. 312–313.
24. Al-ʿAṭṭār's interest in music and musical instruments is mentioned by his son (see Mubārak, *Al-Khiṭaṭ al-tawfīqīya al-jadīda*, IV, 30). Al-ʿAṭṭār's theories are discussed in "Ḥāshiyat al-ʿAṭṭār ʿalā sharḥ Qāḍī Zadeh fīʾl-handasa," folio 52. For a discussion of the Ikhwānian theory of music and the intellectual unity which al-ʿAṭṭār opposed, see Seyyid Hossein Nasr, *An Introduction to Islamic Cosmological Doctrines*, p. 45.
25. Al-ʿAṭṭār, "Risāla fī taḥqīq al-khilāfa al-Islāmīya wa manāqib al-khilāfa al-ʿUthmānīya," no date (App. III, no. 58), manuscript thanks to Nijāh Maḥmūd al-Ghunaymī of Al-Azhar University. The work resembles one of its most probable sources, Ḥusayn Khuja b. ʿAlī (d. 1735), "Bashāʾir Ahl al-ʾimān bi futūḥāt Āl ʿUthmān"; cf. Abdesselem, *Les Historiens tunisiens*, pp. 208, 219–220. Husayn Khuja was a Tunisian writer influenced by Ibn Khaldūn.
26. Al-ʿAṭṭār, "Risāla fī taḥqīq al-khilāfa al-Islāmīya wa manāqib al-khilāfa al-ʿUthmānīya," folio 13.
27. Ibid.
28. Ibid., folio 15.
29. Ibid., folios 33–34.
30. Al-ʿAṭṭār, *Ḥāshiya ʿalā sharḥ jāmiʿ al-jawāmiʿ*, II, 487.
31. Al-Maqrīzī, *Al-Bayān waʾl-ārāb ʿan mā bi arḍ Miṣr min al-aʿrāb* (App. III, no. 59), utilizing in part the manuscript of al-Maqrīzī, on which were written some comments by Ḥasan al-ʿAṭṭār, which comments the editor retained in the printed edition; see esp. p. 73, also pp. 9–10.
32. Ibid., p. 73. Al-ʿAṭṭār was in a sense imposing these categories on the *muḥaddith* al-Maqrīzī. The background for al-ʿAṭṭār was the eighteenth-century fascination with, and dependence on, commercial tribes. He attacks their ʿAlidism and even attacked the commercial Fāṭimids while praising the Khilāfa of the agrarian ʿAbbāssids and Ottomans.
33. Al-Ṭahṭāwī, *Takhlīṣ al-ibrīz fī talkhīṣ Bārīz*, p. 244. Elsewhere he gave a typology

of nations based on their levels of development: barbarism—human community—civilization, a sort of pre-Comtian evolutionism based on Ibn Khaldūn (ibid., pp. 60–61).

34. Lane, *Manners and Customs of the Modern Egyptians*, p. 227.

35. Al-Ṭahṭāwī, *Takhlīṣ al-ibrīz fī talkhīṣ Bārīz* (al-ʿAṭṭār's comments on pp. 53, 56). In this period (1830), the idea of travel was increasingly connected with government mission to Europe and much less associated with travel to Islamic countries as in the past. There is thus in these comments a certain obvious social orientation.

36. Al-Ṭahṭāwī, *Manāhij al-albāb al-miṣrīya*, pp. 375–376, stated that he had read "Kitāb taqwīm al-buldān" of Abūʾl-Fidāʾ, as well as other books, with al-ʿAṭṭār. This contains a number of marginal comments by al-ʿAṭṭār dated 1833. Professor Layla ʿAbd al-Laṭīf of ʿAyn Shams University copied the relevant portions for me.

37. The section is called "Dhikr umam al-ʿArab wa Aḥwāluhum wa mulūkuhum qabla al-Islām," which is pp. 160–193 of *Bidāyat al-qudamāʾ*.

38. Abūʾl-Fidāʾ, "Kitāb taqwīm al-buldān," p. 3 (marginal notes of al-ʿAṭṭār) (App. III, no. 60); al-ʿAṭṭār also wrote in an earlier work, however, that Damāʾwund, a mountain supposedly in Ceylon (Sarandīb), was the highest in the world (al-ʿAṭṭār, "Sharḥ al-ʿAṭṭār al-musammā bi rāḥat al-abdān ʿalā nuzhat al-adhhān," folio 22A). On folio 139A, he cites "Kitāb al-buldān" as a medical source. "Sharḥ al-ʿAṭṭār al-musammā bi rāḥat al-abdān ʿalā nuzhat al-adhhān" is the earliest writing by al-ʿAṭṭār to discuss equivalents such as the above (Indian, Turkish, Arabic); cf. folio 40B.

39. Abūʾl-Fidāʾ, "Kitāb taqwīm al-buldān," p. 4. The book was not identified. Other Turkish historical books which al-ʿAṭṭār referred to gave accounts of al-Azīq, whom he said were Turks now living under Turkish rule; and (p. 12) he mentioned the Kupchiks from still other sources.

40. Ibid., p. 3; J. Heyworth-Dunne, "Rifāʿah Badawī Rāfiʿī al-Ṭahṭāwī: The Egyptian Revivalist," *Bulletin of the School of Oriental and African Studies* 10 (1940–1942): 399–415, esp. p. 412; F. Taeschner, "Djugrāfīya," *Encyclopedia of Islam*, 2d ed., II, 575–590.

41. Al-Ṭahṭāwī, *Takhlīṣ al-ibrīz fī talkhīṣ Bārīz*, pp. 107–108. Among the classical works which influenced al-Ṭahṭāwī was al-Qazwīnī's "ʿAjāʾib al-makhlūqāt wa gharāʾib al-mawjūdāt." This book included the idea of America and five continents, according to al-Ṭahṭāwī (ibid., p. 69), but where the Europeans had more precise information (as opposed to theories), al-Ṭahṭāwī was prepared to accept it. Al-Qazwīnī claimed, according to al-Ṭahṭāwī, that palm trees existed only in Islamic countries. However, the French, he said, found them in America (ibid., p. 112).

42. Al-Ṭahṭāwī, *Al-Kunūz al-Mukhtār fī kashf al-arāḍī waʾl-buḥār*, pp. 129–143, esp. p. 131. It seems worth noting that this decisive break occurred in his thinking at the moment of the greatest strength of his social class vis-à-vis the traditional middle class. It is worth asking why he relied on Newton rather than Kepler, the mystic.

43. Edward W. Lane, *A Thousand and One Nights*, II, 65.

44. A. Demeerseman, "Une mémoire célèbre qui préfigure l'évolution moderne en Islam," *Institut des Belles Lettres Arabes* (1955): 7.

45. Alexander Scholch, *Agypten den Agyptern: Die Politische und Gesellschaftliche Krise der Jahre 1878–1882 in Agypten*, pp. 53–125. Thanks to Eric Davis of Rutgers University.

9. The World Market as a Limiting Factor in the Development of Neoclassicism

1. An article on the history of Egyptian and Turkish medicine in the eighteenth century is forthcoming.
2. Al-ʿAṭṭār, "Sharḥ al-ʿAṭṭār al-musammā bi rāḥat al-abdān ʿalā nuzhat al-adhhān," folio 5A, 212A. He gave an incident in his life as a reason for his decision to seriously study medicine. He was traveling to Izmir with a servant boy who contracted smallpox and began perspiring heavily. Al-ʿAṭṭār attempted to apply henna, according to a well-known remedy, to close the pores. But every day the boy got sicker until he died (folio 250A). On henna as a treatment, see G. S. Colin, "Ḥinnāʾ," *Encyclopedia of Islam*, 2d ed., III, 461. The use of this anecdote by al-ʿAṭṭār was to dissociate himself from popular medicine.
3. Dāʾūd al-Anṭākī, "Nuzhat al-adhhān fī iṣlāḥ al-abdān," folios 7–8. A discussion of occult elements in Dāʾūd's best-known work, the *Tadhkara*, and notably some references to Idrīs (Hermes Trismegisthus) are contained in Martin Plessner, "Dāʾūd al-Anṭākī's Tenth-Century Encyclopedia on Medicine, Natural History, and Occult Sciences," *Congrès d'Histoire des Sciences* 10 (1962): 635–637.
4. For Dāʾūd al-Anṭākī in the tradition of medicine and *ḥadīth*, see Ḥasan ʿAbd al-Salām, *Dhakīrat al-ʿAṭṭār aw tadhkarat Dāʾūd fī rawīyatihi fī ʿilm al-ḥadīth*, not located.
5. There can be no doubt of the later influence of the *Tadhkara*, but the *Nuzhat al-adhhān* is far more obscure. One commentary was located which was written before that of al-ʿAṭṭār in 1757/1170 by al-Sayyid Muḥammad Riḍā b. al-Sayyid al-Fayḍullah.
6. Al-ʿAṭṭār, "Sharḥ al-ʿAṭṭār al-musammā bi rāḥat al-abdān ʿalā nuzhat al-adhhān," folios 5–11. Concerning the charge that al-Anṭākī was merely a collector, one of course cannot easily judge. Al-Anṭākī indicates that he worked from his own experiences ("Nuzhat al-adhhān fī iṣlāḥ al-abdān," folios 5A, 12B). These might of course have been the common experiences of everyone. Al-ʿAṭṭār also accused Dāʾūd of including material which was not part of medicine (folios 12–13), for example, on plants and animals, which he said were part of agricultural sciences. These are mistakes of logic.
7. M. Meyerhof and J. Schacht, "ʿAlāʾ al dīn . . . al-Qurashī," *Encyclopedia of Islam*, 2d ed., III, 897–898. Al-ʿAṭṭār, "Sharḥ al-ʿAṭṭār al-musammā bi rāḥat al-abdān ʿalā nuzhat al-adhhān," folio 102B. This is not the well-known ʿAbd al-Laṭīf al-Baghdādī (Mawāqif al-dīn al-Mawaṣilī), known as Ibn al-Labbād (born 1162/557), also a critic of Ibn Sīnā.
8. Seyyid Hossein Nasr, *Science and Civilization in Islam*, pp. 213–214; Paul Ghaliunjī, *Ibn al-Nafīs*, pp. 102–104. Nasr erred here in identifying the correct work of Ibn al-Nafīs.
9. Al-ʿAṭṭār, "Sharḥ al-ʿAṭṭār al-musammā bi rāḥat al-abdān ʿalā nuzhat al-adhhān," folio 98B. Why on this crucial passage did al-ʿAṭṭār actually agree with al-Qurashī, whose relevant work he cites (p. 35A), and yet claim that he opposed him? Was he undermined by his copyist, or were the "circumstances" in Damascus, which he referred to above, not conducive to an onslaught on Ibn Sīnā?
10. Seyyid Hossein Nasr, *Islamic Studies*, chapters on Hermes, the chemistry of Rāzī, and Rāzī's rejection of prophecy and *taʾwīl*.
11. Al-ʿAṭṭār, *Ḥāshiyat al-ʿAṭṭār ʿalā sharḥ jāmiʿ al-jawāmiʿ*, II, 512.
12. Al-ʿAṭṭār, "Sharḥ al-ʿAṭṭār al-musammā bi rāḥat al-abdān ʿalā nuzhat al-adhhān," folios 72–73. Similarly, the importance of empirical anatomy for being able to

diagnose correctly genito-urinary diseases (folio 104A).

13. Ibid., folio 248A, attacking the "Sharḥ al-Kazarūnī ʿalā al-qānūn." He was of course also attacking the mid-eighteenth-century tradition of European medicine, aligning himself with the findings of the new positivist tradition.
14. Al-ʿAṭṭār, "Sharḥ al-ʿAṭṭār al-musammā bi rāḥat al-abdān ʿalā nuzhat al-adhhān," folio 78A. In this way he was able to introduce a range of figures including Qusṭāʾ b. Lūqāʾ on the subject of insomnia (folio 117B). This distinction could not have endeared him to the Damascenes of 1814.
15. Ibid., folio 109, on living in the wind, etc.; folio 134C on the winter in Damascus versus the winter in Cairo; folios 153B–154 on the clothes and foods used, etc.; on public baths, folio 155A, where he reveals great familiarity with their construction. Such knowledge was presumably available; see Dāʾūd al-Anṭākī, "Al-Tuḥfa al-bakrīya fī aḥkām al-istiḥmām al-kullīya waʾl-juzʾīya."
16. Al-ʿAṭṭār, "Sharḥ al-ʿAṭṭār al-musammā bi rāḥat al-abdān ʿalā nuzhat al-adhhān," folios 109 and 134B on climatic regions; folio 225A on the Delta and the habits of its people.
17. Article on Egyptian science forthcoming.
18. Lane, *Manners and Customs of the Modern Egyptians*, pp. 227 and 223, respectively.
19. Al-ʿAṭṭār, *Ḥāshiya ʿalā sharḥ al-Balīdī ʿalā al-maqālāt* (App. III, no. 18). This is a Māturīdite approach.
20. Ibid., pp. 16, 296–297, 301. Here Māturīdite theology merges with utilitarianism.
21. Al-ʿAṭṭār, *Ḥāshiya ʿalā sharḥ jāmiʿ al-jawāmiʿ*, II, 506. This remark has been quoted in a number of books. See ʿAbd al-Mitʿāl al-Ṣaʿīdī, *Tārīkh al-iṣlāḥ fīʾl-Azhar*, pp. 20–21; al-Ḥusaynī, "Sharḥ al-umm al-musammā bi murshid al-anām li bīrr umm al-imām," p. 34.
22. Al-ʿAṭṭār, "Sharḥ al-ʿAṭṭār al-musammā bi rāḥat al-abdān ʿalā nuzhat al-adhhān," folio 67A. Al-ʿAṭṭār's sources on medicine, apart from al-Rāzī, include "Al-Qiff," "ʿUmda fī ṣināʿat al-jirāha," and the "Book" of al-Zahrāwī (folio 219B), al-Jāḥiẓ, "Kitāb al-ḥayawān," and the "Sharḥ qānūnjā" of Ibn Rushd (folio 51A).
23. Al-ʿAṭṭār, *Ḥāshiyat al-ʿAṭṭar ʿalā sharḥ al-Balīdī*, p. 301.
24. Sami Bey, "Fī shukr al-ʿināya wa bayān al-ḥikma," *Al-Waqāʾiʿ al-Miṣrīya*, no. 33 (June 3, 1828/end of Dhūʾl-Ḥijja 1244), discusses his view on *al-ḥikma* and on Shaykh ʿAbd al-Qādir al-Jilānī. See also al-ʿAṭṭār's student al-Ṭanṭāwī, who wrote a work on the gloss of al-ʿAṭṭār on al-Sījāʿī (Kratchkowsky, *Ḥayat Muḥammad ʿIyād al-Ṭanṭāwī*, p. 71), but it was not located. There is, however, an unidentified manuscript in al-Azhar which fits the description but which is defective: "Taqrīr ʿalā ḥāshiyat al-ʿAṭṭār ʿalā maqālāt al-Sijāʿī."
25. In the eighteenth century, *ʿilm al-hayʾa* as astronomy was scarcely studied in Egypt. A possible exception is the work of Muḥammad al-Ṣabbān (unlocated) called *Kitāb fī ʿilm al-hayʾa*. Ibrāhīm Khūrī, *Makhṭūṭāt Dār al-Kutub al-Ẓāhirīya: ʿIlm al-hayʾa*, lists works by Ḥasan al-Jabartī on astronomy (!).
26. Al-ʿAṭṭār's previous Wafāʾīya formation still showed when he wrote a commentary on an essay by al-ʿĀmilī ("Risālat tashrīḥ al-aflāk fī ʿilm al-hayʾa"; App. III, no. 22). While al-ʿAṭṭār's commentary could not be located, the original was obviously part of the Ikhwānian corpus. The text cited above was commented on at least six times before al-ʿAṭṭār wrote his commentary (Brockelmann, *Geschichte der Arabischen Litteratur*, S2, p. 595), mainly by Persians and Indians.
27. Al-ʿAṭṭār, "Ḥashīyat al-ʿAṭṭār ʿalā sharḥ Qāḍī Zadeh al-Rumi ʿalā ashkāl al-taʾsīs fī ʿilm al-handasa." The basic text was written by Shams al-dīn Muḥammad b.

Ashrāf al-Samarqandī. A partial translation of this is Hamid Dilgan, "Demonstration du Ve postulat d'Euclide par Shams al-dīn al-Samarqandī: Traduction de l'ouvrage aschkal-ut-tasis de Samarkandi," *Révue de l'Histoire des Sciences et de Leurs Applications* 13 (1960): 191–196. The name of the commentary is *Ta'sīs al-ashkāl.*

28. Al-ʿAṭṭār, "Ḥāshiya ʿalā sharḥ ta'sīs," folios 41–50; Nasr, *Science and Civilization*, pp. 80–82. Al-ʿAṭṭār's source of information on Qāḍī Zadeh, he said, was a work (unlocated) called "Tārīkh bashā'ir al-īmān fī dawlat al-ʿUthmān" (folios 41–42). He was attracted to the scholars who were involved in the astronomical observatories, perhaps because the observatory was an Islamic invention which was accepted as modern by the West. Whatever the reason, al-Ṭahṭāwī was also particularly interested in observatories and spent some time in the one in Paris (*Takhlīṣ ibrīz fī talkhīṣ Bārīz*, p. 213).
29. Among the early figures whom he correctly saw as "continuators of Euclid" were Ibn Haytham (al-ʿAṭṭār, "Ḥāshiya ʿalā sharḥ ta'sīs," folio 69B), Thābit b. Qurra (71B), and Ḥunayn b. Ishāq (87A). He then listed later India figures whose identification is rather problematic: Zuhayr al-dīn al-Hindī (86A), and Khalīl al-dīn al-Hindī (87B). The only Arab source he respected was Tāj al-dīn al-Ṣaʿīdī. He cited "Ḥāshiyat al-Birghundī ʿalā mulakhkhaṣ al-Jaghmīnī" on the subject of the relation of the point to the line (folio 36B).
30. Al-ʿAṭṭār, "Ḥāshiya ʿalā sharḥ ta'sīs," folio 54A. This was "Taḥrīr al-manāẓir" (not located). Al-ʿAṭṭār was partially aware that in following al-ʿĀmilī he was taking a false step, but in this work (1817) there is no criticism voiced of him. He noticed, for example, that the theorems in geometry were used by the *ishrāqiyīn* as the basis of their system, and he wished to dissociate himself from them (folio 56B). He likewise opposed the theory of the *ṭabīʿiyīn* (56B). Elsewhere al-ʿAṭṭār criticized their views on *al-handasa* and in other fields (51B).
31. Ibid., folio 40. "The cosmos of the Ikhwān is the traditional, finite cosmos beyond which there is 'neither void nor plenum.' Moreover, they equate the heavens of the fixed stars with the *kursī*, or pedestal (Qur'ān, II/255) and the ninth heaven with the 'arch or throne' (Qur'ān, IX/129) in order to conform to Quranic cosmology" (Nasr, *Introduction to Islamic Cosmological Doctrines*, p. 76).
32. Al-ʿAṭṭār, "Ḥāshiya ʿalā sharḥ ta'sīs," folios 50–51. Here he cites the *Kashkūl* in solving a problem in the measurement of angles.
33. Al-ʿAṭṭār, "Ḥāshiya ʿalā sharḥ ta'sīs," folios 50–51; Nasr, *Introduction to Islamic Cosmological Doctrines*, pp. 46–47, 48–49.
34. David Pingree, "ʿIlm al-Hay'a," *Encyclopedia of Islam*, 2d ed., III, 1135–1138. Pingree discusses the School of Marāgha and the star charts, but does not see them, as al-ʿĀmilī did, in terms of their relationship to the Persian mystical tradition.
35. Hobsbawm, *Age of Revolution*, p. 282; see also p. 293.
36. Georges Gurvitch, *The Social Frameworks of Knowledge*, pp. 174–198, on European cognitive systems in different historical epochs.
37. Hobsbawm, *Age of Revolution*, p. 285.

Appendix I. The Maqāmat al-ʿAṭṭār

1. Al-ʿAṭṭār, *Maqāmat al-ʿAṭṭār.* This is published in conjunction with a longer *maqāma* of Imām al-Suyūṭī, the full title of which is *Hadhihi al-maqama al-*

suyūṭīya li'l-imām al-ḥāfiẓ Jalāl al-dīn Sīdī 'Abd al-Raḥman al-Suyūṭī wa fī mayzala bi maqāma li mawlāna al-Ḥammām al-shaykh Ḥasan al-'Aṭṭār. The *maqāma* of al-'Aṭṭār appears on pp. 91–96 (Dār al-Kutub, 7574 Adab). This work was translated by Oscar Rescher, *Orientalische Miszellen*, pp. 229–234; also discussed in al-Kilānī, *Fī rubū' al-Azbakīya*, pp. 51–65 passim.

2. Al-'Aṭṭār, *Maqāmat al-'Aṭṭār*, pp. 92–94.
3. Ibid., pp. 94–96. It is a matter for regret that in all the printed sources by the French for this period, al-'Aṭṭār's name does not appear. This makes even the identity of those French Orientalists whom he knew a matter for conjecture. We conclude that it was R. Raige whom al-Khashshāb and al-'Aṭṭār were both fond of to the point of a certain rivalry. Al-Jabartī, *'Ajā'ib al-āthār fī'l-tarājim wa'l-akhbār*, IV, 230, records some amatory poetry which al-'Aṭṭār wrote for Raige which is very similar to the text of the *maqāma* presented above. R. Raige (1770–1807), who lived in the shadow of a better-known Orientalist, Venture de Paradise, was an Arabic translator who had only minor responsibilities. Information concerning Raige is quite limited because of his early death and relatively uneventful life. He is remembered in the *Déscription de l'Egypte* only for his involvement in an Egyptological controversy concerning the age of the Zodiac of Dandara; see Gabriel Guémard, *Histoire et bibliographie critique de la Commission de Science et Artes de l'Institut de l'Egypte*, p. 58; G. Guémard, "Les Orientalistes de l'Armée de l'Orient," *Revue de l'Histoire des Colonies* (1928), pp. 140–142. The friendship of Raige and al-'Aṭṭār would make a certain amount of sense in that they were the same age and both rather uninvolved in the events of the day. Al-Kilānī, *Fī rubū' Azbakīya*, pp. 56–57, also states that his French friend was Raige.

Appendix II. Al-'Aṭṭār's Itinerary from 1802 to 1810

1. *Ḥāshiyat al-'Aṭṭār 'alā sharḥ al-azharīya*, pp. 1, 125. In the information which is presented here, we find al-Ḥusaynī ("Sharḥ al-umm al-musammā bi murshid al-anām li birr umm al-imām," p. 37) in more or less agreement that the period in Damascus was the last (he relies on Damascus sources), but he contradicts himself in presenting another account (p. 35), which appears to be a paraphrase of Mubārak *Al-Khiṭaṭ al-tawfīqīya al-jadīda*, IV, 38–39. Al-Ḥusaynī wrote in the exact phrases of Mubārak: "Then he traveled at that time to Syria [i.e., on leaving Egypt] and he stayed in Damascus for a while, as the poets say, 'without a care,' as was the custom of many *'ulamā'*." Al-Ḥusaynī then omits Mubārak's long description of what supposedly transpired and jumps to the statement that upon leaving Damascus he went to the Turkish lands, stayed there a long time, went to Albania, and then came back to Egypt. All sources agree that he came back to Egypt in 1815. However, following al-'Aṭṭār's own words, this would suggest that he was in Damascus between 1810 and 1815, with perhaps short trips from the city, and that he had finished his sojourn in Turkey. Al-'Aṭṭār must be regarded as his own best witness in these details, as Mubārak and al-Ḥusaynī gathered their materials from his relatives in Egypt long after he was dead. Thus, the first tentative conclusion which we may state is that Mubārak inverted al-'Aṭṭār's visit to Syria by putting it first instead of last. Evidence which will be presented in the next section, on al'Aṭṭār in Syria, also supports this view. Al-Bayṭār, *Ḥilyat al-bāshir fī tārīkh al-qarn*

al-thālith ʿashar, I, 490, an important source, stated that, when he went out of Egypt in 1812/1217, he went to the Turkish lands, then went to Damascus after staying in Turkey for a long time; then he came to Damascus in 1225/1810. This is drawn from the life of Muḥammad al-ʿAṭṭār.

2. Al-ʿAṭṭār, "Ḥāshiyat al-ʿAṭṭār ʿalā sharḥ Qāḍī Zadeh," folio 100B.
3. Al-ʿAṭṭār, "Ḥāshiyat al-ʿAṭṭār ʿalā sharḥ natāʾij al-afkār," p. 407.
4. Ibid., pp. 252, 406. More collateral evidence might exist from Alexandretta. On p. 406 he indicates that his gloss on this grammar book was greatly delayed by the poorness of the copy which he had access to, forcing him to reconstruct it piece by piece and finally to procure additional copies, and that this occurred while he was teaching in Alexandretta. Al-Ḥusaynī, "Sharḥ al-umm al-musammā bi murshid al-anām li birr umm al-imām," p. 38, states that this was a very detailed work written for Turkish students. This would tend to support the view of a longer stay in Alexandretta, dating at least from 1806.
5. Al-ʿAṭṭār, "Ḥāshiyat al-ʿAṭṭār ʿalā sharḥ Muḥammad al-Bahnisī ʿalā risālat al-walādīya li Muḥammad al-Marʿashī," folios 71B–72A.
6. Ibid., p. 35. The work called "Tuḥfa" (not located) was probably entitled in full "Tuḥfat gharīb al-waṭan fī taḥqīq naṣrat al-Shaykh Abīʾl-Ḥasan." This was described as an attack on the commentary of Khadimi-Zadeh on the text called "Al-Ṭarīqa al-muḥammadīya." Al-ʿAṭṭār was defending an Ashʿarite position (see Chapter 7). Mubārak, *Al-Khiṭaṭ al-tawfīqīya al-jadīda*, IV, 39.
7. Al-Bayṭār, *Ḥilyat al-bāshir fī tārīkh al-qarn al-thālith ʿashar*, I, 490–491.
8. Sāmī al-Badrāwī, "Ḥasan al-ʿAṭṭār," in *Aʿlām al-fikr al-islāmī fīʾl-ʿaṣr al-ḥadīth*, ed. Aḥmad Taymūr, p. 26.
9. Muḥammad al-ʿAṭṭār, "Sharḥ ʿalā manẓūmat al-ʿAṭṭār fīʾl-tashrīḥ," folio 1A.
10. Al-ʿAṭṭār, *Ḥāshiyat al-ʿAṭṭār ʿalā sharḥ ʿalā jāmiʿ al-jawāmiʿ*, II, 533.
11. Unsigned article, "Scutari," *Grand dictionnaire universel du XIX siècle*, ed. Pierre Larousse, XIV, 437. Among those who were buried there were some of the Badrīyīn.
12. Adnan Abdulhak, *La Science chez les Turcs ottomans*, p. 142. It is clear that the intent was to provide needed skills in military engineering.
13. Guémard, *Une Oeuvre française*, p. 40. Stanford Shaw discounts the significance of these schools, pointing out that the technical schools went into a state of eclipse after 1788, when Louis XVI pulled out the French advisors, and that in any case instruction in them had been limited to elementary mathematics and the use of artillery. However, elsewhere Shaw characterizes the navy and army engineering schools as the most important part of the Niẓām al-Jadīd because they created a corps of Western-trained, reform-minded specialists. Cf. Shaw, "The Established Ottoman Army Corps under Sultan Selim III," *Der Islam* 90 (1964): 177–178. Shaw also refers to the press in Scutari, which was, he states, founded in 1800 because of the growing need for textbooks in technical subjects for these schools (ibid., p. 183).
14. Sylvestre de Sacy, *Bibliothèque imprimé*, pp. 331–333 nn. 1498–1506. See his article in *Mines de l'Orient* 4 (n.d.): 296 n. 593.
15. For a discussion of the backward, pastoral economy of Scutari, Albania, see F. C. H. L. Pouqueville, *Voyage en Morée à Constantinople et en Albanie*, III, chap. 28–29, which convey a sense of the sheer difficulty of travel through the region. In the late eighteenth century, the region was in considerable turmoil. See Dennis N. Skiotis, "From Bandit to Pasha: First Steps in the Rise to Power of ʿAlī of Tepelen, 1750–1784," *International Journal of Middle East Studies* 2

(1971): 243 n. 3. This source showed, for example, that ʿAlī Bey was at war after 1787 with the rebellious Pasha of Scutari, Kārā Maḥmūd Bushātlī. In 1807, a Bektashi Dervish opened a branch lodge in Kruya, near Scutari, but was later expelled. Little other intellectual life is reported in the early nineteenth century (F. W. Hasluck, *Christianity and Islam under the Sultans*, II, 590).

Glossary

ādāb al-baḥth: argumentation
ʿadd: numbers
adīb: litterateur
al-afātīn: troublemakers
akhbār: events
ʿālim, ʿulamāʾ (pl.): an elite cleric
amīr: provincial bureaucrat
ʿāmm: that which is general in logic
ʿaqīda: dogmatics, a special field in the scholastic corpus
ʿaṣaba: a social solidarity
al-ʿaṣabīya: group loyalty; solidarity
asānīd: chains
awliyāʾ: saints
aʿyān: provincial notables

badal al-musallaḥa: a fee paid to create an inherited tax farm
al-balāgha: the general field of rhetoric
barāʾa: innocence
baraka: magical spiritual power
bāṭinan: hidden; esoteric
beratli: beneficiaries of capitulation agreements, such as the Syrian Christian community in Egypt
bey: an Ottoman official
burhān, barahīn (pl.): logical proof

dallāla: a woman who was able to enter the harems as both seller and creator of new tastes and new consumption habits
al-dawāʾir al-fālakīya: the domain of the stars
al-dhikr: meditation
dīn wa dawla: an expression conveying the unity of religion and state
dirāya: analysis of *ḥadīth* evidence
dīwān: a decision-making body

efendī: an urban functionary

fahrasa: courses taught by the *shaykh*
fallāḥ, fallāḥīn (pl.): a peasant
falsafa: peripatetic philosophy
faqīh, fuqahāʾ (pl.): a systematic theologian
farāsikh: units of distance
fatwa, fatāwī (pl.): legal opinion on points of *fiqh*
fiqh: systematic theology

ghayb: the world of the unknowable
ghazal: love poetry
ghazwa: raid

ḥadīth, aḥādīth (pl.): the studies of the sayings of the Prophet
ḥadīth qudsī: sacred tradition
ḥālu maʿlūm: his condition is known, i.e., a homosexual
al-handasa: geometry, with topics in astronomy and engineering
ḥāra: quarter, in a city
ḥāshiya, ḥawāshī (pl.): a gloss; commentary on commentary
al-hayʾa: astronomy with geometry
ḥayl: a part of the medieval science of mechanics
Ḥijj: the pilgrimage to Mecca
al-ḥikma: gnosis; wisdom literature
ḥisba: urban maintenance system
ḥiyal: devices for getting around the prohibition of changing interest; lit., tricks
ḥukamāʾ: specialists in *al-ḥikma*, or wisdom science
ḥulwān: annual tribute to the Porte from Egypt

iftāʾ: the issuing of legal opinions
ijāza, ijāzāt (pl.): an academic diploma
ijmāʿ: consensus as a method of resolving jurisprudential impasses, one of the roots of jurisprudence
ijtihād: reliance on self-judgment in theological matters
iktisāb: excessive profiteering
ilahīyāt: theology
ʿilm: scholastic science
ʿilm al-bayān: a part of rhetoric
ʿilm al-ḥadīth: the science of *ḥadīth* study
ʿilm al-manāẓir: spherical geometry
ʿilm al-qawāfa: the science of rhyme
ʿilm al-tashrīḥ: empirical anatomy
ʿilm al-waḍʿ: the rules of composition
iltizām, iltizāmāt (pl.): tax farm
imām: the continuator of the Prophet's divine nature
imāma: spiritual leadership of an *imām*
al-inshāʾ: letter writing of an elegant type; composition writing
al-inshād: recitation
ishrāq: illuminationist, the quietist way in mysticism
al-ishtiqāq: the deriving of words from their roots
isnād: chains of authorities used as proof
istidlāl: deduction

jabrīya: philosophical determinism
al-jadal: argumentation
jalāʾ: the activist way in Ṣūfism
jarr al-athqāl: gravity, as a branch of medieval mechanics
jihād: intense spiritual struggle; sometimes, holy war

kalām: speculative theology
karāmāt: divine blessings

kasb: gain
kashf: illumination
khalīfa, khulafā' (pl.): lieutenant in a Ṣūfī *ṭarīqa*
khalwa: seclusion; lit., a cell
khāṣṣ, khawāṣṣ (pl.): the elite
kiswa: the cover of the Maḥmal, part of the Egyptian expenditure for the upkeep of the holy cities
kuhl: a salve used to treat bienorrheal ophthalmia
kunya: a surname

laqab: an honorific name

mabādi': principles
madhhab: orthodox legal tradition
madrasa: a religious training school associated with a mosque
maḥall tijāra: a place of trade
mahdī: a charismatic leader claiming divine inspiration
Maḥmal: a sacred litter; see also *kiswa*
majlis, majālis (pl.): a salon
ma'mūrs: provincial administrators
manāqib: special virtues
maqām: a shrine
maqāma, maqāmāt (pl.): an Arabic prose genre
māristān: a hospital
al-maṣlaḥa: general welfare
mawlāna: the lord or master
mawlid: an annual religious celebration commemorating a birthdate
Mawlid al-Nabī: the celebration of the Prophet's birthday
mawqūf: willed
mawwāl: colloquial poetry often sung to the accompaniment of a reed pipe
al-mīqāt: the science of time measurement
mīrī: the state land tax
mollas: religious bureaucratic officials
muftī: a state functionary and leading theologian
muḥaddith, muḥaddithīn (pl.): a specialist in *ḥadīth* studies
muḥaqqiq, muḥaqqiqūn (pl.): one who takes an approach based on reason but within the bounds of the Sharī'a
muḥtasib, muḥtasibūn (pl.): a market inspector
mujtahid, mujtahidūn (pl.): one engaged in the practice of *ijtihād*, or self-judgment in jurisprudence
mulk: the secular aspect of rule in medieval political theory
multazim, multazimūn (pl.): a tax farmer
muqāṭa'a: a tax area
murattabāt: illegal fees paid to bureaucrats to retain land
murīd, murīdīn (pl.): a follower of the way of a Ṣūfī master
mursal: the chain of authorities for a given report back at least unto the second generation
murshid, murshidūn (pl.): a Ṣūfī guide, mentor
muṣṭalaḥ al-ḥadīth: lit., the study of the technical terms of *ḥadīth*
mutakallim, mutakallimūn (pl.): a student of speculative theology
muwashshaḥa, muwashshaḥāt (pl.): an Arabic poetry form

al-naḥt: the derivation of words
al-najāsa: ritual impurity
naqīb: a functionary
nasab: genealogy
nāẓir, nuẓẓār (pl.): a superintendent of *awqāf*
nisba: attribution of occupation

qāḍī: the chief Ottoman judicial official in Egypt; judge
qafīya: rhyme scheme
qaṣīda: a classical form of Arabic poetry
qiyās: analogy
qulluq: a police station

raḥīm: an adjective expressing God's attribute of mercifulness
raḥman: an adjective expressing God's attribute of mercifulness
ra'īs al-kuttāb: a high official of the central government
rajaz: a poetic metre
rak'a: the bending of the torso in prayer
raml: astrology
rāwī: a *ḥadīth* transmitter
al-ra'y: self-judgment, i.e., not drawn in a literal way from the Qur'ān or *sunna*
ribḥ: interest
rīf: the [Egyptian] countryside
riḥla: spiritual travel
riwāq: the administrative and residential component of al-Azhar
riwāya: recounting of *ḥadīth*, in contrast to *dirāya*
ruḥ: soul, vital spirit (in medicine)

ṣaḥāba: the Companions of the Prophet Muhammad
saj': rhymed prose
sarrājūn: servants mounted on horseback as a new form of soldiery
shahāda: a diploma of spiritual progress in this period
shawāhid: sources of words; lit., witnesses
shaykh: an instructor in a mosque; other meanings include tribal chief, or village headman
shishm: a salve used to treat bienorrheal ophthalmia
shuhadā': martyrs
shurūṭ: conditions, here in the study of *ḥadīth*
sijāda: as in phrase Shaykh al-Sijāda, i.e., leader of a Ṣūfī order
silsila: a chain; *silsila* literature may give the links between the life of a Ṣūfī *shaykh* and the founder of his order
sunna: part of *ḥadīth*; lit., custom, usage, tradition

tabarruk: an inner religious strengthening
tafsīr: commentary on the Qur'ān
tahdhīb: spiritual training
taḥrīf: inaccuracies
taknīya: the giving of an honorary name
talqīn: instruction
taqlīd: adherence to a tradition

taqrīr: a commentary on a gloss
tārīkh: history
ṭarīqa, ṭuruq (pl.): a mystical confraternity
tarjama, tarājim (pl.): the life of a notable individual
taṣawwuf: mysticism
tawakkul: trust in God, often manifested in withdrawal from earthly affairs
tawḥīd: theology of unity
ta'wīl: a derived meaning
tekke: a Ṣūfī monastery
ṭuhr: purity

'ulūm: scholastic sciences
umūr mawhūma: imaginary subjects
uṣūl al-fiqh: the science of the roots of jurisprudence, here used as *uṣūl al-dīn*
uṣūliyūn: orthodox jurisprudents who use the traditional roots of jurisprudence

wajba: forced labor erratically extracted in the precapitalist land system of Egypt
Wālī: a high urban functionary
waqf, awqāf (pl.): property deeded by will
waṭanīya, waṭanīyāt (pl.): patriotic themes; poetry of the bureaucratic age
wazīr: a plenipotentiary
wikālāt: wholesale trade houses
wilāya: guardianship

zaghal: an Arabic poetry form
zā'irjā: astrology
zāwiya: a Ṣūfī monastery
ziyārāt: visits for spiritual purposes to the tombs of the saints or the *ṣaḥāba*

Selected Bibliography

Reference Works

Al-Baghdādī, Isma'īl. *Hidāyat al-'ārifīn asmā' al-mu'allifīn āthār al-muṣannifīn*. 2 vols. with supplement. Istanbul: Maṭba'at al-Bahīya, 1955.

Al-Bayṭār, 'Abd al-Razzāq. *Ḥilyat al-bāshir fī tārīkh al-qarn al-thālith 'ashar*. 3 vols. Damascus: Majma' al-Lugha al-'Arabīya, 1961.

The major source for Syrian cultural life in the eighteenth and the first half of the nineteenth centuries. Supplemented by al-Shaṭṭī (see below).

Brockelmann, Carl. *Geschichte der Arabischen Litteratur*. 5 vols. Leiden: Brill, 1937–1949.

Al-Brussawi, Muhammad Tahir. *Uthmanliri muallifliri*. 2 vols. Istanbul, 1928/1346.

Al-Daghastānī, 'Alī Ḥilmī. *Fihris al-kutub al-Turkīya al-mawjūda fī'l-Kutubkhāna al-Khidīwīya*. Cairo: al-Maṭba'a al-'Uthmānīya, 1888/1306.

Dār al-Kutub al-Miṣrīya. *Fihris al-Khizāna al-Taymūrīya*. 4 vols. Cairo: Dār al-Kutub, 1948–1950.

———. *Fihris al-kutub al-'arabīya al-maḥfūẓa bi Dār al-Kutub al-Miṣrīya*. 8 vols. Cairo: Dār al-Kutub, 1924–1942.

———. *Fihris al-kutub al-'arabīya al-maḥfūẓa bi'l-kutubkhāna al-khidīwīya*. 7 vols. Cairo: Dār al-Kutub, 1887.

Ellul, Jean, *Index des communications et memoires publiés à l'Institut de l'Egypte, 1849–1952*. Cairo: Imprimerie de l'Institut Français d'Archaeologie Orientale, 1950.

Encyclopedia of Islam. 4 vols. Leiden: E. J. Brill, 1913–1937. 2 vols. Leiden: Brill, 1960–.

Al-Ḥasanī, 'Abd al-Ḥā'ī b. Fakhr al-dīn. *Nuzhat al-khawāṭir wa bahjat al-masāmi'wa'l-nawāẓir*. 10 vols. Hyderabad: Maṭba'a Dā'irat al-Ma'ārif, 1946.

Kahhāla, 'Umar Riḍā. *Mu'jam al-mu'allifīn wa tarājim al-'arabīya*. 15 vols. Damascus: al-Maktaba al-'Arabīya, 1937.

Al-Kattānī, 'Abd al-Ḥā'ī. *Fihris al-fahāris wa āthbāt wa mu'jam al-ma'ājim wa'l-mashīkhāt wa'l-musalsalāt*. 2 vols. Fās: al-Maṭba'a al-Jadīda, 1927/1346.

Al-Khālidī, Aḥmad Samīḥ. *Ahl al-'ilm bayn Miṣr wa Filisṭīn*. Jerusalem: al-Maṭba'a al-'Aṣrīya, n.d.

Contains biographies of eighteenth- and nineteenth-century Palestinian intellectuals.

Khalīfa, Ḥājjī. *Kashf al-ẓunūn 'an asāmī al-kutub wa'l-funūn*. 4 vols. Istanbul: Wikālat al-Ma'ārif, 1941.

Al-Khānī, 'Abd al-Majīd al-Khālidī. *Al-Anwār al-qudsīya fī manāqib al-Sādāt al-Naqshbandīya*. Cairo: Maṭba'at al-Sa'āda, 1926/1344.

A useful work for the lives of Naqshbandīs, whose order was the most important of the Ṣūfī orders of the Arab world between the seventeenth and nineteenth centuries.

Khūrī, Ibrāhīm. *Makhṭūṭāt Dār al-Kutub al-Ẓāhirīya: ʿIlm al-hayʾa.* Damascus: Maṭbaʿa Majmaʿ al-Lugha al-ʿArabīya, 1969.
Al-Marāghī, Abūʾl-Wafāʾ. *Fihris al-kutub al-mawjūda biʾl-maktaba al-Azharīya ilā 1952/1371.* 6 vols. Cairo: Maṭbaʿat al-Azhar, 1952.
Mukhtār, Muḥammad. *Al-Tawfīqāt al-ilhāmīya.* Cairo: Būlāq, 1898.
Al-Murādī, Muḥammad Khalīl. *Silk al-durar fī aʿyān al-qarn al-thānī ʿashar.* 4 vols. Cairo: Dār al-Ṭibāʿa al-Kubrā, 1874–1883.
Rawḍat al-madāris al-miṣrīya.
An important cultural journal of the last half of the nineteenth century.
Sezgin, Fuat. *Geschichte des Arabischen Schriftums.* Leiden: Brill, 1967.
Al-Shalabī, Dāʾūd. *Makhṭūṭāt al-Mawṣil.* Baghdad: Euphrates Press, 1927.
Al-Shaṭṭī, Muḥammad Jamīl. *Rawḍ al-bashar fī aʿyān Dimashq fīʾl-qarn al-thālith ʿashar.* Damascus: Dār al-Yaqza al-ʿArabīya liʾl-taʾlīf waʾl-tarjama waʾl-nashr, 1946.
Al-Shūrbajī, Jamāl al-dīn. *Qāʾima bi awāʾil al-maṭbūʿāt al-ʿarabīya al-maḥfūẓa bi Dār al-Kutub.* Cairo: Dār al-Kutub, 1963.
Among the most useful reference works for cultural history of the period from 1800 to 1850.
Al-Ziriklī, Khayr al-dīn. *Al-Aʿlām.* 3 vols. Cairo, 1928.

Unpublished Materials

ARABIC

Al-Alūsī, Shihāb al-dīn Maḥmūd. "Al-Ṣādiḥ bi shahīq al-nujūm ʿalā afnān tarjamat Shaykh al-Islām wa Walī al-Niʿam." Manuscript. Al-Azhar, Cairo. 724 al-Tārīkh, Abāẓa.
Al-ʿAṭṭār, Muḥammad. "Sharḥ ʿalā manẓūmat al-ʿAṭṭār fīʾl-tashrīḥ," 1813/1228. Manuscript. Al-Azhar, Cairo. 6509 Abāẓa.
Al-ʿAwaḍ, al-Ḥasan al-Badrī. "Al-Lawāʾiḥ al-anwārīya." Manuscript. Dār al-Kutub, Cairo. 1419 Adab.
Card File (Sijillāt) of Arabic Manuscripts in Istanbul. Dār al-Kutub, Cairo.
Lists the contents of twenty-eight mosque libraries in Istanbul.
Al-Dimardāsh, Amīr Aḥmad. "Kitāb al-durra al-muṣānaʾ fī akhbār al-kināna min mā waqaʿa fī dawlat al-mamalīk min al-sanājiq waʾl-dawla wa ʿawāʾidihim waʾl-bāshā." 2 vols. Manuscript. British Museum, London. No. 488 Arabic Manuscripts.
Al-Ḥusaynī, Aḥmad. "Sharḥ al-umm al-musammā bi murshid al-anām li birr umm al-imām." Manuscript. Dār al-Kutub, Cairo. 1411 al-Tārīkh, Taymūr.
Al-Majīd, ʿAbdullah b. al-ʿĀrif billāh Shaykh ʿAlī al-ʿUdwī. "Hadhihi risālat al-tabshīr fī faḍl man banī masjidān aw farrasha biʾl-ḥaṣīr," 1844. Manuscript. Al-Azhar, Cairo. 430 Majāmīʿ, no. 3.
Al-Sijāʿī, Aḥmad. "Al-Ruwwād al-naḍīra fī mā yataʿalliq biʾl-bayt al-bashīr al-nadhīr." Manuscript. Al-Azhar, Cairo. Majāmīʿ 430, no. 3.
al-Zabīdī, Muḥammad Murtaḍā. "Tuḥfat al-qamāʿīl fī madīḥ Shaykh al-ʿArab Ismaʿīl," 1770/1184. Manuscript. Dār al-Kutub, Cairo. 616 Taymūr Adab, 1770/1184.

EUROPEAN LANGUAGES

Algar, Hamid. "Shaykh Muḥammad As'ad and the Naqshbandī Ṭarīqat in the Turkish Republic." Report. Middle East Studies Association of North America, Conference no. 5, 1971.

Darwīsh, 'Abdullah 'Abd al-Fattāḥ. "Al-Khalīl Ibn Aḥmad and the Evolution of Arabic Lexicography." Doctoral dissertation, School of Oriental and African Studies, University of London, 1955.

Digby, Simon. "Changing Horizons of Thought in Eighteenth-Century Muslim India." Conference paper. Colloquium on the Muslim World in the Eighteenth Century, Philadelphia, 1971.

Great Britain. Public Record Office. Foreign Office, Egypt, Series 142, vol. I (1805).

Kuhnke, Laverne. "Resistance and Response to Modernization: Preventive Medicine and Social Control in Egypt, 1825–1850." Doctoral dissertation, History Department, University of Chicago, March 1971.

Marsot, Afaf Lutfi al-Sayyid. "The Role of the '*Ulamā*' through the Nineteenth Century." Conference paper. American University in Cairo—Columbia University Conference, Cairo, 1968.

A pioneering article on the '*ulamā*' of Egypt.

Moreh, S. "The Sociological Role of the Ṣūfī Shaykh in Eighteenth-Century Egypt." Doctoral dissertation, School of Oriental and African Studies, University of London, 1964.

Verdery, Richard. "'Abd al-Raḥman al-Jabartī as a Source for the Early History of Muḥammad 'Alī, 1807–1821." Doctoral dissertation, Oriental Studies, Princeton University, 1967.

Walz, Terence. "The Trade between Egypt and Bilād As-Sūdān." Doctoral dissertation, History Department, Boston University, 1974.

Published Materials

ARABIC

'Abd al-Karīm, Aḥmad 'Izzat. *Tārīkh al-ta'līm fī aṣr Muḥammad 'Alī.* Cairo: Maktabat al-Nahḍa al-Miṣrīya, 1928.

'Abd al-Raḥīm, 'Abd al-Raḥman 'A. *Al-Dawla al-su'ūdīya al-ūlā.* Cairo, 1969.

The most detailed study of the rise of the Wahhābīs.

———. "Dirāsa nuṣṣīya li'l-kitāb hazz al-quhūf fī sharḥ qaṣīdat Abī Shadūf." *Al-Majalla al-Miṣrīya li'l-Dirāsāt al-Tārīkhīya* 20 (1973): 287–316.

A study of a literary source for the study of the Egyptian countryside in the seventeenth century.

———. *Al-Rīf al-Miṣrī fī'l-qarn al-thāmin 'ashar.* Cairo, 1972.

'Abd al-Salām, Ḥasan. *Dhakīrat al-'Aṭṭār aw tadhkarat Dā'ūd fī rawīyatihi fī 'ilm al-ḥadīth.* Cairo, 1947.

'Abduh, Ibrāhīm. *Tārīkh al-Waqā'i' al-Miṣrīya.* Cairo: al-Maṭba'a al-Amīrīya, 1942.

Al-'Allāf, 'Abd al-Karīm. *Al-Ṭarab 'inda-l-'arab.* Baghdad: Maṭba'at As'ad, 1963.

One of the few works containing material on Arabic music in the later Middle Ages.

Al-ʿĀmilī, Muḥammad Bahāʾ ad-dīn. *Kashkūl.* Cairo: Maṭbaʿat al-ʿĀmira al-Ḥamīdīya al-Miṣrīya, 1916.

Al-Amīr, Muḥammad. *Ḥāshiya ʿalā sharḥ ʿAbd al-Salām li jawharat al-tawḥīd liʾl-Laqānī.* Cairo: Muṣṭafā al-Bābā al-Ḥalabī, 1948.

———. *Ḥāshiya ʿalā sharḥ matn mughnī al-labīb.* Cairo: al-Maṭbaʿa al-Sharqīya, 1874/1299.

———. *Ḥāshiyat al-Amīr ʿalā sharḥ al-azharīya.* Cairo: al-Maṭbaʿat al-Amīrīya, 1869/1286.

———. *Sharḥ majmūʿ Muḥammad al-Amīr.* 2 vols. Cairo: al-Maṭbaʿa al-Khayrīya, 1884/1302.

Among the most influential works on Mālikī *fiqh* until the early twentieth century.

Anīs, Muḥammad. "Ḥaqāʾiq ʿan ʿAbd al-Raḥman al-Jabartī." *Al-Majalla al-Tārīkhīya* 9 (1962): 66–115.

ʿĀnūtī, Usāma. *Al-Ḥarakat al-adabīya fīʾl-Shām fīʾl-qarn al-thāmin ʿashar.* Beirut: St. Joseph University Press, 1971.

The first study of Syrian intellectual life in the eighteenth century.

Al-Bahī, Muḥammad. *Al-ʿIlmānīya waʾl-Islām bayn al-fihr waʾl-taṭbīq.* Cairo: Dār al-Ṭibāʿa al-Muḥammadīya, n.d.

Al-Bājūrī, Ibrāhīm. *Tuḥfat al-murīd ʿalā jawharat al-tawḥīd.* Cairo: Muṣṭafā al-Bābā al-Ḥalabī, 1939.

Al-Bakrī, Muṣṭafā. *Risāla fī rudd ʿalā manʿ al-ziyāra li qubūr al-anbiyāʾ waʾl-awliyāʾ.* Cairo: Muṣṭafā al-Bābā al-Ḥalabī, 1932/1351.

Al-Bakrī, Tawfīq. *Bayt al-Sādāt.* Cairo, n.d.

The main source for the study of the *mashāyikh al-sijāda* of the Wafāʾīya.

———. *Bayt al-Ṣiddīq.* Cairo: Maṭbaʿat al-Muʿīd, 1905–1906/1323.

The main source for the study of the *mashāyikh al-sijāda* of the Bakrīya.

Al-Balīdī, Aḥmad. *Sharḥ al-Balīdī ʿalā al-maqālāt.* Cairo: al-Maṭbaʿa al-Khayrīya, 1910.

An example of eighteenth-century science in Egypt.

Al-Dajjānī, Aḥmad Ṣidqī. *Al-Ḥaraka al-ṣānūsīya nashʾatuhā wa numūʾuhā fīʾl-qarn al-tāsiʿ ʿashar.* Beirut: Dār al-Lubnān liʾl-Ṭibāʿa waʾl-Nashr, 1967.

Compare to the older work by Muḥammad Fūʾād Shukrī, which is much more difficult to obtain.

Al-Darwīsh, ʿAlī Efendī. *Al-Ishʿār bi ḥamīd al-ashʿār.* Cairo, 1855.

Al-Disūqī, ʿUmar. *Fīʾl-adab al-ḥadīth.* 2 vols. Cairo: Maṭbaʿat Lajnat al-Bayān al-ʿArabī, 1954.

Fahmī, Naʿīm Zakī. *Ṭuruq al-tijāra al-duwalīya wa maḥaṭṭātuhā bayn al-sharq waʾl-gharb.* Cairo: al-Hayʾa al-Miṣrīya, 1973.

Ghaliunjī, Paul. *Ibn al-Nafīs.* Cairo: al-Dār al-Miṣrīya liʾl-Taʾlīf waʾl-Nashr, n.d.

Ḥāmid, Rāʾūf ʿAbbās. *Al-Niẓām al-ijtimāʿī fī Miṣr fī ẓill al-milkīya al-zirāʿīya al-kabīra, 1837–1914.* Cairo: Dār al-Fikr al-Ḥadīth liʾl-Ṭibāʿa waʾl-Nashr, 1973.

A socioeconomic analysis drawing on archival materials.

Ḥasan, Muḥammad ʿAbd al-Ghanī. *Ḥasan al-ʿAṭṭār.* Cairo: Dār al-Maʿārif, 1968.

The first and only book on Ḥasan al-ʿAṭṭār. It is especially useful for the poetry of al-ʿAṭṭār, which it reprints. The author is himself a poet.

Al-Ḥifnāwī, Muḥammad b. Sālim. *Al-Thamāra al-bahīya fīʾl-ṣaḥāba al-badrīya.* Introduction by Muṣṭafā ʿAbd al-Rāziq. Cairo: Maṭbaʿat al-Anwār, 1945.

Al-Ḥulwānī, Aḥmad. *Al-Sumūw al-rūḥī fīʾl-adab al-ṣūfī.* Cairo: Muṣṭafā al-Bābā al-Ḥalabī, 1948.

A very useful work for identifying the influence of mystical thought in modern Egyptian poetry.

Ibn al-ʿArabī, Muḥiy ad-dīn. *Al-Futūḥāt al-Makkiya*. Beirut: Dār al-Ṣādir, 1968.

Ibn Suʿūd, ʿAbd al-Salām. *Dalīl muʾarrikh al-Maghrib al-Aqṣāʾ*. Ribāṭ: Dār al-Kitāb, n.d.

Al-Jabartī, ʿAbd al-Raḥman. *ʿAjāʾib al-āthār fīʾl-tarājim waʾl-akhbār*. 4 vols. Cairo: Būlāq, 1879.

See also the French translation, *Merveilles biographiques et historiques*. 9 vols. Cairo, 1888–1898.

———. *Maẓhar al-taqdīs fī dhahāb dawlat al-faransīs*. Cairo: Lajnat al-Bayān al-ʿArabī, 1969.

Karāma, Buṭrus. *Sajʿ al-ḥamāma aw dīwān al-maghfūr lahu al-muʿallim Buṭrus Karāma*. Istanbul: Maṭbaʿat al-Jawāʾib, 1886.

Al-Khashshāb, Ismaʿīl. *Dīwān al-Khashshāb*. Istanbul: Maṭbaʿat al-Jawāʾib, 1884.

An important literary work of the early nineteenth century. The poems to al-Zabīdī form the most important part.

Khayret Efendī. *Riyāḍ al-kutabāʾ wa ḥiyāḍ al-udabāʾ*. Cairo: Būlāq, 1878.

Al-Kilānī, Muḥammad Sayyid. *Al-Adab al-Miṣrī fī ẓill al-ḥukm al-ʿUthmānī*. Cairo: Dār al-Qawmīya al-ʿArabīya liʾl-Ṭibaʿa, 1965.

The first important study of the literature of Ottoman Egypt.

———. *Fī rubūʿ al-Azbakīya: Dirāsa adabīya, tārīkhīya, ijtimāʿīya*. Cairo: Dār al-ʿArab, 1958–1959.

An excellent short work on the social history of literature, focusing on the famous suburb of al-Azbakīya in Cairo.

Kratchkowski, Ignatius. *Ḥayat Muḥammad ʿIyād al-Ṭanṭāwī*. Cairo: al-Majlis al-Aʿlā li Riʿāyat al-Funūn waʾl-Ādāb, 1964.

Al-Madanī, Muḥammad Ẓāfir. *Al-Nūr al-sāṭiʿ waʾl-burhān al-qāṭiʿ*. Cairo: 1883.

Al-Maghribī, Ismaʿīl ʿAbdullah. *Kitāb nūr al-waḍʿ fī manāqib wa karāmāt ʿumdat al-awlīyāʾ*. Cairo: Maṭbaʿat al-Ṣādiq al-Khayrīya, 1928.

Maḥmūd, ʿAlī b. al-Khalwatī. *Hadhā minḥat al-majīd ʿalā sayf al-murīd*. Cairo: al-Maṭbaʿa al-Ḥusaynīya, 1911.

Al-Majdī, Ṣāliḥ. *Ḥilyat al-zamān bi manāqib khādim al-watan, sīrat Rifāʿa Rāfiʿī al-Ṭahṭāwī*. Cairo: Muṣṭafā al-Bābā al-Ḥalabī, 1958.

Al-Maʿlūf, ʿIsā Iskandār. *Al-Usra al-ʿarabīya al-mushthara biʾl-ṭibb al-ʿarabīya wa ashhara al-makhṭūṭāt al-ṭibbīya al-ʿarabīya*. Beirut: al-Maṭbaʿa al-Adabīya, 1935.

Mandūr, Muḥammad. *Al-Naqd waʾl-nuqqād al-muʿāṣirūn*. Cairo: Maṭbaʿa Miṣr, n.d.

Al-Marṣafī, Ḥusayn. *Al-Kilām al-thamān*. Cairo: Maṭbaʿat al-Jumhūrīya, 1903.

———. *Al-Waṣīla al-adabīya*. 2 vols. Cairo: Maṭbaʿat al-Madāris al-Mālikīya, 1877.

Mubārak, ʿAlī. *ʿAlām al-dīn*. 4 vols. Alexandria, 1299.

———. *Al-Khiṭaṭ al-tawfīqīya al-jadīda*. Vols. I–XX. Cairo: al-Maṭbaʿa al-Kubrā, 1886–1888.

Mursī, Ṣāliḥ. "Thawrat al-ʿumyān." *Al-Hilāl* 78 (1970): 76–84.

Al-Nashshār ʿAlī Sāmī. *Manāhij al-baḥth ʿinda mufakkirī al-Islām wa naqd al-Muslimīn liʾl-manṭiq al-Arisṭū*. Cairo: Dār al-Fikr al-ʿArabī, 1947.

Qasṭūn, Wadīʿ ʿAbdullah. *Al-Afrānj fī Ḥalab fīʾl-qarn al-thāmin ʿashar*. Aleppo: Maṭbaʿat al-Ḍad, 1968.

Al-Rāfiʿī, ʿAbd al-Raḥman. *Shuʿarāʾ al-waṭanīya, tarājimuhum wa shiʿruhum al-waṭanī*. Cairo: Maktabat al-Nahḍa al-Miṣrīya, 1954.

Ramaḍān, ʿAbd al-Jawwād. "Bayn al-ʿAṭṭār waʾl-Khashshāb min udabāʾ al-qarn al-tāsiʿ ʿashar." *Majallat al-Azhar* 19 (1948): 139–144, 220–225.

Al-Rashīdī, Aḥmad Ḥasan. *Bahjat al-ruʾasāʾ fī iʿlāj amrāḍ al-nisāʾ*. Cairo: Būlāq, 1845.

One of many early texts in medicine, an area which has yet to be studied.

Al-Riḍwān, Abūʾl-Futūḥ. *Tārīkh maṭbaʿat Būlāq*. Cairo: al-Maṭbaʿa al-Amīrīya, 1953.

Ritter, Helmut, ed. *Asrār al-balāgha (The Mysteries of Eloquence of ʿAbd al-Qāhir al-Jurjānī)*. Istanbul: Istanbul Government Press, 1954.

Al-Ṣabbān, Muḥammad. *Ḥāshiya ʿalā sharḥ Mullā Ḥanafī ʿalā al-ādāb al-ʿaḍudīya*. Cairo: al-Maṭbaʿa al-Ẓāhira, 1908.

———. *Ḥāshiyat al-Ṣabbān ʿalā sharḥ al-Ashmūnī ʿalā alfīyat Ibn Mālik*. 2 vols. Cairo: Maṭbaʿat al-Saʿāda, 1924.

This was a major grammar text of the eighteenth century used in al-Azhar until the twentieth century.

———. *Kitāb isʿāf al-rāghibīn fī sīrat al-Muṣṭafā wa faḍāʾil ahl al-bayt*. Cairo: al-Maṭbaʿa al-Azharīya, 1929.

Al-Ṣaʿīdī, ʿAbd al-Mitʿāl. *Tārīkh al-iṣlāḥ fīʾl-Azhar*. Cairo, 1947.

Salām, Muṣṭafā Yūsuf al-Shādhilī. *Jawāhir al-iṭṭlāʿ wa durr al-intifāʿ ʿalā matn Ibn Shajāʿ*. Cairo: al-Tadamun al-Ikhwī Ḥāfiẓ Muḥammad Dāʾūd, 1931.

This work contains the texts of ʿAlī al-Bayyūmī.

Sāmī, Amīn. *Taqwīm al-Nīl*. 2 vols. Cairo, 1928.

Al-Sānūsī, Muḥammad. *Shifāʾ al-ṣadr bi ārāʾ al-masāʾil al-ʿashar*. Cairo: Dār al-Maʿārif, 1966.

Al-Sharqāwī, ʿAbdullah. *Fatḥ al-mubdī bi sharḥ mukhtaṣar al-Zabīdī*. Cairo: Muṣṭafā al-Bābā al-Ḥalabī, 1955.

A major work of the post-Napoleonic period in *ḥadīth*. Useful for research in a wide range of fields, including economy and medicine.

———. *Tuḥfat al-nāẓirīn fī man wālī Miṣr fī wilāyat al-Salāṭīn*. Cairo, 1892.

Shaybūb, Khalīl. *ʿAbd al-Raḥman al-Jabartī*. Cairo: Dār al-Maʿārif, 1948.

The outstanding work on the cultural context of al-Jabartī.

Al-Shayyāl, Jamāl al-dīn. *Al-Ḥarakāt al-iṣlāḥīya wa marākiz al-thaqāfa*. 2 vols. Cairo: Arab League, 1958.

———. *Tārīkh al-tarjama waʾl-ḥarakat al-thaqāfīya fī ʿaṣr Muḥammad ʿAlī*. Cairo: Maṭbaʿat al-Iʿtimād, 1951.

———. *Al-Taʾrīkh waʾl-muʾarrikhūn fī Miṣr*. Cairo: Maktabat al-Nahḍa al-Miṣrīya, 1958.

An English translation is *A History of Egyptian Historiography in the Nineteenth Century*. Alexandria: Alexandria University Press, 1962.

Shihāb al-dīn, Muḥammad. *Dīwān Muḥammad Shihāb al-dīn*. Cairo: Muḥammad Shāhīn, 1860/1277.

Al-Shubrāwī, ʿAbdullah. *Al-Itḥāf bi ḥubb al-ashrāf*. Cairo: Muṣṭafā al-Bābā al-Ḥalabī, 1900.

Shukrī, Muḥammad Fūʾād. *Al-Sānūsīya, dīn wa dawla*. Cairo: Dār al-Fikr al-ʿArabī, 1948.

Al-Taftazānī, Abūʾl-Wafāʾ al-Ghunaymī. "Al-Ṭuruq al-ṣūfīya fī Miṣr." *Majallat Kullīyat al Ādāb* 25 (1963): 55–85.

Al-Ṭahṭāwī, Rifāʿa. *Al-Kunūz al-Mukhtār fī kashf al-arāḍī waʾl-buḥār*. Cairo: Maktabat al-Ṭubḥīya, 1835.

This is perhaps the first sustained presentation of the Copernican theory in the Arab world.

———. *Bidāyat al-qudamā'*. Cairo: Būlāq, 1838.
———. *Manāhij al-albāb al-miṣrīya fī mabāhigh al-adab al-'aṣrīya*. Cairo: Maṭba'at Sharīkat al-Raghā'ib, 1912/1330.
———. *Nihāyat al-i'jāz fī sīrat sākin al-Ḥijāz*. Cairo: Maṭba'at al-Madāris al-Mālikīya, 1876.
A work of equal importance for sociology as the author's *Manāhij*.
———. *Takhlīṣ al-ibrīz fī talkhīṣ Bārīz*. Cairo: Muṣṭafā al-Bābā al-Ḥalabī, 1958.
Taymūr, Aḥmad, ed. *A'lām al-fikr al-islāmī fī'l-'aṣr al-ḥadīth*. Cairo: al-Lajna al-Taymūrīya, 1967.
Tizīnī, Ṭīb. *Mashrū' rawīya jadīda ilā al-fikr al-'arabī*. Damascus: Dār Dimashq, 1971.
A major study of the history of Arabic philosophy which appears to follow the "Frankfurt School."
Ṭūsun, 'Umar. *Al-Ba'thāt al-'ilmīya fī 'ahd Muḥammad 'Alī*. Alexandria: Maṭba'a Ṣalāḥ al-dīn, 1934.
Wali'ullah, Shāh. *Ḥujjat allah al-bāligha*. Cairo: Dār al-Kutub al-Ḥadītha, n.d.
Al-Waqā'i' al-Miṣrīya. Cairo. 1828–.
The official newspaper, published irregularly in the early years.
Al-Zabīdī, Muḥammad Murtaḍā. *Ḥikmat al-ishrāq ilā kuttāb al-āfāq*, 1770/1184. Edited by 'Abd al-Salām Hārūn. Baghdad: Maktabat al-Mathāna, 1954.
———. *Itḥāf al-sādāt al-muttiqīn bi sharḥ asrār iḥyā' 'ulūm al-dīn*. 12 vols. Cairo: al-Maṭba'a al-Maymanīya, 1893/1311.
———. *Tāj al-'arūs min sharḥ jawāhir al-qāmūs*. 10 vols. Banghāzī: Dār Lībīya li'l-Nashr wa'l-Tawzī', n.d.
This should be taken with al-Jabartī's *'Ajā'ib* as one of the two major sources for eighteenth-century Egyptian culture. It is a prodigious work of scholarship, far exceeding the bounds of lexicography.
Al-Zayyātī, Abū'l-Qāsim. *Al-Turjumān al-kubrā*. Ribāṭ: Wizārat al-Anbā', 1967.

EUROPEAN LANGUAGES

Abdel-Malek, Anouar. *Idéologie et renaissance nationale de l'Egypte moderne*. Paris: Editions Anthropos, 1969.
Abdesselem, Ahmed. *Les historiens tunisiens des XVIIè, XVIIIè, et XIX siècles: Essai d'histoire culturelle*. Paris: Klincksieck, 1973.
Abdulhak, Adnan. *La Science chez les Turcs ottomans*. Paris: Maisonneuve, 1939.
Abir, M. "The 'Arab Rebellion' of Amīr Ghālib of Mecca, 1788–1813." *Middle East Studies* 5 (1972): 191–220.
Amin, Samir. *Accumulation on a World Scale: A Critique of the Theory of Underdevelopment*. New York: Monthly Review Press, 1974.
Ayalon, David. "Studies in al-Jabartī, I: Notes on the Transformation of Mamlūk Society in Egypt under the Ottomans." *Journal of the Economic and Social History of the Orient* 3 (1960): 148–174, 275–325.
Badawi, M. M. "Al-Bārūdī, Precursor of the Modern Arabic Poetic Revival." *Der Welt des Islams* 22 (1969): 228–244.
Baer, Gabriel. "Urbanization in Egypt, 1820–1907." In *The Beginnings of Modernization in the Middle East in the Nineteenth Century*, edited by W. R. Polk and R. L. Chambers, pp. 155–171. Chicago: University of Chicago Press, 1968.

Baldwin, George. *Memorial Relating to the Trade in Slaves.* Alexandria, 1789.
Bannerth, Ernst. "La Khalwatiyya en Egypte." *Mélanges Institut Dominicains Etudes Orientales* 8 (1964–1966): 1–75.
Bergeron, L., ed. *L'Ankylose de l'économie Mediterranéenne au XVIIIième et au début du XIXième siècles: Le rôle de l'agriculture.* Nice: Centre de la Mediterranée Moderne et Contemporaine, 1973.
Berkes, Niyazi. *The Development of Secularism in Turkey.* Montreal: McGill University Press, 1964.
Bianchi, T.-X. *Notice sur un ouvrage d'anatomie et de médecin.* Paris: L.-T. Cellat, 1821.
———. "Recueil de Fetvas." *Journal Asiatique* 1st ser., 2 (1822): 3–16.
Birge, John Kingley. *The Bektashi Order of Dervishes.* Hartford: Hartford Connecticut Seminary, 1937.
Bombaci, Alessio. *Histoire de la littérature turque.* Paris: Klincksieck, 1968.
Bosworth, C. E. "A Maqāma on Secretaryship: Al-Qalqashandī's *Al-Kawākib al-durrīya fī manāqib al-badrīya.*" *Bulletin of the School of Oriental and African Studies* 27 (1964): 291–299.
Brown, John P. *The Dervishes or Oriental Spiritualism.* London: Trubner and Company, 1868.
Burckhardt, John. *Arabic Proverbs, or the Manners and Customs of the Modern Egyptians.* London: Bernard Quaritch, 1875.
———. *Notes on Bedouins and Wahabys.* London: Henry Coulbourn and Richard Bentley, 1830.
———. *Travels in Arabia.* Reprint, London: Cass, 1968.
C.-D., N. "L'Aristocratie religieuse en Egypte." *Revue du Monde Musulmane* 2 (1908): 241–283.
This article deals with the Wafāʾīya and the Bakrīya.
Cachia, Pierre. *Ṭaha Ḥusayn: His Place in the Egyptian Literary Renaissance.* London: Luzacs and Company, 1956.
Capper, James. *Observations on the Passage to India through Egypt.* London: Faden, 1785.
Charles-Roux, François. *Bonaparte, gouverneur de l'Egypte.* Paris: Plon, 1935.
———. *Les Origines de l'expédition de l'Egypte.* Paris: Plon, 1910.
Le Chatelier, A. *Les Confréries musulmanes du Hedjaz.* Paris: Ernest Leroux, 1887.
Chejne, Anwar. *The Arabic Language: Its Role in History.* Minneapolis: University of Minnesota Press, 1969.
Choiseul-Gouffier, L. P. *La France en l'Orient sous Louis XVI.* Paris: Alphonse Piscard, 1887.
Colloque Internationale sur l'Histoire du Caire. Cairo: Ministry of Culture, 1972.
Copies of Original Letters from the Army of General Bonaparte in Egypt. London: J. Wright, 1798.
Daressy, M. G. "Les maladies fréquentes au Caire au XVIIe siècle." *Bulletin de l'Institut de l'Egypte* 5 (1923): 67–82.
Demeerseman, A. "Une mémoire célèbre qui préfigure l'évolution moderne en Islam." [*Bulletin de l'*] *Institut des Belles Lettres Arabes* 18 (1955): 5–33.
Dény, J. "Quatre lèttres de Mehmet Ali de l'Egypte." In *Mélanges offerts à Wm. Marçais*, pp. 125–146. Paris: Maisonneuve, 1950.
———. *Le Sommaire des archives turques au Caire.* Cairo: La Société Royale de Géographie de l'Egypte, 1930.

Depont, Octave, and X. Copolani. *Les Confréries religieuses musulmanes.* Algiers, 1897.
Déscription de l'Egypte—Etat Moderne. 4 vols. Paris, 1809–1812.
Dodwell, Henry. *The Founder of Modern Egypt.* Cambridge: At the University Press, 1967.
Douin, G. "Le Carrosse de Mohamed Bey." *Bulletin de l'Institut de l'Egypte* 8 (1926): 165–184.
Elgood, Cyril. "Medicine of the Prophet." *Osiris* 14 (1962): 33–192.
The main source on al-Suyūṭī's medicine.
Farhat, Germanos. *Dictionnaire arabe.* Marseilles: Imprimerie Carnaud, 1849.
Fazlur-Rahman, I. *Islamic Methodology in History.* Karachi: Central Institute of Islamic Research, 1965.
Forbin, Count de. *Travels in Egypt, Being a Continuation of Travels in the Holy Land.* London: Sir Richard Philipps and Company, 1819.
Foucault, Michel. *Madness and Civilization: A History of Insanity in the Age of Reason.* New York: Random House, 1973.
Frank, A. G. *Capitalism and Underdevelopment in Latin America.* New York: Modern Reader, 1969.
Gibb, H. A. R. "Studies in Contemporary Arabic Literature, IV: The Egyptian Novel." *Bulletin of the School of Oriental and African Studies* 7 (1933–1935): 1–22.
Gibb, Sir Hamilton, and Harold Bowen. *Islamic Society and the West.* Vol. I, parts 1 and 2. Oxford: Oxford University Press, 1950.
Goldmann, Lucien. *Immanuel Kant.* London: NLB, 1971.
———. *The Philosophy of the Enlightenment.* London: Routledge and Kegan Paul, 1973.
Goldziher, Ignace. *Muhammadan Studies.* Edited by S. M. Stern. 2 vols. London: George Allen and Unwin, 1971.
Guémard, Gabriel. *Aventuriers Mamluk de l'Egypte.* Alexandria: Société Royale d'Archaeologie d'Alexandrie, 1928.
———. "Les Auxiliares de l'armée de Bonaparte." *Bulletin de l'Institut de l'Egypte* 9 (1926): 1–17.
———. "De l'Armement et de l'équipement des Mamelouks." *Bulletin de l'Institut de l'Egypte* 8 (1926): 1–19.
———. "Essai d'histoire de l'Institut de l'Egypte." *Bulletin de l'Institut de l'Egypte* 6 (1924): 43–84.
———. *Histoire et bibliographie critique de la Commission de Science et Arts de l'Institut de l'Egypte.* Cairo: Paul Barbey, 1936.
———. "Trois témoins de la campagne de l'Egypte, Lascaris et Corancel en Syrie, Jaubert en Perse et le rêve Oriental de Bonaparte." *Bulletin de l'Institut de l'Egypte* 7 (1925): 9–31.
———. *Une Oeuvre française: Les réformes en l'Egypte d'Ali Bey el-Kebir à Mehemet ʿAli, 1760–1848.* Cairo: Paul Barbey, 1936.
Gupta, Ashin Das. "Trade and Politics in the Eighteenth Century in India." In *Islam and the Trade of Asia*, edited by D. S. Richards, pp. 181–215. Oxford: Bruno Cassirer, 1970.
Gurvitch, Georges. *The Social Frameworks of Knowledge.* New York: Harper and Row, 1971.
Guys, Henri. *Esquisse de l'état politique et commerciale de la Syrie.* Paris: Chez France, 1862.

Haddad, Robert. *Syrian Christians in Muslim Society.* Princeton: Princeton University Press, 1970.

Hamont, P. N. *L'Egypte sous Mehmet Ali.* 2 vols. Paris: Leautey et Lecointe, 1843.

Hasluck, F. W. *Christianity and Islam under the Sultans.* 2 vols. Oxford: Clarendon Press, 1929.

Hayyim, J. Cohen. "The Economic Background and the Secular Occupations of Muslim Jurisprudents and Traditionalists in the Classical Period of Islam until the Middle of the Eleventh Century." *Journal of the Economic and Social History of the Orient* 13 (1970): 16–61.

Heyd, Uriel. "The Ottoman Ulema and Westernization in the Time of Selim III and Mahmud II." In *Studies in Islamic History and Civilization*, pp. 48–104. Jerusalem: Magnes Press, 1961.

Heyworth-Dunne, J. "Arabic Literature in Egypt in the Eighteenth Century with Some Reference to the Poetry and the Poets." *Bulletin of the School of Oriental and African Studies* 9 (1937–1939): 675–689.

———. *Introduction to the History of Education in Modern Egypt.* London: Cass, 1967.

———. "Rifāʿah Badawī Rāfiʿī al-Ṭahṭāwī: The Egyptian Revivalist." *Bulletin of the School of Oriental and African Studies* 10 (1940–1942): 399–415.

Hobsbawm, Eric J. *The Age of Revolution.* Cleveland: World Publishing Company, 1962.

———. "The Crisis of the Seventeenth Century." In *Crisis in Europe*, edited by Trevor Ashton, pp. 5–58. New York: Doubleday Press, 1967.

Holt, Peter M. "Al-Jabartī's Introduction to the History of Ottoman Egypt." *Bulletin of the School of Oriental and African Studies* 25 (1962): 38–52.

———., ed. *Political and Social Change in Modern Egypt.* London: Oxford University Press, 1967.

Hopwood, Derek. *The Russian Presence in Syria and Palestine, 1843–1914.* Oxford: Clarendon Press, 1969.

Ibn Khaldūn. *The Muqaddimah.* Edited by Franz Rosenthal. 3 vols. New York: Bollingen Foundation, 1958.

Issa, Hossam. *Capitalisme et sociétés anonymes en l'Egypte.* Paris: R. Pichon et R. Durand-Auzias, 1970.

Issawi, Charles. *The Economic History of the Middle East, 1800–1914.* Chicago: University of Chicago Press, 1966.

Jargy, Simon. *La Musique arabe.* Paris: Presses Universitaires de France, 1971.

Juynboll, G. H. A. *The Authenticity of the Tradition Literature—Discussion in Modern Egypt.* Leyden: Brill, 1969.

Khalīfa, Ḥājjī. *The Balance of Truth, by Kātib Chelebi.* Translated by G. L. Lewis. London: Allen and Unwin, 1957.

Kissling, Hans Joachim. "Aus der Geschichte des Chelvetijje-Ordens." *Zeitschrift der Deutsches Morgenlander Gesellschaft* 103 (1953): 233–289.

Kopf, L. "Religious Influences on Mediaeval Arabic Philology." *Studia Islamica* 5 (1956): 33–59.

Lampton, Ann K. S. "Persian Trade under the Early Qajars." In *Islam and the Trade of Asia*, edited by D. S. Richards, pp. 215–244. Oxford: Bruno Cassirer, 1970.

Landau, Rom. *The Philosophy of Ibn al-ʿArabī.* London: George Allen and Unwin, 1959.

Landberg, Carlo Von. *Primeurs Arabes.* Leiden: Brill, 1886.

Lane, Edward W. *Arabic-English Lexicon.* 9 vols. London: Williams and Norgate, 1863.

———. *The Manners and Customs of the Modern Egyptians.* Reissue, London: J. M. Dent, 1963.
———. *A Thousand and One Nights.* 3 vols. London: C. Knight and Company, 1839–1841.
Laoust, Henri. *Contribution à une étude de la méthodologie canonique de Taqī al-dīn Aḥmad b. Taimīya.* Cairo: Imprimerie de l'Institut Français d'Archaeologie Orientale, 1939.
———. *Essai sur les doctrines sociales et politiques de Taqī al-dīn Aḥmad b. Taimīya.* Cairo: Imprimerie de l'Institut Français d'Archaeologie Orientale, 1939.
Larousse, Pierre. *Grand dictionnaire universel du XIX siècle.* Paris: Administration du grand dictionnaire universel, 1875.
Levey, M. *The Medical Formulary of al-Samarqandī.* Philadelphia: University of Pennsylvania Press, 1967.
Livingston, John W. "ʿAlī Bey al-Kabīr and the Jews." *Middle East Studies* 7 (May 1971): 221–229.
———. "The Rise of Shaykh al-Balad ʿAlī Bey al-Kabīr: A Study of the Accuracy of the Chronicle of al-Jabartī." *Bulletin of the School of Oriental and African Studies* 33 (1970): 283–294.
Lukacs, George. *History and Class Consciousness.* Cambridge, Mass.: Massachusetts Institute of Technology Press, 1972.
Lusignan. *A History of the Revolt of Ali Bey against the Ottoman Porte.* London, 1784.
Madkour, Ibrāhīm. *L'Organon d'Aristote dans le monde arabe.* Paris: J. Vrin, 1969.
Marcel, Jean-Joseph. *Contes du Cheykh el-Mahdy, traduite de l'arabe.* 3 vols. 2d ed. Paris, 1835.
A literary work of the early nineteenth century which has not yet been studied.
Marsot, Afaf Lutfi al-Sayyid. "The Political and Economic Functions of the ʿUlamāʾ in the 18th Century." *Journal of the Economic and Social History of the Orient* 16 (1973): 130–154.
———. "The Role of the ʿUlamāʾ in Egypt during the Early Nineteenth Century." In *Social Change in Modern Egypt,* edited by P. M. Holt, pp. 264–280. Oxford: Oxford University Press, 1968.
Martin, B. G. "Notes sur l'origine de la ṭarīqa des Tījānīya et sur le début d'al-Ḥājj ʿUmar." *Revue des Etudes Islamiques* 37 (1969): 267–290.
———. "A Short History of the Khalwatīya Order of the Derviches." In *Scholars, Saints and Sufis,* edited by Nikki R. Keddie, pp. 275–307. Berkeley: University of California Press, 1972.
Masson, P. *La Histoire du commerce français dans le Levant au XVIIIe siècle.* Paris: Hachette, 1911.
Mémoires sur l'Egypte publiées pendant les campagnes du General Bonaparte. 4 vols. Paris, 1797–1801.
A partial English translation is *Memoirs Relative to Egypt.* 2 vols. London: N. R. Philipps, 1800.
Meyerhof, Max. "Sur le nom Dardar (orme et frêne) chez les Arabes." *Bulletin de l'Institut de l'Egypte* 18 (1935–1936): 137–149.
Molès, Marijan. "Les Kubrawīya entre Sunnisme et Shīʿisme aux huitième et neuvième siècles de l'hégire." *Revue des Etudes Islamiques* 29 (1961): 61–142.
———. *Les mystiques musulmanes.* Paris: Presses Universitaires de France, 1965.
Moore, Barrington, Jr. *The Social Origins of Dictatorship and Democracy.* Boston: Beacon Press, 1966.

Moosa, Matti. "Napoleon's Islamic Policy in Egypt." *Islamic Quarterly* 9 (1965): 103–116.

Moreh, S. "Blank Verse (al-Shiʿr al-Mursal) in Modern Arabic Literature." *Bulletin of the School of Oriental and African Studies* 29 (1966): 483–506.

———. "Reputed Autographs of ʿAbd al-Raḥman al-Jabartī and Related Problems." *Bulletin of the School of Oriental and African Studies* 28 (1965): 524–540.

El-Mouelhy, Ibrāhīm. "L'Enregistrement de la propriété en l'Egypte durant l'occupation française." *Bulletin de l'Institut de l'Egypte* 30 (1949): 197–228.

Nasr, Seyyid Hossein. *An Introduction to Islamic Cosmological Doctrines.* Cambridge, Mass.: Harvard University Press, 1964.

———. *Islamic Studies.* Beirut: Librairie du Liban, 1967.

———. *Science and Civilization in Islam.* Cambridge, Mass.: Harvard University Press, 1968.

Nizami, K. A. "Naqshbandī Influence on Mughal Rulers and Politics." *Islamic Culture* 39 (1965): 41–52.

North, Douglas C., and Robert Paul Thomas. *The Rise of the Western World.* Cambridge: At the University Press, 1973.

Olivier, G. A. *Voyage dans l'empire Othman.* Vols. I and II. Paris: Chez Henri Agasse, 1804.

Owen, E. R. J. *Cotton and the Egyptian Economy, 1820–1914.* Oxford: Clarendon Press, 1967.

Pallary, Paul. "Les Rapports Originaux de Larrey à l'armée d'Orient." *Mémoires de l'Institut de l'Egypt* 30 (1936): 1–85.

Palmer, R. R. *Twelve Who Ruled.* Princeton: Princeton University Press, 1941.

Pérès, Henri. "L'Institut de l'Egypte et l'oeuvre de Bonaparte jugés par deux historiens Arabes contemporains." *Arabica* 4 (1957): 113–130.

Peters, F. E. *Aristotle and the Arabs.* New York: New York University Press, 1968.

Plessner, Martin. "Dāʾūd al-Anṭākī's Tenth Century Encyclopedia on Medicine, Natural History and Occult Sciences." In *Congrès d'Histoire des Sciences.* Vol. 10 (1962), pp. 635–637. Paris: Hermann, 1964.

Politis, A. G. *L'Hellènisme et l'Egypte moderne.* Vols. I and II. Paris: Librairie Félix Alcan, 1929.

A valuable source for late eighteenth-century Egypt.

Pouqueville, F. C. H. L. *Voyage en Morée à Constantinople et en Albanie.* Paris: Chez Gabon et Cie., 1805.

Prinsep, James. "Notes on the Nautical Instruments of the Arabs." In *Une Introduction à l'astronomie nautique Arabe*, edited by Gabriel Ferrand, pp. 1–30. Paris: Paul Geuthner, 1928.

Rahbar, Dāʾūd. "Shāh Walīʾullah and Ijtihād: A Translation of Selected Passages from his ʿIqd al-Jīd fī Aḥkām al-Ijtihād waʾl-Taqlīd." *Muslim World* 45 (1955): 346–358.

Raymond, André. *Artisans et commerçants au Caire au XVIIIième siècle.* 2 vols. Damascus: IFAO, 1973–1974.

———. "Essai de géographie des quartiers de résidence aristocratique au Caire au XVIIIième siècle." *Journal of the Economic and Social History of the Orient* 6 (1963): 58–103.

———. "Quartiers et mouvements populaires au Caire au XVIIIième siècle." In *Political and Social Change in Modern Egypt*, edited by P. M. Holt, pp. 104–116. Oxford: Oxford University Press, 1968.

———. "Tunisiens et Maghrebins au Caire au dix-huitième siècle." *Les Cahiers de Tunisie* 7 (1959): 336–371.

Reinaud, Joseph-Toussaint. "De la gazette arabe et turque imprimée en l'Egypte." *Journal Asiatique* 1st ser., 8 (1831): 238–249.

———. "Notice des ouvrages Arabes, Persans et Turcs imprimées en l'Egypte." *Journal Asiatique* 1st ser., 8 (1831): 333–344.

Rescher, Nicholas. *The Development of Arabic Logic.* Pittsburgh: University of Pittsburgh Press, 1964.

Rescher, Oscar. *Orientalische Miszellen.* Constantinople, 1925.

Rivlin, Helen. *The Agricultural Policy of Muḥammad ʿAlī in Egypt.* Cambridge, Mass.: Harvard University Press, 1961.

Rodinson, Maxime. *Islam et capitalisme.* Paris: Editions de Seuil, 1966.

An English translation is *Islam and Capitalism*, translated by Brian Pearce. Austin: University of Texas Press, 1978.

Romano, Ruggiero. *Commerce et prix du blé à Marseilles au XVIIIième siècle.* Paris: Colin, 1956.

Rudé, Georges. *The Crowd in the French Revolution.* Oxford: Oxford University Press, 1959.

Sacy, Sylvestre de. *Bibliothèque Imprimé.* Paris, 1843.

This library lists many rare items from the period of the author's life, supplementing al-Shūrbajī. There is a copy in the Bibliothèque Nationale in Paris.

Saint-Martin, J. "Critique Littéraire." *Journal Asiatique* 1st ser., 1 (1822): 109–115.

Saint-Simon, Claude Henri and Enfantin. *Oeuvres de Saint-Simon et d'Enfantin.* Paris: E. Dentu, 1873.

Salāma, Ibrāhīm. *Bibliographie analytique et critique.* Cairo: Paul Barbey, 1938.

———. *Enseignement islamique en l'Egypte.* Cairo: Imprimerie Nationale, 1938.

Contains material not found elsewhere on cultural life for the eighteenth and nineteenth centuries.

Savant, Jean. *Les Mamelouks de Napoleon.* Paris: Calmann-Levy, 1949.

Sayili, Aydin. "Islam and the Rise of the Seventeenth Century Science." *Turk Tarih Kurumu, Belleten* 22 (1958): 353–368.

Schacht, Joseph. *Classicisme et déclin culturel dans l'histoire de l'Islam.* Paris: Editions Besson Chante-Merle, 1957.

Scholch, Alexander. *Agypten den Agyptern: Die Politische und Gesellschaftliche Krise der Jahre 1878–1882 in Agypten.* Freiburg: Atlantis Verlag, 1972.

Shaw, Stanford. "The Established Ottoman Army Corps under Sultan Selim III." *Der Islam* 90 (1964) 142–184.

Excellent article on the late eighteenth century in Turkey, which covers much more than the title implies.

———. *The Financial and Administrative Organization of and Development of Ottoman Egypt, 1517–1798.* Princeton: Princeton University Press, 1962.

———. "Landholding and Land Tax Revenues in Ottoman Egypt." In *Political and Social Change in Modern Egypt*, edited by P. M. Holt, pp. 91–103. Oxford: Oxford University Press, 1969.

———. *Ottoman Egypt in the Age of the French Revolution.* Cambridge, Mass.: Harvard University Press, 1964.

Al-Shayyāl, Jamāl al-dīn. "Doctor Peron and Two Shaykhs, al-Tūnisī and al-Ṭanṭāwī." *Majallat Kullīyat al-Ādāb* 2 (1944): 1–16.

Skiotis, Dennis N. "From Bandit to Pasha: First Steps in the Rise to Power of ʿAlī of Tepelen, 1750–1784." *International Journal of Middle East Studies* 2 (1971): 219–244.

Sobhy, George. *Lectures in the History of Medicine.* Cairo: Fuad I University Press, 1949.

Stetkevych, Jaroslav. *The Modern Arabic Literary Language: Lexical and Stylistic Developments.* Chicago: University of Chicago Press, 1970.
Strauss, Leo. *Natural Right and History.* Chicago: University of Chicago Press, 1953.
Thédenat-Duvent, M. P. P. de. *L'Egypte sous Mehemet-Ali.* Paris: Chez Pillet-Ainé, 1822.
Toderini, Abbé. *De la littérature des Turcs.* 2 vols. Paris: Chez Poincat, 1789.
A work of great insight and depth on eighteenth-century Turkish culture.
Tomiche, N. "La Situation des artisans et pétits commerçants en Egypte de la fin du XVIIIième siècle jusqu'au milieu du XIX." *Studia Islamica* 12 (1960): 79–94.
Toussoun, Omar [Ṭūṣun, ʿUmar]. "La Fin des Mamelouks." *Bulletin de l'Institut de l'Egypte* 15 (1933): 187–205.
Trécourt, Jean-Baptiste. *Mémoires sur l'Egypte, 1791.* Edited by Gaston Wiet. Cairo: Royal Geographical Society of Egypt, 1942.
A primary source written by a French consul. Exceedingly useful for economic details.
Trimmingham, John Spencer. *Sufi Orders in Islam.* Oxford: Clarendon Press, 1971.
Ulken, Hilmi Ziya. "L'Ecole wujūdite et son influence dans la pensée Turque." *Wiener Zeitschrift für die Kunde des Morgenlandes* 112 (1969): 193–208.
Volney, Constantine. *Voyage en l'Egypte et en Syrie.* The Hague: Mouton and Co., 1959.
Walz, Terence. "Notes on the Organization of the African Trade in Cairo, 1800–1850." *Annales Islamologiques* 11 (1972): 263–286.
A study of Egyptian-African commerce based on Egyptian and Sudanese archives.
Watt, Ian. *The Rise of the Novel.* Berkeley: University of California Press, 1957.
Wilson, Bryan. *Religion in Secular Society.* London: Watts, 1966.
Wood, Alfred C. *A History of the Levant Company.* Oxford: Oxford University Press, 1935.
Ziadeh, Nicola A. *Sānūsīya: A Study of the Revivalist Movement in Islam.* Leiden: E. J. Brill, 1958.
Zolondek, Leon. "The French Revolution in Arabic Literature in the Nineteenth Century." *Muslim World* 57 (1967): 202–211.

Index of Terms and Concepts

In this section I wish to share with my fellow Arabists my conviction of the need for a new type of Arabic lexicographical work. I have defined in context the technical terms of this study as they would be found in a dictionary. Yet I am aware that I have given meanings which applied in many cases one thousand or more years before. While this did not matter in the case of highly technical words, such as *qiyās*, meaning analogy in logic, when I came to define *ḥadīth* or *fiqh* or a number of other words which form the conceptual basis of this study, I was struck by the inadequacy of relying on their generic meaning. I had the feeling that I was giving the Latinate meaning of an English word without suggesting the way the meaning has evolved. In eighteenth-century Egypt the *ḥadīth* revival arose because of the situation in which the merchants found themselves. To say that *ḥadīth* is the sayings of the Prophet Muḥammad is not very helpful. To say that it is one of a number of mutually reinforcing aspects of law would be to ignore the features of the period which found *ḥadīth* in conflict with *fiqh*. A solution occurred to me while reading Raymond Williams' *Keywords: A Vocabulary of Culture and Society* (1976). While I cannot work out, as he has, the history of the key words which are indices of social change, I might on a more modest scale try to define words to fit the study of the period of this book in a very brief way, and to hope that this idea will be taken up by linguists interested in the historical development of language. I justify my venture by pointing to the fact that the changes in culture and society in the eighteenth century called forth in the mind of al-Zabīdī the need for a total dictionary. As a first step, I decided to organize terms according to their social relationships, for the changing society highlighted the new relationships of terms to each other. There is a considerable risk inherent in this. The meaning of a given term depends on conflict. Categories derive their meaning not from being juxtaposed here but from being in conflict in certain concrete ways.

I. Law and Its Cultural Buttressing
  A. Bureaucratic/Landowning Regimes (*fiqh* of the rulers), 53, 133ff
    1. Institutions
      a. Mosques, 33, 45, 124, 130, 140
      b. Translation centers, missions, presses, 113, 123, 130, 145
    2. Genres
      a. Scholastic (the rational sciences as the base of *fahrasa* logic, *ādāb al-*

Index of Names